The Air War in Indochina

REVISED EDITION

With a Preface by Neil Sheehan

Raphael Littauer and Norman Uphoff, editors
Air War Study Group
Cornell University

BEACON PRESS *BOSTON*

We dedicate this report to the memory of Frank Rosenblatt *whose enthusiasm did much to launch the Study Group and whose unstinting work contributed greatly to our progress. He died in a boating accident July 11, 1971.*

Library of Congress catalog number: 72-490
International Standard Book Number: 0-8070-0248-8 (hardcover)
International Standard Book Number: 0-8070-0249-6 (paperback)
Beacon Press books are published under the auspices of
the Unitarian Universalist Association
Published simultaneously in Canada by Saunders of Toronto, Ltd.

Printed in the United States of America

THE AIR WAR IN INDOCHINA

Prepared Under the Auspices of the

CORNELL UNIVERSITY PROGRAM ON PEACE STUDIES

A Preliminary Report was Issued

November 8, 1971

PREFACE

The quantum advances in military technology since World War II have given the American Presidency a substantial degree of independence from Congress and the general public in the waging of war. When future historians ask how the current Administration of President Richard M. Nixon was able to continue an unpopular war in Indochina for four years after the country had voted against that war in the presidential election of 1968, technological advances in weaponry, chiefly in air power, will be one of the answers the historians discover. The development of the air weapon to its present responsiveness to centralized control, its remoteness from the tides of the ground battle, and its vast destructive force have created the opportunity for an American President and the state machinery that serves him in the Executive Branch to conduct war with little reference to the wishes of the body politic at home. The reason is simple. War from the air is not very tangible to the average American.

Over the seven years from 1965, when sustained bombing raids against North Vietnam began, to the end of 1971, the United States dropped 6,300,000 tons of bombs and other aerial munitions on Indochina. This fact means that our country has loosed upon a region about the size of Texas three times the total tonnage of bombs dropped on Europe, Africa, and Asia during World War II. In the spring of 1972, the bombs were still falling on Indochina at the rate of about 55,000 tons a month and yet their crash and thunder seemed to be only dimly heard in the homes of America. The public has appeared to sense the existence of the Indochina war in proportion to the number of American ground combat troops in South Vietnam and to the casualties they suffer in the ground fighting there. Because President Nixon has steadily withdrawn troops and has drastically reduced American casualties by ordering those who remain to fight as little as possible, the war has seemed to be going away.

Air warfare in Indochina is cheap in terms of American lives. Two men fly an F-4 Phantom fighter-bomber that can carry 14,000 pounds of explosives. Six men form the flight crew of a majestic B-52 Stratofortress that lofts one hundred and eight 500-pound bombs for an area obliteration strike from 18,000 to 30,000 feet above the earth.

The dollar cost of the air war is also not perceptible to the citizenry. In 1972 the entire costs of the Indochina war, including those of maintaining a million-man Saigon government force in action, were estimated at about $7 billion a year. The Nixon Administration was careful not to publicize this figure. The cost of the war thus tended to become lost in a total federal budget of $236 billion for fiscal year 1972. And the cost of the air war itself was estimated at about a quarter of the $7 billion price for the war.

Furthermore, the President can swiftly escalate the air war in Indochina without arousing much public attention. One of the tactical advantages of air power, in fact, is that it can be turned on and off, up or down, with a simple order from the White House. In February of 1972, when the North Vietnamese and the Viet Cong guerrillas were reported to be assembling for a major offensive in the central highlands of South Vietnam, the Administration doubled the number of B-52s stationed at air bases on Guam and in Thailand for raids over Indochina. The regular complement of about 40 B-52s was reinforced by approximately 40 more of the great bombers deployed from the United States. For two weeks, a third aircraft carrier, with its 65 fighter-bombers, was added to the two carriers that normally fly attack sorties from the Gulf of Tonkin. More Phantoms, slightly less than 20, were flown in to augment the approximately 300 fighter-bombers stationed at fields in South Vietnam and Thailand. During those two weeks in February this air fleet loosed an inferno of high explosive on the central highlands. Sorties by the fighter-bombers (a sortie is a strike by a single plane) went from twelve in South Vietnam on February 9 to 242 on the 15th of the month. B-52 raids, most of them single-plane strikes, rose from eight missions on February 11 to twenty-seven on February 14. All the while, other aircraft continued the work-a-day bombing of the Ho Chi Minh supply road network through southern Laos, the communist-held areas in the north and central part of that country, and in Cambodia, where 80 percent of the territory is now dominated by communist forces and thus subject to American aerial bombardment. The newspapers took note of this surge in the air war with a few articles that did not provoke any outcry.

The air war seems to be perceived by the American public only intermittently, when the Administration varies the pattern of raids over South Vietnam, Cambodia, and Laos with a series of heavy strikes against North Vietnam itself for military or psychological purposes. Even then, once the initial brouhaha subsides, those pilots who survive the downing of their planes by anti-aircraft fire and are captured become objects of pity and patriotic outrage which the Administration has been able to exploit to its advantage with the public.

But if the fact that the United States dropped 764,000 tons of bombs and other aerial explosives on Indochina in 1971 is not known to most Americans, it is agonizingly sensed by the peoples of Cambodia, Laos, and North and South Vietnam. Their most tangible perception of America is death from the sky. The cost of the air war is very high in Cambodian and Laotian and Vietnamese lives. Unlike the human terrorist, the mechanical bomb cannot discriminate among its victims. It kills and maims willy nilly.

Senator Edward M. Kennedy's Senate Subcommittee on Refugees, which has relied on official reports to compile its record of the devastation wrought in Indochina since 1965 by the Johnson and Nixon Administrations, has estimated civilian casualties from military action by the United States and the Saigon government at a minimum of half a million persons. At least 150,000 non-combatants, men, women, and children, have been killed and another 350,000 wounded or permanently maimed, according to the Subcommittee record. Five million persons, approaching a third of South Vietnam's population, have been turned into refugees by the creeping ruination of the rural society. Unrestrained use of air power by the United States, the Subcommittee record shows, has been responsible in large measure for the casualties and the destruction of peasant homes.

In Laos, the Subcommittee discovered, civilian casualties, again in large measure from relentless American air bombardments, were exceeding 30,000 a year, including more than 10,000 dead, out of a population of only three million people. Where Laos is concerned, classified American military documents have specifically mentioned bombing civilian villages in communist-held areas "to deprive the enemy of the population resource." The population, in short, was deliberately made the principal target of American war planes.

No one knows what the civilian casualty toll has been in Cambodia, partly because the Nixon Administration and its client in Phnom Penh, the regime of General Lon Nol, have avoided statistics. The Kennedy Subcommittee has guessed that the war there has created about a million and a half refugees, in a population of 6.5 million persons, and is killing or wounding civilians at the rate of tens of thousands a year.

There can be no doubt that President Nixon, and President Johnson before him, have used air power with the knowledge that this weapon exacts a terrifying price from the civilian population of Indochina. The record shows that neither President has acted in ignorance. During the air war against North Vietnam from 1965 to 1968, the Johnson Administration insisted in public that American planes bombed only military targets and that the strikes were made with surgical-like precision. When Pentagon spokesmen were asked about civilian casualties in the North, they maintained that they knew of none. The publication of the *Pentagon Papers* in the summer of 1971 disclosed that in January of 1967 the Central Intelligence Agency informed the Administration in a secret report that American bombing raids had caused an estimated 29,000 civilian casualties in North Vietnam during 1965 and 1966.

There can also be no doubt that both Presidents decided that the value to American foreign policy of preserving a non-communist South Vietnam justified the death and suffering inflicted on the Indochinese peoples by American air power. Indeed, with his strategy of Vietnamization, Mr. Nixon depends far more than his predecessor did upon the air weapon, for he seeks to use it as a substitute for American ground combat troops to prop up the Saigon government and his other allies in the capitals of Laos and Cambodia.

Professor Raphael Littauer and his colleagues at Cornell began their study of the air war in Indochina from anti-war motives. Once at work, however, they decided to approach their subject in a detached and scholarly manner. The result is a pioneer study, the first of its kind, which assembles the vast array of information concerning the air war and subjects that information to careful and searching analysis.

Their statistics are sometimes rough because the once secret records on the air war available from the *Pentagon Papers* end with March 31, 1968, and the study group had to rely on material in the public domain for the Nixon years. Many, as this reader did, will also find themselves in varying states of agreement and disagreement with the study group's analyses and conclusions. What one must respect is the integrity of their effort and the enduring value of their work.

Although Professor Littauer and his colleagues do not come to a firm judgment on the question of war crimes, the facts they gathered demonstrate that the employment of American air power in Indochina years ago reached a level of calculated slaughter which may gravely violate the laws of war, laws the United States has pledged itself to uphold and enforce. The evidence speaks for those who wish to hear it. The air war may constitute a massive war crime by the American government and its leaders.

The final irony this study suggests is that the air weapon may prove militarily ineffective in the end. After long years of subjecting impoverished peoples to the multifaceted cruelty of its technological might, the richest and most powerful nation on the earth may ultimately find itself driven from the Indochinese peninsula by the Vietnamese communists. If this proves to be the case, and the outcome is still uncertain, then the victory of the Vietnamese will be an unparalleled example of the triumph of the spirit of man over the machine.

March 13, 1972
Washington, D.C.

Neil Sheehan

ACKNOWLEDGEMENTS

This study was sponsored by the Peace Studies Program of the Center for International Studies and the Program on Science, Technology and Society at Cornell University, with an initial grant and with generous advice and guidance. We are also much indebted to the D.J.B. Foundation of Scarsdale, New York, who covered the greater part of the expenses with a grant-in-aid, and to the Fund for Peace for supporting reproduction and distribution of the preliminary report of our Study Group which has been expanded and revised here. None of these institutions is of course in any way responsible for the opinions expressed here.

Over eighty consultants gave their time and knowledge in interviews or discussions, and several have reviewed sections of the manuscript for us. Rather than list them individually, we summarize their institutional affiliations to indicate the range of their experiences and views on the air war:

Brookings Institution
Congressional staffs
Cornell University
Department of Defense
Department of State
Dispatch News Service
Friends Comm. on Natl. Legislation
Harvard University
Institute for Policy Studies
International Voluntary Service
Massachusetts Inst. of Technology
New York Times
National Security Council
Princeton University
Senate Foreign Relations Committee
Senate Judiciary Committee Subcommittee on Refugees
South Vietnamese Embassy, Washington
St. Louis Post-Dispatch
U.S. Agency for International Development
U.S. Air Force
U.S. Army
University of Pittsburgh
Washington Star
Windham College

In addition, we had access to transcripts obtained in Indochina by interviewing Embassy personnel, local administrators, base commanders, pilots and other servicemen; also to personal reports from Americans living for extended periods in Indochina, as well as from some Vietnamese citizens. To all these consultants we express our sincere thanks. Responsibility for the analysis and conclusions which follow rests of course with us.

In addition, we wish to thank Mr. William Broydrick for his help with the production and distribution of our preliminary report in November 1971. Circulation of this report resulted in our receiving some corrections, some additional data, and many helpful suggestions. We are particularly indebted to Mr. Maurice Rosenblatt for his continued interest in the study. His guidance and advice have been invaluable throughout, and his unstinting help has greatly facilitated the logistics of our Washington contacts.

*STUDY GROUP PARTICIPANTS**

Raphael Littauer (Coordinator), Professor of Physics
James Allaway, Doctoral Candidate, Natural Resources
Saha Amarasingham, Doctoral Candidate, Government
Thomas Bjorkman, Doctoral Candidate, Government
Curtis Christensen, Undergraduate Major in Government
Paul Feeny, Assistant Professor of Entomology, Ecology and Systematics
John Harding, Professor of Human Development and Family Studies
Fred Heidtman, Undergraduate Major in Economics
George Hildebrand, M.A. (Chinese History)
Chris Jenkins, M.A. (Asian Studies), University of California, Berkeley
Peter Kimball, Undergraduate Major in Government
Chandler Morse, Professor Emeritus of Economics
Judy Reynolds, M.A. (American Studies), University of Michigan
Frank Rosenblatt, Associate Professor of Neurobiology
deceased July 11, 1971
Arthur Rovine, Assistant Professor of Government
Carl Sagan, Professor of Astronomy
Mark Sharefkin, Doctoral Candidate, Economics
Peter Sharfman, Assistant Professor of Government
John Lee Smith, Acting Director, Center for Religion, Ethics, and Social Policy
Norman Uphoff, Assistant Professor of Government

**All affiliations are with Cornell University unless otherwise noted.*

CONTENTS

APPENDIXES

ILLUSTRATIONS

CHINA
RED RIVER
HANOI
Haiphong
RED RIVER DELTA
GULF OF TONKIN
Samneua
NORTH
MEKONG RIVER
Luang Prabang
Thanh Hoa
PLAIN OF JARS
Xieng Khouang
LAOS
ANNAMITE
Vinh
VIETNAM
MEKONG RIVER
VIENTIANE
Mu Gia Pass
Udorn Air Base
Nakhon Phanom Air Base
Dong Hoi
Yankee Station
Ben Hai River
(1954 Demarcation Line)
Tchepone
Muang Phine
Hue
SOUTH
Da Nang
CHINA
THAILAND
Saravane
SEA
MTNS
SEKONG RIVER
BOLOVENS
PLATEAU
Ubon Air Base
Khorat Air Base
SOUTH
Pleiku
Angkor Wat
Tonle Sap
CAMBODIA
U-Tapao Air Base
VIETNAM
Kampong Cham
Snuol
Da Lat
PHNOM PENH
Kampong Som
SAIGON
MEKONG DELTA

INDOCHINA

The states of Laos, Cambodia, and Vietnam, collectively known as Indochina, lie in the eastern half of the Indochinese peninsula. Although the name "Indochina" has had no political meaning since 1954, when French dominion over the region came to an end, it does reflect the early cultural influence of both India and China on mainland Southeast Asian states. While Cambodia and Laos are part of what may be called Indianized or Hinduized Southeast Asia, the area now comprising North and South Vietnam was exposed primarily to Chinese culture. The two forms of Buddhism represented in Indochina illustrate what the area owes to the two great centers of Asian civilization. The majority of Laotians and Cambodians practice Theravada Buddhism, which they share with the other peoples of Indianized Southeast Asia, while the majority of lowland inhabitants of Vietnam follow the Mahayana Buddhist tradition of China's imperial past.

The three Indochinese states describe an "S" shape following the north-south orientation of the Annamite mountain chain. Two major river deltas dominate the lowland geography. The Mekong or "great river" flows from Tibet through China, marking the border between Thailand and Laos. At Phnom Penh the Mekong divides into branches and fans out in a delta to deposit its rich soils through 26,000 square miles of South Vietnam. From its headwaters in China the shorter Red River flows southeast into Vietnam, where it forms a smaller delta of 5,750 square miles, and then into the Gulf of Tonkin. Hanoi and Haiphong, the capital and major port of North Vietnam, are both situated on the main branch of the Red River. Still smaller deltas deposited by rivers originating in the Annamite mountains lie along the east coast of central Vietnam.

With an area of 283,988 square miles Indochina is no larger than the state of Texas. When Vietnam, the largest of the three Indochinese states, was divided into North and South Vietnam at the Ben Hai River near the seventeenth parallel in 1954, its land area (128,190 square miles) and population were divided approximately in half. Nine million of the 18,000,000 inhabitants of North Vietnam live along the Red River Delta, the most densely populated area of Indochina, and an additional 2,500,000 people live in the smaller central Vietnamese deltas.* The mountainous inland regions are sparsely populated. About 6,500,000 of the 16,000,000 South Vietnamese live in the Mekong delta, including the population of Saigon which is located on a small river on the northern side of the delta. Most of the rest of the people live along the coastal lowland. As in North Vietnam, the highlands are sparsely populated; they are inhabited more commonly by hill tribe peoples (Montagnards) than by ethnic Vietnamese.

*Approximate population figures are from surveys taken in the early 1960s.

Laos is the second largest Indochinese state with an area of 85,900 square miles, mostly rugged mountain terrain. Its population of only about 2,500,000 is the smallest of the three states. Most population centers are found along the lowland Mekong valley which Laos shares with Thailand.

The area of Cambodia is 69,898 square miles and, as in South Vietnam, its people are concentrated along the Mekong river valley and the delta which begins at Phnom Penh. However, the population is only 5,736,853, about one-third the size of South Vietnam's.

All of Indochina lies south of the Tropic of Cancer, within the tropical zone, a transitional climate between those of continental Asia and equatorial Southeast Asia. It is often referred to as Monsoon Asia, after the region's most distinctive climatic feature. Despite popular usage, the term "monsoon" describes a periodic wind, not a heavy rainfall.

In Indochina itself the prevailing Northeast Monsoon from mid-September to March brings cool, wet weather with continuous drizzle, fogs, and poor visibility to Tonkin or northeastern Indochina; dry weather to Laos and the mountainous areas of north and central Vietnam; cool rains to the east coast; and dry sunny weather to the southern plain that includes Cambodia and the delta region of South Vietnam. The Southwest Monsoon prevails from June to September, bringing tropical heat and humidity and the season of heaviest rainfall to the entire region. From July through November typhoons are common. These tropical cyclones are accompanied by torrential rains which cause drastic changes in river levels. The Red River at Hanoi drops to a height of only nine feet from January to May, but reaches an average height of 27 feet from June through October. Because the Mekong is longer and has a natural flood reservoir formed by the large lake Tonle Sap in Cambodia, its fluctuations are less dramatic. Even so the waters of the Mekong inundate the southern plain of Indochina regularly. It is flooding in both the Red River and Mekong deltas that allows the planting of wet rice, the area's most important subsistence and export product.

Indochina is primarily an agricultural region, and its demography is a function of the geography and the climate. Religious ritual, as well as the rhythm of the agricultural cycle, depends on the arrival and departure of monsoon winds and the rains which they bring to this naturally beautiful, potentially prosperous, but historically unfortunate region.

FOREWORD

American ground troops are scheduled for withdrawal from Vietnam. Whether or not this policy is to be implemented literally, by now it is clear that a major reduction of U.S. ground involvement in the Indochina war has taken place and that public opinion is strongly in favor of disengagement. But will this disengagement imply the end of *all* U.S. combat activity in the war? The answer is uncertain. Americans have somehow come to regard air power as a distinct entity--pristine, not subject to the same restrictions as ground warfare. Air power has played a major, even a dominant role in U.S. military actions in Indochina. Yet it appears that the air war--less well known and understood than the ground war--may continue for some time.

This study was undertaken to ascertain the manner in which American air power has been used in Indochina. How far and in what ways has it furthered U.S. policy aims, announced or implicit, and at what cost? Has it been suited to the military and political tasks confronted, or did its main virtue lie in being conveniently at hand when U.S. policy makers faced a military crisis? Though the air war had been raging for more than six years, these questions were still open when we started this study in May 1971. They had a special importance since it seemed clear that the effect of the Nixon Doctrine and of the policy of Vietnamization would be to augment the role played by American air power in the future.

In June came the publication of the *Pentagon Papers* and, with it, a closer look at the evolution of American policy for Indochina. Public pronouncements, it was seen, were often a very uncertain guide to the thinking which underlay the policy planning. Military moves were, on the one hand, a response to a chain of developing crises. On the other hand, they played an active part in the considerations which shaped the very policy itself; the availability of American air power--flexible, responsive, and overwhelming in the relatively uncontested skies of Indochina--played an important role in setting the U.S. on the path it has followed.

The documents in the *Pentagon Papers* do not cover events beyond the early months of 1968. The facts from that date on are not so intimately or authoritatively revealed, but rather must be pieced together from fragmentary information. But if a realistic understanding of future policies is to be gained, it becomes urgent to examine the premises which motivate the deployment of air power, now that it promises to remain as the only instrument of active American military involvement in Indochina. This has been underscored by events as we have been finalizing this report in the latter part of

February 1972.

Our group, working from an academic base and without access to classified data, gathered its material from the literature and the press, from Congressional hearings, and from interviews with many experts who generously shared their views with us. In some areas our information is incomplete or tentative, though occasional "leaks from well-informed sources" were helpful. Information was cross-checked wherever possible. On the whole, the internal consistency of the material was very gratifying.

Obviously we could not hope to assemble at this time a historically complete and balanced assessment of the air war with the resources and skills available to us. Such an assessment remains for others to make at some future time. Instead, our aim was to place in perspective those aspects of air warfare in Indochina which distinguish it from other military operations: above all, its ability to extend enormous firepower from distant and secure bases, over contested territories, and almost by remote control. Among other matters, we were concerned with the match--or the mismatch--in a confrontation between a major industrial power and a predominantly rural, even underdeveloped country. In such a confrontation, reciprocity is absent, and the struggle raises political, legal and moral issues beyond the more straightforward technical and military factors. Air power enhances this aspect of imbalance between the adversaries. The technological developments now in progress foreshadow a completely automated and computerized warfare, with far-reaching consequences.

Though we have considered a broad range of questions related to the air war in Indochina, we did not deal with all of its aspects. For example, the logistic and reconnaissance functions of aircraft are not discussed. More importantly, perhaps, the use of helicopters is considered only peripherally. This may be thought by some a serious omission in connection with a war that has frequently been dubbed a "helicopter war"; but we see helicopters as intimately bound to the control of territory by virtue of their vulnerability and short operating range, and thus we think of them more as elements of mobile artillery or transport.

It is the speed, range, remoteness, and vastly increased destructive power brought by fixed-wing aircraft to contemporary air war which most significantly alter the character of modern warfare. Our treatment of the air war therefore deals primarily with these aircraft. Their employment and further evolution are of greatest significance for the future--in Indochina as American ground involvement is cut back, and more generally as the Nixon doctrine for limited wars further emphasizes the use of U.S. air and naval support forces.

There are some inherent problems in the task we have tried to tackle. In assessing the record of past actions, it is often impossible to separate the effects of air warfare from those of the rest of the fighting. In this area one must be content with finding mixed causes and mixed consequences. This blurring does not invalidate analysis and discussion; it is clear that the air war, if not always dominant, is certainly a major element in the Indochina conflict. If our conclusions are not rigorously quantitative, at least their validity appears to be independent of detailed numerical findings. Where we show graphs or tabulations, we realize that the data are often more suggestive than definitive. This cannot be avoided, given the limitations of the undertaking at this time. Yet we find that the basic impact of the air war is quite distinct and ascertainable, and it is this impact which we attempt to present.

A similar difficulty arises when the merits of air war policies are examined. The air war is obviously an integral part of the American Indochina involvement as a whole, and any final conclusions must relate to an assessment of the overall policy for the war. It has been our decision, however, not to present a judgment on the Indochina involvement *per se*. No matter what one's judgment about the wisdom or folly of this involvement, it is still possible, and we think necessary, to make a specific assessment of air power as a *tool*--whether it is contributing to announced objectives, and whether the costs to Americans and Indochinese can be considered acceptable.

We conclude the study with a consideration of the future course of American policy toward Indochina, where the successes and shortcomings of air power may play a determining role. In this way we hope to provide a basis for better informed judgments about the consequences of a continued air war.

March 1972

Raphael Littauer
Norman Uphoff

for the Study Group on the
Air War in Indochina

CHAPTER 1

INTRODUCTION

This is an account of the air war in Indochina. It focuses on the impact that U.S. air power has had there, and on its implications for the future--not on the broader questions of whether and how the U.S. should have become involved in the war in the first place. To be sure, we do have to consider the context in which the air war was fought: but we hope to steer clear of the doctrinaire arguments which generally characterize debate on this broader question.

Air power is not the only tool that the U.S. has used in pursuing its Indochina policies; more than half a million American soldiers were at one time deployed on the ground in Vietnam, and various diplomatic initiatives have been pursued through the years. Air power, however, symbolizes the main thrust of U.S. strategy, bringing to bear America's outstanding military strength--the massive firepower made available through advanced technology and material wealth. As Vietnamization reduces the number of U.S. ground forces, American air power becomes markedly more important. To analyze the impact of this air power therefore sheds light both on past U.S. involvement and on future prospects for the Indochina conflict.

This introductory chapter sets the stage for subsequent detailed discussions of the air war. First, we consider the special nature of the fighting in South Vietnam, which has been at the focus of U.S. involvement in Indochina. Both sides in the conflict regard the basic character of the military struggle there to be *insurgency warfare*, in which both modern and guerrilla forces, techniques, and strategies have been employed by the protagonists. Vietnam thus confronts the U.S. with some particular and unaccustomed problems. Second, we explore the nature of the U.S. response, which has been to concentrate heavily on mechanized warfare and massive firepower--a strategy which can be characterized as *capital-intensive* warfare. Last, to convey an idea of the scope and deployment of American air power over Indochina, we give a brief overview of the five major air campaigns, indicating how they interact and how emphasis has shifted among them.

Though we confine our study to the use of air power in Indochina, we have considered prior uses during the last three decades. Some historical notes on air power from World War II to Indochina are presented in Appendix B to provide the reader with an idea of the context in which military air action has evolved.

A. THE WAR IN VIETNAM, AND THE U.S. RESPONSE

> A guerrilla war differs from traditional military operations because its key prize is not control of territory but control of the population. This depends in part on psychological criteria, especially a sense of security. No positive program of counterinsurgency can succeed unless the population feels safe from terror or reprisal. Guerrillas rarely seek to hold real estate.
>
> Henry Kissinger[1]

The conflict in Vietnam is commonly considered a *guerrilla war* inasmuch as there are no clear lines of battle, most engagements involve small units, and one side generally employs irregular, semi-modern forces. There is a measure of agreement on the abstract model of guerrilla warfare, with its characteristic rules and dynamics.[2] Yet this designation belies the tactical complexity of the war, which has changed repeatedly in scale and style. At times, when the NLF[3] has been militarily weak, the fighting has been intermittent and dispersed; when they have been relatively strong, the fighting has taken on a more conventional character. Indeed, flexibility has been a central theme in NLF/NVA doctrine--both in the tactics of the moment and in the overall strategy. This underscores the difficulty which the U.S. has faced in dealing with the forces of the insurgency. The other side has usually had the initiative in seeking engagements, choosing what it considers the most favorable terms.

Henry Kissinger's analysis emphasizes that one cannot judge success in combating a guerrilla war by conventional military criteria. When he speaks of control of the population as the key prize, this should not conjure up an image of two rival but similar armies seeking to impose their will on the populace, if need be by conquering it outright. The struggle tends to be waged on grounds where the great military strength of the U.S. is offset at least in part by a fundamental weakness. The U.S. is foreign--in language, in ma-

[1]Henry Kissinger, "The Vietnam Negotiations," *Foreign Affairs* (January 1969), p. 212.

[2]See, for example, Vo Nguyen Giap, *People's War, People's Army* (Praeger, 1962); Roger Trinquier, *Modern Warfare* (Praeger, 1964); Nathan Leites and Charles Wolf, Jr., *Rebellion and Authority* (Markham, 1970). The latter is a RAND Corporation study. An earlier guerrilla war some 50 years ago displaying most of the same rules and dynamics as that in Vietnam is described in John Womack, *Zapata and the Mexican Revolution* (Vintage, 1967). This was a completely indigenous struggle predating communist ideological involvement in such conflicts.

[3]The use of acronyms and abbreviations is not very elegant, but it facilitates writing and reading. A glossary of terms appears in App. A. NLF is the well-known abbreviation for the National Liberation Front of South Vietnam, known pejoratively as the Viet Cong. The NLF, formed in 1960, is a direct descendant of the Viet Minh, the nationalist movement which fought against French colonial rule between 1945 and 1954. The NLF has received increasing support from North Vietnam since 1960. Where appropriate, forces arrayed against the Army of South Vietnam (ARVN) will be referred to as the NLF/NVA (NVA stands for North Vietnamese Army).

chines, in appearance, and in its failure to appreciate fully the political and cultural factors fueling the insurgency. Such factors have proved to be as important as military ones. As Kissinger notes,

> . . . the American strategy produced what came to be the characteristic feature of the Vietnamese war: military successes that could not be translated into permanent political advantage.[4]

Prior to the Korean war, American strategic doctrine presupposed conflict with industrialized foes. Factories, stockpiles, transportation networks, power systems--the whole of the enemy's military and economic apparatus--offered targets which could be attacked and destroyed by strategic air power. In the Korean war the U.S. for the first time faced an adversary too underdeveloped to present many lucrative targets for such strategic weapons.[5]

In Vietnam, the U.S. confronts not only a non-industrialized enemy, but a foe with political roots firmly established in numerous sectors of the population. This base enables him to make use, more or less permanently, of the "classical" advantages of guerrilla warfare. These include drawing strength from the population, relying on it for recruits, for food, for information, and for cover. Guerrilla forces can take war materiel from the government they are fighting--by raids, ambushes, or subversion. They can when necessary merge with the noncombatants to elude government forces. They are mobile, picking the time, place, and scale of armed encounter to their own advantage.

Conventional military forces operating in a guerrilla war thus face a serious dilemma. Killing off the guerrillas does not necessarily deplete their number. In the Algerian war, for example, in order to reduce the rebel forces from 40,000 to 12,000 men, the French army had to kill 120,000 insurgents and capture another 60,000. As reported in Appendix B, even this degree of "success" was made possible only by favorable terrain which permitted cutting off supplies and reinforcements from the guerrillas in a way that is not possible in Vietnam. Moreover, despite military "success," the war was lost politically.

The principal strategic target in counterinsurgency warfare becomes the population itself. If government forces want to attack the guerrillas in their base of strength, they are usually forced to attack the population whose loyalty it is hoped to obtain, so as to deny resources and support to the guerrillas. The dilemma is sharpened if the military forces are highly

[4] Kissinger, *op. cit.*, p. 212.

[5] Gregory Carter, "Some Historical Notes on Air Interdiction in Korea, September 1966" (a RAND Corporation study); reprinted as App. A in the *Air War Hearings* (1967), Part 4, p. 375. See also App. B-3. (For a key to abbreviated titles of hearings, see App. A.)

mechanized. Their massive firepower, which is an asset in a set-piece, conventional battle, becomes a liability if used among the people it is intended to "save."[6] At some point the political and ideological objectives of modern counterinsurgency warfare must be called into question if, in the process of rooting out the insurgents, it destroys the very society that is being contested.

When the U.S. militarily entered the Vietnam war in earnest in 1965, the Army of South Vietnam (ARVN) was on the point of collapse, and only rapid, forceful action could have forestalled the imminent defeat of the Saigon government. The number of U.S. ground troops that could be deployed in South Vietnam was limited, since the Administration in Washington did not believe partial mobilization and calling up the reserves would be politically acceptable at home. With the Korean war experience in mind, U.S. planners also did not want American ground forces committed to a war of attrition involving heavy casualties. For a combination of reasons, therefore, American military strategists in Vietnam emphasized the use of maximum firepower to replace reliance on manpower. American casualties were still unacceptably heavy, in domestic political terms, but technology and firepower helped to reduce them substantially.

What are the possible roles for air power in counterinsurgency warfare? The primary military missions in Indochina are: (1) direct support for troops in firefights; (2) interdiction of the insurgents' supply lines; and (3) a general harassment of the enemy in his base areas.[7]

1. Close air support for troops in action is likely to be most effective under conventional battlefield conditions; snipers are not easily attacked by air. Should the insurgents mass their forces, they expose themselves to an all-out attack; in such circumstances air power can be used to decisive advantage.[8] The availability of air power thus tends to inhibit the insurgents from abandoning smaller guerrilla action in favor of conflict with larger units. Conversely, the counter-insurgent forces try to maneuver or lure the insurgents into open battle.

2. The effectiveness of air interdiction is contingent on many factors.

[6] This is strongly supported by British and American officers with anti-guerilla experience in Malaya and the Philippines. See App. B-4.

[7] We note again that attention in this account of the air war is focused almost entirely on the use of fixed-wing aircraft, with little consideration of helicopters. The helicopter's range is short, its endurance limited, and its deployment almost entirely conditioned by control of the adjacent territory. Thus the helicopter may frequently be regarded as a direct extension of artillery, of the firepower of ground troops, and of their logistic, reconnaissance, and communications functions.

[8] Unless the contact between opposing forces becomes so close that friend and foe can no longer be distinguished from the air.

In the early stages of an insurgency, the guerrillas usually do not need to rely on external sources for their supplies, and so to a large extent they may be independent of identifiable lines of support which could be interrupted. External aid may become essential to success in insurgent war when the scale of conflict outstrips the yield of supplies from local sources, or the government under attack has, itself, brought in outside assistance (as in Vietnam). Even then, the external supply lines are likely to prove elusive targets. The guerrilla does not rely so much on railroads or highways as on jungle tracks; if need be he can resort to bicycle or foot porterage since his mode of warfare is sparing with material inputs.

3. General harassment of the enemy in his base areas can disrupt his organization and deprive him of sanctuaries where he can rest and regroup. In guerrilla warfare, however, the enemy may choose to mingle with the noncombatant population and not present a separate target for air attack.

One of the central problems for pro-government forces, then, is to separate the insurgents from the population. This separation must be sought not only to permit selective attacks on the insurgents, but also to deprive them of their main source of strength--the population, which yields new recruits as well as food and shelter.[9] When this separation is frustrated by the guerrillas' mobility and anonymity, the problem is often attacked in reverse. Rather than driving the guerrillas away from the population, the population is moved away from those areas in which the insurgents are established and into refugee camps or other locations under effective government control. Adopting Mao Tse Tung's simile that a guerrilla lives among the population "like a fish in the sea," this tactic has been described as "draining the sea away from the fish."[10]

The strategy of using air power in this way leads to large-scale population displacements, after which air strikes can be called freely against the areas so defined. Anyone remaining behind is considered the enemy.[11] It seems clear that such a gross definition of who is "friend" and who "foe"

[9]This greatly simplified argument ignores the possibility that the "population" and the guerrillas may not be as distinct from one another as counterinsurgency doctrine implies. The problem is of course simplified where there are ethnic differences between guerrillas and the majority of the population, as for example in Malaya.

[10]As an American working in Vietnam explained to a French student of guerrilla warfare: "There have been three choices open to the peasantry. One, to stay where they are; two, to move into areas controlled by us; three, to move off into the interior towards the Vietcong. The application of our air power since February [1966] has made the first choice impossible from now on. It is not possible to stay in the line of fire and live." Robert Guillain, *Vietnam: The Dirty War* (Housmans, 1967), p. 16.

[11]There are some practical reasons which may thwart this attempted separation: the population may not be willing to move away from their homes or may be unable to do so in the short time allowed them; once moved out they may be tempted to return, to resume working their land or to retrieve belongings left behind.

cannot do justice to the complex realities of the situation in either political or human terms.

U.S. military operations, characterized by this approach to the use of firepower, can seldom actually provide safety and security to noncombatants--the condition for success which Kissinger and others have pointed out.[12] Instead, as Arthur Schlesinger has put it, "our strategy in Vietnam today is rather like trying to weed a garden with a bulldozer. We occasionally dig up some weeds, but we dig up most of the turf too."[13]

There may well be conditions under which the use of massive air power could be effective against a guerrilla adversary; to judge any particular case, however, one must consider not only military factors, but the political nature of the adversary's goals and the crucial role of the noncombatant population in its relationship to the insurgents.

B. CAPITAL-INTENSIVE WARFARE

> . . . there is also a constant effort going on within the Department [of Defense] to find ways to reduce manpower and more highly mechanize. In the private sector we would be talking about how to industrialize our operations which means, how can we get more firepower with less manpower.
>
> Defense Hearings for 1972[14]

"Capital-intensive" is a term used in the economic analysis of production processes, but it is also descriptive of recent trends in warfare. In both cases, labor, capital, and other inputs are combined to achieve some purpose--production in one case and destruction in the other. It is easy to see how capital used in warfare--essentially physical capital, in the form of weapons and aircraft--can make labor inputs more efficient, *i.e.*, destructive. The combat capabilities of soldiers can be multiplied manyfold and the range of their effectiveness can be extended to great distances by guns, rockets, and aircraft.

12 This point is argued also by Leites and Wolf, *op. cit.*, who reject the idea that the "hearts and minds" of the population need to be won, but insist that provision of security is the key to success.

13 Arthur M. Schlesinger, Special Assistant to President John F. Kennedy, *The Bitter Heritage* (Houghton Mifflin, 1967), pp. 47-48. He elaborates: "If we continue the pursuit of a total military victory, we will leave the tragic country gutted and devastated by bombs, burned by napalm, turned into a wasteland by chemical defoliation, a land of ruin and wreck. This is the melancholy course to which the escalation policy commits us. The effect will be to pulverize the political and institutional fabric which alone can give a South Vietnamese state that hope of independent survival which is our presumed aim. Our method, in other words, defeats our goal."

14 U.S. House of Representatives, Committee on Appropriations, *Defense Hearings for 1972*, Part I, p. 1130.

When relatively more labor is used in combination with other inputs, the process is described as *labor-intensive*; when relatively more capital is employed instead of other inputs, this is called *capital-intensive*. The mix of factors used depends on their relative abundance and cost. When capital is plentiful and cheap--or when labor is scarce and expensive--there is an incentive to substitute capital for labor. If the existing technology, as embodied in machines, processes, and materials, sets limits on this substitution, there is an inducement to devise and adopt new labor-saving technologies. Such an effort is underway in U.S. military planning.[15]

This development seems natural for America. It parallels in the military realm the trend toward capital-intensive production in the American economy, which has augmented productivity and prosperity in such spectacular fashion. Mechanization and automation of warfare might be expected to produce analogous benefits, achieving large results at small cost. This is correct if "large results" are equated with large-scale and widespread destruction. When judged from a broader viewpoint, however, the politico-military results of capital-intensive warfare may not prove to be as impressive. A major reason for this lies in the character of the objectives. Mechanically concentrated firepower can destroy objects and people, but it cannot always bend wills to conform with American aims: achieving a goal such as nation building is a subtler process, not necessarily susceptible to coercion.[16] Obtaining compliance with political terms through the use of force may also be difficult; in fact a reverse psychological effect has been attributed to bombing by several studies.[17]

15 Former Secretary of Defense McNamara spoke of this attitude as it relates to U.S. military strategy in Indochina. "He [McNamara] discoursed on the 200,000 troops then in Vietnam and on the enormous mobility and firepower of the American soldier. 'The thing we prize most deeply,' he said, 'is not money but men . . . We have multiplied the capability of our men. It's expensive in dollars but cheap in life.'" Henry F. Graff, *The Tuesday Cabinet* (Prentice-Hall, 1970), pp. 81-82. "[The use of B-52s in Indochina] was admittedly an expensive operation. Secretary of Defense McNamara estimated that the cost of the bombs alone was $30,000 a sortie. But the Secretary had also said earlier that what the U.S. sought in South Vietnam was a limited objective, and it would be accomplished with the lowest possible loss of lives and not necessarily with the lowest expenditure of money." Robert M. Kipp, "Counterinsurgency From 30,000 Feet: The B-52 in Vietnam," *Air University Review*, XIX, No. 2 (January-February 1968), p. 16.

It goes without saying that we do not question the validity of doing everything possible to save American lives. A balanced assessment of methods of warfare must however take into account the cost in non-American lives also, as well as the overall cost in disruption and destruction of the society.

16 "In coordination with our military operations, the task of nation building in South Vietnam, *the ultimate goal of our struggle*, received its full share of attention" (emphasis added). Admiral U.S.G. Sharp, in *Report on the War in Vietnam* (USGPO, 1968), p. 9.

17 A study by the JASON Division of the Institute for Defense Analyses, sponsored by the Department of Defense (see Chap. 3), summarized the psychological effects of the North Vietnam air campaign: "The indirect effects of the bombing on the will of the North Vietnamese to continue fighting and on their leaders' appraisal of the prospective gains and costs of maintaining the present policy have not shown themselves in any tangible way." "The bomb-

When capital is relatively plentiful and cheap, or manpower costly and scarce, pressures for escalation in capital-intensive warfare become hard to resist. If an impressive show of destructive force does not produce a measurable reduction in the enemy's military capability or make him accept terms at the bargaining table, a greater effort can be ordered. If the existing equipment and ordnance prove imperfectly effective against their intended targets, a research and development program can improve their operation, at least according to technical specifications. But as these efforts and innovations escalate, the war becomes not only more indiscriminate in its effects, but more impersonal and more remote from those who conduct it as well.

The juxtaposition of these two models--capital-intensive warfare and guerrilla warfare (which is labor-intensive)--points up the dynamics of the conflict on both sides, and indicates the possibility that the two modes of warfare may be mismatched. We do not draw any final conclusions on the basis of such models, but the importance of the overall strategic context for evaluating the air war in Indochina should be clear. Body counts, truck kills, sortie rates, and tonnages expended cannot tell the whole story: much more is at stake in the deployment of air power than technical or material forces alone.

C. THE CAMPAIGNS OF THE AIR WAR--AN OVERVIEW

U.S. air power has played an important, and often dominant, role in all theaters of the Indochina war. In this section we will set the stage for the more detailed discussions which follow by giving a brief outline of how the air war has evolved geographically, and in what context. For the sake of exposition we consider the five major air campaigns separately, labelling them according to the theater of war in which they unfolded. These are: (1) North Vietnam, (2) South Vietnam, (3) the Ho Chi Minh trail, mainly in the southern part of Laos, (4) northern Laos, and (5) Cambodia. Of course these five air campaigns interact and overlap to some degree, so the separation is somewhat artificial. However, it is instructive to trace the changes of emphasis which have occurred as the conflict has evolved and as U.S. policy aims have shifted in response to that evolution.

ing clearly strengthened popular support of the regime by engendering patriotic and nationalistic enthusiasm to resist the attacks." The study noted further that the planners of the campaign exhibited "a general failure to appreciate the fact, well-documented in the historical and social scientific literature, that a direct, frontal attack on a society tends to strengthen the social fabric of the nation, to increase popular support of the existing government, to improve the determination of both the leadership and the populace to fight back . . ." The conclusions of the JASON study are quoted in *The Senator Gravel Edition, The Pentagon Papers* (Beacon, 1971), Vol. IV, pp. 117-118, 224.

To comprehend the magnitude of the air war, and the relative intensity of the several campaigns within it, some quantitative indicators are helpful. Unfortunately, no single set of numbers conveys a complete picture. Figures on attack sortie rates or tonnages of aerial munitions do not indicate clearly the effects of the bombing--population density, degree of industrialization, target selection, and defensive measures all affect the actual impact of air power.[18] In this section, where we are interested in only the most marked overall trends within the air war, we have chosen to use bomb tonnage figure as a gross measure of activity. While this neglects the detailed influence of the variable factors just mentioned, the trends reveal some unmistakable features.

The standards of comparison usually quoted to place bomb tonnages in perspective are taken from the Second World War and from the Korean War. During all of World War II, the U.S. dropped about 2,000,000 tons of air ordnance in all theaters; during the Korean War, about 1,000,000 tons.[19] In Indochina, by the end of 1971, the total weight of air-drop munitions was about 6,300,000 tons. However, the fact that these figures are drawn from vastly different contexts makes a comparison of consequences difficult. In a more closely related case, we find that the British in their counterinsurgency effort in Malaya employed during ten years of that war a total of only 33,000 tons of aerial munitions.[20]

How can one assess figures like these? What material or human destruction results from a hundred, a thousand, or a million tons of ordnance? The Indochina experience in general remains to be studied and documented in detail; however, one of the campaigns comes closer than any other to providing a yardstick for gauging the effects of aerial bombardment. Naval and ground attacks against North Vietnam were on a relatively minor scale; the impact of the war on North Vietnam can thus be ascribed to *air action alone*. Moreover, both the effort and its results have been reasonably well documented.[21] The figures show that during the intense phase of the North Vietnam bombing, 100,000 to 200,000 tons of munitions per year were dropped. This bombing inflicted 25,000 to 50,000 casualties per year, 80 percent of whom were civilians. (An equivalent rate in the U.S., given its greater population, would be 300,000 to 600,000 casualties per year.)

[18] This important point emerges, for example, from the Strategic Bombing Surveys made after World War II in the European and Pacific theatres (cf. App. B).

[19] These are the figures quoted in *Impact of the Vietnam War*, prepared by the Congressional Research Service of the Library of Congress for the Committee on Foreign Relations, U.S. Senate, June 1971 (USGPO, 1971), pp. 8-9.

[20] *Symposium on the Role of Airpower in Counterinsurgency and Unconventional Warfare: The Malayan Emergency* (RAND Corporation, 1963), p. 49.

[21] There were many detailed studies of the bombing of North Vietnam, some sponsored by the

These facts suggest that an air war involving 100,000 or 200,000 tons of ordnance per year must be regarded as an intense attack, with severe civilian impact, in the Indochina context.[22]

Figure 1-1 shows the approximate weights of aerial munitions expended in the different Indochina air campaigns, as well as for the theater as a whole. These figures give a reasonably accurate picture of the patterns of air activity over Indochina since 1965 and of the shifts among the different campaigns.

1. *South Vietnam*

The intensity of the air war for some time was greatest within South Vietnam, which is the focus of ground conflict and where large numbers of U.S. troops have been deployed. During the years of most intense fighting, 1968 and 1969, the air war resulted in the dropping of almost 1,000,000 tons of ordnance (one megaton) per year on South Vietnam. This is five times the maximum annual tonnage deployed against North Vietnam, and it is tonnage used within a country which was in military terms to be defended, not attacked, from the air. Since then the pace of the air war in South Vietnam has slackened, presumably in response to the diminished intensity of the ground fighting and to the withdrawal of American troops. Even so, the rate for 1971 was almost 250,000 tons per year, a figure that can be considered small only in comparison with what went before.

The numbers indicate the scale on which the air war is being waged in South Vietnam; they do not show the kinds of targets against which it is directed. As mentioned previously, we do not deal here with the activity of helicopters (about which, in any event, only very sparse statistical information is available). Of the fixed-wing air strikes, a surprisingly small fraction--well below ten percent--actually involves air support of friendly troops engaged in battle. The rest goes for interdiction, harassment, and sometimes reprisal, a wide span of objectives which reflects the heterogeneous and fluid structure of the conflict itself. In the remoter, sparsely populated regions often used by the NLF/NVA for staging, regroupment, and infiltration, area saturation bombing is common. In those zones which are pre-

Department of Defense and by the CIA. See Sec. 2, below, and Chap. 3 for references.

[22]There are obvious local variations within Indochina and no precise generalizations are possible. North Vietnam has a higher population density than most other regions; on the other hand, it had instituted significantly more effective civil-defense measures. North Vietnam has better anti-aircraft defenses, whose effect is to reduce the accuracy of bombing; but the official American bombing policy was to attempt greater care and precision in attacking primarily military targets. Moreover, it should be remembered that the casualty figures quoted in the official U.S. studies are based on indirect estimates; other reports suggest higher casualty rates, and one might expect the official numbers to err, if anything, on the low side. For the purposes of the present discussion we are content to accept the DoD figures.

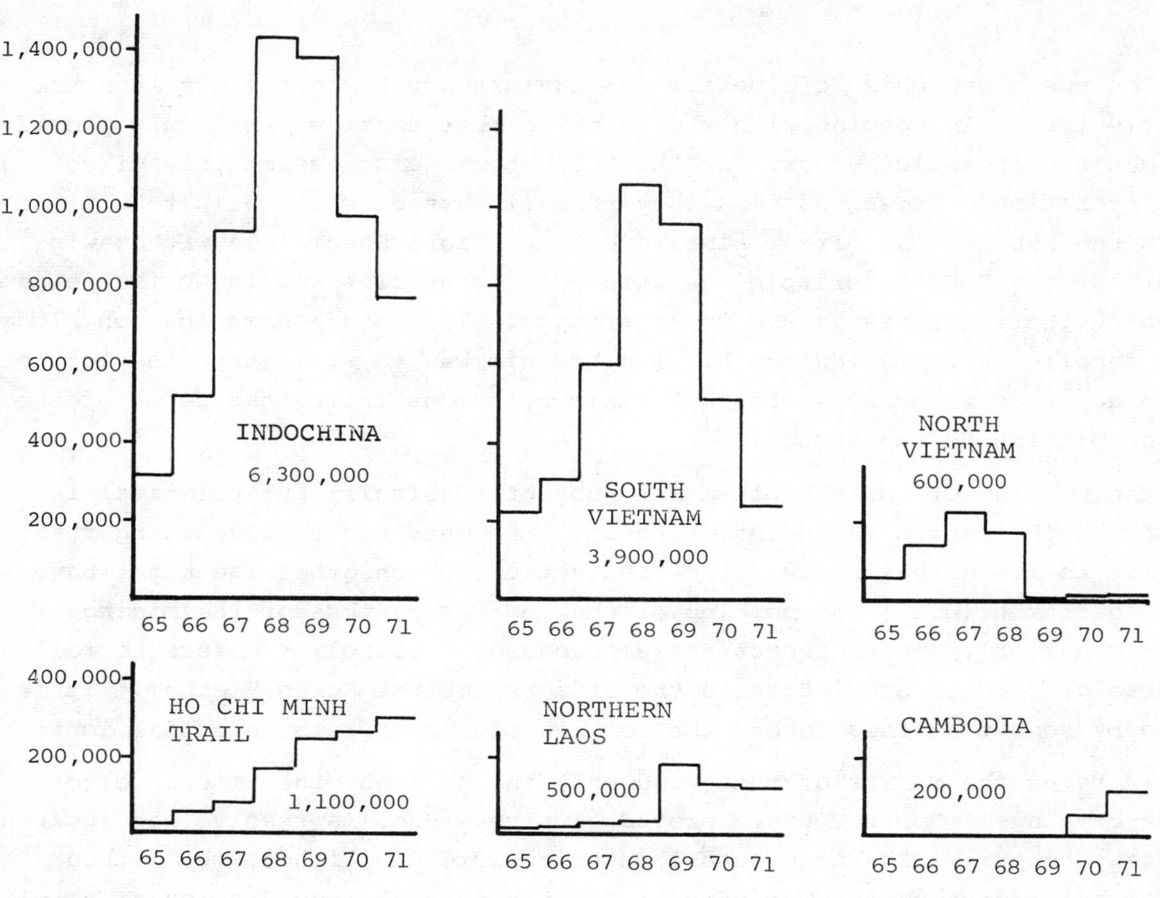

Figure 1-1

ANNUAL TONNAGE OF AERIAL MUNITIONS*

*Cf. Statistical Summary, Sec. SS-8. 1965-1971 totals are rounded to nearest 100,000 tons.

dominantly under NLF control, attacks may be motivated to influence the population: to cause them to move into areas under government control, or to make them stop supporting the insurgency. During the fighting which followed the Tet offensive of 1968, tactical air strikes extended even into the cities themselves.

Because of this wide range of targets and objectives, no unique characterization of the bombing in South Vietnam is possible. However, it can clearly not be considered to have been restrained or highly discriminating, if only because of the sheer volume of activity; and, though strikes may have been motivated by military objectives, the intermingling of combatants and civilians in South Vietnam results in severe social and political consequences from the massive deployment of air power.

2. *North Vietnam*

The sustained phase of the air war against North Vietnam was launched in early 1965. In keeping with the thinking that Hanoi was not only providing men and logistic support for the NLF but was also effectively directing their operations, it was assumed that this air attack would help to win the war in the South. The direct aims were to pressure Hanoi into withdrawing its support of the NLF, to cripple the strategic industries within North Vietnam (of which there were few), and to interrupt the lines of communication along which supplies were moving south. Another aim was to strengthen the morale of pro-government forces in South Vietnam by demonstrating the depth of the U.S. commitment to the struggle.

The bombing of North Vietnam was subject to significant political restraints. The fear of bringing China into the war, and of escalating the conflict to the global scale, precluded actions which otherwise might have been undertaken (e.g., the bombing of the Red River dikes or the mining of Haiphong harbor). These restraints also caused U.S. policy makers to follow a course of gradual escalation in the attacks against North Vietnam. It is argued by some that this robbed the bombing of much of its potential impact.

Whatever the merits of that argument, in the event the immediate goals of the bombing of North Vietnam proved elusive. Hanoi's resolve was apparently strengthened; North Vietnamese industries were demolished, but without significant effect on the war effort; and the partial interdiction of supplies was not sufficient to limit military actions in the South.[23] The air war no doubt exacted a heavy price from North Vietnam in terms of civilian and economic losses, but Hanoi accepted this. Why then did the bombings continue?

Washington was committed for two reasons. First, to convince Hanoi that the air war would be waged with ever increasing force, and that there would be no respite while the insurgency in the South continued, official pronouncements had tied U.S. prestige to the successful prosecution of the air war against the North. Second, the deployment of large numbers of U.S. ground soldiers in Vietnam called for pressing any military action which could be construed as being in their support: "Any limitation on the bombing . . . will cause serious psychological problems among those of our people who cannot understand why we should withhold punishment from the enemy."[24] Retaliation, then, must be seen as an important component in the motivation for the bombing of the North; the official rationale for the first few air attacks

[23] See testimony by Secretary of Defense Robert S. McNamara at the *Air War Hearings* (1967), pp. 276-282.

[24] Secretary McNamara in Draft Presidential Memorandum, October 14, 1966. *Pentagon Papers, op. cit.*, p. 548.

against North Vietnam in fact described them as being retaliatory in nature.[25]

The attacks against North Vietnam continued at a high level long after their military effectiveness had been seriously questioned within the American government. The first break came in March 1968, when President Johnson announced that bombing would be limited to below the twentieth parallel. This amounted to a concentration of the entire air effort, with almost no reduction in total volume, on the interdiction mission against the supply lines. Finally, on November 1, 1968, the intensive bombing of North Vietnam came to an official halt.[26]

3. *The Ho Chi Minh Trail*

Concurrently with the air war against North Vietnam, interdiction efforts were escalated against the Ho Chi Minh trail, a network of supply routes leading from North Vietnam to the South. This was part of a unified attempt to stop or reduce the flow of supplies reaching the insurgents in South Vietnam.[27] Especially after March 1968, air missions against North Vietnam were concentrated on the interdiction mission in the southern part of the country. With the bombing halt in November, a substantial volume of air power was freed for use elsewhere. This force was transferred almost entirely to Laos, in greater part to Trail interdiction. As indicated in Figure 1-1, Trail interdiction has since received steadily increasing emphasis, and it now represents the greatest part of the U.S. air effort. This is central to current U.S. policy:

> The pace of Vietnamization and of U.S. withdrawal from South East Asia rests heavily on reducing the flow of enemy supplies along the Ho Chi Minh trail.[28]

Beyond the escalation in volume of U.S. air power devoted to the interdiction mission, there has been a determined effort to develop radically new technologies for countering infiltration. Indochina, and more particularly the area around the Trail, has thus become the laboratory for the evolution of the *electronic battlefield*. This development promises to have important repercussions on the conduct of limited warfare in general; for the first time it may become possible to confront insurgencies with remote-controlled weapons capable of deploying overwhelming firepower without direct involvement of fighting personnel. This represents the ultimate stage in the juxtaposition of capital-intensive and labor-intensive warfare referred to in the previous section.

[25] For further discussion, see Chap. 11.

[26] At least as a concerted, offensive effort. Surveillance flights over North Vietnam continued, while sporadic attack missions, classified by the U.S. as "protective reaction," have followed with increasing intensity since late 1971.

[27] Another supply route existed, through Cambodia via the port of Sihanoukville (now Kompong Som); we will consider this below.

[28] John L. Frisbee, "Igloo White," *Air Force* (June 1971), p. 48.

There have been impressive claims for the efficacy of the new technology. Though such claims are necessarily based on tentative estimates and are often received with considerable skepticism, doubtless a far greater fraction of supplies coming down the Trail is now being intercepted and destroyed than was possible in earlier years. This obviously exacts a greater effort from the infiltrators and may circumscribe the style of warfare accessible to the NLF, the NVA, and their Cambodian allies. However, significant offensive actions by these forces do continue.[29]

4. *Northern Laos*

In Laos since the early 1960s there has been considerable ground fighting not directly connected with the Trail. The forces of the Royal Laotian Government (RLG) and their supporters have been opposed by those of the Pathet Lao (PL) and the North Vietnamese Army (NVA).[30] The fighting had a fairly well defined front which shifted east or west seasonally along the entire length of Laos. Since its focus was in the central and northeastern provinces, the conflict is commonly referred to as the war in *northern* Laos to distinguish it from the Trail activity in the southern panhandle. The U.S. has strongly supported the RLG in this war. Air power played a rather minor combat role at first. The Royal Laotion Air Force (RLAF), which was effectively under U.S. control, was flying some close-support missions. In 1964 U.S. planes began to participate directly; their activity increased sharply late in 1968, culminating in a dramatic escalation in the summer of 1969. In that year the U.S. expended 200,000 tons of bombs over northern Laos, a rate equal to the peak rate reached in the war against North Vietnam.

In 1969 RLG forces retook the Plain of Jars, a strategically important region in central Laos which for several years had been under PL/NVA control; this success was attributed to the effects of U.S. air support, and optimistic predictions were made about holding Laos against communist pressure, at low cost, through the "proper" application of air power. It was thought possible for air power to maintain a military balance even without the presence of effective ground forces. In the event, the demonstration failed. The PL/NVA soon recaptured the Plain, and though it has changed hands several times since then, it is now firmly under PL/NVA control, as is more territory in Laos than ever before.

[29]The wider implications of the automated warfare now being adopted appear of great importance; they are considered in Chap. 12.

[30]The main fighting strength of the RLG has been the *Armee Clandestine,* composed largely of Meo tribesmen and led by General Vang Pao. Thai mercenaries and U.S. advisors have also participated. These forces are now known as the *Bataillons Guerriers* (BG) and are under the close control of the U.S. Central Intelligence Agency (CIA). See *Laos: April 1971,* Staff Report, Subcommittee on U.S. Security Agreements and Commitments Abroad, Committee on Foreign Relations, U.S. Senate, August 3, 1971 (USGPO, 1971), p. 14.

The relatively clear separation between territories controlled by the RLG and by the PL/NVA brings into focus in Laos some of the results of U.S. bombing. In many areas threatened by a PL/NVA advance the population has been evacuated, leaving the area a free-fire zone. Regions under PL/NVA control are subjected to continuous bombing, to the point where normal life for the remaining population becomes virtually impossible and many villages and towns are levelled. This strategic bombing aims implicitly, if not consciously, at the population--to deprive the PL/NVA of needed services, and to inhibit, insofar as possible, the establishment of normal social patterns in communist-controlled zones. Strategic air warfare exacts enormous costs from the people of Laos, both those remaining in their homes and those made into refugees (about one-third of the population).

5. *Cambodia*

Cambodia occupies a strategic position in Indochina: because of its frontier with South Vietnam, across which NLF/NVA forces may withdraw when pressed; because of its frontier with Laos, across which branches of the Ho Chi Minh trail emerge to continue toward South Vietnam; and because of its port on the Gulf of Siam (Sihanoukville, now Kompong Som), which offers an alternative supply route into South Vietnam.

Until the U.S.-South Vietnamese invasion of Cambodia in April 1970, air activity over that country had at most been sporadic, confined to the regions near the South Vietnamese frontier. Since that date, ground fighting has been heavy and continuous, with U.S. air power engaged both in direct support of Cambodian and South Vietnamese soldiers and in interdiction raids against communist base areas in the northeast. The pattern of this conflict is reminiscent of that seen elsewhere in Indochina. The intensive deployment of air power, though it clearly confers local tactical advantages, does not seem to stabilize the overall military situation. In December 1971, 80 percent of Cambodia was reportedly under communist control.

As in Laos, the impact of air power on the country is severe. Dispatches from the front routinely mention villages that, once taken by the communist forces, are levelled by the bombers. In Cambodia, as in Laos, more than one-third of the population has been made into refugees. It is impossible at this juncture to identify what proportion of the destruction and dislocation should be attributed to the use of air power and what proportion to ground action. Given the magnitude of bombing in both countries, however, air power must be considered a major cause of the destructive effects of the war, and indeed the few studies which have been undertaken on this question have clearly implicated it in this way.

* * * * *

This brief summary of the major campaigns of the Indochina air war will give the reader not only an overview of their objectives, scale, and interrelationship, but also an idea of the approach we have adopted in this report. Notably absent from most of the discussion will be any fundamental ethical judgments concerning the air war. There is little doubt that moral issues will underlie a final judgment; but we believe that moral assessments must be made by the reader himself. We have taken it as our task to gather and present information as coherently as possible so that more informed judgments may follow.

In adopting this approach we in no way wish to imply that moral judgments cannot or should not be made. We noted in our interviews that readiness to reach such judgments was often determined by personal experience. Most consultants who had spent a significant amount of time in Indochina and witnessed the effects of the air war at first hand displayed a certain impatience with detailed discussion of the marginal utility of that war. For them, the overwhelming consideration was the enormous cost inflicted on the people of Indochina; in the face of this cost the other questions tended to fade into insignificance. Others, ourselves included, who had not had such personal acquaintance, found it more difficult to imagine in realistic terms the full impact of what we learned about the air war. This in itself is not surprising; but the lesson emerges that--failing an unusual ability to sense unfamiliar proportions correctly--it is easy to overlook the basic realities and reduce the problem to purely schematic terms.

A second choice that we have deliberately made is to utilize, as the basis for our discussions, official figures released by American authorities or Western journalists in preference to those which originate from communist sources. This does not imply an unreasoning acceptance of American data over others. It simply establishes a common point of reference and avoids the numerology game which often results when data from various sources are mixed. The factual information in this report, though by no means complete or firm in every detail, has not been seriously challenged.[31] The temptation to become sidetracked by the search for exact numbers is great. To establish a sense of proportion, however, questions such as the following should be asked: Would the conclusions be greatly different if the war were shown to cost twice, or half, the amount currently estimated? If the planes lost were twice or half as numerous? If the casualties inflicted were doubled or halved? In most cases the problem lies not in ascertaining the numbers with sufficient precision but in knowing how to *interpret* their magnitude and their meaning.

[31] A preliminary report was circulated November 8, 1971 (500 copies) to invite criticism and comments. It contained almost all the data presented here, none of which were challenged.

CHAPTER 2

THE USE OF AIR POWER

> *Strategic air warfare:* Air combat and supporting operations designed to effect, through the systematic application of force to a selected series of vital targets, the progressive destruction of the enemy's war-making capacity to a point where he no longer retains the ability or will to wage war. Vital targets may include key manufacturing systems, sources of raw material, critical material, stockpiles, power systems, transportation, communication facilities, concentrations of uncommitted elements of enemy armed forces, key agricultural areas, and other such target systems.
>
> *Dictionary of U.S. Military Terms*[1]

A. STRATEGIC AND TACTICAL AIR MISSIONS

In conventional warfare, the objectives of air missions are classified as strategic or tactical. In contrast with the aims of strategic warfare, given above, which have no immediate connection with actual combat and which are intended as a long-term attack on the enemy's war posture, *tactical air warfare* consists of operations carried out "in coordination with ground or naval forces,"[2] i.e., in a direct relationship to the conflict on the battlefield and against military forces in being.

Guerrilla warfare with its shifting "battlefield" does not permit such a clear distinction between strategic and tactical operations, and there is a temptation to classify as tactical a large group of tasks or missions that are actually of ambiguous nature.[3] In order to avoid confusion we will use more specific terms to describe the various kinds of mission. A brief discussion of the necessary terminology follows.

Air superiority is the first-priority mission; if air superiority is not established none of the other missions can be performed without severe interference from enemy aircraft. In the long run, losses would become crippling.

Close air support is "air action against hostile targets which are in close proximity to friendly forces and which require detailed integration of

[1] *Dictionary of U.S. Military Terms* (Public Affairs Press, 1963), pp. 203-204. We quote these definitions from official sources even though they are often not sufficiently precise to serve as a basis for analytical discussion without further elucidation.

[2] *Ibid.*, p. 211.

[3] "In 1966, some 65 percent of the total tonnage of bombs and artillery rounds used in Vietnam was expended against places where the enemy *might* be, but without reliable information that he *was* there." Alain C. Enthoven and K. Wayne Smith, *How Much is Enough?* (Harper & Row, 1971), p. 305. Mr. Enthoven was formerly Assistant Secretary of Defense for Systems Analysis.

each air mission with the fire and movement of those forces."[4]

Interdiction means "to prevent or hinder, by any means, enemy use of an area or route."[5] It "should be a selective campaign waged by aerospace forces against the enemy's total logistic organization."[6] This very general category covers a wide range of missions, and it will be helpful to distinguish between *battlefield interdiction*, which is directed against enemy men and materiel already deployed in the battlefield area, and *deep interdiction*, which is directed against lines of communication with the enemy's remoter base areas, against men and materiel en route to the area of operations. Deep interdiction merges with strategic bombing when it is directed against targets whose military significance is only indirect.[7] Similarly, we shall see that even battlefield interdiction may have a strategic character in a guerrilla conflict because of the difficulty of isolating specifically military targets in such a context.

Logistic air support facilitates the movement of men and materiel, often into areas that would otherwise be inaccessible, e.g., besieged garrisons. The speed and flexibility of air transport, especially by helicopter, may have a critical impact on the outcome of an engagement. On the other hand, "commuting into battle" tends to remove soldiers further from the realities of the conflict, which transcend the military problems of the moment. Since we are concerned primarily with the uses of aerial firepower, logistic missions will not be considered here.

Aerial reconnaissance and communications represent important tactical uses of air power but, again, we will be dealing with them only peripherally.

Psychological operations include loudspeaker announcements, leaflet drops, and drops of gift packages with a message. Our main interest in this mission is due to the fact that the leaflets are often coordinated with air strikes and announce the reasons for the associated attacks.

Defoliation missions involve chemical attacks on the environment rather than on people directly. Their purpose is to deprive the enemy of the cover afforded by heavy vegetation, to deprive him of the food resources of a region, or, ultimately, to force the population of that region to move away. Because these missions involve chemicals rather than conventional munitions they will be dealt with separately.

[4] *Dictionary, op. cit.*, pp. 14-15.

[5] *Ibid.*, p. 115.

[6] *Fundamentals of Aerospace Weapons Systems* (Air University, 1961), p. 313.

[7] Enthoven and Smith use this same distinction between deep interdiction and "local battlefield interdiction"; *op. cit.*, p. 21. Their description of the former as seeking to "limit the enemy's ability to sustain operations at the front by destroying and disrupting his in-

In the Indochina war, the bombing of power plants or of a cement factory in North Vietnam is strategic. Bombing the Ho Chi Minh Trail is deep interdiction; bombing NLF strongholds in the Iron Triangle is battlefield interdiction. Breaking the siege of Khe Sanh in 1968, when 95,000 tons of ordnance were delivered by air to help U.S. and ARVN soldiers, involved elements of close air support as well as battlefield interdiction.[8]

Air missions may be further divided into categories which describe the manner in which individual strikes are initiated. An *immediate* strike is called by ground forces in contact with the enemy, or by reconnaissance plane pilots who have spotted a specific enemy target. Such a strike should be carried out as quickly as possible, before the target information becomes obsolete. Ground forces desire a reaction time measured in minutes, but it is more typical in South Vietnam for the "immediate" strikes to be delayed a half-hour or more. To provide the quickest possible response, planes may be "stacked" on airborne standby duty; otherwise, they may be diverted from lower-priority missions or they may be "scrambled" from their bases.

Preplanned strikes, which are usually scheduled a day or more in advance, normally fall into the interdiction or strategic categories because of the extremely fluid nature of most of the fighting in Indochina.

Armed reconnaissance is defined as

> an air mission flown with the primary purpose of locating and attacking targets of opportunity, i.e., enemy materiel, personnel, and facilities in assigned general areas or along assigned ground communication routes, and not for the purpose of attacking specific briefed targets.[9]

Armed reconnaissance is an important element in interdiction campaigns and a high percentage of strikes are missions of this type. In a large-scale air effort, more missions tend to be directed into "armed recce" as the list of worthwhile fixed targets diminishes.[10]

Harrassment and interdiction is a term more often applied to artillery fire than to aerial fire, though it may be applicable to the latter in some cases. We treat it here as one aspect of general interdiction.

Reconnaissance by fire is a probing attack on an area where enemy presence is suspected. Its purpose is to flush out the opposing forces.

dustry and transportation system" emphasizes the close relationship between deep interdiction and strategic missions.

8 "B-52s Prove Tactical Value During Siege of Khe Sanh," *Aviation Week & Space Technology* (May 13, 1968).

9 *Dictionary, op. cit.*, pp. 22-23.

10 See Admiral U. S. Sharp's testimony in *Air War Hearings* (1967), pp. 6 and 39. [For a key to abbreviated titles of hearings, see App. A.]

With this brief summary of the terminology as a basis, we can now turn to a more detailed description of the actual manner in which air missions are organized and directed against their targets.

B. THE DEPLOYMENT OF AIR POWER[11]

The delivery of ordnance against selected targets from an aircraft is a complex management problem. In principle the mission might seem simple: load the aircraft with the desired munitions, fly to the target, and drop the bombs. In practice the problems to be faced include (1) establishing and maintaining sufficient air superiority to permit unimpeded penetration of the selected air space; (2) countering and avoiding any ground defenses which the enemy may be able to mount; (3) identifying the correct target from the air; and (4) delivering the ordnance with sufficient precision of aim and at the appropriate time to find and destroy the selected target.

1. *Air Superiority.* As noted earlier, the establishment of air superiority is the priority mission in U.S. Air Force doctrine.[12] Key factors are numerical superiority, technical dominance, and favorable basing and logistics. Once air superiority is established in a given area, its grip is hard to break. In Indochina, the U.S. Air Force acquired air superiority by default, only on occasion encountering a challenge over North Vietnam where Russian-made fighters have been intermittently deployed against American planes.[13]

Once air superiority has been effectively established, missions over territory that might be contested--North Vietnam or Laos--are provided with a fighter escort ("MIG cap") to protect them against possible interference. Otherwise, surprise attacks could take an occasional heavy toll.

Air-to-air combat involves highly specialized aircraft in terms of their speed, maneuverability, armaments, and electronic support systems ("black boxes"). The F-4 Phantom is at present the U.S. workhorse in air-to-air battle. Designing an aircraft for the air superiority mission tends to lessen its effectiveness for other tasks. Subsonic and even propeller-driven craft are preferred in close air support and interdiction missions; their lower speed and their ability to dive at steeper angles improve the accuracy of their bomb delivery, and they can loiter for longer times over the target

[11] A brief summary of aircraft types, of their basing in Indochina, and of aerial munitions appears in App. C. We would like to acknowledge extensive discussions with several consultants who helped us develop a picture of air power deployment in Indochina. Among them were William D. White (Brookings Institution) and Brian Eden (Institute for Policy Studies), as well as Air Force and Navy personnel.

[12] *Tactical Air Hearings* (1968), p. 102.

[13] Air superiority does not, however, assure immunity from ground fire.

region.[14]

The type of aircraft available for deployment in Indochina derives to a large extent from the decisions made previously by each of the Services in building up its own inventory. Since the Air Force contributes the greater fraction of U.S. air activity, its emphasis on the air-superiority mission results in the deployment of more tactical air fighters, and fewer close-support planes, than would normally be appropriate in the permissive Indochina air environment.[15]

2. *Ground Defenses.* The presence of heavy ground defenses imposes severe limitations on the patterns in which attack aircraft may be used. Anti-aircraft (AA) weapons may be grouped as follows:

a. *Small arms:* rifles, light automatic weapons. Effective only up to altitudes of about 1,500 feet, but inexpensive and capable of wide and diverse deployment.

b. *Anti-aircraft artillery (AAA):* these weapons begin with heavy machine guns (.50 caliber) and extend through guns with five-inch bore. Because of its high rate of fire the .50 gun is particularly effective against low-flying aircraft up to about 4,500 feet.[16] The larger calibers have a ceiling which extends to over 20,000 feet, but beyond this altitude their accuracy diminishes. The lateral range is a few miles at most. AAA can be radar-controlled for increased precision and for nighttime use.

c. *Surface-to-air missiles (SAMs):* these missiles, radar-controlled, have virtually no ceiling. The SAM-2, deployed in North Vietnam, is effective only above about 1,500 feet.[17] SAMs can be extremely efficient unless effective countermeasures are taken. Such countermeasures include electronic devices and special flight formations, direct evasive tactics (by maneuverable aircraft), and the technique of flying below the altitude at which the missile's control radar is first able to pick up the approaching aircraft in time. The presence of SAMs may therefore force the aircraft into the envelope of AAA or even small-caliber defenses. An aircraft coming in "on the deck" is exposed to these hazards; moreover, it eventually has to climb to higher altitudes to deliver its ordnance against the target, and it is during this period of "popping up" that it is most vulnerable to conventional AAA fire.

The air-to-ground duel is a complicated game in which neither side has

[14] See Enthoven and Smith, *op. cit.*, pp. 220-221; also, *Tactical Air Hearings* (1968), p. 92.

[15] Cf. General G. P. McConnell, Chief of Staff, U.S. Air Force, in *Tactical Air Hearings* (1968), p. 129: ". . . for a long time the national policy was that we were not going to fight anything except a nuclear war at places and with weapons of our own choosing. We did not even start doing anything about tactical fighter aviation until about 1961 or 1962."

[16] *Air War Hearings* (1967), p. 110.

[17] *Ibid.*, p. 483. More recently it has been reported that the newer SA-3 missiles are being supplied to Hanoi. *Washington Post,* April 27, 1971.

the decisive advantage. If, in the long run, the ground defenses can inflict sufficiently high losses on the attacker, the latter will have to change tactics or the cost will outweigh any gains. Attacking aircraft can, of course, fire on the ground defenses. They can seek out radar controls by using specialized missiles such as the Shrike; they can attempt to destroy the installations by conventional bombing, although the small size and "hardness" of these entrenchments is commonly such that decisive scoring is rather unlikely; and, finally, they can suppress such defenses temporarily by the use of anti-personnel weapons which force the crews attending the AA weapon to take shelter.

AA suppression is a function routinely assigned to some of the aircraft making up a typical attack formation.[18] Counting these escort planes and those in the MIG cap, less than half the planes participating in a mission may be actual strike aircraft. A large fraction of the ordnance carried on the mission is thus likely to be expended against ground defenses rather than the target itself; and much of this "extra" ordnance will be in the form of missiles, strafing fire, or anti-personnel weapons, particularly cluster bomb units (CBUs).[19]

In considering where this extra ordnance is likely to fall, the following points should be borne in mind: AA defenses are generally located close to the targets, which in a strategic bombing campaign are situated near predominantly civilian areas. The AA guns are small, highly mobile, and readily camouflaged; SAM sites can be prepared in large numbers, not all necessarily containing missiles.[20] Neither SAMs nor AAA are likely to fire except at worthwhile targets since they expose their location and lay themselves open to attack; conversely, aircraft rarely go on missions specifically to search for and destroy AA sites, since the cost of such missions is likely to exceed their benefit. The air-to-ground duel, then, is deadly business for both sides; each tends to husband its forces.

3. *Target Identification.* This is obviously a difficult problem from the air, particularly in a fast-moving aircraft. Wherever possible, planes are guided to their targets by forward air controllers (FACs) who ride slow-moving spotter planes which can hover over the target regions. Where there are no substantial ground defenses, airborne FACs are so widely used that "FACing" has become a common term, and a pilot attacking without such help is said to FAC for himself.

[18] Ground-fire suppression must also precede defoliation missions, which are not normally pictured as involving any lethal firepower. The low-flying, slow spray planes are very vulnerable targets and thus call for suppressive escort even in areas where other aircraft can operate with relative safety.

[19] *Air War Hearings* (1967), p. 66.

[20] *Ibid.*, p. 498.

Use of a FAC, familiar with his section of terrain and perched in a relatively slow plane, obviously increases the discrimination with which ground targets can be identified and marked for actual strike, usually with the help of a phosphorus rocket. However, even a FAC may have difficulty with target identification, particularly if he attempts to work on his own in separating friend from foe. To do this from the air he may have to rely on criteria which can at best be called subtle, at worst misleading.[21] If he is directing localized air support at the request of ground forces, communicating the desired target location to him from the ground may still be surprisingly difficult, because of the different perspectives involved.[22]

FACs cannot venture into areas with heavy ground defenses: the faster strike aircraft are then obliged to pick out the targets for themselves. Where the targets are prominent and can be readily described in the advance briefing, this may present no problems. More frequently the desired targets are not easily distinguished and so must be specified by their map coordinates, which is at best accurate to within a few hundred feet;[23] the pilot may make additional errors in locating his own position on the map. The situation becomes worse in bad weather or at night when visual navigation and weapon delivery must be abandoned altogether.[24] Instrument navigation is subject to many errors. Its best potentialities are realized when the systems can be calibrated by reference to nearby prominent ground features, which may be picked up on the plane's radar to serve as a reference. Under optimal circumstances, instrument-guided bombing may be accurate to within a few hundred feet.

Particular identification problems arise during armed reconnaissance missions, during which fast attack aircraft are out looking for targets of opportunity. Such targets (trucks, barges, etc.) may in principle be easy to identify. However, because of his plane's fuel consumption, the pilot has

[21]Jonathan Schell writing from Quang Ngai province in 1967 described how FAC pilots identified the enemy: "Captain Reese came to think that he could spot, on the trails, grass that had been freshly bent by the passage of enemy troops, and that he could distinguish enemy houses from civilian houses by whether they were in the tree line or not; . . . Lieutenant Moore came to think he could tell a farmer from a soldier by the way he walked; and . . . Major Billings came to believe he could tell enemy soldiers from civilians by making a low pass over the fields and seeing who ran for cover, and that he could judge whether a wisp of smoke hanging over the woods was rising from the fire of a Montagnard or from the fire of a Vietcong soldier. *The Military Half* (Vintage Books, 1968), p. 181.

[22]Often ground forces do not want to mark a target themselves since this might reveal their own position and draw hostile fire.

[23]James A. Donovan, *Militarism, U.S.A.* (Scribners, 1970), p. 186: "The map's grid squares are one kilometer and the squares are identified by numbers. The target location on the map can be located within about one tenth of a kilometer [about 330 feet]."

[24]Powerful flares can be dropped to illuminate the countryside, but they have several shortcomings. Among them is the "washbowl effect," an optical illusion which makes the ground seem to curve up on all sides of the plane and causes the pilot to become disoriented.

only a limited time to search for them, and he may be tempted to make snap decisions. For example, if he observes tracks leading into a village he may suspect a truck park under some trees. He gets no more than a short glimpse of his possible target, and what he decides to fire on may bear no resemblance to what he thought it was.[25] The combination of technical and human factors involved in armed reconnaissance make it a relatively indiscriminate form of air power deployment.

4. *Precision of Delivery.* Targeting accuracy is usually measured in terms of the circular error probable (CEP).[26] This is the radius of a circle centered on the actual aiming point such that, on the average, half of the bombs are expected to strike inside the circle, with the other half falling somewhere outside. The CEP varies dramatically with circumstances: under ideal conditions of visual dive bombing from low altitudes, and with no interference from enemy defenses, CEPs as low as 100 feet may be achieved, although a figure of 250 feet is quoted as typical in combat today.[27] Since the CEP varies so widely and is, in any event, no more than a statistical measure of how the bombs are likely to be distributed, generalizations about bombing accuracy are difficult to make: but it is clear that the concept of "pinpoint bombing" is a gross idealization, at least so long as conventional unguided weapons are considered. The advent of sophisticated armaments may change this picture; such developments are already well under way and are likely to continue in the future.[28] Air war may then undergo a technological revolution of great importance. However, almost all the bombing in Indochina to date has used conventional munitions, the limitations of which make it inaccurate and often indiscriminate except presumably against large targets such as factory complexes, oil depots, railroad marshalling yards and the like.[29]

[25] Cf. this query from Senatory Stuart Symington: "You say the operation constitutes armed recce--how do you know a certain moving vehicle is not full of schoolchildren instead of soldiers, on the road, when you use napalm?" In response, Colonel Robert Tyrell, Air Attache in Vietiane, emphasized that this would be unlikely because of "source intelligence," concluding, however, by saying, "I would not deny that it would not be impossible." [I.e., he agreed that it would be possible.] *Security Agreement Hearings* (1969), p. 510.

[26] *Dictionary, op. cit.*, p. 45.

[27] Barry Miller, *Aviation Week & Space Technology* (May 3, 1971): "When American bombing began in Vietnam, the Air Force cited in Congressional testimony its ability to achieve CEPs of 750 feet. Only two or three years ago pilots of Republic F-105 fighter-bombers were achieving CEPs in Vietnam of 365 feet against undefended targets; 540 feet against moderately defended targets, and 575 feet against highly defended targets. The same pilots and same aircraft were doing 125 feet in training at Nellis Air Force Base during the same period. Today, these figures in combat are roughly 250 feet."

[28] For a fuller discussion, see Chap. 12.

[29] See the description of how one such large target was bombed, given by Chester L. Cooper, former Assistant for Asian Affairs on the White House staff: "The President agreed to postpone his decision to limit the bombing until the [Joint] Chiefs [of Staff] had been given their opportunity to 'take out' Hanoi's thermal power plant. It would be a simple matter that could be executed with 'surgical precision'; one strike would do the job. . . . On

If the target is a smaller one, such as a bridge, a truck, or a railroad car, many bombing attempts may be made before the target is actually hit.[30]

To offset bombing inaccuracy, many more bombs are dropped than are in principle necessary to destroy the target. This overkill is most dramatically illustrated by the pattern bombing of high-flying strategic bombers (B-52s), where no attempt is made to hit specific point targets. Instead, a whole area is saturated with bombs. The destruction within this area is extremely heavy.[31] The use of such saturation tactics is not dictated entirely by the technical inaccuracies of the bombing process itself. The difficulty of target identification, outlined in the preceding subsection, is often such that the desired aiming point is uncertain. This is particularly true of guerrilla war, and all the more so in a jungle environment.

Other means of improving the effectiveness of air attack rely on the use of *area weapons* to compensate for inaccuracies of aim. Napalm and CBUs are well-known examples and have been, by all accounts, the weapons of preference for close-support operations.[32] Rapid-firing cannon and mini-guns are also

May 19th, the Joint Chiefs were given their chance to get the last piece of candy out of the box. The power plant was bombed. But the target was not destroyed with 'one strike.' Nor was the raid characterized by the precision that had been advertised. Many more attacks over many more months were necessary before it was put out of operation; in the process the surrounding area took a beating. The power plant was located in downtown Hanoi and was bounded on two sides by residential areas. 'Subsidiary damage' was significant, and it was another case of 'sorry about that.'" *The Lost Crusade* (Dodd, Mead & Co., 1970), pp. 375-376.

[30] Examination of aerial photographs from target areas quickly brings home this point. Cf. *Report on the War in Vietnam* (U.S. Government Printing Office, 1968), pp. 26, 28, 32, 37-40, 45.

[31] *Ibid.*, p. 329. For the sake of illustration, the area covered by a single mission of six B-52 bombers, about one-half mile wide and three miles long, is shown below superimposed on a section of a street map of Washington, D.C. About 150 tons of bombs are dropped onto this area within a fraction of a minute.

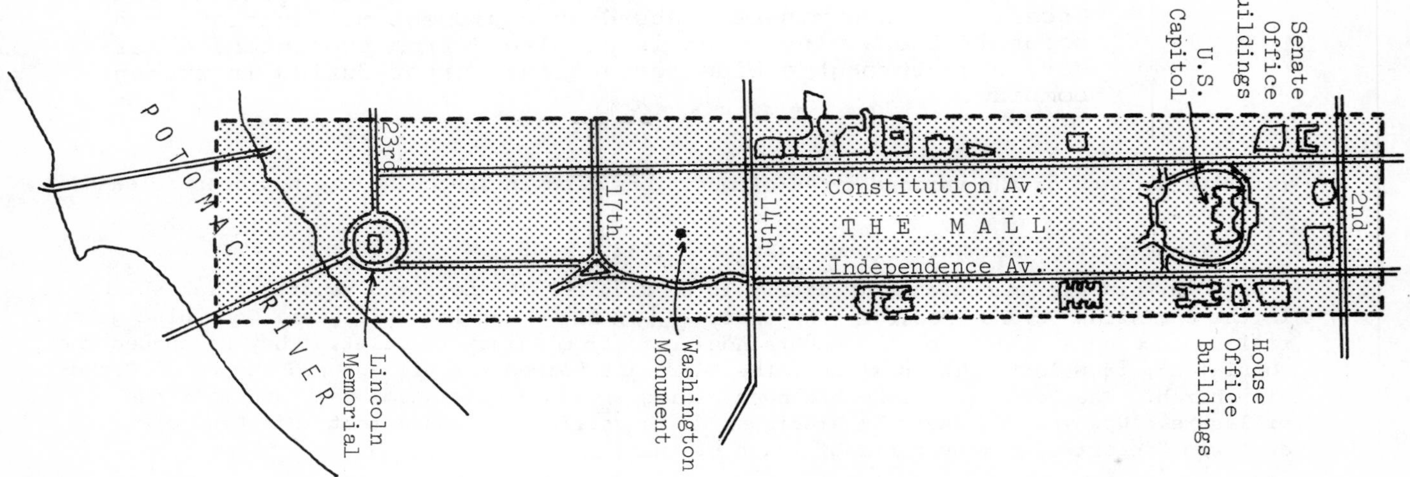

[32] We came across various indications that ground troops felt aircraft did not arrive with enough of these and instead carried too many conventional bombs. However, data on the

area weapons, with the motion of the aircraft helping to distribute the projectiles. With one pass a gunship can put a bullet per square foot into an area the size of a football field.[33]

Targeting accuracy must be considered in terms of time as well as space. This does not apply to stationary targets such as power stations, but in a guerrilla war mobility is the chief military asset of the insurgents; once identified, most targets have to be struck quickly or the information becomes valueless. In practice, even for "immediate" air strikes, despite great efforts at organization, reaction times have varied widely--from a few minutes up to as much as an hour. Preplanned strikes usually rely on target intelligence that is at least a day or two old. Thus in the Indochina context such strikes should generally be considered strategic missions with little tactical value. The intended specific target is "volatile" and likely as not to be absent at the time of the strike.[34]

C. PROBLEMS OF CONTINGENT ORDNANCE

We are concerned here not only with the degree of effectiveness with which targets are bombed, but also with the effects of ordnance dropped on areas outside the target region itself. We refer to this as *contingent* bombing, since it is likely but not certain to occur in the course of a mission.[35] Obviously, the fraction of total ordnance which is deployed against non-targets will vary greatly with the circumstances, and will be affected by both technical and human factors.

1. *Technical Factors*

   a. *Inaccuracy of delivery* (as measured by CEP). Contingent ordnance falls into a region adjacent to the aiming point; its composition will be the same as that used against the target. Occasional wide misses, caused by equipment malfunction, can occur if the aiming point is displaced from the intended target, e.g. through a wide navigational error during instrument bombing.

relative amounts of the various types of munitions used in Indochina has not been released officially.

33 See Frank Harvey, *Air War--Vietnam* (Bantam, 1967), p.45.

34 Data on this are understandably difficult to acquire. We note the report of Takashi Oka in the *Christian Science Monitor* (September 30, 1965): "Earlier this year, Communist guerrillas occupied a village on the mountainous road from Saigon to Dalat. They harangued the population, then left. The next day, the Americans bombed the village and its Roman Catholic church. The Communists, who had been hiding in the jungle, came back and told the villagers, 'Now you see what the Americans do to you.'" Oka added that this kind of incident was "reported in many parts of South Vietnam."

35 Finding an inclusive term, not burdened with connotations, to describe this aspect of the air war was not easy. We use the term "contingent" according to its meaning in *Webster's Third New International Dictionary:* likely but not certain to happen; intended for use in

b. *Target misidentification.* This accounts for much contingent ordnance that strikes regions without apparent military significance. It also accounts for concentrated attacks on unintended targets such as a "friendly" village.[36]

c. *AA-suppression fire.* In regions with substantial ground defenses, AA-suppression becomes an important part of the mission. Contingent ordnance of a type suitable to this function will fall into the vicinity of those installations participating in the defense. Most of these are adjacent to the target itself, or at least near the normal flight path of the mission to its target. Often they are located in or near population centers. The ordnance used typically includes rockets, strafing fire, CBUs and napalm--antipersonnel weapons with an area coverage that is likely to extend over the surroundings.

d. *Armed reconnaissance.* Contingent ordnance on such a mission is usually due to target misidentification. We call attention to it separately because of the large percentage of air sorties that are actually flown as armed reconnaissance in many theaters (e.g., 75 to 90 percent during the bombing attacks on North Vietnam).

e. *Surplus ordnance.* This category includes ordnance remaining in an aircraft when its primary mission has either been achieved or had to be aborted for technical or circumstantial reasons. Planes are not allowed to land with explosives aboard; surplus ordnance can be dumped harmlessly into the sea or into a safe dumping area, but this is considered a waste and is avoided if possible. The surplus may be used against secondary targets, sometimes chosen beforehand. However, their selection tends to be less careful than that of primary targets and is often left to the pilots themselves.[37]

f. *Emergency dumping.* In the case of unexpected attack by hostile fighters, or of partial damage from enemy action or technical failure, a pilot may be obliged to dump his ordnance quickly. Fighter-bombers, for example, cannot fly supersonically while they carry exterior bomb loads, so these bombs will be jettisoned if MIGs are sighted.[38]

circumstances not completely unforseen; dependent on or conditioned by something else.

[36]If a "friendly" village is mistakenly attacked under conditions of good visibility, it may be due to an error of navigation, but it is clear at least that the intended target was another *village*. An example of a well documented incident of this type is the attack on the village of Lang Vei by two U.S. fighter-bombers on March 2, 1967, during which they strafed the village with cannon fire, dropped high-explosive bombs, and scattered antipersonnel bombs. Seventy percent of the village was laid in ruins, 100 persons were killed and 200 more were injured. The incident was witnessed by a U.S. Special Services officer from a camp just outside the village; one of the men from the camp, who tried to signal the planes away with a flare, was also killed. In the subsequent discussions, Pentagon spokesmen would not admit that the pilots had consciously attacked a village, but laid the blame on equipment malfunction. See "Incident in Vietnam," *Center Diary* (Center for the Study of Democratic Institutions, March 4, 6, 21; April 5, 13, 15, and 24 (1967). It may be noted that the attack occurred about five hours after ground fire downed a U.S. helicopter in the area.

[37]For example, pilots returning from North Vietnam with surplus ordnance were authorized to expend this against lines of communication.

[38]For example, Col. Jack Broughton, USAF (ret.), veteran pilot of many missions over North Vietnam, recounts how bombs had to be jettisoned as MIGs approached to give battle to his

In summary, though no specific figures can be given, it is likely that more than half of the ordnance delivered falls outside the intended target zones because of technical factors inherent in the nature of the air mission itself.

2. *Human Factors.* In discussing the effects of the air war, it is of course tempting to focus on those aspects which are most easily quantifiable or described. Thus, in the preceding sections, we have dealt with the technical factors which govern the progress of an air mission. However, there are equally relevant human limitations, which must not be ignored. Though our remarks are confined to some general observations on the subject, it should not be assumed that we consider these factors less important. War is ultimately waged by men, and the men who operate the machines are an essential element in the outcome of the operation.

There are numerous situations in which human judgment may become a limiting factor:

--a FAC has to identify suitable targets for air strikes on the basis of highly ambiguous clues: the way people in the field react when he flies over them, some apparently new tracks in the grass, some unexpected smoke in the forest;

--a fighter-bomber pilot on an armed reconnaissance mission must identify targets while passing over them at high speed: his glimpse of them may last only a second or two;

--a FAC, a helicopter, or a gunship takes hostile fire from the ground: even if the source of the fire can be identified, how can it be ascertained whether or not civilians are nearby?

A basic fact of air war is responsible for such dilemmas: it is war waged at a distance, both physically and psychologically. Participants remain emotionally detached, not only because flying the plane and operating its complicated gadgets demand all their attention, but also because the magnitude of the forces they control, the extent of the destruction they unleash, would otherwise overload their emotional reserves. These men operate in an atmosphere where professionalism is essential not only for technical reasons, but for psychological ones as well.[39]

Professionalism means concentrating on the technical aspects of the mis-

group of aircraft. He notes thus bombing a target which was in a category at that time not authorized for American strikes. *Thud Ridge* (Lippincott, 1969), p. 76.

39 Pilots often say that they are not bothered by their work; they regard it as "a job that needs doing." When the question is pursued in greater detail, however, they may readily concede that they would "go crazy" if they thought about what was happening on the ground as a result of their bombs [*CBS Evening News* with Walter Cronkite, December 23, 1971]. The recurrent use of the surgical analogy for bombing (a "surgical" strike, "surgical" precision) appears symptomatic of the need to take emotional shelter in the emphasis on professionalism.

sion, substituting a formal set of immediate objectives for the actual, long-term aims of the conflict. It often encourages competition on these formal grounds: which group, which service, flies the greatest number of sorties, which delivers most ordnance "on target"? Competition also arises at the top of the chain of command, where a good showing must be made at appropriations hearings: furtherance of the overall aims of the war cannot be readily quantified, so the performance record of each service comes to depend on such criteria as the aircraft utilization ratio--the number of sorties flown per aircraft deployed, with the real results of those sorties left out of consideration.

General David M. Shoup, former commandant of the U.S. Marine Corps, reports:

> So by early 1965 the Navy carrier people and the Air Force initiated a contest of comparative strikes, sorties, tonnages dropped, 'Killed by Air' claims, and target grabbing which continued up to the 1968 bombing pause. Much of the reporting on air action has consisted of misleading data or propaganda to serve Air Force and Navy purposes. In fact, it became increasingly apparent that the U.S. bombing effort in both North and South Vietnam has been one of the most wasteful and expensive hoaxes ever to be put over on the American people. Tactical and close air support of ground operations is essential, but air power use in general has to a large degree been a contest for the operations planners, 'fine experience' for young pilots, and opportunity for career officers.[40]

The professional structuring of situations defines them in controlled ways. There are no spaces on bomb-damage assessment forms for reporting civilian damage--the targets hit are assumed to be those described in the original briefing for the mission, however tentative their identification may have been. Jargon proliferates. A hootch (house) destroyed becomes a "military structure," a sampan is a "waterborne logistic craft." The jargon pervades the reports, invades the intelligence accounts and finally comes to influence even the policy thinking.

These human factors are basic to the problem of applying air technology to a guerrilla conflict. They generate their own pressures for escalation, and in turn the escalation magnifies the human failings. One can conceive of a small, highly trained and tightly supervised team of men operating an air force, limiting their actions wherever the dangers of their weapons seemed disproportionate to the potential military gains. Such a team could remain responsive to the technical shortcomings of its weapons and make all possible allowances for them. But if this controlled operation did not yield the desired results, or did not yield them quickly enough, the standard response

[40] David M. Shoup, "The New American Militarism," *The Atlantic Monthly* (April 1969), p. 55.

would be a call for more air power, and yet more again. The pattern in Indochina has been one of repeated escalation. This changes the very atmosphere in which air power is exercised. The criteria for selecting targets must be broadened. Pilots must be encouraged to bomb more rather than less. Volume becomes an end in itself. Many of the participants eventually come to accept the view that everything on the ground (at least in some regions) is "the enemy" and that all ordnance expended helps "save the lives of our boys."

In summary, air technology applied to a guerrilla conflict leads to an interaction in which the tasks that pilots are formally asked to perform are frequently beyond the limits of their actual capabilities, both technical and emotional. Frustration, rivalry, and the effects of escalation combine to create a set of performance criteria whose relevance to the actual goals of the operation is indirect at best.

CHAPTER 3

THE AIR WAR AGAINST NORTH VIETNAM

A. EVOLUTION OF THE INSURGENCY IN SOUTH VIETNAM

The conflict in South Vietnam is central to the war in Indochina. Before turning to the description of the air campaigns in North and South Vietnam, it is worthwhile recalling some of the milestones in the evolution of the South Vietnamese insurgency.[1] U.S. involvement in the area predated the Geneva Conference of 1954; but up to that point the U.S. had played an indirect role supporting the French colonial effort to prevail against the rising movement of nationalism in Indochina. By 1954, Viet Minh insurgents had gathered enough strength to overcome the French forces in Indochina, notably at the battle of Dien Bien Phu. Following the Geneva Conference and the French withdrawal, there was to be a period of political restructuring to succeed the years of armed conflict between nationalist and communist forces on the one side, and pro-Western, anti-communist forces on the other.

However, the political interlude did not last. A military regroupment of opposing forces to either side of the 17th parallel had been agreed upon, to precede nationwide elections which would reunite the whole nation; but these elections were not held, and the separation took on a more permanent character. The Democratic Republic of Vietnam (DRV), from Hanoi, claimed jurisdiction over the whole of Vietnam, as did the Government of the Republic of Vietnam (GVN), formed on October 26, 1955, in Saigon under President Ngo Dinh Diem.

The Viet Minh had left political cadres in the South to organize for the elections scheduled for 1956; these cadres were enjoined at the time to wage only political struggle. When the elections were not held, and arrests made by Diem threatened to destroy these political cadres, armed insurgency began

[1] This brief summary is drawn mostly from a synopsis given by Neil Sheehan and others, in *The Pengtagon Papers* (Bantam, 1971), pp. 72-78. This work is the well-known first publication, by the *New York Times*, of a summary and extracts from *United States-Vietnam Relations, 1945-1967,* a study prepared under the direction of Leslie Gelb for the Department of Defense. This study remained classified until 1971, when a restricted selection from it was made available in a very limited edition by the Government Printing Office. A different, and in many respects more extensive, version was published under the title *The Senator Gravel Edition, The Pentagon Papers* (Beacon, 1971). Material from this work will be referenced, wherever possible, from the Bantam edition by reason of its greater availability. The reader is referred also to Bernard B. Fall, *The Two Vietnams,* 2nd ed. (Praeger, 1967); Douglas Pike, *Viet Cong* (M.I.T. Press, 1966); George McT. Kahin and John Lewis, *The United States in Vietnam,* 2nd ed. (Delta, 1969).

once again in South Vietnam. In 1959 Hanoi abandoned its policy of endorsing only political action in the South, and with this the amount of armed action grew. Men began to infiltrate to the South from the North along a system of trails that came to be known as the Ho Chi Minh trail, and a period of successes for the insurgents ensued. From December 20, 1960, the insurgents officially described themselves as the National Liberation Front for South Vietnam (NLF); by the end of 1961 the NLF claimed to have 300,000 members.

Though the communist associations of the NLF were repellent to some, it gained more and more support as a political force pledged to national liberation. President Diem's government was seen to be dependent on outside support, the manner of his rule autocratic and corrupt. In the Strategic Hamlet program, Diem had ordered the forced relocation of Montagnard tribesmen and Vietnamese peasants from remote areas to more easily defended locations, but the result was that those forced to move often became easy recruits for the NLF. Diem further angered rural Vietnamese by abolishing their elected village councils (1956) and replacing them with political appointees loyal to himself--often strangers to the area under their administrative control. The "land reform" program was another case in point: it often took away land given to the peasants by the Viet Minh and required them to resume paying rent, whether to landlords or to government officials. Diem also succeeded in alienating large numbers of South Vietnamese intellectuals and members of the armed forces.

The NLF was thriving on support from various sections of the population: the infiltration of men and supplies from the North was of relatively little importance. U.S. intelligence estimates were that 80-90 percent of the NLF forces were locally recruited; "there was little evidence that the Viet Cong relied on external supplies."[2] A report prepared for President Kennedy in March 1961 stated that internal security in South Vietnam was deteriorating rapidly and was likely to continue deteriorating under Diem. This was not new. The previous year, the American Ambassador in Saigon had explained to Washington that the "Diem government is in quite serious danger," and requested that some drastic action be taken.[3]

The action taken by the Kennedy administration was indeed drastic in its implications, though not dramatic at first sight. Kennedy secretly ordered 400 Special Forces and 100 other military advisors to South Vietnam in the spring of 1961. By the end of 1962 there were 11,000 U.S. military men in South Vietnam. Among them were two helicopter companies, with thirty-three H-21C helicopters, who flew combat support missions, and an air commando unit

[2] *Pentagon Papers, op. cit.*, p. 98.

[3] *Ibid.*, p. 116.

which instructed the South Vietnamese air force (VNAF) in the techniques of close air support. In addition, American planes based in Thailand and on carriers in the China Sea flew surveillance and reconnaissance missions. Six C-123 aircraft based in South Vietnam began defoliation operations.

While this increasing military aid was being given to the Diem regime, there was an awareness in Washington that social and political reforms were needed in South Vietnam before that regime could hope to become viable. However, beyond suggesting such reforms and obtaining vague promises from time to time, U.S. policy makers did not insist on actual results before proceeding with further military steps. Thus the technological approach to counterinsurgency outstripped the political one from the beginning.

At the end of 1963, in the confusion following the coup against Diem, Washington learned that the degree of NLF administrative and military strength was much greater than it had been led to believe by the Diem government.[4] Assuming that Hanoi played an important role in creating political instability in the South, Washington undertook clandestine military operations against North Vietnam.[5] The clandestine military action, however, did not stop the process of military and political disintegration in the South. In September 1964, Assistant Secretary of Defense John T. McNaughton wrote that

> The situation in South Vietnam is deteriorating. Even before the government sank into confusion last week, the course of the war in South Vietnam had been downward, with less and less territory meaningfully under the control of the government.[6]

Secretary of Defense McNamara observed in December 1964 that the guerrillas controlled the population and rice production heartland of the Mekong Delta, south and west of Saigon.[7] On December 26, 1964, and January 2, 1965, two South Vietnamese Marine battalions were defeated by guerrilla forces in a battle at Binh Gia, southeast of Saigon.[8] The Army of the Republic of South Vietnam (ARVN) was collapsing rapidly.

In January 1965 William Bundy wrote, in a memorandum to Secretary of State Rusk, that

4 Roger Hilsman, *To Move a Nation* (Dell, 1967), pp. 522-524.

5 *Pentagon Papers*, *op. cit.*, Chap. 5 and p. 239. The covert war took on greater military emphasis at this time as the bombing of Laos was also begun then. Already in 1961 the U.S. Joint Chiefs of Staff had made tentative plans for air strikes against North Vietnam and possibly southern China in response to the deterioration of Diem's control at that time [*Ibid.*, p. 89]. U.S. air power was used clandestinely over North Vietnam, beginning in 1961, for harassment, intelligence and sabotage missions. [*Ibid.*, pp. 91-93.]

6 *Ibid.*, p. 355. The pro-American government in Laos was also deteriorating.

7 *Ibid.*, p. 242.

8 *Ibid.*, p. 340.

> The situation in South Vietnam is now likely to come apart more rapidly than we had anticipated in November. We would still stick to the estimate that the most likely form of coming apart would be a government of key groups starting to negotiate covertly with the Liberation Front or Hanoi, perhaps not asking in the first instance that we get out, but with that necessarily following at a fairly early stage.[9]

In the National Security Action Memorandum 288 of March 1964, the Johnson Administration had committed itself to maintaining an independent, non-communist South Vietnam.[10] If a government willing to negotiate with the NLF were to emerge in Saigon, achievement of this objective would be frustrated. It was in this crisis atmosphere that plans were made for bombing the North in order to rescue some remnant of American policy in South Vietnam.

B. INCEPTION OF THE AIR WAR AGAINST NORTH VIETNAM

To support the highly unstable government in Saigon, Washington decided to use air strikes against the North as a means of undermining Hanoi's support of the NLF. McNaughton summarized the relationship between the situation in the South and the bombing of the North:

> Action against North Vietnam is to some extent a substitute for strengthening the government in South Vietnam. That is, a less active VC (on orders from DRV) can be matched by a less efficient GVN. We therefore should consider squeezing North Vietnam.[11]

The air war against the North was begun with three primary objectives in mind: to provide a morale boost for Saigon, and an incentive for it to carry out reforms; to force Hanoi to cease its support of the insurgency; and to gain a bargaining position from which the U.S. could insure a non-communist government in the South.[12] The first strikes were begun with the expectation that they would bring Hanoi to its knees in two to six months.[13] The high expectations that Washington placed on the bombing can be traced to the assumptions that Hanoi had direct control over the NLF, that the guerrilla movement

[9] *Ibid.*, pp. 340-341.

[10] *Ibid.*, p. 323.

[11] *Ibid.*, pp. 365-366.

[12] *Ibid.*, pp. 324, 327.

[13] *The New York Times* (June 5, 1967) and *Pentagon Papers, op. cit.*, pp. 374-375. We note that General Maxwell Taylor advised President Kennedy in 1961 that "North Vietnam is extremely vulnerable to conventional bombing." [*Ibid.*, p. 85.] See also analysis of these decisions by William E. Simons, "The Vietnam Intervention, 1964-65," in Alexander L. George, David K. Hall, and William E. Simons, *The Limits of Coercive Diplomacy: Laos, Cuba, Vietnam* (Little Brown, 1971), esp. p. 172 on the decision makers' expectations. This analysis is based on a RAND study by Colonel Simons.

in the South would fail if its outside source of supplies were cut off, and that the North would be willing to stop support of the NLF if its small but hard-won industrial capacity were threatened with destruction.

In spite of the high expectations, policy planners apparently realized in a matter of weeks that the bombing was stiffening, not weakening, Hanoi's resolve and consequently that ground troops would be required to halt the collapse of the Saigon government.[14] American Marines already on defensive duty in South Vietnam were put on offensive duty. The objectives of the bombing of the North also shifted somewhat with this realization. The hope of coercing Hanoi into concessions remained, but the military objective of interdicting lines of communication from North to South became the primary purpose.[15]

The importance attached to various air war objectives varied from planner to planner in the Johnson Administration. When the sustained bombing of North Vietnam began in February 1965, expectations about the effects of the air war were of two types. The Joint Chiefs of Staff (JCS) favored large-scale strategic bombing, believing that Hanoi could be intimidated into ceasing support for the NLF only if air power was massively employed. At one point, for example, they suggested that it would take only twelve days to destroy a series of initial targets--bridges and depots of ammunition and petroleum--if all U.S. air power in the western Pacific were used.[16]

Most other planners favored a gradual increase in the scope and intensity of the bombing, hoping to deter Hanoi from further prosecution of the war before heavy damage was actually inflicted. They believed that this approach would make clear the Administration's limited objective, and, by holding North Vietnam's economy hostage to further attacks, would pressure Hanoi into concessions. Larger political considerations obviously played an important part in this line of thinking. The fear that China might be brought into the war, as in Korea, and the possibility of ultimately triggering World War III, dictated a restrained approach.

The step-by-step escalation permitted continuous monitoring of the international reactions. One the other hand, in the opinion of many, it robbed the bombing of much of its deterrent effect: on the psychological level, the people of North Vietnam were given a chance to become gradually accustomed to the air attacks; on the practical plane, Hanoi had time to institute effective countermeasures. These included greatly strengthened anti-aircraft defenses,

[14] *Pentagon Papers, op. cit.*, pp. 382-383.

[15] This emphasis can be seen in the way aircraft were used: most additional planes deployed between 1965 and 1966 were absorbed in the interdiction campaign against infiltration routes. See George *et al.*, *op. cit.*, pp. 179 ff. Data on missions are given in *Gravel Edition, Pentagon Papers*, *op. cit.*, Vol. IV, p. 373.

[16] *Pentagon Papers, op. cit.*, pp. 247, 330.

dispersal of industry, alternative lines of supply and communication, and negotiations for increased material help from both Moscow and Peking.

In what follows we will be analyzing the effectiveness of the bombing of North Vietnam, given the actual, gradual escalation that took place and the targeting restraints that American policy makers accepted. This must be clearly understood. It would be a matter of speculation, today, to ask whether a different bombing policy would have had more definite results. One can certainly imagine a level of bombing, suddenly applied, which would have deterred (or directly prevented) Hanoi from further support of the fighting in the South. Breaching the Red River dikes, for example, has been compared in its predicted impact with the dropping of a nuclear weapon. However, it would be equally realistic to say that such an action would have brought China into the war, if not started World War III. We therefore prefer not to enter into speculation about "what might have been." There is no basis to saying with any certainty that air power unfettered by political considerations could have "won" the war in Vietnam. Various outcomes of a more rapid escalation are possible, not all of them favorable to "victory."

As the war continued, a point of view opposing escalation, sudden or gradual, began to emerge. While the Joint Chiefs continued to emphasize the importance of strategic bombing and pressed for rapid increases in its scope and intensity, Secretary of Defense McNamara began to doubt as early as the fall of 1965 that it was possible for the U.S. to achieve its goals in Vietnam; by 1966-67 a few other policy planners had come to share McNamara's doubts. They suggested both scaling down the level of air activity and modifying the objective of preserving a non-communist government in South Vietnam.

Most high officials in the State Department and the White House comprised a third group which tried to mediate between the escalators and the de-escalators. The resulting compromises usually entailed piecemeal escalation of air activity.[17]

Each time the war widened, the prestige and credibility of the U.S. were more heavily invested in the effort, making it more difficult for Washington to do anything but go on with the air war. At stake too was the U.S. plan of making Vietnam a "test case," a proof that wars of national liberation were not "cheap," because the U.S. was prepared to engage in counterinsurgency.[18]

The first American air strikes on North Vietnam, carried out after the Tonkin incident in August 1964, were meant to punish North Vietnam for actions

[17] *Ibid.*, p. 511.

[18] *Ibid.*, p. 255; and Henry F. Graff, *The Tuesday Cabinet* (Prentice-Hall, 1970), pp. 42-43. The author quotes President Johnson as saying that the Americans in Vietnam could not be "tucking tail and coming home" [p. 54].

believed to have been taken by North Vietnamese PT boats. The two air strikes which took place in February 1965, however, were clearly designed to broaden the concept of reprisal by way of preparation for the sustained bombing of North Vietnam.[19] Thus the first strike on February 7, 1965, in response to an NLF attack on a U.S. military installation in the South, held the North responsible for action taken by the NLF in the South. The public rationale for the air strikes emphasized Hanoi's infiltration of men and materiel to the South.[20] The second strike on February 11, 1965, again blamed the North for NLF action in the South (an attack on a U.S. billet at Qui Nhon), but instead of explaining the U.S. attacks on the North as reprisals, Washington chose to describe the air strikes as a response to continued aggression from the North.[21] Punishment for continuing infiltration from the North then became the public rationale for the sustained bombing of North Vietnam which, under the code name ROLLING THUNDER, was approved on February 13 by President Johnson and began March 2.

Because of the political sensitivity of the air war in the North, the targets struck by U.S. bombers were chosen in Washington on a weekly basis and needed the approval of the Office of Secretary of Defense, the Department of State, and the White House. There were two types of targets: fixed or numbered, and unnumbered. The fixed targets were listed individually by the Joint Chiefs and every strike or restrike on them had to be approved separately. In 1965 no attacks were permitted within a 30 nautical-mile radius of Hanoi, within a 10 nautical-mile radius of Haiphong, and in a buffer zone along the Chinese border.[22] The JCS list included strategic targets such as factories and power plants, but North Vietnam offered very few such targets. A November 1965 report from the Defense Intelligence Agency to Secretary McNamara stated:

> What intelligence agencies like to call the "modern industrial sector" of the economy was tiny even by Asian standards . . . There were only a handful of "major industrial facilities." When North Vietnam was first targeted, the JCS found only eight industrial installations worth listing.[23]

Debate raged, however, on which targets should be approved and which should be considered too "politically sensitive," or else too trivial, for air

[19] *Pentagon Papers, op. cit.*, pp. 388-389 and Document 92, pp. 423-425.

[20] White House Statement, Department of State *Bulletin* (February 22, 1965), pp. 238-239.

[21] *Pentagon Papers, op. cit.*, p. 389.

[22] *Gravel Edition, Pentagon Papers, op. cit.*, Vol. IV, p. 29. The sizes of these prohibited zones were later reduced and occasional raids were authorized even within the narrower limits.

[23] *Pentagon Papers, op. cit.*, p. 469.

strikes.[24] The kingpin among the sensitive targets was the harbor of Haiphong, through which many of the imports were entering North Vietnam from the USSR and from China, but in which the danger of hitting foreign shipping made air strikes a risky proposal. Dock installations at Haiphong were ultimately bombed, but the harbor itself was not attacked, nor were the proposals for closing it by aerial dissemination of mines accepted.

Air strikes against North Vietnam were flown by the Air Force, the Navy (from carriers at Yankee Station, 100 miles north-east of Da Nang), and the Marines. These services had different "route packages" allotted to them within North Vietnam, and the number of sorties they were scheduled to fly was strictly regulated:

> The total number of sorties over the North was carefully controlled by allotment to each service for a two-week period, regardless of weather or technical military considerations, General Meyers said. This procedure was to insure that the Air Force and the Navy each received its fair share of the action so that their periodic reports would not reveal that one service was more effective or efficient than the other. As a result, sorties were often ordered in bad weather to meet what commanders considered to be a "quota."[25]

Such inter-service rivalry may have been a contributing factor to the escalation of the bombing of North Vietnam, and it very likely caused many missions, rather than being cancelled because of poor flying conditions, to be diverted to secondary targets selected with lesser care.

Sometimes the list of authorized fixed targets was exhausted before the scheduled number of sorties had been flown; in that case, the pilots flew additional armed reconnaissance missions against targets of opportunity within certain specified categories such as trucks, railroad cars, and barges.[26] Armed reconnaissance is a normal component of any aerial interdiction campaign; but, as a result of the scarcity of worthwhile fixed targets, the fraction of missions flown in this mode over North Vietnam was unusually large.[27] Such

[24] The list of numbered targets became a political football and was the subject of what can only be described as a highly cynical numbers game; this comes out particularly strongly in the *Air War Hearings* (1967), Part 4. (For a key to abbreviated titles of hearings, see App. A.)

[25] James A. Donovan, *Militarism, U.S.A.* (Scribner's, 1970), pp. 180-181.

[26] ". . .these targets had all been struck and many of them heavily damaged. Our efforts in the vital northeast area over the last two months have consisted principally of armed reconnaissance . . ." Admiral U. S. Sharp in *Air War Hearings* (1967), Part I, p. 6. Also, p. 39: "When we had hit all the assigned targets we were working on armed recce alone." A relevant comment on armed reconnaissance appears on p. 30: "Sometimes people go out on an armed reconnaissance mission. They are not fortunate enough to find anything, and so then they let go on a less important target, in order not to haul the bombs back and drop them in the ocean."

[27] During 1965, "nearly three-fourths" of the sorties were flown on armed reconnaissance;

missions may account for much of the incidental civilian damage that has been reported, since pilots flying fast fighter-bombers are not in a good position to make unambiguous target selections.

C. THE PHASES OF THE AIR WAR

The air war over the North can be divided into five phases.

The first phase began in the summer of 1965 and was directed primarily at North Vietnam's transportation system.[28] The bombing concentrated on infiltration routes, beginning in the panhandle of North Vietnam and moving slowly northward and hitting a wider variety of targets. This interdiction campaign remained one aspect of the air war throughout; other important elements were added.

The second phase of the air war lasted only a month from June 29, 1966 until the end of July 1966; in this time 70 percent of North Vietnam's oil storage capacity was destroyed.[29] Though brief in its duration, the attack on the oil-storage facilities was the subject of an Administration debate characterized by extravagant predictions about the importance and vulnerability of these targets and a subsequent demonstration of their marginal importance to the war in the South. During the winter of 1965-66 the JCS prepared a program for full strategic bombing of the industrial, economic resources of North Vietnam which eventually centered on the possibility of striking petroleum, oil, and lubricant (POL) storage facilities. The JCS claimed that destruction of this target system would prove more damaging to the North's ability to send war-supporting material south than an attack on any other system. Admiral U. S. Grant Sharp, Commander-in-Chief, Pacific, told the JCS in January 1966 that the destruction of the sites would either bring about negotiations or cause the insurgency to wither for lack of support.[30]

The start of the attacks was delayed until Washington had assurances that the strikes could be carried out with a minimum of civilian casualties. *The list of precautions taken to reduce the non-combatant casualties is a catalog of the factors affecting air strike and anti-aircraft suppression*

Pentagon Papers, op. cit., p. 468. For the later years no such precise figures are given, but it is significant that during 1966 only one percent of all sorties flown was directed against the JCS numbered targets. [*Gravel Edition, Pentagon Papers, op. cit.*, Vol. IV, p. 138.] We estimate that armed reconnaissance constituted about 90 percent of the sorties in 1967.

28 *Report on the War in Vietnam* (U.S. Government Printing Office, 1968), p. 17.

29 *Pentagon Papers, op. cit.*, p. 480.

30 *Ibid.*, pp. 475-476.

accuracy. The JCS included the following requirements in their order to begin the bombing: use of the most experienced pilots; detailed briefing of pilots; execution of strikes only when visual identification of targets permitted; selection of the best axis of attack in order to avoid populated areas; maximum use of electronic equipment to hamper SAM and AAA fire, thereby limiting possible distractions for pilots; use of weapons of high precision delivery; and limitation of SAM and AAA suppression to sites outside populated areas.[31]

When, by the end of July, 70 percent of the storage facilities had been destroyed it seemed futile to continue the campaign against the remaining 30 percent of these targets because they were small and had been dispersed. The effects of the destruction could not be seen in the pattern of infiltration; the flow of men and materiel continued unabated. A study examining the discrepancy between prior claims and the results of the bombing showed that the North Vietnamese had been able to disperse their storage and distribution systems. Additional imports supplemented their supplies without much strain, since the volume of petroleum, oil, and lubricants in question was not great.[32]

Neither the strikes against oil storage facilities nor the continuing interdiction campaign appeared to have any effect on the war in the South, although the interdiction of lines of communication was costing $250 million per month by the fall of 1966.[33] Winter again brought renewed pressures for escalation, which during the spring of 1967 culminated in the third phase of the air war, directed against a series of targets within previously restricted zones. The JCS recommended a "'sharp knock' on North Vietnamese military assets and war-supporting facilities rather than the campaign of slowly increasing pressure," to be accomplished by striking strategic targets in urban areas.[34] In spite of the fact that few of the President's civilian advisors believed that the resulting damage would affect Hanoi's determination to continue the war, the President decided to approve a series of new targets as a demonstration of U.S. determination. Urban power plants, a steel plant, an airfield, an urban power transformer, a petroleum storage facility, an ammunition dump, and a cement plant were approved for air strikes between February and May. The President also approved the mining of rivers and estuaries along the coastline up to the 20th Parallel.[35] After these targets

[31] *Ibid.*, p. 500. Note that most other strikes against North Vietnam, or against targets elsewhere in Indochina, were *not* made subject to such careful restrictions.

[32] *Ibid.*, p. 480.

[33] *Ibid.*, pp. 554-555.

[34] *Ibid.*, p. 553.

[35] *Ibid.*, p. 526.

located within previously restricted areas were approved, General Wheeler reported that there were no important military targets remaining to be struck in the North. The only remaining possibilities for increased military action against the North were mining and bombing of ports, bombing dikes and locks, and a land invasion of North Vietnam.[36]

In spite of General Wheeler's views, President Johnson did approve 44 new targets and expand the area subject to armed reconnaissance missions during July and August of 1967. Many of the targets were within the inner circle of Hanoi and Haiphong and the buffer zone along the Chinese border. These actions were probably an attempt to blunt criticism of his restrictions on aerial bombardment from the Senate Armed Services Committee, which had scheduled hearings to begin in August.[37] The Senate hearings themselves may have been a reaction to knowledge reaching the Senate and the public of the debate going on within the Administration over the air war, a debate caused by a sense of stalemate and a lack of additional significant targets to hit.

The *New York Times* had accurately reported in June 1967 the three possible choices then under discussion in the Administration for the future of the air war: (a) bombing or blockading Haiphong, forcing the North to depend on land routes from China; (b) maintaining the status quo, restriking fixed targets and continuing the same level of activity against lines of communication to the South; and (c) decreasing the level of bombing by confining air strikes to interdiction south of the 20th Parallel.[38]

The third alternative, de-escalation of the bombing, was supported by McNamara, Rostow, and McGeorge Bundy, among others, and although they argued from different points of view, their conclusions seemed to reflect agreement that bombing north of the 20th Parallel was simply not worth the cost.[39] Pilot and aircraft losses in the panhandle region of the North were far lower than losses over the heavily defended regions in the Red River Delta, where the U.S. was losing one plane in every 40 sorties.[40] The JCS favored escalation once again, this time proposing that foreign shipping be forced out of Haiphong by bombing dock facilities and then mining the harbor.[41] Neither the McNamara nor the JCS proposals were accepted. With the exception of the

[36] *Ibid.*, p. 578.

[37] *Ibid.*, p. 540.

[38] *The New York Times* (June 13, 1967).

[39] *Pentagon Papers, op. cit.*, pp. 579 and 584; p. 576; p. 570.

[40] *Ibid.*, pp. 576 & 580. This loss ratio appears to have exceeded the implicit bounds of acceptability in cost terms. It meant that each sortie flown with a $3 million plane effectively cost $75,000 for replacement of lost aircraft, over and above the normal operating costs. (The normal cost of a fighter-bomber sortie is about $8,500; cf. App. D-6.)

[41] ". . . an attack of Haiphong, conducted first by surgically 'shouldering out' foreign

additional 44 targets approved in July and August, the air war neither escalated nor de-escalated until April 1968.

The fourth and last phase of the sustained bombing of the North began when President Johnson announced a partial bombing halt to begin on April 1 1968. This represented precisely that de-escalation which had been discussed the previous spring, although in effect it did not reduce the level of the bombing; indeed, the intensity of the bombing south of the 20th parallel increased. President Johnson's decision was motivated partially by military and economic factors; but if the air war against North Vietnam had been launched partly for political-strategic motives, then the bombing halt, too, was conditioned by political considerations. There was continuous concern over the domestic and international spectacle of massive air power brought to bear on a small, underdeveloped, agricultural country which represented no direct threat to the security of the U.S.;[42] moreover, the whole American posture on the Vietnam war had undergone a drastic change in the aftermath of the NLF Tet offensive early in 1968.[43] The shock of that offensive, demonstrating a wholly unexpected striking power and determination on the part of the NLF, was great. After Tet, Administration thinking turned to de-escalation rather than escalation; this attitude, culminating in what is today known as the policy of Vietnamization, is directed toward disengaging U.S. forces and shifting the burden of ground fighting to the ARVN. The U.S. supportive role is to be restricted to the minimum needed for ARVN to operate with success. Interdiction of supplies and men going south from North Vietnam is a key factor in this supportive role. The partial bombing halt represented precisely such a concentration of U.S. air power over North Vietnam on the interdiction mission. Moreover, when the air war against North Vietnam was "stopped" on November 1, 1968, many of the planes thus made available immediately took up interdiction duty over the same supply routes further west and south, known collectively as the Ho Chi Minh trail.[44]

The fifth phase of the air war against North Vietnam began as a covert continuation of the war on a much reduced scale. Sporadic attacks were made on targets in North Vietnam, mostly near the Demilitarized Zone and at the entrances to the Ho Chi Minh trail. The official rationale was stated as "protective reaction": U.S. aircraft overflying North Vietnam or flying

shipping and then mining the harbor and approaches." *Gravel Edition, Pentagon Papers, op. cit.*, Vol. IV, p. 490.

[42]These are Secretary McNamara's words, to which he added: "There may be a limit beyond which many Americans and much of the world will not permit the United States to go." *Pentagon Papers, op. cit.*, Document 129, p. 580.

[43]*Pentagon Papers, op. cit.*, Chap. 10: "The Tet Offensive and the Turnaround," pp. 589 ff.

[44]See Chap. 5.

missions in neighboring Laos would carry out attacks against anti-aircraft installations when fired on or even when tracked by associated radars. As justification, the U.S. claimed the right of self-defense for its aircraft.

With the passage of time, the rationale was gradually broadened through a series of public announcements until it came to encompass any action deemed necessary to protect American soldiers in South Vietnam in the course of their gradual withdrawal. President Nixon outlined a policy of reprisal by air if the NLF/NVA "took advantage" of the U.S. ground withdrawal; bombing would be authorized if the level of fighting in the South increased.[45] In January 1971 he stated that "key areas" would be struck upon evidence of increased infiltration into the South, and, in February, that he would put no limit on the use of U.S. air power in Indochina, and would not be bound by previous understandings about the bombing of North Vietnam.[46]

Raids are classified by the Defense Department as Type I, immediate protective reaction for reconnaissance missions over North Vietnam; Type II, immediate protective reaction for aircraft in Laos or South Vietnam; and Type III, limited duration protective reaction strikes. Types I and II generally involve few aircraft; Type III encompasses very massive attacks, as in May and November of 1970, and February, March, September, and December of 1971. The latest such raids, a five-day series launched December 26-30, 1971, totalled about 1,000 sorties--a daily average comparable to that achieved during the intensive phase of the air war against North Vietnam. This type of attack is now officially called "reinforced protective reaction." Its targets are listed as airfields, supply depots, and anti-aircraft sites.[47]

Thus the air war against North Vietnam continues. According to Secretary of Defense Melvin Laird, "the major difference, of course, is that these [strikes] are of limited duration."[48] The significance of this continued air action against North Vietnam is discussed further in Section 13-C and in Chapter 14; beyond its direct military effects it has important political motivations. In this respect the air war situation at the beginning of 1972 is not unlike that in early 1965, when the major attacks on North Vietnam were first launched.

D. AIR OPERATIONS AND COSTS

To summarize U.S. activity over North Vietnam, Figure 3-1 shows the

[45] *New York Times*, December 11, 1970.

[46] *New York Times*, January 5, 1971 and February 24, 1971.

[47] *New York Times*, December 28, 1971 and December 31, 1971.

[48] *New York Times*, December 28, 1971.

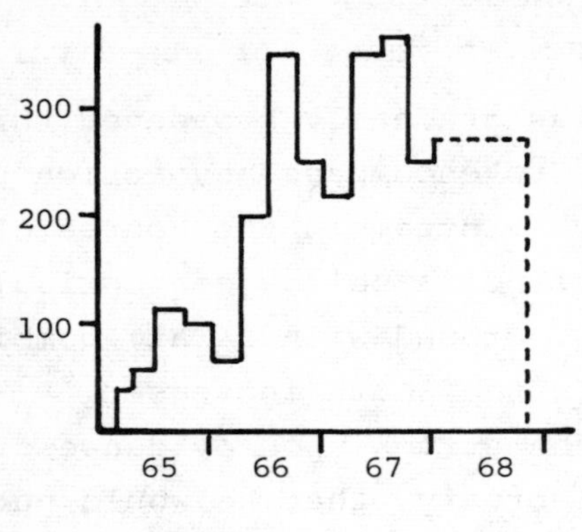

Figure 3-1

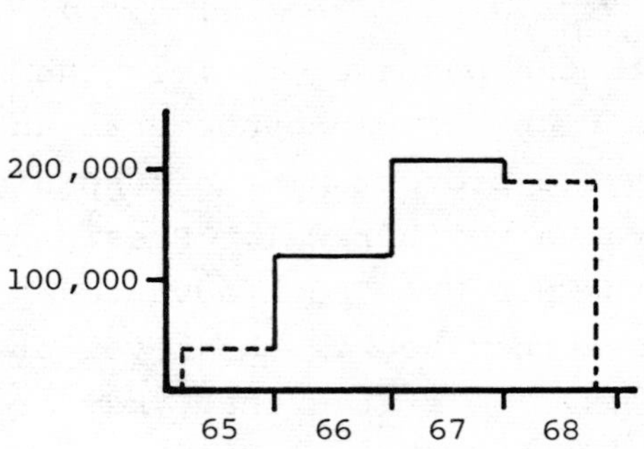

200,000
100,000
65
66
67
68

Figure 3-2

NORTH VIETNAM:

AVERAGE DAILY FIGHTER-BOMBER ATTACK SORTIES*

*Cf. Statistical Summary, Sec. SS-5 (Quarterly breakdown not available for 1968.)

ANNUAL TONNAGE OF AERIAL MUNITIONS**

**Cf. Statistical Summary, Sec. SS-8 (1965 & 1968 prorated to equivalent full-year rates.)

average daily number of attack sorties flown by fighter-bombers for the years 1965 through 1968.[49] Figure 3-2 shows the total tonnages of air-drop munitions delivered. Very few B-52 bomber attacks were directed against North Vietnam; the total number of missions through 1968 was 141, with an additional 270 missions directed into the Demilitarized Zone.[50] Protective reaction strikes, of all types, are listed by the Department of Defense as follows: November and December, 1968, 25; 1969, 75; 1970, 20; and 1971, 108. During early 1972 their rate was approaching one a day.

The direct cost of the air war against North Vietnam was estimated for the years 1965 and 1966 at about $1.7 billion, including the cost of operating the aircraft, the munitions, and the replacement cost of aircraft lost, but not the cost of basing and other support items. In the same period, the economic and military damage inflicted on North Vietnam was estimated to be about $200 million. About 500 aircraft were lost to North Vietnamese defen-

[49] The classification of sorties flown as attack sorties, or as another type, is not a rigid one. Hence figures for attack sorties do not always prove entirely consistent, and they should be regarded as an *approximate* indicator for attack activities. (In 1964 there was a total of 64 attack sorties against North Vietnam.) Approximately one-half of the sorties over North Vietnam were flown by the Air Force, the remainder by the Navy and the Marines.

[50] *1969 Summary*, MACV Office of Information, Saigon; p. 98. B-52 bombers were not used extensively over North Vietnam, other than in the immediate vicinity of the demilitarized zone, because of their vulnerability to surface-to-air missiles [Donovan, *op. cit.*, p. 182]. B-52 strikes against the southernmost provinces of North Vietnam have, however, been carried out with increasing frequency since the early months of 1971.

ses, mostly to anti-aircraft artillery; 46 were shot down by SAMs and 11 were lost to MIGs.[51] For later years no such detailed figures have been released, but the total losses of fixed-wing aircraft are now quoted as 928.[52] If losses of support aircraft and those due to operational causes are included this figure rises substantially.

E. EVALUATION

Criticism of the assumptions basic to the air war against the North began before the bombing itself had started and continued throughout,[53] but the most extensive examination was the special seminar study sponsored by the Department of Defense and contracted to the Jason Division of the Institute for Defense Analyses. Forty-seven of "America's most distinguished scientists, men who had helped the Government produce many of its most advanced technical weapons systems since the Second World War, and men who were not identified with the vocal academic criticism of the Administration's Vietnam policy," concluded that "the bombing of North Vietnam was ineffective."[54]

A year later, many of the people who had participated in this Jason study were called together once again for another look at the effectiveness of the bombing. Their report, submitted in December 1967, was "probably the most categorical rejection of bombing as a tool of our policy in Southeast Asia to be made before or since by an official or semi-official group." The scientists had access to secret documents and briefings by Pentagon, CIA, State Department, and White House officials. They evaluated the bombing in terms of its achievement of the objectives that Secretary McNamara had defined for it:

> (1) To reduce the flow and/or to increase the cost of the continued infiltration of men and supplies from North to South Vietnam.
>
> (2) To raise the morale of the South Vietnamese people who, at the time the bombing started, were under severe military pressure.

[51]These figures are quoted in *Gravel Edition, Pentagon Papers, op. cit.*, Vol. IV, pp. 136-137.

[52]*Impact of the Vietnam War,* Report prepared by the Congressional Research Service for the Committee on Foreign Relations, U.S. Senate, 92nd Congress, 1st Session (June 30, 1971), p. 7.

[53]See, for example, *Pentagon Papers, op. cit.*, pp. 242, 331-332, 459, 550, 570.

[54]The results of the two Jason studies are summarized in the *Pentagon Papers*. Individual quotations will not be referenced. The relevant material can be found at the following locations: *Pentagon Papers* (Bantam) pp. 483-485 for the first study; *The Gravel Edition, Pentagon Papers* (Beacon), Vol. IV: pp. 115 ff. for the first study, pp. 222 ff. for the second study. *Emphasis in the quotations is in the original, throughout.*

> (3) To make clear to the North Vietnamese political leadership that so long as they continued their aggression against the South, they would have to pay a price in the North.

On the first of these objectives, the conclusion was emphatically negative: "As of October 1967, the *U.S. bombing of North Vietnam has had no measurable effect on Hanoi's ability to mount and support military operations in the South.*" The reasons for this lack of success were that damage to the North was more than offset by military and economic aid from China and the USSR, that even a small portion of the transportation and trail system to the South was sufficient to maintain an adequate flow of men and materiel, and that the North Vietnamese possessed a more than adequate supply of manpower for repair, reconstruction, and work on the Trail.

The study concluded that there had been an appreciable improvement in South Vietnamese morale immediately after the bombing began, but that the bombing could never constitute a permanent support for morale.

With regard to the third objective, *"The bombing has not discernably weakened the determination of the North Vietnamese leaders to continue or direct and support the insurgency in the South."*

> That the bombing has not achieved anticipated goals reflects a failure to appreciate the fact, well-documented in the historical and social scientific literature, that a direct, frontal attack on a society tends to strengthen the social fabric of the nation, to increase popular support of the existing leadership, to improve the determination of both the leadership and the populace to fight back, to induce a variety of protective measures that reduce the society's vulnerability to future attack and to develop an increased capacity for quick repairs and restoration of essential functions.

The effectiveness of North Vietnamese countermeasures was underscored as a factor neglected in earlier planning and intelligence studies of the air war over North Vietnam. Moreover, the scientists observed that there had been little attempt made in current intelligence and analyses to relate the effects of military operations to the intended objectives:

> Instead, the tendency is to encapsulate the bombing of North Vietnam as one set of operations and the war in the South as another set of operations, and to evaluate each separately; and to tabulate and describe data on the physical, economic, and military effects of the bombing, but not to address specifically the relationship between such effects and the data relating to the ability and will of the DRV to continue its support of the war in the South. . . . Bridging this gap still requires the exercise of broad political-military judgments that cannot be supported or rejected on the basis of systematic intelligence indicators.

They concluded, after studying nine different bombing strategies which included mining the ports, attacking the dikes, and various combinations of attack emphasis on the lines of communications:

> *We are unable to develop a bombing campaign in the North to reduce the flow of infiltrating personnel into South Vietnam.*

The Jason studies were not the only negative assessments of the effectiveness of the air war against the North. Three studies done by the CIA in the spring of 1967,[55] and a late 1967 study by the Joint Chiefs and the International Security Agency of the Department of Defense,[56] reached substantially the same conclusions.

In sum, the bombing of North Vietnam failed to achieve most of the objectives for which it had been launched. The only undisputed result that could be claimed was that a heavy penalty had been inflicted on North Vietnam for continuing the support of the NLF in the South. This penalty was large both in economic and in human terms.

The amount of economic damage inflicted on North Vietnam cannot be stated with precision, but the Jason study completed in mid-December 1967 concluded that

> The bombing of North Vietnam has inflicted heavy costs not so much to North Vietnam's military capability or its infiltration system as to the North Vietnam economy as a whole. Measurable physical damage now exceeds $370 million. . . . Virtually all of the military and economic targets in North Vietnam that can be considered even remotely significant have been struck, except for a few targets in Hanoi and Haiphong. Almost all modern industrial output has been halted and the regime has gone over to decentralized, dispersed, and/or protected modes of producing and handling essential goods, protecting the people, and supporting the war in the South.

The dollar value of the economic damage must be viewed in its relationship to North Vietnam's annual GNP, which was about $1,700 million in 1967.[57] Translating the figure proportionately, it is about the same as if $200 *billion* physical damage had been inflicted on the U.S. In the course of the air war, North Vietnamese cities sustained heavy damage. Reports indicate that the cities of Dong Hoi, Ninh Binh, Phu Ly, Bac Giang, Yen Bai, and Son La were virtually levelled. Serious damage was sustained in the larger cities such as Nam Dinh, Thai Nguyen, Viet Tri and Vinh.[58]

[55] *Pentagon Papers*, *op. cit.*, p. 535.

[56] *Gravel Edition, Pentagon Papers*, *op. cit.*, Vol. IV, pp. 217 ff.

[57] *Ibid.*, p. 225.

[58] "The Vietnamese People and the Impact of War," *Studies in Progress* (Institute for Peace and Conflict Research, Denmark, December 1969), No. 3, p. 92.

This massive economic damage did not in fact cripple North Vietnam's capacity for supporting the war because additional aid from the USSR and China more than compensated for the dollar value of the losses. This aid was mostly in the form of military supplies, however, so that it did not replace the civilian facilities lost through the bombing. Consequently, while North Vietnam's military position was actually strengthened, the bombing inflicted severe damage on the civilian society as a whole.

In human terms, North Vietnam paid a painful penalty also. During 1965 and 1966 alone, U.S. bombings produced more than 36,000 casualties, 80 percent of whom were civilians.[59] In the spring of 1967, when Admiral Sharp was predicting that civilian casualties during the POL campaign soon to begin could be held below 50,[60] Secretary McNamara was writing a draft memorandum for the President in which he estimated that the U.S. was "killing or seriously injuring 1,000 non-combatants a week."[61] Scaled in proportion to the total population, such a casualty rate inflicted on the U.S. would amount to more than 600,000 per year.

Though the bombing of North Vietnam was officially stopped in November 1968, sporadic attacks have continued since then under the classification of "protective reaction." These raids, gradually intensified as the military situation in Laos and Cambodia deteriorates and as the communist ground and air defenses for the first time threaten to challenge U.S. air power, are bringing the air war against North Vietnam full circle. A senior Pentagon official is quoted as saying:

> Look, these so-called reinforced protective reaction strikes amount to a limited, selective resumption of the bombing. They are limited in time and in geographic area. But, as the President and Mr. Laird have said repeatedly, we don't intend to allow Hanoi to take advantage of our troop drawdown to threaten a rout against those who remain. Every once in a while we feel we have to remind Hanoi of this.[62]

Reminding Hanoi was, of course, one of the objectives of the original air war, particularly the first strikes in 1964 and 1965. The deterrent did not work then, and it appears unlikely that it will work now.

However, the air war against North Vietnam was instrumental in bringing about disenchantment with the war among a great segment of the American public; this disenchantment no doubt played a part in the decision to halt the bombing, and more generally in motivating the overall policy of American with-

[59] *Pentagon Papers, op. cit.*, p. 523.

[60] *Ibid.*, p. 479.

[61] *Ibid.*, p. 580.

[62] *New York Times*, December 28, 1971.

drawal. For the moment, the public outcry in response to the "reinforced protective reaction" strikes has been muted by their limited duration. While a series of raids is in progress, discussion is avoided for security reasons; when it is over, the situation has already been defused. However, the total weight of air power that can be brought to bear on Hanoi in this manner is obviously limited. If the Administration wishes to exert greater pressure without ending the public acquiescence, other formulations will have to be found.

These aspects of present and future air war policy are taken up again in greater detail in Chapters 13 and 14.

CHAPTER 4

THE AIR WAR IN SOUTH VIETNAM

> The unparalleled, lavish use of firepower as a substitute for manpower is an outstanding characteristic of U.S. military tactics in the Vietnam war.
>
> *Air University Review*[1]

A central and constant component in the announced U.S. objectives for Indochina has been the preservation of a non-communist government in Saigon.[2] Such a government was established, under President Ngo Dinh Diem, after the Geneva conference of 1954; in subsequent years it enjoyed U.S. endorsement and support in increasing measure. The underlying motives for U.S. actions derived from the policy of Containment: communist expansion was to be met wherever it threatened. In Indochina, in particular, the Domino Theory contended that allowing a communist takeover in one state would inevitably lead to a sequence of similar takeovers in the other states of the region. Soon it was claimed that the U.S. had a commitment to maintaining the independence of South Vietnam from communist domination, and the survival of a Saigon regime friendly to the U.S. was seen as a test of the credibility and strength of this commitment. The U.S. would demonstrate with deeds as well as words its unalterable opposition to communist encroachment by subversion or aggression.

At the beginning of the previous chapter, the evolution of the insurgency in South Vietnam was sketched briefly, indicating the deterioration of the military and political position of successive South Vietnamese governments after 1959, especially following the fall of Diem in November 1963. By the end of 1964 the situation had become desperate, and decisive military intervention by the U.S. was seen as the only way of preventing a total collapse. This action first took the form of an air attack on North Vietnam. The hope was that the military and political effects of such an attack would quickly pressure Hanoi into stopping its support of the insurgency in the South, and that the NLF would thereby be so weakened as to permit the Saigon regime to

[1] Robert M. Kipp, "Counterinsurgency From 30,000 Feet: The B-52 in Vietnam," *Air University Review*, XIX, No. 2 (January-February 1968), p. 17.

[2] Though the most recent pronouncements by President Nixon have been somewhat more restrictive: "I have strongly supported ending this war, ending our involvement as we are, withdrawing Americans, but ending in a way that we do not turn the country over to the communists, ending it in a way that we give the South Vietnamese a reasonable chance to defend themselves against communist aggression." Press conference, June 1, 1971; *Department of State Bulletin*, LXIV, No. 1669, June 21, 1971, p. 790.

regain a tenable position.

Within a few weeks of the onset of the bombings, however, it became clear that this strategy was not having the desired effect. With the realization that the South Vietnamese insurrection would have to be tackled within South Vietnam itself, the style of American ground operations changed. U.S. combat troops in South Vietnam were put on offensive rather than defensive missions and their numbers were dramatically increased.[3] A major involvement of American soldiers, fighting on the ground in Vietnam, was begun: a correspondingly major involvement of American air power to support these men followed.

On the eve of the escalation of American military action in South Vietnam, one high Pentagon official assessed the relative importance of American objectives there as

> 70%--To avoid a humiliating defeat (to our reputation as guarantor).
>
> 20%--To keep South Vietnam (and the adjacent territory) from Chinese hands.
>
> 10%--To permit the people of South Vietnam to enjoy a better, freer way of life.
>
> ALSO--To emerge from crisis without unacceptable taint from methods used.
>
> NOT--To "help a friend," although it would be hard to stay in if asked out.[4]

In examining the "methods used" we shall see that U.S. strategists, for reasons outlined previously in Chapter 1, turned to such weapons as aircraft and heavy artillery for fighting an opponent who, for his part, resorted extensively to the methods of guerrilla warfare.[5] As one American expert put it, however, the best weapon for fighting a guerrilla is a knife, the worst a bomber; the second best is a rifle, the second worst, artillery.[6]

> In a jungle environment attacks on Government outposts are carried on most frequently by platoon or company-sized units at night. These small units are armed with mortars, recoilless rifles, machine-guns, and automatic weapons. They do not have tanks or armored per-

[3] National Security Action Memorandum 328, April 6, 1965, Point 7: "The President approved a change of mission for all Marine Battalions deployed in Vietnam to permit their more active use . . ." A previous section of the Memorandum approved an 18,000 to 20,000 man increase in military forces. See Neil Sheehan *et al.*, *The Pentagon Papers* (Bantam, 1971), pp. 382-383, 398-399, 442.

[4] John J. McNaughton, Assistant Secretary of Defense for International Security Affairs, March 24, 1965; *Pentagon Papers, op. cit.*, p. 432.

[5] Even Ambassador Taylor was surprised when Marines came ashore with tanks, self-propelled artillery, and other heavy equipment which was not "appropriate for counterinsurgency operations." *Pentagon Papers, op. cit.*, p. 406.

[6] Quoted by Roger Hilsman, *To Move a Nation* (Doubleday, 1967), p. 443.

> sonnel carriers, and they walk into battle. They would be hard to find in a jungle environment in the daytime. They are harder to find during the nighttime, which they claim for their own.
>
> Arrayed against these small and elusive units is the military power of America. We have all the tanks that there are in South Vietnam. We have almost all of the artillery, and retain complete mastery of the skies. Over 20 different models of American aircraft, undisturbed by enemy aircraft, roam the skies of South Vietnam at will, subject only to the danger of ground fire from conventional small arms.
>
> Many voices have been raised asking why our air power is unable to find and destroy the Vietcong in South Vietnam.[7]

Just how lavish the use of American aerial firepower became can be seen from figures released by the Department of Defense: the weight of air-drop munitions deployed by the U.S. in the years 1965-1969 was more than 200 times the total weight of all types of munitions used by the insurgents during the same period.[8] Some of this air power was used in support of U.S. or allied ground forces involved in more or less conventional types of military action. A large fraction, however, was directed to missions very specific to the Vietnam war, and in the sections which follow we present a description of the most important functions of air power as they evolved in that conflict.

A. THE USE OF AMERICAN AIR POWER

1. *Close Air Support.* The use of air power for direct support of troops in action has developed in Vietnam into a primary tactic. As Army Brig. Gen. Glenn D. Walker said, "You don't fight this fellow rifle to rifle. You locate him and back away. Blow the hell out of him and then police up."[9] An explicit rationale for this method was given in the field to reporter Peter Arnett:

> The Ninth Division practices the "pile on" concept. A Vietcong force, once located, is surrounded by as many troops as are necessary to block it. Then fighter-bombers and artillery pound the enemy positions into the the gray porridge that the green Delta land becomes when pulverized by high explosives. "This way we don't waste American life," commented an officer.[10]

[7] From the opening statement by Representative Otis Pike in *Close Air Support Hearings* (1965), pp. 4639-4640. (For a key to abbreviated titles of hearings, see App. A.)

[8] Edward S. Herman, *Atrocities in Vietnam: Myths and Realities* (Pilgrim Press, 1970), p. 57, quotes the following figures: U.S. airdrop munitions, 1967-1969, 3,751,131 tons; total munitions of all kinds used by insurgents in the same period, 17,500 tons.

[9] "Counterinsurgency From 30,000 Feet," *op. cit.*, p. 11. The ecological consequences of this approach are discussed in Chap. 8.

[10] Peter Arnett, "After Two Years in Mekong Delta, U.S. Goal is Still Elusive," *New York Times*, April 15, 1969.

Saving American lives is certainly an objective beyond question. But how much of this was actually being done? Official accounts of U.S. air activity naturally lay heavy stress on the close-support function; yet even from their figures a rather surprising picture emerges. Close air support constituted a very small fraction, well below 10 percent, of U.S. fixed-wing air activity.[11] In view of the large overall scale of the U.S. air effort, it is unlikely that U.S. and allied ground forces could not get all the close air support they wanted. Had there been the need, the fraction of missions flown for close support could easily have been increased. The real question is a different one. Given that less than ten percent of the sorties satisfied the close-support requirement, what were the other 90 percent being used for? This surprising distribution of the air missions provides an eloquent commentary on the lavish nature of the U.S. air operations.

An air strike giving close-support is, almost by definition, directed against a military target. Perhaps it would be more realistic to say, "directed against what is thought to be a military target," considering the problems of target identification which have been previously pointed out in Chapter 2. As an example of the difficulty of dealing with a volatile target, consider the maneuver of surrounding a Vietcong force in order to be able to "pile on" firepower. The majority of air strikes used in such a maneuver would certainly be of the preplanned type, arriving in the target area with considerable delay. But the Vietcong are notoriously mobile, seeping out of the areas where they were thought to have been contained. Roger Trinquier, the French student of guerrilla warfare with long experience both in Vietnam and in Algeria, comments on this type of maneuver:

> Large-unit sweeps, conducted with conventional resources within a framework similar to that of conventional warfare, and invariably limited in time, temporarily disperse guerrilla bands rather than destroy them.
>
> A normal operation of this type usually consists in the attempted surprise encirclement of a well-defined zone in which guerrillas are thought to be located . . .
>
> Surprise, that essential factor of success, is practically never realized. As we have seen, the people among whom our troops live and move have as their mission the information of the guerrillas, and no movement of troops can escape them. The noose is never completely tightened.[12]

Another example, illustrating the difficulties of target identification in the space dimension rather than in time, is the type of situation described by Schell, who for several weeks accompanied FAC pilots on their missions:

[11]Official data are available for 1968, 1969, and the first half of 1971. During these periods the percentages of total attack sorties devoted to close air support were, respectively, 8%, 5%, and 6%. *Summaries,* MACV Office of Information, Saigon.

[12]Roger Trinquier, *Modern Warfare* (Praeger, 1964), p. 58.

> . . . the ground commander guided Captain Reese [the FAC pilot] to the target by describing it in relation to landmarks on the ground. "It's five hundred meters east of that pagoda on the road there. Have you got the pagoda?" the ground commander asked. Captain Reese . . . answered, "I see a church but no pagoda." "It's right under you now." "I don't see it." "OK, well, there's one hootch down there about a klik south of us that we want you to get. We've got sniper fire out of that tree line." Captain Reese flew over the area indicated, and found that it was occupied by a village of sixty or seventy houses . . . "I see a village down there," he said. "No, this is just one hootch," said the ground commander, who was apparently unable to see the village from his spot on the ground because of a thick cover of trees . . . [After more discussion and the firing of some marker rockets, without success]: "That's the general area," said the ground commander, apparently tired of trying to pinpoint the one house. "Do you want us to pretty well cover this general area?" Captain Reese asked. "Affirmative. Hit the whole area We've seen activity all through this area." . . . "OK, I'll put in a can of napalm and see what it looks like." . . . "Any civilians in this area are Charlies, or Charlie sympathizers, so there's no sweat there."[13]

The upshot of all this was that the village was struck, and also two prominent houses with red tile roofs, none of which had been identified as the source of the sniper fire against which the strike had originally been called. "Did we get that hootch you wanted?" "Well, you pretty much covered that whole area." The bomb-damage assessment report later said that an Enemy Sniper Position and seven structures had been destroyed.

Some light is also shed on the nature of close air support in Vietnam by the fact that the munitions preferred for such strikes were napalm and cluster-bomb units (CBUs).[14] These weapons have an area coverage and thus do not need to be aimed very precisely; dropping a high-explosive bomb is perhaps more devastating locally, but the radius of destruction is only ten or twenty feet. To wipe out a sniper generally requires dropping many such bombs; napalm or CBUs are far more effective. Interviews suggest that, in the opinion of most ground soldiers, strike aircraft arrived with too little of this type of ordnance, and with too many high-explosive bombs.[15] Napalm and CBUs are usually considered "dread" weapons, however, because of the

[13] Jonathan Schell, *The Military Half* (Vintage, 1968), pp. 172 ff.

[14] For a discussion of the various types of munitions, see App. C-3.

[15] The following exchange occurred between Representative Pike and Sergeant Damron, an Army Assistant Advisor with experience in Vietnam:
Rep. Pike: "Sergeant, can you just explain, if you know, the reasoning that napalm would have killed civilians and that the high explosive bombs and the cannon doesn't kill civilians?"
Sergeant Damron: "Well, the napalm burns all the houses, sir. In fact, if an area is saturated with napalm, it just about burns everything in it . . ." *Close Air Support Hearings* (1965), pp. 4643-4644.

terrible wounds they inflict and the obvious human suffering they cause. Using such weapons too freely would be tantamount to an official admission about the inherently indiscriminate nature of air warfare.[16]

Close air support is certainly a potent and efficient weapon when applied in the appropriate circumstances. Its maximum effect is achieved when the conflict takes on a more or less conventional character, and under these conditions it becomes a weapon of decisive impact. One effect of this impact is to take a heavy toll of the insurgents whenever they mass their forces for large-scale battle: it effectively restricts them to waging the war guerrilla style. Where this guerrilla warfare is extensive, however, close air support is not as appropriate a weapon as some military strategists would like to suggest. Small mobile units are elusive targets.

2. *Interdiction.* More than 90 percent of the air strikes in South Vietnam fall into this wide and diffuse category. Interdiction is defined as preventing or hindering enemy use of an area or route, or as a selective campaign against the enemy's total logistic organization.[17] These definitions are readily applied so long as the area to be interdicted is occupied by the "enemy" alone; then air strikes will indeed hinder him, or disrupt his logistics. But what if the enemy is a guerrilla, or uses guerrilla techniques extensively? Then he may live intermingled with the population or may actually *be* the population. His main-force detachments are mobile, here one day and somewhere else the next: he cannot readily be struck without assaulting the civilian population at the same time. To interdict such an enemy means to blanket all possible areas with firepower.[18] Whether this means that interdiction as an objective must be renounced depends on a judgment of the military, political, moral, and human factors involved. In Vietnam the judgment evidently was in favor of interdiction. The political costs that this entailed need not be stressed again. U.S. strategists were prepared to bear these costs, or, to put it more realistically, they were prepared to inflict these penalties on the population of South Vietnam.[19]

[16] The Department of Defense has released only sparse data on the amount of napalm used in Vietnam, and none on the tonnage of CBUs deployed. Figures quoted by J. B. Neilands, "Napalm Survey," in: *The Wasted Nations* (Harper & Row, to be published), indicate that napalm tonnages were as follows: 1963, 2,181 tons; 1964, 1,777 tons; 1965, 17,659 tons; 1966, 54,620 tons. From January 1969 through June 1971 the estimated amount dropped in Indochina was 125,000 tons. (The legality of using napalm and CBUs is considered in Chap. 11.)

[17] See Sec. 2-A.

[18] General Johnson, Army Chief of Staff, is reported to have said to Moshe Dayan, after the latter expressed astonishment at the amount of firepower being used by Americans in Vietnam: "We have not enough information. We act with ruthlessness, like a steamroller, bombing extensive areas and not selected targets based on detailed intelligence." Quoted in Arthur M. Schlesinger, Jr., *The Bitter Heritage* (Houghton Mifflin, 1967), p. 47.

[19] Gabriel Kolko has pointed out the logic which inevitably led to this situation. "War

Seen in this light, generalized interdiction in Vietnam takes on the character of *strategic* warfare. The targets are not well enough defined to qualify as tactical objectives. Rather, the attacks are directed against the overall reserves of the insurgents, which are in the population itself, and against the will to continue the fight. It is a war of attrition.[20] The criteria for success in such a war are body counts and weapons captured, more permanent indicators of military success being unavailable.

A paradoxical side effect of the widespread bombing may be noted in passing. Bombs do not always explode: a certain fraction of duds is inevitably present. These duds may be disassembled by the NLF, yielding explosive material which can be fashioned into grenades or booby traps. As an example we quote the figures from a study of the effects of bombing which was done for the Pentagon Office of Systems Analysis. This study covered the year 1966, during which the number of NLF/NVA soldiers killed by air strikes was estimated at less than 100. However, these strikes provided the enemy with about 27,000 tons of dud bombs and shells, more than enough to make all the mines and booby traps which were thought to have killed over 1,000 U.S. soldiers that year.[21]

The most dramatic illustration of generalized interdiction is provided by the use of B-52 strategic bombers for this mission. The B-52 Stratofortress was originally meant to deliver the atom bomb, but its enormous cargo capacity suggested a new concept in the conduct of the Indochina air war. Outfitted with racks to carry conventional bombs, a B-52 can deliver up to thirty tons of explosives in a dense pattern.[22] A typical mission, consisting of six of these bombers flying in formation, saturates an area of more than a square mile with bombs. Everything within this area is demolished. To witness such a raid is to witness a disaster of major proportions.

Crimes and the Nature of the Vietnam War," *Journal of Contemporary Asia,* Vol. I, No. 1 (1970).

[20] "We fought a military war; our opponents fought a political one. We sought physical attrition; our opponents aimed for our psychological exhaustion. In the process, we lost sight of one of the cardinal maxims of guerrilla war: the guerrilla wins if he does not lose. The conventional army loses if it does not win." Henry Kissinger, "The Vietnam Negotiations," *Foreign Affairs, 47* (1969), No. 2, p. 214.

[21] The study referred to is quoted in Alain C. Enthoven and K. Wayne Smith, *How Much is Enough?* (Harper & Row, 1971), pp. 305-306. The authors note that not long after the study was circulated, U.S. forces captured a Vietcong training film that showed recruits how to dismantle American dud bombs, recover the explosive, and make grenades out of it. The Directorate for Defense Information, Southeast Asia Division, states that the dud rate experienced for general-purpose high-explosive bombs in the latter half of 1970 was "less than 2%."

[22] Colonel James A. Donovan, *Militarism, U.S.A.* (Scribner's, 1970), pp. 181-184: "As 'limited war' became the new 'thing' in the defense establishment, SAC jumped on the bandwagon and procured iron [i.e., conventional high-explosive] bomb racks for B-52s. . . . As the countryside disappeared under a storm of high explosives it was vividly explained how this was just the ticket for dealing with 'communist aggressors' and guerrillas."

More than half of the tonnage of aerial munitions dropped on South Vietnam was delivered by B-52s. The first B-52 strike was carried out by twenty-seven of the bombers in June 1965. When ground troops afterwards penetrated the target area they did not find evidence of any NLF casualties, nor significant damage to facilities.[23] However, these raids continued and were intensified. The NLF probably had advance warning in many cases through security leaks; but the purpose of the bombing was not so much its direct military effectiveness as its psychological and strategic impact:

> The B-52s' mission would be to harass the enemy, disrupt his normal activities, permit him no respite from attack even in his jungle redoubts, and wear him down psychologically.
>
> . . . .
>
> It seems reasonable to suggest that the main contribution of B-52s to date in the Vietnam war has been the constricting effect the bombings have had on the enemy's freedom of movement and range of action. Emphasis then focuses on the psychological effect on the enemy of being bombed--or what is perhaps almost as disturbing, the threat of being bombed--and its debilitating effect on enemy plans for major operations.[24]

The peak year for B-52 activity in South Vietnam was 1969. In that year, two-thirds of the missions went into III Corps.[25]

No doubt the U.S. Command was aware of the limitations of interdiction bombing in South Vietnam; deliberate attacks on the civilian population were not part of the official policy. So the rationale must be sought in a variety of special situations, some of which are outlined below.

Free-fire zones. The connotations of this term are unpleasant, conjuring up a picture of wanton bombing, strafing, and artillery fire. Perhaps at times these connotations are not far from the truth; but there is a *formal* function for free-fire zones, and to emphasize this the Defense Department in 1965 renamed them Specified Strike Zones (SSZ).[26] The purpose of the SSZ is

[23]"Counterinsurgency From 30,000 Feet," *op. cit.*, p. 13.

[24]*Ibid.*, pp. 13 and 18.

[25]*1969 Summary*, MACV (Military Assistance Command, Vietnam) Office of Information, Saigon, p. 90: there were 2,636 B-52 missions, 319 in I Corps, 440 in II Corps, 1,777 in III Corps, and 98 in IV Corps. (Figures for B-52 missions in South Vietnam for other years are given in the Statistical Summary, Sec. SS-6b.) III Corps includes the famous Iron Triangle and the northern Delta region, of which Peter Arnett wrote: "Vietcong strength is drawn from the two million people who inhabit the northern Delta, an area that includes Kienhoa, Dingtuong, Gocong and Longan provinces. The rabid South Vietnamese nationalists have traditionally come from these regions. All but ten percent of the enemy forces of 40,000 men in the area are South Vietnamese, recruited locally. The rest are North Vietnamese." *New York Times*, April 15, 1969.

[26]"Specified Strike Zones are specifically designated areas within a unit's area of operations. These areas have been cleared by responsible local Vietnamese authority for firing on specific military targets. Before firing is initiated into these areas it must be cleared each time by military authority. Usually, the Specified Strike Zones are in areas

to isolate areas where the conflict can be considered in conventional terms--friendly forces here, the enemy there. Once the enemy is isolated, interdiction strikes make perfectly good sense. The description of an SSZ makes it clear how this isolation is obtained: it is a formal one, based on definitional logic. Areas which have been longtime NLF strongholds, and often Viet Minh strongholds before that, are defined as free of friendly inhabitants. By virtue of residence, anyone who lives there is the enemy. Fine distinctions are glossed over, the area is ascribed to the insurgents *en bloc*.[27] Formally, the judgment is referred to the local Vietnamese authorities, who are supposed to be familiar with the details. However, there is testimony that the Vietnamese Province Chiefs do not always approach this question with the necessary competence or seriousness.[28]

Where NLF strongholds are not so readily identified, an SSZ can be created by moving the friendly population out of the area first. This involves various techniques, but aerial leaflet warnings and loudspeaker announcements from helicopters are common. The leaflets provide one of the few documentary records which speak to the objectives of much of the bombing in South Vietnam.[29] One leaflet reads:

> People of the Song Ve Valley, the GVN urges those of you that are still living in the mountains to come down and move to Nghia Hanh. There you will be protected and cared for by the GVN and Allied Forces. Your friends who have moved to Nghia Hanh have received food and medical care. At Nghia Hanh you will be safe. There will be shelter for you and your family. Those of you who choose to remain in the area will be considered hostile and in danger.[30]

Often, ground forces move through villages which are to be cleared, providing transportation for the inhabitants and for some of their belong-

which are virtually uninhabited by non-combatants such as War Zone "C" and War Zone "D," which were known enemy strongholds. They usually contain no friendly forces. Areas where non-combatants live in villages or hamlets are not included in Specified Strike Zones. Specified Strike Zones exist for a limited amount of time and are used to protect Allied Troops from enemy attack." (Descriptive text obtained from Department of Defense.)

[27] See testimony by Vietnam veteran Everett Carson, a Platoon Commander in I Corps between October 1968 and February 1969, that 90 percent of I Corps was a free-fire zone and that the homes, rice, and livestock of Montagnards in this area were commonly destroyed to deny their possible use by the NLF. *Refugee Hearings* (1971), Part III, pp. 25-27.

[28] Schell, *op. cit.*, p. 151: ". . . to find out about the clearance system I spoke with the province chief. . . . All in all, my investigation disclosed that the procedures for applying these restraints were modified or twisted or ignored to such an extent that in practice the restraints evaporated entirely, though enough motions were gone through to create the illusion of restraints in the minds of the officers."

[29] Psychological Warfare operations involving leaflet drops were a major part of U.S. air strategy. Some 26 *billion* leaflets have been dropped to date: almost 6 billion were dropped over South Vietnam alone in 1967. See *Report on the War in Vietnam* (USGPO, n.d.), App. E, p. 238.

[30] Text of a leaflet, quoted by Schell, *op. cit.*, p. 67.

ings. These organized relocations do not usually unfold along as smooth a schedule as desired, however, as the villagers are understandably reluctant to move.[31] In any event, once relocation attempts have been made and warnings given, the area can then be considered free of friendly noncombatants: it can become an SSZ.[32]

Retaliatory strikes. Where a massive relocation of the population is not desired, air strikes are used for *indirect* interdiction: if the population can be stopped from supporting the NLF, the chief resource of the insurgents is interdicted. To this end, warnings are given to villagers not to collaborate with the NLF; if the warnings are not heeded, retaliation strikes are promised:

> . . . The hamlets of Hai Mon, Hai Tan, Sa Binh, Tan Binh, and many others have been destroyed because of this. We will not hesitate to destroy every hamlet that helps the Vietcong. . . . The U.S. Marines issue this warning: THE U.S. MARINES WILL NOT HESITATE TO DESTROY, IMMEDIATELY, ANY VILLAGE OR HAMLET HARBORING THE VIETCONG. WE WILL NOT HESITATE TO DESTROY, IMMEDIATELY, ANY VILLAGE OR HAMLET USED AS A VIETCONG STRONGHOLD TO FIRE AT OUR TROOPS OR AIRCRAFT. . . .[33]

After a reprisal bombing, the survivors may be showered with leaflets explaining the action. "The Vietcong caused this to happen! Your village was bombed because you harbored Vietcong in your village. . ."[34] An Air Force news release claimed this "I Told You So" technique, i.e., warning plus subsequent

[31] There is a suggestion that illiteracy in rural Vietnam may have handicapped some leaflet campaigns. We do not have any systematic data on this point, however. Cf. Helen Emmerich, *San Francisco Chronicle,* December 2, 1969: "At dusk the helicopters came, . . . dropping thousands of leaflets . . . Colonel William Kitterman said they were warning leaflets, urging the villagers to move out before dark . . . No one came out . . . Kitterman put down the glasses and looked at me. 'Well, they had their chance. Now, we just assume they're VC.' . . . I finally asked a gunnery sergeant why the villagers hadn't come out after the leaflets were dropped. He took a hard drag on his coffee, looked around, then whispered to me, 'Look, don't say I told you this--but don't you know--they couldn't read the leaflets.'"

[32] The forcible movement of civilians from their villages has not come to a halt with the deescalation of military activity in recent years. A U.S. military catalog prepared in February 1971 lists taped messages to be broadcast to the inhabitants: "You must evacuate this area immediately as the GVN and Allied Forces are beginning an operation. If you stay you will be considered Viet Cong. Evacuate immediately!" (*IMP Taped Propaganda Catalog,* Combined Psychological Operations Center, 7th Psyop Battalion, Message Number T7-12-70.) An official, though indirect, acknowledgment of the mass-relocation policy was given by Dr. Johannes U. Hoeber, Senior Refugee Officer, Vietnam Bureau, U.S. Agency for International Development (AID): "The 1968-69 programs of mass movements of people to create free-fire zones have long been terminated." Dr. Hoeber confirmed that relocations are still being carried out, but denied they were undertaken to create free-fire zones. *Ithaca Journal* (February 11, 1972).

[33] Leaflet No. 244-286-67, "Marine Ultimatum to Vietnamese People," quoted by Schell, *op. cit.,* pp. 17-18. Cartoon drawings on one side show a gory scene in which a jet has bombed a house, alongside a picture of a house with a soldier setting up a mortar, another leaning out of a window firing an automatic weapon. The caption reads, "If the Vietcong do this, your village will look like this."

[34] Leaflet No. 244-068-68, *ibid.*

explanation, was surprisingly successful when used during actual ground combat operations.[35]

Beyond the moral and legal problems raised by this procedure, there is a question which must be asked: do the villagers have any option in this process? However one visualizes the relationship between the villagers and the NLF--the groups may not be as clearly separable as these terms imply--it is unlikely that every person in a village can exert control over whether a shot is fired at a passing helicopter or not.[36] On the one hand, the villager is under the threat of massive retaliation from U.S. air power. On the other, should he refuse to collaborate in order to avoid such retaliation he exposes himself to assassination some night: the insurgents make use of terror, too. In a war of competing forces of terror the population becomes a helpless victim.[37]

Motivational bombing. In regions where most of the population is thought to be with the NLF or at least to support them, generalized bombing can be used in an attempt to motivate a return to the Government side:

> As has been announced before, when the plane returns to sow death, you will have no more time to choose. Be sure to follow the example of 70,000 compatriots who have used the free-movement pass to return and reestablish a comfortable life in peace; or stay to die in suffering and horrible danger. All who stay will never be able to know when other bombs will fall. Be sure to be wise and don't be undecided any more. Be sure to use the free-movement pass of the Government printed on this leaflet and hurry to return to the righteous cause.[38]

On the reverse side of the leaflet, a dramatic picture of a B-52 strike is shown. "Do not let this happen again."

3. *Defoliation and Crop Destruction.* Spraying herbicides and defoliants from the air constitutes a special form of interdiction. Defoliating the heavy vegetation along trails, roadsides, base perimeters, and suspected assembly areas is one way of denying the enemy effective concealment, which is his chief asset in many cases.[39] More serious and contestable in its impact is the de-

[35]USAF Directorate of Information, Tan Son Nhut Air Base, News Release No. 4016: *"I Told You So" New Psyops Technique*. In discussing the number of enemy troops that had been persuaded to rally to the Government side by this technique, the release states: "When operation in that province [Kien Hoa] first began the number of ralliers doubled and in one high month, after liberal saturation with psyops missions the number averaged nearly two ralliers per day."

[36]Schell quotes a captain in the ARVN: "The Americans are destroying everything. If they get just one shot from a village, they destroy it . . . Just one VC--just one--can enter a village with a machine gun and the people are helpless against him . . . He shoots, and then their village is bombed." *Op. cit.*, p. 165.

[37]See Chap. 11 for a discussion of the legality of reprisal bombing.

[38]Leaflet No. 147-66-R, original in our possession.

[39]A paradoxical situation arose after strips along each side of a road had been cleared, to

struction of crops, whereby the flow of food to the enemy is stopped at the source; however, the civilian population is also deprived of its sustenance and livelihood and is often driven out of the area.[40] Soldiers are usually able to look after their own needs and interests: if food becomes short, it is likely to be the civilians who suffer first. Moreover, herbicides have toxic effects on humans, as well as an overall ecological impact which so far has not been fully assessed, beyond the recognition that it is likely to be severe.[41]

Herbicide use has drawn much public attention and unfavorable comment. In December 1970, the White House announced that an "orderly yet rapid phase-out" of all herbicide operations in Vietnam had begun. In March 1971, the Secretary of State informed Congress that chemical crop destruction had been stopped; however, the disposition of the remaining stocks of herbicide and of the spray equipment has not been made clear.

B. STATISTICAL SUMMARY OF AIR OPERATIONS

The average daily rates for attack sorties flown by fighter-bombers and by helicopters in South Vietnam, and the monthly rate for B-52 missions, are shown in Figure 4-1.[42] Through the end of 1971, the sortie rates for U.S. fighter-bombers have decreased sharply, to the point where VNAF was carrying the major share of this air activity. A major re-escalation of American bombing in South Vietnam, which does not show on the graphs of Figure 4-1, took place however in February 1972. This resurgence of air activity was suppor-

deny cover to any guerrillas ambushing convoys along the road. The guerrillas merely mounted their ambushes from the newly defined edges of the forest, but the men on the road now had no cover into which they could quickly run to take shelter from the attackers.

[40] Crop destruction may also have had the objective of driving the population out of the remoter mountain regions, which were hard to control, and into the Strategic Hamlets set up by the Government. See Ngo Vinh Long, "Leaf Abscission?," *Bulletin of Concerned Asian Scholars,* Vol. II, October 1969, p. 54.

[41] See the detailed discussion in Chapter 8.

[42] A *sortie* is one flight made by one aircraft; a *mission* is an air strike which may be carried out by several aircraft working in collaboration. A *strike* is an indefinite term which is sometimes used to denote a sortie, sometimes a mission. Attack sorties are distinguished from other sorties which may include reconnaissance or transport of men or materiel; the exact line separating an attack sortie from a non-attack sortie is open to definitional manipulation, so that the resultant figures are not always easily interpreted. For example, the MACV Monthly Summaries for 1970 changed column headings for these tabulations three times in the course of the year, using the titles sortie, strike, and mission in what ostensibly described the same category in the listing.

B-52 activity is not broken down into sorties by official figures; instead, the number of missions flown is listed. Over the course of the war, each mission has averaged about seven planes; most recently, missions have reportedly consisted of fewer planes. The average bomb load for a B-52 has increased with successive modifications of the aircraft; cf. Statistical Summary, Sec. SS-6. A typical figure for the average load has been 28 tons.

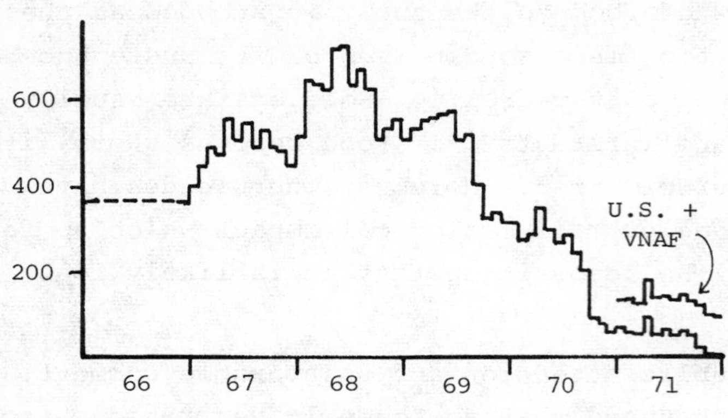

AVERAGE DAILY FIGHTER-BOMBER SORTIES

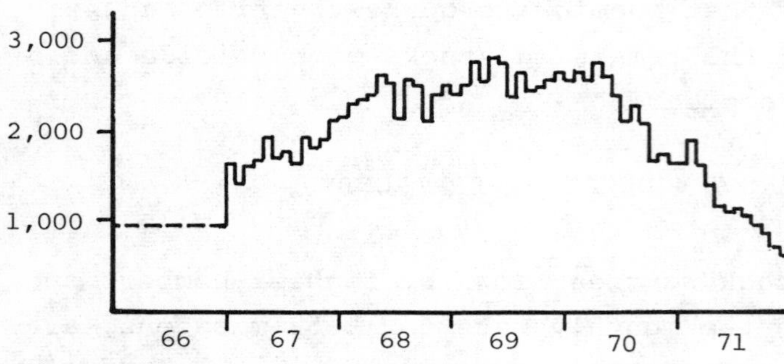

AVERAGE DAILY HELICOPTER ATTACK SORTIES

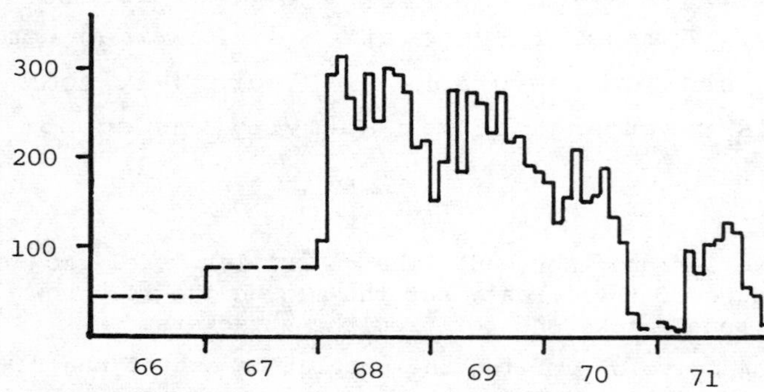

AVERAGE MONTHLY B-52 STRATEGIC BOMBER MISSIONS

Figure 4-1

SOUTH VIETNAM: ATTACK AIRCRAFT ACTIVITY

ted by important redeployments of U.S. aircraft, both land-based and carrier-based, to the Southeast Asian theater.

B-52 activity has also decreased substantially. It now shows a variability which is characteristic of the flexible manner in which U.S. air power in Indochina is deployed. The B-52s, whose standby mission is the bombing of the Ho Chi Minh trail, are readily diverted to troublespots anywhere in the theater.[43]

The total weight of bombs dropped on South Vietnam through the end of 1971 is about 3.9 million tons. U.S. aircraft losses over South Vietnam are given as 429 fixed-wing and 1,886 helicopters through hostile action, plus a rather larger number (which, however, is not broken down by theater of action) from operational and other causes.[44]

C. SOCIAL AND POLITICAL CONSEQUENCES

The massive use of American firepower led to a movement of civilians on a scale so large as to have the effects of a social upheaval. In the early 1960s, 80-85 percent of the population of South

[43]The peak in mid-summer, 1971, reflects the intensified fighting in MR I near the demilitarized zone. The B-52 raids, involving at times as much as half of the active fleet in Southeast Asia, were credited with blunting an NLF/NVA offensive against ARVN firebases. *New York Times*, August 19, 1971. [B-52 activity, too, was re-escalated in a major way in February 1972. The number of these strategic bombers deployed for service in Indochina was doubled at that time. Cf. Chap. 13 for present trends in the air war.]

[44]*Impact of the Vietnam War,* Report prepared by the Congressional Research Service of the Library of Congress for the Committee on Foreign Relations, U.S. Senate, June 30, 1971 (USGPO, 1971), p. 7.

Vietnam lived in the countryside. Today the number of urban dwellers has increased two- or threefold: according to one estimate made in 1968, 6,800,000 or 40 percent of the 17,200,000 South Vietnamese people live in urban areas, making South Vietnam more urbanized than Sweden, Canada, the U.S.S.R., Poland, Austria, Switzerland, Italy, and all other Southeast Asian states.[45]

The responsibility for the remarkable movement of population cannot be laid entirely to the air war. It is impossible to say what percentage of deaths and injuries or what number of refugees are directly traceable to American use of air power in South Vietnam. Artillery bombardment and ground sweeps by infantry units have taken a considerable toll of civilian life and have been responsible for creating refugees. One can only look at the overall consequences of the war with the understanding that aerial bombing and defoliation have contributed significantly to civilian casualties, mass movements of people, and destruction of forests and farmlands.[46] In many areas the military forcibly moved whole settlements of people. The purpose of such resettlements was, in the words of one U.S. military advisor engaged in moving 8,000 Montagnards in Pleiku province in 1967, "to create free artillery and air-strike zones in the area without endangering friendly villages."[47]

While figures alone never convey the suffering caused by death of a family member or friend, by lifelong disfigurement and disability, or the economic, spiritual, and psychological disorientation of being uprooted from one's home, occupation, possessions and familiar surroundings, the figures which describe the number of civilian casualties and refugees in South Vietnam are nevertheless awesome. For the period from 1965 to April 1971, the estimate of civilian casualties in South Vietnam is 1,050,000 including 325,000 deaths, while over 6,000,000 South Vietnamese (one-third of the population) are thought to have become refugees.[48] These figures mean that there is hardly a family in South Vietnam that has not suffered a death, injury or the anguish of abandoning an ancient homestead.

[45] Samuel P. Huntington, "The Bases of Accommodation," *Foreign Affairs* (July 1968), pp. 648-649.

[46] Ambassador Colby in his statement at the *Refugee Hearings* (1971) gave a breakdown of civilian casualties by the method of their creation (p. 62). Even in official estimates, shelling and bombing account for significant if declining percentages of total civilian war casualties. However, these figures are extremely misleading since they do not include casualties inflicted in the NLF-controlled zones of South Vietnam where heavy bombing and artillery strikes have occurred.

Civilian Casualties by Method

Year	Shelling and Bombing	Total
1967	18,811 (43%)	43,849
1968	28,052 (38%)	74,403
1969	16,183 (31%)	52,645
1970	8,607 (22%)	38,306

[47] *New York Times*, June 22, 1967.

[48] *Refugee Hearings* (1971), p. 2, and *Refugee and Civilian War Casualty Problems in Indochina*, Staff Report, Subcommittee to Investigate Problems Connected with Refugees and Escapees, Committee on the Judiciary, U.S. Senate, September 28, 1970 (USGPO, 1970), p. 3. Official

The massive dislocation of population has continuing costs for the refugees and for the GVN. The influx to cities and refugee camps has caused unemployment on a large scale. In 1970, AID estimated that 600,000 refugees had found jobs created by the American forces,[49] but even these relatively fortunate ones face an uncertain future as U.S. troops are withdrawn. The South Vietnamese Minister of Finance has called unemployment "the big challenge of the Thieu Government."[50] With rural society pulverized in various sections of the country, the unemployed cannot return to productive lives in the countryside for some time to come, if ever.

Inflation is a concomitant problem. Prices in urban areas are reported to be 700 percent higher now than in 1965.[51] This is partly due to sectoral imbalance created by the movement of population from rural to urban areas. There is more demand for foodstuffs while at the same time less are being produced. The combination of unemployment and higher prices is fuel for political turmoil. It is reported that American and South Vietnamese officials fear the possibility of large-scale urban violence "spearheaded by disabled

U.S. Government estimates have consistently been much lower than those of the Refugee Subcommittee. The table shown here gives both sets of figures as of December 1969 (Source: *Refugee and Civilian War Casualty Problems, op. cit.*, p. 68). The Subcommittee estimates are higher for several reasons. Official government estimates are based on inpatient admissions to U.S. and GVN provincial hospitals and do not take into account GVN hospital underreporting, reports from private hospitals, outpatient admissions to GVN provincial hospitals, casualties treated at hamlet and village medical facilities or at Special Forces hospitals, casualties treated by the NLF, casualties who are never treated at all, and casualties who die before reaching any treatment facility.

Vietnamese Civilian War-Related Casualties, December 1969

Year	U.S. Government Estimates	Subcom. Estimates
1965		100,000
1966		150,000
1967	48,734	175,000
1968	88,116	300,000
1969 (10 months)	58,698	200,000

The table showing South Vietnamese refugee figures represents the most recent government estimates. The statistics for 1970 and 1971 indicate that the number of refugees being created has actually risen recently. These statistics may be low, since on June 24, 1970, President Thieu declared that no new refugees were to be added to the rolls. (See *Refugee and Civilian War Casualty Problems, op. cit.*, p. 9; this report also cites other reasons why the figures may be low.)

Refugees, South Vietnam

Year	Refugees Generated
1964-66 (est.)	2,400,000
1967	435,000
1968	340,000
1969	115,000
1970	135,000
Cambodian Repatriates	210,000
1971 (1st Quarter only)	70,400
Total	3,705,400

Source: *Refugee Hearings* (1971), p. 47

[49] See *Refugee and Civilian War Casualty Problems in Indochina, op. cit.*, p. 8.

[50] "With the coming of the Americans, many laborers were trained. Now the Americans leave behind a reservoir of talent. But the economy cannot develop fast enough to create more jobs." Pham Kin Ngoc, *New York Times*, July 18, 1971.

[51] *Impact of the Vietnam War, op. cit.*, p. 33.

veterans and/or other war victims" in the Mekong Delta area.[52]

The relocation of people has also made the relations between antagonistic groups in South Vietnam more difficult. Although mutual antagonisms and hostility have existed between the Montagnards and ethnic Vietnamese for centuries, geography has aided accommodation between the two groups by separating them from each other; the hill tribes inhabited the rugged highlands while the Vietnamese have preferred lowland habitation. At moments of strain between the two groups, settlements and understandings have been negotiated by the political leaders from each side.

Now, however, large numbers of Montagnards have been moved off their land, many into lowland regions, a move which has forced them into closer contact with the Vietnamese, destroyed their political institutions, adversely affected their health, and threatened their claim to land titles. Some wealthy Vietnamese have moved into the more fertile areas of what were formerly Montagnard lands and claimed them for their own.[53]

The Refugee Subcommittee reported in 1968 that there was "a great deal of resentment toward the United States among the refugees." Subcommittee investigators often found that

> the refugees are bitter and disillusioned and in many cases are hostile to the South Vietnamese government and the U.S. officials. . . . The refugee program was failing to win the allegiance of this significant segment of the South Vietnamese population and was resulting in a partial disaffection of these people away from the South Vietnamese Government.[54]

That the NLF is present among the urban refugees is no secret.[55] The ability of the NLF to release prisoners from city jails in 1967 and launch the Tet offensive of 1968 depended in part on the cooperation of refugees who served as protective shields to NLF infiltration.

When all the numbers describing deaths, injuries, and refugees have been listed, examined, and absorbed, one has only begun to comprehend the effect of the war on South Vietnam. To many an American the possibility of physical mobility is desirable. To a Vietnamese peasant, the opposite is true. To be removed from his land is not only to be removed from the source of a subsistence crop of rice but also from the site of ancestral graves which must be venerated if he is to fulfill his religious duties. His children may

52 *New York Times*, July 11, 1971.

53 *New York Times*, January 6, 1971; *Refugee Hearings* (1971), Part II, pp. 67-72.

54 *Report on Civilian Casualty and Refugee Problems in South Vietnam*, May 9, 1968, Subcommittee to Investigate Problems Connected with Refugees and Escapees, Committee on the Judiciary, U.S. Senate.

55 *Ibid.*, p. 13.

never practice the veneration of ancestors, a rite exemplifying the transmission of culture and shared experience from one generation to the next. More than human life, rice fields, livestock, homes and local institutions of social and political accommodation have been destroyed. Some of the living links to the past are gone.

Still more abstract bonds to the past were obliterated when aerial and artillery bombardment were employed against the Citadel at Hue in order to retake the city from the NLF during the Tet offensive. Again, it is difficult for an American to comprehend the place of Hue as the single most important center of culture, history, and learning to Vietnamese both North and South. Our own great centers of history, culture, learning, and government are plural. Hue must be understood as a city that combines all these as do such cities as London, Paris, and Berlin. Furthermore, Vietnam possesses no large industry devoted to the accumulation, reproduction, and dissemination of materials recording the experiences of the Vietnamese throughout history. Their archival and artistic collections are the more precious for their precarious and limited existence. It was some of these treasures which were destroyed when the Hue Citadel was bombed. Their loss cannot be compared to the loss of an American museum or library. Their destruction is more akin to the loss suffered by European civilization when some of the records of Greek and Roman antiquity were ruined in the sacking of monastaries.

To speak in this manner of rites, architecture, art and annals is not to revere the artifacts of civilization more than human life. It is to recognize that a nation's historical and cultural birthright is more than a decorative frill or grist for the scholar's mill; even if all damaged and destroyed physical structures were to be replaced in a program of postwar reconstruction and rehabilitation and a healthy economic life restored, the South Vietnamese would continue to suffer the disruption of complex and fragile patterns of social and cultural life which comprise the ties to the past. At the same time, the world's most superb program of public health and education will not erase the experiences of a generation of children raised amidst violence and exploitation, many of them urban urchins schooled only in the cunning of street life.

CHAPTER 5

SOUTHERN LAOS: AIR INTERDICTION OF THE HO CHI MINH TRAIL*

A. OBJECTIVES AND ACTIVITY

The main supply line linking North Vietnam and South Vietnam, other than the direct crossing at the Demilitarized Zone, has become known as the Ho Chi Minh trail. From North Vietnam it crosses into eastern Laos through various mountain passes, such as the Mu Gia Pass (see map, Figure 5-1), then continues south through the panhandle of Laos, finally to emerge in South Vietnam through passes into Military Regions I and II (MR I and MR II). Branches of the Trail also extend into Cambodia and thence into the more southern sections of South Vietnam. Though the Trail is referred to in the singular, it must be emphasized that it actually comprises a whole network of paths. This network has evolved and widened as the need arose--primarily, in fact, in response to attempts at interdiction. The paths run, for the most part, through rough terrain with heavy jungle forests. In some sections waterways, such as the Sekong river, form part of the network.

In February 1971, the South Vietnamese Army (ARVN), with heavy U.S. air support, invaded Laos in the region of the Trail (Operation Lam Son 719). This invasion provided a dramatic object lesson illustrating three important points about the Trail. First, the fact that an attempt at ground interdiction was made at all reflects the difficulty of impeding the flow of men and supplies down the Trail by air action alone. Second, the stiff resistance with which the NLF/NVA met the invasion is an indication of the large value they attach to this supply line. Third, the fact that the incursion, which reached as far west as Tchepone, did not significantly reduce the volume of supplies travelling down the Trail is evidence of the effectiveness of this diffuse system of jungle paths.[1]

Activity along the Trail varies seasonally: it is heaviest in the dry

*The focus of U.S. air activity over southern Laos is certainly interdiction of the movement of supplies and men over the Ho Chi Minh trail, although a fraction of the air effort is also linked with the ground conflict between opposing forces in the region. We were unable to determine the exact amount devoted to this latter objective, and so have arbitrarily assigned all sorties reported for southern Laos to "Trail interdiction," which is the subject of the present chapter. The air activity associated with the ground fighting, however, should more properly be considered part of the Laotian air war, which is discussed in Chap. 6, below.

[1] *Laos: April 1971*, Staff Report, Subcommittee on U.S. Security Agreements and Commitments Abroad, Committee on Foreign Relations, U.S. Senate, August 3, 1971 (USGPO, 1971), p. 9. See also page 4: "To the west of the area in which South Vietnamese forces were active, a whole new network of trails has been constructed."

Figure 5-1

HO CHI MINH TRAIL
(schematic)

season, from October to May; in the summer and early fall, monsoon rains severely restrict ground mobility. Material is transported down the Trail by stages, with well-concealed storage depots and rest and repair areas distributed along its length. Most of the transportation is by truck convey; however, the NVA/NLF have improvised with bicycles and even foot porterage when the need arose, and their repair of damaged sections of the Trail has been rapid and efficient.

Of the various U.S. air efforts over Indochina, interdiction of the Trail supply lines has been the most concerted and continuous. Given its diffuse nature, the Trail is not a very rewarding target. In addition to the usual problems associated with air interdiction, particularly in jungle terrain,[2] there are factors peculiar to the Indochina war which make effective interdiction an even more elusive goal.[3] The relatively small volume of supplies needed to sustain military effort in South Vietnam--a generous estimate was 75 tons per day in a time of relatively high activity[4]--implies that very thorough interdiction is required before significant military effects will be visible. Partial destruction of materiel in transit can be offset by extra supplies fed into the supply lines at their points of origin.

Interdiction attempts began in 1964 with occasional raids by planes of the Royal Laotian Air Force (RLAF). The U.S. greatly escalated the effort in 1965, at about the time the air war against North Vietnam was launched, and gave it the code name STEEL TIGER. Its relative scale can be judged from Figure 5-2, showing sortie rates for fighter-bombers, which were flying most of the attack missions at first.

There was a close relationship between Trail interdiction and the air war against North Vietnam, which of course included interdiction among its objectives also. The two operations competed for aircraft, and planes which were unable to strike their scheduled targets in North Vietnam were often diverted onto the Trail in Laos. After bombing in North Vietnam was halted in November 1968, the sortie rate against the Trail rose suddenly. Figures on the total amount of air power used for interdiction, whether in North Vietnam or along the Trail, show that this was kept roughly constant in spite of the much-publicized bombing halt which affected only North Vietnam.

Trail interdiction has been made difficult by the fact that movement of

[2]See "Some Historical Notes on Air Interdiction in Korea," by Gregory A. Carter, RAND Corporation; reprinted in *Air War Hearings* (1967), Part 4, August 25, 1967, pp. 375 ff. (For a key to abbreviated titles of hearings, see App. A.)

[3]Summarized by Secretary of Defense Robert S. McNamara, *ibid.*, p. 276.

[4]*Ibid.*, p. 277. The intelligence estimate prepared for the Secretary was actually only 15 tons per day, but, to strengthen his point, he allowed for the possibility that the estimate might be low by as much as a factor of five.

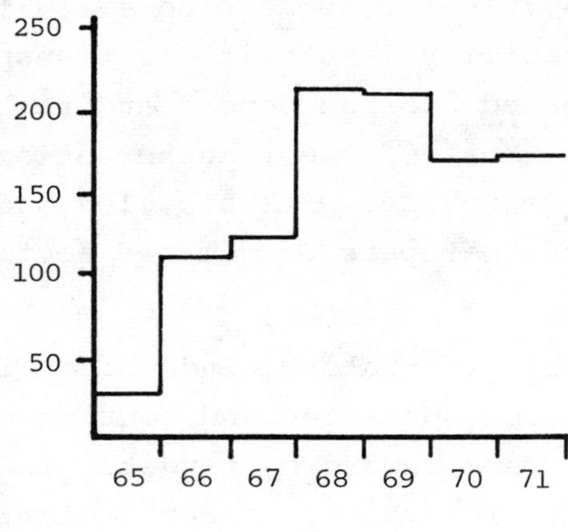

Figure 5-2

HO CHI MINH TRAIL:
AVERAGE DAILY FIGHTER-BOMBER SORTIES*

*Cf. Statistical Summary, Sec. SS-5

men and supplies can be concentrated during night hours when aerial interdiction is greatly hampered by lack of visibility. Recently, however, as discussed in more detail in Chapter 12, special electronic techniques for improving nighttime interdiction have been under development by the U.S. Air Force through a project named IGLOO WHITE. Initial operation of some of the components began in December 1967, and since that time a whole family of electronic devices has come into being.[5] The Trail has in effect been a field laboratory for testing and perfecting the apparatus for an *electronic battlefield*. To detect movement of trucks or personnel along the Trail, sensors are implanted on the ground or suspended in the foliage by air drop. Aircraft overhead receive electronic messages from them and relay the information to a central computer control station. Strike aircraft are then directed to the designated area.

For interdiction of trucks on the move, a specialized type of aircraft known as a gunship has been developed.[6] The craft may be equipped with nighttime viewing aids such as low light-level television systems and infrared detectors. The combination of new technical capabilities has radically al-

[5] "Igloo White," *Air Force*, June 1971, p. 48. See also "The Components and Manufacturers of the Electronic Battlefield," August 1, 1971, a preliminary summary compiled by Gene Massey, available from NARMIC (National Action/Research on the Military Industrial Complex), American Friends Service Committee, 160 North 15th Street, Philadelphia, Penna. 19102.

[6] The aircraft referred to here are fixed-wing aircraft, not the more familiar helicopter gunships. Armaments include various combinations of 7.62mm miniguns, 20mm cannon, and 40mm cannon.

tered the nature of the interdiction effort directed against individual transportation targets.[7]

Another facet of interdiction is the destruction of the Trail itself rather than of materiel moving along it. This is less effective because of the speed with which repairs can usually be made, unless the destruction is aimed at particularly vulnerable spots like mountain passes, bridges, or fords--the *choke points*. Much of this type of interdiction is still being carried out by fighter-bombers, although B-52 strategic bombers have come into very heavy use. The B-52s can "clear" whole sections of the terrain, removing all cover from the Trail, converting forests into wasteland. They can also modify the contours of the land with their heavy bomb loads, causing landslides or other massive blockages. Finally, B-52 bombing may be used against areas thought to contain storage or truck depots, devastating any area which might conceal a military target.

The Trail defenders have been steadily increasing their anti-aircraft defenses in response to this escalated interdiction, but they are hampered by the rough terrain and the long lines of supply. An effective anti-aircraft barrage consumes large amounts of ammunition, and bringing this ammunition down the Trail subtracts from the net flow of other supplies.[8] Moreover, the anti-aircraft weapons have to be transported into difficult terrain and any large, complex or sensitive hardware is likely to be a hindrance. Refined radars are difficult to maintain.[9]

Nevertheless, the defenses have taken their toll. From January 1970 to April 1971, announced losses over the Trail for the Air Force alone totalled 65 planes.[10] The defense has certain advantages since it knows when the trucks will be moving while the attackers do not. The slower aircraft, such as gunships, FAC planes, and helicopters, are easy targets and are forced by ground fire to fly at higher than optimum levels. Accounts of how Trail traffic is moved suggest a duel between the ground and the air, with neither side in a totally dominant position.[11]

[7] *Armed Forces Journal,* February 15, 1971, pp. 18 ff.

[8] During the North Vietnam campaign, the North Vietnamese were estimated to have used 25,000 tons per month of anti-aircraft munitions in their ground defenses, which were of course more extensive than the Trail defenses are. See *Air War Hearings* (1967), Part 2, p. 170.

[9] The use of SAMs along the Trail has been reported only recently; see Drew Middleton, *New York Times,* July 18, 1971, and *Laos: April 1971, op. cit.,* p. 5.

[10] *Laos: April 1971, op. cit.,* p. 12. The Navy flies about half as many sorties over the Trail as the Air Force. Detailed loss figures were not available to us; one report [*New York Times,* December 13, 1970] stated that 400 combat aircraft had been lost over all of Laos up to that date. The U.S. began to announce losses over Laos in March 1970. By the end of 1970, 48 fixed-wing aircraft and 38 helicopters had been lost. The fraction lost over the Trail has averaged about two-thirds of the total for Laos.

[11] Foreign Broadcast Information Service, *Daily Report (North Vietnam),* March 17-30, 1971.

The present air activity over the Trail (calendar year 1971) can be summarized as follows: The fighter-bomber sortie rate in all of Laos is about 250 per day, about 70-80 percent of which is reportedly directed against the Trail.[12] This represents by far the heaviest commitment of U.S. fighter-bomber attack sorties in Indochina. There are about 1,000 B-52 sorties per month in Indochina, most of which are also directed against the Trail. The gunship activity has actually been increasing, with important new equipment being added to the fleet in Thailand.[13] Indications are that Trail interdiction will continue to be the dominant part of the U.S. air war in Indochina. (Neither B-52 nor fighter-bomber sorties are scheduled for any major reductions in the coming year;[14] in fact a 50 percent *increase* has recently been reported.[15])

B. EVALUATION

Interdiction of the enemy's supplies and lines of communication is a normal part of military strategy; in Indochina it has taken on a special significance because of the difficulty of forcing the enemy into a telling confrontation on the battlefield. The main supply lines linking the areas of combat in the South with North Vietnam, Moscow, and Peking are the Ho Chi Minh trail and the Sihanouk trail. The latter runs through Cambodia from the port of Sihanoukville (now Kampong Som). This route once carried a significant fraction of the supplies, a fact often deemphasized in arguments advocating continued bombing of North Vietnam and the supply lines through Laos. However, starting about 1969 Prince Norodom Sihanouk was reported to have curbed the communists' access to supplies stockpiled in Sihanoukville.[16] With the ouster of Sihanouk in March 1970 the port was closed to communist shipping and the Ho Chi Minh trail gained a unique significance.

Many U.S. strategists consider Trail interdiction a prerequisite for the

[12] *Refugee Hearings* (1971), Part II, p. 43. *Washington Post*, January 17, 1972.

[13] Twenty B-57 Canberra bombers modified into a gunship configuration began operations on October 1, 1970, just in time for the dry season and the consequent increase in truck traffic; about 10 new AC-130 gunships are now being outfitted; and twelve C-130s requested in the FY 1972 budget are intended for gunship programs. *New York Times*, December 14, 1969; *Armed Forces Journal*, February 15, 1971; *Aviation Week and Space Technology*, May 10, 1971. Since the total inventory of gunships has never been large, this is a major augmentation. (There were about ten AC-130s in 1969).

[14] *Associated Press* dispatch of April 27, 1971.

[15] Jack Anderson, *Washington Post*, January 20, 1972, and private communication. *Added note:* the redeployment of additional aircraft carriers, land-based fighter-bombers and B-52s to Southeast Asia is now in progress. See, e.g., *Washington Post*, February 10, 1972.

[16] *New York Times*, April 4, 1970.

success of the Administration's Vietnamization policy.[17] Evaluation of the present status and prospects of this interdiction program thus takes on a special interest.

Measuring the "success" of an interdiction effort is a difficult problem, however. The results achieved are hard to verify; the volume of supplies reaching their destination is precisely known only to the enemy's quartermaster corps. Interdiction is in essence a long-term effort; results can be masked, for a certain period, by stockpiling. Besides, the enemy may adjust the level and style of his fighting to accommodate his actual supply situation. Without definite knowledge of his original intentions, interpretation again becomes indefinite. Finally, the enemy may respond by stepping up his infiltration activities. He may start a much larger volume of supplies down the trail routes to obtain the amount he actually needs at the other end, and he may disperse the trails by means of many parallel paths to reduce the effectiveness of the interdiction. Of course the efforts he is forced to make in this way can be counted among the positive results of interdiction; but this limited success could influence the outcome of the fighting only if the enemy were supply-limited or labor-limited in an overall sense, a condition which does not seem to apply in Indochina.

As mentioned above, trail interdiction has been intensified not only by increasing the mere volume of the effort, but also by the development of a specialized technology adapted to this function. The evolution of these new techniques is described in Chapter 12, below. Here we summarize some of the performance figures cited by Secretary of the Air Force Robert C. Seamans:[18]

--during the 1969/70 season, of 68,000 tons of materiel that started down the Trail routes, 21,000 tons managed to reach their final destination;

--in the 1970/71 season, the corresponding figures given were 9,500 tons out of 68,500 tons;

--in the 1970/71 season, 23,000-25,000 enemy trucks were hit, with about one-half that number actually destroyed.

Mr. Seamans estimated that the 1970/71 volume of supplies getting through was only about one-half of what the communists need to "fight effectively." In spite of this judgment the communist forces have indeed been fighting very effectively during 1971, making unprecedented gains both in Laos and in Cambodia. Moreover, their supply situation appears to have been good enough to permit them to build up what is described as a supply stockpile of "historic

[17] *Laos: April 1971, op. cit.*, p. 22. See also "Igloo White," *Air Force*, June 1971, p. 48.

[18] *Washington Post*, December 17, 1971. (Detailed figures taken from charts released at press conference.)

proportions" in the central highlands of South Vietnam as well.[19]

Similarly optimistic estimates for the successes achieved by the new interdiction technology were reported earlier from Vientiane. However, the figures "are regarded with considerable skepticism by some U.S. officials"; it was suggested that "the North Vietnamese were intelligent enough to set off decoy explosions when trucks were being attacked so that they would be counted as destroyed or damaged even if not hit."[20]

We dwell on these details mostly to illustrate how difficult it is to measure the direct effectiveness of an aerial interdiction campaign. There can be little doubt that the interdiction is seriously hampering the flow of supplies down the Ho Chi Minh trail, and that the enemy is being forced to make vastly increased efforts to maintain the net flow of materiel received. However, it is not correct to proceed from these observations to the conclusion that interdiction has altered the struggle decisively. Nor should one be confident in predicting that the effort can be augmented in the future to achieve such a decisive role. The search for a "decisive" effect from interdiction appears misguided; the interdiction is only one of a number of factors affecting the war's outcome. (Future prospects and the influence of interdiction bombing on other issues are explored in greater detail in Section 13-C.)

An evaluation of the bombing of the Ho Chi Minh trail must include, besides a discussion of its military effectiveness, some consideration of its costs. Beyond the direct operating expenses and aircraft losses, mentioned in the preceding section, there are indirect costs, economic, political, and social. Some portion of the cost of supporting Souvanna Phouma's regime should be charged against the interdiction campaign.[21] Bombing of the Trail has been a bargaining counter in the relationship between Souvanna and his Pathet Lao/NVA opponents. At times it seemed that an accommodation could have been reached had Souvanna been willing to forbid U.S. bombing of the Trail.[22] The bombing question will also play a central role in the overall

[19] *Washington Post*, January 4, 1972.

[20] *Laos: April 1971, op. cit.*, pp. 8-9.

[21] Initially, Trail interdiction had to be carried out covertly, from bases in Thailand from which "cover" strikes were simultaneously flown into South Vietnam. See "Summary of Actions within Present Guidelines which would result in Added Pressure on the Enemy," JCS Document, October 1967. [*The Senator Gravel Edition, The Pentagon Papers* (Beacon, 1971), Vol. IV, p. 535, Item 7.] Permission for unrestricted bombing of the Trail was subsequently obtained from Souvanna Phouma, but no doubt at the cost of U.S. commitments, mostly in the form of economic and military aid. "The Royal Lao Government continues to be almost totally dependent on the United States, perhaps more dependent on us than any other government in the world. . . ." *Laos: April 1971, op. cit.*, p. 3.

[22] Robert Shaplen, "Our Involvement in Laos," *Foreign Affairs*, April 1970, pp. 484, 486. Also *Laos: April 1971, op. cit.*, p. 21.

Indochina picture when negotiations for a settlement get under way in earnest.

Beyond this there are the human costs. The civilian impact of the Trail bombing has been relatively small, at least when compared with the effects such tonnages would have had in more densely populated regions. Unfortunately, information on the subject of refugees and civilian casualties is usually kept secret. The Trail does not run through entirely deserted landscapes, and the persons killed or displaced by the bombing have been the beneficiaries of only somewhat remote official sympathy.[23] It was confirmed, however, that 10,000 refugees had been created in the Trail area by 1970, and that 3,000 more came in 1970 from the area around Muong Phine alone.[24] The total population of the provinces through which the Trail runs is about 250,000: one can only speculate on the impact the bombing will have as the Trail expands further west, into the regions (including the Bolovens Plateau) now under PL/NVA control.[25]

[23] *Refugee Hearings* (1971), p. 43, *inter alia*.

[24] Secretary of State Rogers, in reply to questions supplied by the Subcommittee to Investigate Problems Connected with Refugees and Escapees, Committee on the Judiciary, U.S. Senate on April 14, 1971. Also *Refugee Hearings* (1971), p. 39.

[25] *New York Times*, March 11 and April 11, 1971; *Evening Star* (Washington), May 21, 1971. See also footnote 1, above, and *Refugee Hearings* (1971), p. 37.

CHAPTER 6

NORTHERN LAOS: THE LAOTIAN AIR WAR

A. OBJECTIVES AND ACTIVITY

President Kennedy's "Country Team" directive of May 1961 placed all U.S. agencies operating within a foreign country under the direct supervision of the U.S. Ambassador.[1] In Laos, a nominally neutral country torn by a serious conflict in which the U.S. was involved, this had the effect of giving the Ambassador direct control over all U.S. military and paramilitary operations. These operations were subsequently escalated to a very high level, and the American Ambassador in effect became the commander in a theater of war, responsible directly to the President.

U.S. military operations in Laos were conducted by decision of the Executive, first using paramilitary organizations directed by the CIA, and later official U.S. air power, but still under the control of the Embassy in Vientiane.[2] For many years these operations were not publicly acknowledged, though occasional newspaper accounts provided a glimpse of them. Because of this official secrecy, Congress was not given an opportunity to participate in shaping American policy in Laos, causing this to be dubbed by some a "presidential war."

Early U.S. air activity in Laos was channeled through Air America, a CIA-sponsored organization, which performed mostly logistical missions in support of Royal Laotian Government (RLG) ground forces and their paramilitary branches. At the same time the U.S. helped outfit the Laotian air force and trained their pilots and ground crews at bases in Thailand.

The first direct involvement of U.S. forces dates from the spring of 1964. In May of that year, the Department of State admitted that U.S. jets had begun reconnaissance flights over the Plain of Jars in Central Laos at the request of the RLG. On June 6 one of these jets was shot down by the Pathet Lao, and an armed escort plane was brought down the next day. In retaliation, six F-100 fighter-bombers from South Vietnam bombed Pathet Lao installations. Although Souvanna Phouma eventually broke his silence on these initial American air activities by threatening to resign unless the

[1] *Security Agreement Hearings* (1969), p. 517. (For a key to abbreviated titles of hearings, see App. A.)

[2] *Laos: April 1971*, Staff Report, Subcommittee on U.S. Security Agreements and Commitments Abroad, Committee on Foreign Relations, U.S. Senate (USGPO, 1971).

U.S. ceased the attacks, and then announcing that they had ceased, two days later he pronounced them necessary and announced their resumption.[3] The summer of 1964 also saw the use of American "civilian" pilots from Thailand flying T-28s with Laotian insignia. In October, U.S. fighter-bombers began flying cover missions for the Royal Laotian Air Force (RLAF). The first independent strike by U.S. aircraft apart from these initial reconnaissance and cover missions occurred in December 1964. It began a growing series of U.S. missions still referred to only as "reconnaissance."[4] No information on specific flights was released and firing on ground targets was not acknowledged.[5]

A decision was made at the Presidential level in late 1964 that enlarged the role of the U.S. Air Force to include interdicting lines of communication.[6] This led to a substantial increase in the scale of air activity in 1965. In March 1965, the Administration approved a division of the air activity over the Kingdom of Laos into two separately commanded programs: (1) interdiction of the Ho Chi Minh trail, code-named operation STEEL TIGER; and (2) close air support and interdiction in support of ground combat, mostly in the northern part of Laos, code-named BARREL ROLL.[7] The Trail interdiction campaign was described in Chapter 5; here we are concerned with U.S. air action in the "other war" in Laos, the conflict between opposing ground factions.[8]

During the 1960s the ground war had a cyclical pattern: Pathet Lao (PL) forces, with their North Vietnamese supporters (NVA), would advance during the dry season (about October to May); during the subsequent wet season, the army of the RLG with their supporters, the *Bataillons Guerriers* (BG),[9] would

[3] *Ibid.*, pp. 370, 476.

[4] The flights were variously classed as "reconnaissance," "armed reconnaissance," or "reconnaissance with armed escort." The technical significance of "armed reconnaissance"--an attack sortie flown in search of targets of opportunity--is not widely understood. Hence the terminology has some potential for deception. See *Security Agreement Hearings* (1969), p. 778.

[5] *Security Agreement Hearings* (1969), p. 370.

[6] *Ibid.*, p. 483.

[7] *The Senator Gravel Edition, The Pentagon Papers* (Beacon, 1971), Vol. III, p. 279. Air activity in support of ground forces also extends into the southern part of Laos, where, however, we are unable to separate it from the air interdiction campaign against the Ho Chi Minh trail (cf. Chap. 5). Because of this lack of information the figures quoted in this chapter represent only a *lower limit* on the volume of air power devoted to the specifically Laotian campaign.

[8] See D. Gareth Porter, "After Geneva: Subverting Laotian Neutrality," in *Laos: War and Revolution*, Nina S. Adams and Alfred W. McCoy, ed., for a discussion of this background. We concentrate on the U.S. part in the air activity, since the RLAF played a relatively minor role throughout the conflict, flying about 5 to 20% of the missions. Moreover, RLAF is effectively under U.S. control. For a discussion of U.S. involvement in Laos prior to 1962, see Jonathan Mirsky and Stephen E. Stonefield, "The United States in Laos, 1945-1962," in Edward Friedman and Mark Selden, eds., *America's Asia* (Vintage, 1971), pp. 253-323.

[9] See *Laos: April 1971, op. cit.*, p. 14. See also footnote 30, Chap. 1.

regain the lost territory. This pattern was related to the fact that the PL/NVA had difficulties bringing in their supplies over long lines during the wet season.

Several developments since 1967 caused this pattern to change. One factor was the increase of U.S. military activity in Laos. Electronic support bases for the North Vietnam air war had been installed in several strongholds within the Pathet Lao-controlled eastern provinces.[10] Following the bombing halt over North Vietnam in November 1968, the U.S. increased its air activity against Laos dramatically, taking advantage of the sudden increase in the number of planes available.[11] Another factor was that the RLG offensive of 1967 had had particularly impressive results, bringing RLG forces to within twenty miles of the North Vietnam border.

Perhaps in reaction to these moves, the PL/NVA offensive during and after 1968 increased substantially in scale and duration. For the first time they failed to conform to the earlier see-saw pattern and extended well into the wet season. In 1968 the PL/NVA captured many of the isolated sites that had previously remained under RLG control. Similarly, in 1969 the PL/NVA offensive was of unprecedented proportions; the key town of Muong Soui was taken and the Royal capital of Luang Prabang was virtually surrounded. These PL/NVA moves may in part have been prompted by events away from the battlefield: there were expectations of renewed negotiations linked with the change of U.S. Administration in 1969, and such negotiations would be better approached from a position of strength. Also, pressure exerted on the RLG might eventually help persuade Souvanna Phouma to withdraw his permission for U.S. bombing of the Laotian portions of the Trail.

As noted above, U.S. air activity over Laos rose sharply when the planes which had been flying missions against North Vietnam became available in November 1968. Much of this additional air power at first went to Trail interdiction missions; however, the bombing in northern Laos was also intensified by a large factor (see Figure 6-1).[12] The sharpest increase came early in 1969. Then, in May, the decision was made to accede to General Vang Pao's request for direct air support of his BG units,[13] including the bombing of

[10] *Security Agreement Hearings* (1969), p. 490; see also Roland Paul, "American Involvement in Laos," *Foreign Affairs*, April 1971, p. 537.

[11] Alternate missions were always promptly found for aircraft that were not momentarily busy; thus even during brief bombing pauses over North Vietnam, the planes flew extra missions against other targets in Indochina. One official, quoted by T. D. Allman in the *Far Eastern Economic Review*, March 12, 1970, stated: "We just couldn't let the planes rust."

[12] The Air Force, Thai-based sortie rate rose from 22 per day in October 1968 to 52 per day in December.

[13] *Security Agreement Hearings* (1969), p. 502. This decision was actually taken during the interregnum between Ambassador Sullivan's departure from Vientiane in March 1969, and the

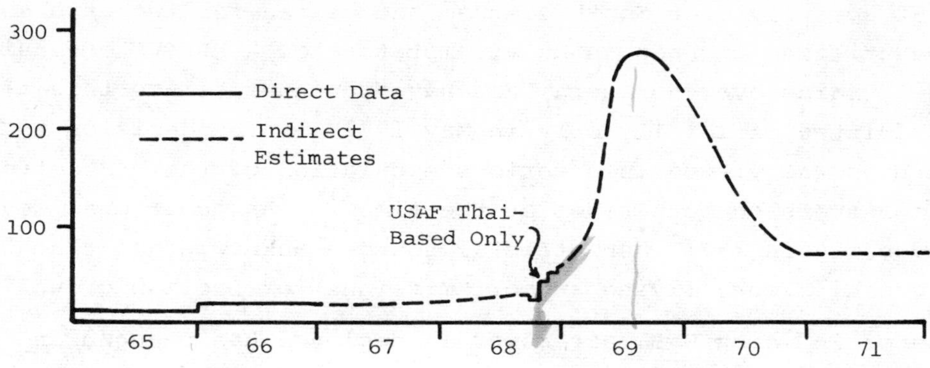

Figure 6-1

NORTHERN LAOS: AVERAGE DAILY FIGHTER-BOMBER SORTIES*

*Cf. Statistical Summary, Sec. SS-5

the town of Xieng Khouang, a long-time Pathet Lao stronghold off the southern edge of the Plain of Jars.[14] Yet another escalation marked the counteroffensive mounted by Vang Pao in the late summer, in which he retook the Plain of Jars for the first time since 1964. Simultaneously with this increase in scale, some of the restrictions on U.S. bombing were relaxed. The result was to give the Air Force a quantity of aircraft and a freedom of use in Laos even beyond that which it had in South Vietnam at the height of the air war there.[15]

Since this peak of activity in 1969, during which the sortie rate reached 300 per day, fighter-bomber activity over northern Laos has been decreasing. This is no doubt due to a reduction in the tempo of ground activity. It is also a part of the general deescalation of U.S. air power in Indochina: aircraft are no longer as readily available.

The sortie rate for fighter-bombers, however, is not the only index for the intensity of the air war. In February 1970, B-52s began saturation-bombing raids in northern Laos.[16] At that time, President Nixon announced only that a single B-52 mission had been authorized, but press reports indicated

arrival of Ambassador Godley in July.

[14] Robert Shaplen, "Our Involvement in Laos," *Foreign Affairs*, April 1970, p. 485; and T. D. Allman, *New York Times*, September 28, 1969.

[15] *Security Agreement Hearings* (1969), p. 784.

[16] There are indications that B-52 raids in support of ground action in Northern Laos may have begun as early as the spring of 1969. Ambassador Sullivan told reporters in May 1971 that B-52s had been flying missions over Northern Laos for "about two years." See article by John W. Finney, *New York Times*, May 4, 1971. See also Harald Munthe-Kaas in *Far Eastern Economic Review*, October 23, 1969.

that all B-52 activity over South Vietnam had ceased for two days as the bombers were utilized in Laos in an attempt to stop a PL/NVA offensive.[17] The fact that B-52 raids over northern Laos have continued since this first instance was admitted officially only in May 1971.[18] The decision to use B-52s in northern Laos was viewed as a serious escalation of the U.S. effort by diplomatic observers on both sides at the time.[19] An additional development was revealed early in 1971 when official sources acknowledged that U.S. helicopter gunships were flying support missions for Laotian ground troops.[20]

The manner in which U.S. air power is deployed has changed in recent years: a strategy was sought which would maximize the effectiveness of abundant air power when used in conjunction with the relatively ineffective ground troops of the RLG. The aim is to turn major battles into contests between U.S. air power and North Vietnamese infantry. During major PL/NVA offensives, such as that of the winter of 1970, the RLG/BG forces held positions only long enough to draw their adversary into the open where he could be attacked effectively from the air:

> [Air power] was used more or less in a classic sense. Vang Pao and his troops would move out, identify the enemy, pull back, and the airpower would come in. They just couldn't stand that weight of effort.[21]

In this sense, the Laos campaign has become a clear application of that aspect of the Nixon Doctrine which rests upon the substitution of American technology, in conjunction with Asian forces, for American manpower.

B. EVALUATION

If all air activity connected with interdiction of the Ho Chi Minh trail is specifically excluded, as in this chapter, the remainder of the Laotian air war represents a campaign with a specific and fairly easily separable objective: to support the forces of the Royal Laotian Government against the Pathet Lao and their North Vietnamese allies, in order to prevent extensive loss of territory and population to them. The U.S. has involved itself in this war not only through its air power, but also by organizing, supplying, and directing irregular ground forces, mostly under control of the CIA.[22] The war in

[17] *New York Times*, February 19, 1970 and *Observer*, February 19, 1970.

[18] John Finney, *New York Times*, May 4, 1971. "B-52s bomb the Plain of Jars daily since its capture by the communists." *Le Monde*, December 31, 1971.

[19] See Allman, *Far Eastern Economic Review*, *op. cit.*, p. 5.

[20] *New York Times*, January 20, 1971.

[21] Maj. Gen. Robert L. Petit, deputy commander, 7/13th Air Force, Udorn, Thailand, in *Security Agreement Hearings* (1969), p. 784. See also *New York Times*, February 13, 1971 and March 6, 1970.

[22] This has become public knowledge only recently; *Laos: April 1971*, *op. cit.*, p. 14.

the air played a major part in the conflict, and it is instructive to ask to what extent this aerial activity has met with the desired successes, and what the costs were for Laotian society in the course of this escalation.

At its peak, the Laotian air war involved up to 300 fighter bomber sorties per day--a rate equal to the average sortie rate flown against North Vietnam at the height of that air campaign. Deployed against a very limited geographical area, such a volume of air attacks must be considered an extreme measure, and one which cannot fail to have the deepest impact on the society against which it is directed.

For a while in 1969 it appeared that this lavish use of air power was meeting with some military success: Vang Pao's capture of the Plain of Jars seemed like a turning point, and questions were being asked in Congressional hearings why air power could not be as successful elsewhere in Indochina as it was in northern Laos. Senator Stuart Symington suggested that if the U.S. used air power properly in Laos, that country could be held at relatively low cost in lives and money.[23] "Properly," in this context, implied a sufficient intensity and a certain lack of restrictions:

> When the situation got close to desperate in June in Laos, certain restrictions were removed and we were allowed to use airpower in a little freer manner. We also had available at this time what might be termed a sufficient quantity of airpower.[24]

Events, however, soon belied the rosy course predicted for them. The PL/NVA in the following dry season rolled back Vang Pao's advance and soon were in control of more territory in Laos than ever before.

It is in the context of such highly temporary military successes that the costs imposed on the people of Laos should be examined. Western journalists who have visited the Pathet Lao headquarters in the province of Sam Neua report a landscape covered with bomb craters, "a chaos of red earth, broken rocks, devastated trees." Most towns and villages in the area have been destroyed. The villagers and Pathet Lao live in trenches and caves; farming, when possible at all, is done at night.[25] Interviews with refugees from the Plain of Jars indicate similar living conditions there. The use of delayed-action antipersonnel weapons on the Plain after 1967 made life above ground very hazardous. By 1969 villages were being abandoned altogether.[26]

[23] *Security Agreement Hearings* (1969), pp. 784-785.

[24] Maj. Gen. Robert L. Petit, *ibid.*, p. 784.

[25] Jacques Decornoy, "Life in the Pathet Lao Liberated Zone," in *Laos: War and Revolution, op. cit.*, p. 411; Richard Ward, *Guardian,* July 18, 1970, August 8, 1970, and September 19, 1970.

[26] Laurence Stern, *Washington Post,* May 23, 1971; *Christian Science Monitor,* March 14, 1970; *Manchester Guardian,* March 14, 1970; and *Far Eastern Economic Review,* February 27, 1971.

> By 1968 the intensity of the bombings was such that no organized life was possible in the villages. The villagers moved to the outskirts and then deeper and deeper into the forest as the bombing climax reached its peak in 1969 when jet planes came daily and destroyed all stationary structures. Nothing was left standing. The villagers lived in trenches and holes or in caves. They only farmed at night. All of the informants, without any exception, had his village completely destroyed. In the last phase, bombings were aimed at the systematic destruction of the material basis of the civilian society.[27]

Similar observations of the destruction in Laos have been reported by virtually all those who have had an opportunity to visit the regions involved.[28] Several observers have actually been led to assert that one of the aims of U.S. bombing policy was "to destroy the social and economic fabric of Pathet Lao areas."[29]

Just how much of the destruction is attributable to the use of air power and how much to conventional warfare is debatable, but air power is the major arm of U.S. firepower, and in the minds of the victims as well as in those of most observers it is responsible for a major portion of the destruction.[30] About one-quarter to one-third of the Laotian population has been made into refugees since 1960;[31] recent studies indicate that the main reason given by the refugees for leaving their homes is the effect or fear of U.S. bombing.[32]

This desolate picture raises some difficult questions about the use of

[27] G. Chapelier and J. Van Malderghem, "Plain of Jars, Social Changes Under Five Years of Pathet Lao Administration," *Asia Quarterly*, I, 1971.

[28] See, for example, the documentation collected by Fred Branfman, printed in *Refugee Hearings* (1971), Part II, pp. 89-113. Mr. Branfman spent four years in Laos and conducted extensive interviews with refugees as well as with American pilots, forward air controllers, and Embassy officials. See also T. D. Allman, *Far Eastern Economic Review*, January 8 and 29, 1972. Mr. Allman was recently permitted to fly by charter airplane over the Plain of Jars and to visit adjacent government outposts. He describes the bombing as "an operation that lies well down the spectrum between a military scandal and a provable war crime." [*FEER*, January 29, 1972, p. 19.]

[29] Shaplen, "Our Involvement in Laos," *op. cit.*, p. 485; see also Tammy Arbuckle, *Washington Star*, April 19, 1970: "Well informed sources said the U.S. is pursuing a 'scorched-earth' policy to force the people to move into the Government areas . . ."; and T. D. Allman, *New York Times*, October 1, 1969: "[T]he main U.S. targets now, according to sources in both the Laotian Government and the Pathet Lao rebels, are the rebel economy and social fabric."

[30] The exact proportion of damage attributable to air power cannot be determined at present, but this does not nullify the reports of observers in Laos, or the inferences which can be drawn from the scale and intensity of the air war there.

[31] *Impact of the Vietnam War*, Report prepared by the Congressional Research Service of the Library of Congress for the Committee on Foreign Relations, U.S. Senate, June 30, 1971 (USGPO, 1971), pp. 24-26.

[32] See, for example, the USIS survey conducted in 1970 and reported in the *Refugee Hearings* (1971), pp. 14 ff: "97% of the people said they had seen a bombing attack. . . . *The Bombing is clearly the most compelling reason* for moving" (p. 17, emphasis in original). Other reports on this subject have been made by Fred Branfman, Walter Haney, and Congressman Paul McCloskey.

American air power. There is a remarkable divergence between the reported effects of the bombing in Laos, which we have just outlined, and the continuing statements on the part of Administration officials that no civilian targets have been attacked except through occasional error. Such a divergence between intent and result is of course a common feature of war, especially where it involves a widespread enterprise requiring the control of many individual elements. Air war, even more than other forms of warfare, has a great potential for striking unintended targets: the human and technical circumstances underlying this have been outlined in Chapter 2. No doubt such considerations account for some of the devastation in Laos, but other factors have also been important.

Among these, the extreme escalation which took place in 1969 must be seen as central. The control of such a large number of sorties, and the selection and verification of so many targets, represent a difficult problem for any organization. We think it fair to say that the Embassy staff in Vientiane, responsible for controlling the bombing, was overloaded. A report for the Senate Subcommittee on Refugees states that "the sheer volume and constancy of bombing activity since 1968 makes effective control of these strikes almost impossible."[33]

The chain of command which controlled the bombing in Laos has been considered in detail in a report prepared for the Senate Committee on Foreign Relations. After discussing the rules of engagement for American aircraft and enumerating the categories of free-fire zone which were established in Laos, the report notes:

> Given the apparent stringency of these rules of engagement, it is difficult to see how roads with civilian traffic, villages and groups of civilians could have been bombed, rocketed, or napalmed. It seems clear, however, that . . . the system itself is so complicated that it cannot possibly be foolproof. Indeed, the effort to provide in the rules of engagement for every contingency appears to create obvious loopholes . . . There are plenty of instances known to American civilian employees who have been in Laos for some years in which civilian targets have been bombed. . .[34]

According to a former senior Air Force photo reconnaissance expert attached to the Embassy in Vientiane, restrictions on American air operations have been quietly relaxed while control over the Laotian air war by the Ambassador has been reduced. "The Rules of Engagement were strictly adhered to from 1966 to 1968 but for all practical purposes after Ambassador [William

[33] *Refugee and Civilian War Casualty Problems in Indochina,* Staff Report, Subcommittee to Investigate Problems Connected with Refugees and Escapees, U.S. Senate, September 28, 1970 (USGPO, 1970), p. 30.

[34] *Laos: April 1971, op. cit.,* pp. 10-11.

H.] Sullivan left [in March 1969] they appear to have been discarded and are only cited to placate Congressmen in Washington."[35] This reported relaxation of enforcement in the rules of engagement coincided with the greatest period of escalation in the bombing, suggesting once again that discrimination is lost as the air war intensifies.

When all the circumstantial factors which may have accounted for civilian bombings in Laos have been enumerated, one is still left with the troubling possibility that the widespread devastation visited on areas under long-time communist control was to some extent an element of overall U.S. policy for the war. The question of intent is ultimately very important, of course. However, the available information does not permit an unambiguous answer; we must leave this question open. Whether the devastation is the result of conscious planning, however, or whether it comes about merely from an unformulated attitude which made civilian damage an acceptable byproduct, the final results for the victims are real enough. Even former Ambassador Sullivan, a staunch witness to the exclusively military orientation of American bombing, has stated that

> most Lao civilians learn very quickly that bombing necessarily follows the North Vietnamese.[36]

A lesson that Lao civilians must learn from this experience is that they remain in areas threatened by a communist advance at their own risk. Government forces have in fact carried out large-scale evacuations of the population from such threatened areas. The merits of such an evacuation were discussed in detail under the heading "Strategic Movement of Refugees" in the staff report previously cited.[37] According to the report,

> Population control and the strategic movement of people in Laos has been justified on two grounds: first, it denies the Pathet Lao the resources of the local population and, second, it secures more of the population under government control.

Among the reasons for "mass evacuation" quoted from a USAID field memorandum is that "such refugee evacuation would clear the Plain [of Jars] for unrestricted military strike operations against the enemy." Anyone remaining in the area after the evacuation is deemed to be the enemy. Most of the Plain has indeed become a free-fire zone:

> Air bombings during the last year have mutilated the economic and ethnographic map of Laos--turning the Plain

[35] Reserve Air Force Captain Jerome J. Brown, quoted in "U.S. Bombing in Laos: An Inside Report," *Bi-Weekly Asian Release*, Dispatch News Service International, November 22, 1971, p. 3.

[36] *Refugee Hearings, op. cit.*, Part II, p. 40.

[37] *Refugee and Civilian Problems, op. cit.*, pp. 24-26.

> of Jars, central Savannakhet province, and the three formerly well established north Laotian towns of Khang Khai, Xieng Kouangville, and Muong Soui for the first time into free fire zones.[38]

Though the evacuation of civilians can also be justified by the desire to shelter them from the impending ground fight, these same civilians had, as the Plain changed hands on previous occasions, opted to weather the storm near their homes; as mentioned above, most of them name the bombing as the main reason for leaving.

Though U.S. air support has undoubtedly slowed enemy advances, and has occasionally produced momentary allied military successes, we have seen that in the long run air power, associated with the relatively weak ground forces in Laos, has been unable to hold the line. It might be argued, moreover, that the use of American air power has actually provoked a counterescalation of the ground conflict. Many observers believe that the communists' objectives do not go much beyond the military achievements already to their credit.[39] In this view, air power has merely heightened the scale of the conflict, without affecting its outcome to a significant extent.

Now raising the stakes may well be an important element in overall U.S. strategy for Indochina. It draws communist forces away from the focus in South Vietnam, providing extra time for South Vietnam's army to better match that of North Vietnam.[40] It may also cause the North Vietnamese to extend themselves beyond their capacity for sustaining long-term activity. In such a view, the wars in Laos and Cambodia are building blocks for the ultimate achievement of a military balance throughout Indochina--a balance principally determined by Vietnamese armies, from the North and from the South.

The immediate effect of this policy, however, is to force the indigenous communist groupings into a much closer dependence on their North Vietnamese allies.[41] One no longer talks about areas in Laos under Pathet Lao control: the North Vietnamese are there. So a concomitant result is that, in the areas lost to government control, an adverse political reorientation is likely to take place.

There is little doubt that widespread devastation has been brought to those areas of Laos, like Sam Neua province and the Plain of Jars, which have

[38] T. D. Allman, *Far Eastern Economic Review*, March 12, 1970.

[39] The RLG defenses have been so shaky that the capture of Luang Prabang and perhaps even of Vientiane might be attainable, though it has not been attempted.

[40] Cf. *Laos: April 1971, op. cit.*, p. 22.

[41] It would be a mistake to assume that the Pathet Lao has always been oriented to the DRV. It began as a nationalist movement and sustained its independence for some time. See Mirsky and Stonefield, *op. cit.*, pp. 255 ff.

for long periods been under communist control. Bombing which results in "destruction of the fabric of society," a phrase recurring in reports from those areas, whether undertaken for deterrent or punitive reasons, is unlikely to contribute to a Laotian nation which is self-sufficient and at all friendly to the United States. The immediate costs of this air war are borne largely by the people of Laos, not by the North Vietnamese forces. The anti-Western political consequences of this suffering will, we believe, seriously erode the American position in Indochina in the long run.

CHAPTER 7

THE AIR CAMPAIGN IN CAMBODIA

A. OBJECTIVES AND ACTIVITY

The events following the fall of President Norodom Sihanouk in March 1970 and the invasion of Cambodia just over a month later by American and South Vietnamese forces have resulted in a large-scale ground and air war there. The ground war is primarily a contest between the army of the Phnom Penh government[1] and ARVN, on the one hand, and about 50,000 NLF/NVA allied with a smaller number of indigenous pro-Sihanouk forces (FUNK) on the other.[2] American air involvement has followed a familiar pattern: official acknowledgment of increasing U.S. participation has not kept pace with the action.

U.S. and VNAF air operations over Cambodia are directed from Saigon, though an American-financed center has reportedly been set up in Phnom Penh to coordinate the bombing efforts of the U.S., South Vietnamese, Thai, and Cambodian air forces.[3] The U.S. embassy in Phnom Penh, established following the ouster of Sihanouk, has attempted to maintain such a "low profile" that one Asian ambassador has described Ambassador Emory C. Swank as "the invisible ambassador."[4] Embassy personnel were uninformed about either the location or the results of bombing missions.[5]

At the time of the initial Cambodian "incursion," President Nixon announced that while the U.S. would continue interdiction bombing of NVA/NLF and FUNK personnel concentrations and military supply targets "with the approval of the Cambodian government," there would be no close support of Cambodian troops or ARVN units operating in Cambodia.[6] This official policy of labelling all U.S. activity "interdiction" and revealing none of the details continued until January 1971, though it was clear from press reports, and later in a staff report to the Senate Committee on Foreign Relations, that some direct support operations were conducted throughout the campaign.[7] In July 1970 it was reported that there were no limitations on how far American

[1]The army of the Phnom Penh government grew from 35,000 men in May 1970 to 165,000 in December. *Cambodia: December 1970*, Staff Report, Committee on Foreign Relations, U.S. Senate, December 16, 1970 (USGPO, 1970), p. 1.

[2]*Ibid.*, p. 3. FUNK is the acronym for the National United Front of Kampuchea (Cambodia).

[3]T. D. Allman, *Far Eastern Economic Review*, August 21, 1971, p. 17.

[4]Henry Bradsher, *Evening Star* (Washington), May 23, 1971.

[5]*Cambodia: December 1970*, *op. cit.*, p. 7.

[6]*New York Times*, July 1, 1970.

[7]*New York Times*, August 9, 1970.

planes were permitted to penetrate into Cambodia.[8] The British press quoted the Second-in-Command of one Cambodian military region as claiming that his troops received American air support "whenever they need it."[9]

In early 1971, in response to what U.S. officials considered a deterioration of the Cambodian governments's position, the scope of American air support rose above the level at which it had stabilized after the initial invasion. At the same time, the policy of referring to all American air activity as interdiction was dropped and the Department of Defense announced that the U.S. intended to employ the full range of its air combat power throughout Cambodia against troop units and supplies that might "ultimately" threaten American military personnel in South Vietnam.[10] In January, American B-52s supported the efforts of Cambodian government forces to reopen the Pic Nil Pass on Route 4 southwest of Phnom Penh, which connects the city with the vital port of Kampong Som (formerly Sihanoukville).[11] After February, South Vietnamese requests for helicopter support of their units in Cambodia no longer had to be cleared individually.

U.S. aircraft from South Vietnam and Thailand, with some help from VNAF, were flying most of the combat sorties in Cambodia in late 1970, when the Cambodian Air Force inventory included 60 fixed-wing and helicopter aircraft. The U.S. role increased in early 1971 after the Cambodian Air Force was virtually wiped out on the ground at the Phnom Penh airport by a guerrilla unit. (There has also been some support for Cambodian government operations by Thai aircraft.)[12] In periods of intense fighting, allied planes have flown hundreds of sorties daily.[13] B-52s, besides carrying out interdiction raids against communist base areas in the northeast, also participate in the close support function.[14] Detailed figures for the overall level of B-52 activity in Cambodia have not been made available; the monthly fighter-bomber sortie rate during 1971 has varied from 1,000 to 1,800 for U.S. planes, with VNAF contributing a rather smaller number.[15]

[8] *New York Times,* July 5, 1970.

[9] *The Times* (London), August 9, 1970. See also Associated Press dispatch in the *New York Times,* August 4, 1970; and *Washington Post,* January 16, 1971.

[10] William Beecher, *New York Times,* January 19, 1971.

[11] *Ibid.*

[12] *New York Times,* July 2, 1970.

[13] *New York Times,* December 5, 1971.

[14] For example, in an action near the town of Krek, B-52s were reported to have dropped 1,000 tons of bombs. *Washington Post,* October 10, 1971. See also *The Times* (London), January 15, 1971.

[15] For details, see the Statistical Summary, Sec. SS-5.

B. EVALUATION

Much of the early fighting in Cambodia, after the U.S.-South Vietnamese invasion in 1970, was small-unit, guerrilla-style warfare. Most of the NLF, NVA, and FUNK troops were engaged in the development of a new base complex in the northeast; only 5,000 to 10,000 men confronted Cambodian government forces directly.[16] As the conflict escalated, however, the military situation changed in character. The communists' position has been consolidated, and the war in Cambodia is now in many ways like that in northern Laos. Saigon reports say that

> highly placed [U.S.] officials estimate communist forces now control as much as 80 per cent of Cambodia and can do anything they want. . . . They could take Cambodia in a week if they tried, if they cut loose everything they had.[17]

U.S. air power has played a crucial role in holding down the losses sustained by the Cambodians and the South Vietnamese in a series of costly encounters.[18] Nevertheless, as in Laos, this air power working with relatively ineffective ground forces has been unable to halt the communists' advance.

Meanwhile, towns and villages taken by the communists are subjected to extensive bombing.[19] Detailed information on the damage, and on the civilian casualties and refugees produced, is not available. Official pronouncements by both the Cambodian government and U.S. sources have minimized these problems.[20] Scattered information indicates, however, that the situation is entirely analogous to the one found in northern Laos. The most recent investigation was carried out by the General Accounting Office, at the request of the Senate Judiciary Subcommittee on Refugees.[21] The report states

> more than two million Cambodians have been driven from their homes at different times since the war spread to their country in the spring of 1970. . . . Bombing is a very significant cause of refugees and civilian casualties. . . . Refugee conditions are deplorable and hospitals are suffer-

[16] *Cambodia: December 1970, op. cit.*, p. 2.

[17] *AP* dispatch, *Ithaca Journal*, December 10, 1971.

[18] *New York Times*, November 19 and 26, 1971.

[19] *Washington Post*, December 17, 1971.

[20] *Refugee and Civilian War Casualty Problems in Indochina*, Staff Report, Subcommittee to Investigate Problems Connected with Refugees and Escapees, Committee on the Judiciary, U.S Senate, September 28, 1970 (USGPO, 1970), pp. 43-44; *Refugee Hearings* (1971), Part II, pp. 69-70. (For a key to abbreviated titles of hearings, see App. A.)

[21] *Problems in the Khmer Republic (Cambodia) Concerning War Victims, Civilian Health, and War-Related Casualties*, Doc. B-169832, Dept. of State (February 2, 1972). Note that the Refugee Committee was motivated to work with the General Accounting Office in these investigations because of the difficulty of access to the required information directly from the concerned agencies both in Washington and in Cambodia. A similar investigation was made earlier by the GAO in Laos.

> ing from severe pharmaceutical shortages. . . . The population of Phnom Penh is estimated to have more than doubled because of the influx of refugees.[22]

On the other hand, the U.S. Administration's attitude is "not to become involved with the problems of civilian war victims in Cambodia." "Since only a limited amount of money is available, we can most effectively focus it on military and economic assistance."[22] This emphasis on the military aspects of the problem, and disinclination to face the civilian consequences of American military actions in Indochina, is a bias in the prevailing official attitudes that can be noted throughout the Indochina debate.

Because events in Cambodia parallel those in Laos, which were discussed extensively in Chapter 6, we will not repeat the discussion here. Some future implications of American air activity in these two countries are considered in Chapters 13 and 14.

[22] The findings of the GAO Report are summarized in the *New York Times*, December 5, 1971

CHAPTER 8

THE ECOLOGICAL IMPACT OF THE AIR WAR*

Only We Can Prevent Forests

Motto over the door to headquarters, Operation Ranch Hand, Saigon

A. DEFOLIANTS AND HERBICIDES

Use of defoliants in South Vietnam began on an experimental basis in 1961 and became fully operational the following year.[1] This program had two major objectives. The first was *defoliation* (operation RANCH HAND), in which forests, roadsides, base perimeters, etc., were sprayed in order to remove the foliage cover which had afforded concealment to the enemy. At low concentrations these chemicals do indeed act merely as defoliants; at the concentrations used in Vietnam, however, they normally act also as herbicides, killing a significant fraction of the plants in addition to defoliating them. The second major objective was the *destruction of crops*, mostly rice, carried out in the hope of denying food to the enemy.[2] Crop destruction was largely confined to the mountainous areas of northern and western South Vietnam, where the impact was felt most severely by the small population of about one million, mostly Montagnards. Crop destruction may also have had the objective of driving South Vietnamese civilians into the "strategic hamlets" set up for them by the South Vietnamese Government.[3]

Though some spraying in Vietnam has been done with helicopters or ground equipment, the principal means of application has been the twin-engine C-123 cargo plane. In the years 1962 through 1968 these aircraft made more than 19,000 individual spray flights. Each plane is fitted with a 950-gallon tank from which the herbicide is pumped to spray booms under each wing and at the tail. When the herbicide hits the airstream it is dispersed into fine droplets. One aircraft flying at about 150 feet above

*A more detailed discussion of many of the issues raised in this chapter is given in App. E.

[1] Herbicide Assessment Commission for the American Association for the Advancement of Science, *Background Material Relevant to Presentations at the 1970 Annual Meeting of the AAAS*, Chicago, Ill., December 29, 1970, p. 14.

[2] Stanford Biology Study Group, 1971, "The Destruction of Indochina," *Bulletin of the Atomic Scientists, 27* (1971), pp. 36-40; A. H. Westing, "Agent Blue in Vietnam," *New York Times*, July 12, 1971.

[3] Ngo Vinh Long, "Leaf Abscission?," *Bulletin of Concerned Asian Scholars* (October 1969), p. 54.

the tree tops produces a swath of affected vegetation about 300 feet wide and ten miles long.[4] Precautions must be taken that the sprayed chemical does not drift into adjacent, non-target areas. Occasional incidents occur in which an aircraft is forced to dump its herbicide quickly; it can pump out the entire 950 gallons in about 30 seconds.[5]

Three formulations account for almost all the herbicides used in Indochina: agents Orange, White, and Blue. The composition and mode of action of these agents are discussed in greater detail in Appendix E, which also contains a listing of appropriate references; a summary of the main facts is given below.

> *Orange:* Composition, 2,4-D and 2,4,5-T; an oily liquid insoluble in water. Mainly used against broad-leaved and woody vegetation. One application defoliates hardwoods and kills some canopy trees; two applications produce a heavy kill of all woody vegetation; the resulting invasion by bamboo and grasses may arrest forest regeneration indefinitely. On mangrove forests Orange kills almost all trees in a single application; mangrove areas sprayed in 1961 have still shown no significant signs of regeneration. The chemical itself persists for only a few weeks, except in stagnant water or poorly aerated ground, where high concentrations could conceivably accumulate. 2,4,5-T or an associated impurity (dioxin) is thought to be a teratogen (causing serious birth deformities, like thalidomide); its use in the U.S. has been restricted since late 1969. Orange accounts for about 60 percent of the herbicide used in Vietnam; it was being sprayed at least until August 1970.
>
> *White:* Composition, butyl esters of 2,4-D and picloram; a solution in water. Used much like Orange, but less volatile and therefore less subject to wind drift; it is preferred near populated areas. Picloram is one of the most potent herbicides known; it is remarkably persistent, like the insecticide DDT; its use on agricultural land in the U.S. is prohibited. Since White is water soluble, it can easily be washed by rainfall into adjacent areas.
>
> *Blue:* Composition, organic arsenates including cacodylic acid; a solution in water. Its prime use is for crop destruction, especially rice. It is more effective against grasses than are Orange or White, and acts more rapidly (within a few days).

Herbicides are sprayed at a rate of about three gallons per acre, the stock solution of each agent being formulated to obtain the desired coverage. In the case of Orange, the rate of application is about 26 pounds per acre, almost ten times the rate recommended for use in the U.S.[6] It is estimated

[4]The C-123 cruises at 230 miles per hour; at this low speed and at minimal altitude, it becomes vulnerable to ground fire from any weapons, even small-caliber. Hence in all areas where hostile elements may be present, even if they have no conventional anti-aircraft capability, the spraying missions are preceded by fighter-bomber sweeps providing maximum-intensity ground-fire suppression (cf. p. 22). The effects of this support activity must be reckoned as a contingent cost of the herbicide program.

[5]Orians and Pfeiffer, "Ecological Effects of the War in Vietnam," *Science*, Vol. 168 (1970), pp. 544-554.

[6]Statement of A. W. Galston before the Subcommittee on National Security Policy and Scien-

that more than 100 million pounds of herbicides have by now been sprayed on Vietnam, covering a total of almost six million acres;[7] details are illustrated in Figure 8-1. The greatest impact has been on tropical hardwood forests. About 35 percent of South Vietnam's 14 million acres of dense forest have been sprayed one or more times, resulting in the destruction of enough merchantable timber (six billion board feet) to supply the country's domestic needs for about 30 years; this also represents a loss of about $500 million in taxes that would otherwise have accrued to the South Vietnamese Government. Of the three-quarter million acres of coastal mangrove forests, mostly in the Delta area, about one-half have been totally destroyed.

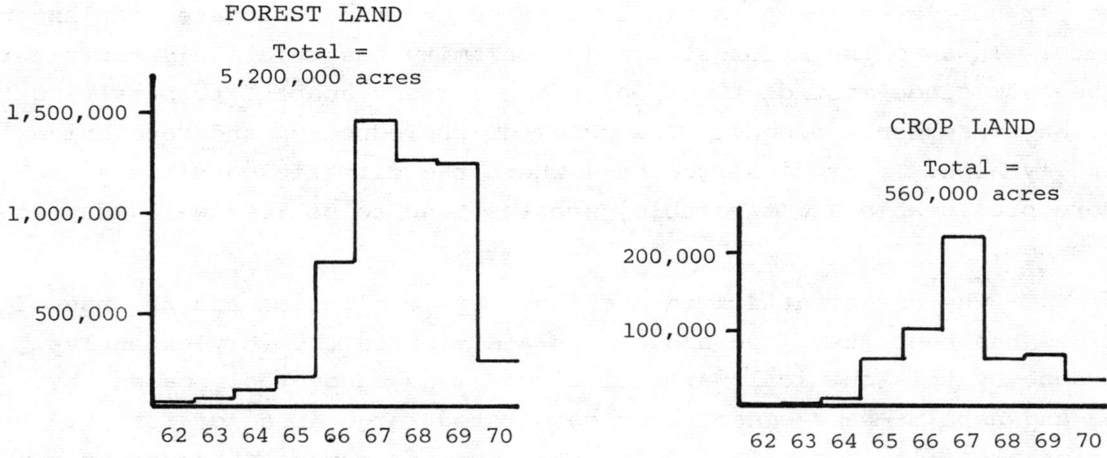

Figure 8-1

SOUTH VIETNAM: ANNUAL ACREAGE SPRAYED BY HERBICIDES

B. BOMBING AND SPRAYING: THE POTENTIAL CONSEQUENCES

Forests are first to go. Then the animals--some, like the elephant, are killed deliberately since they could be used to transport supplies; others just happen to be in the wrong place at the wrong time. Finally, the land itself is destroyed: farms, rice paddies, and village sites in many regions are bomb-pocked and barren.

tific Developments, U.S. House of Representatives, December 1969; reprinted in T. Whiteside, *Defoliation* (Ballantine, 1970), p. 107.

[7] "Impact of the Vietnam War," a report prepared for the Committee on Foreign Relations, U.S. Senate, by the Congressional Research Service of the Library of Congress, June 30, 1971 (USGPO, 1971). The figures which follow are abstracted from the excellent summary presented in this report, pp. 10 ff.

In the brief discussion that follows, only the most obvious environmental effects of the air war will be mentioned, but even such a superficial enumeration conveys an idea of the pervasiveness of the damage. The very fact that data on the present extent of this damage are scant, combined with the virtual impossibility of predicting future consequences, is in itself one of the most ominous signs of danger.

The air war has been a severe shock to all the natural ecosystems of Indochina. Such damage would be of concern wherever it occurred since it affects an intricate web of relationships; but Indochina is especially sensitive because tropical ecosystems are thought to be less resilient than those of temperate regions. Tropical systems are characterized by many more species per unit area; each is finely adapted and food webs are complex and intricate. In a northern forest a major calamity has relatively short-term consequences, since most of the species are already adapted to surviving frosts, and unseasonal floods. The rates of reproduction and recolonization are usually high. In tropical regions, where the climatic conditions are much more predictable and favorable, species tend to be less well adapted to rapid change.

Flora. The direct attack on the flora by defoliation and the use of herbicides has been described above. In addition to the very extensive damage done by this chemical warfare, fires--many undoubtedly caused by bombing and napalm--have consumed or defoliated large areas of forest. Revegetation of soils in severely defoliated forests may be retarded by rapid loss of plant nutrients following defoliation and by invasion of bamboo and other grasses. Tropical forests carry most of their nutrients in the vegetation itself, rather than in the soil; hence, following decomposition of the plants, most of the nutrients are lost directly, with the remainder being subject to leaching from the soils.[8]

Mangrove forests have suffered particularly severe damage from defoliation--about half have been totally destroyed in South Vietnam--and so far there is no evidence of regeneration. These forests play an important part in the natural process of delta formation, and stabilize the coastline and river banks. They also provide essential cover and food during the life cycles of many fish and other animals.

Fauna. The weapons of air warfare affect animals directly by killing them, and indirectly by changing the environment, with the result that

[8]In temperate zones, by contrast, most of the nutrients reside in the soil rather than in the flora of the forest. L. E. Rodin and N. I. Bazilevich, *Production and Mineral Cycling in Terrestrial Vegetation* (Oliver & Boyd, Edinburgh and London, 1967), p. 246. (Translated from Russian edition, 1965.)

populations are changed and the diversity of species is reduced. Natural checks and balances to pests and disease vectors may be upset, particularly as predatory fauna are killed. The invasion of destroyed areas by other plant groups may result in larger populations of undesired animals favoring this new habitat--rats, for example, often thrive in bamboo, which is a predominant regrowth species in defoliated forest areas. The population of the tiger has apparently increased as its natural food supply has been augmented by battlefield casualties.

There are contradictory claims about the toxicity of herbicides to animals. Though some authorities claim there is little danger, evidence indicates that 2,4-D in moderate doses may be toxic to some fish, that plants treated with 2,4-D may accumulate toxic quantities of nitrates (which could affect domestic stock as well as wild fauna), and that dioxin, a contaminant of some 2,4,5-T solutions used, is toxic and concentrates in the food chain since it does not break down with time. Finally, domestic livestock are affected by herbicides, both directly and indirectly, as they eat plants that have been contaminated.

Agriculture. Agriculture, and land utilization in general, are affected not only by chemical warfare but also directly by bombing. One may estimate that at least 12,000,000 craters have been produced in the Indochina air war so far, covering an area of at least 200,000 acres and excavating about 1.5 billion cubic yards of soil.[9] (Roughly two-thirds of the bomb tonnage was deployed within South Vietnam, whose total area is 42 million acres.) Some areas in Indochina have been likened to moonscapes. The long-term effects of this cratering are hard to assess, but the fact that craters do not naturally fill in is evidenced by craters from World War II which are still found in the jungles of New Guinea. A bomb crater destroys the surface organic layer and throws up subsoil; it creates severe local relief and erosion in the soil and may disrupt drainage patterns. Usually it fills with water and becomes very difficult to drain, making heavily bombed areas virtually unsuitable for cultivation.

Flooding. The control of water flow is a vital problem in many areas of Indochina. Defoliation and laterization lead to more rapid runoff of rain water; the destruction of many man-made control structures compounds the problem. The destructiveness of the floods in central South Vietnam in November 1970 was blamed in part on defoliation and bomb damage. People

[9]Total expenditure of aerial munitions through 1971 is about 6,300,000 tons. If half of this is crater-producing, in the form of 500-pound bombs, there will be about 12,000,000 craters. Taking each to be 30 feet in diameter, conical in shape and with a maximum depth of 15 feet, the quoted figures for area and volume can be derived. [We are indebted to Professor A. H. Westing for discussion of this point. See also the estimates of reference 11, App. E.]

were driven by the floods out of refugee camps to which they had come, in the first place, because of crop destruction or bombing in their native highlands.

Malnutrition. It is generally recognized that crop destruction has had its chief impact on the civilian population rather than on enemy soldiers, who are in the best position to obtain food in times of scarcity. The Herbicides Assessment Commission has concluded that the food destroyed would have been enough to feed 600,000 persons for a year, and that nearly all of it would have been consumed by civilians. Although the amount destroyed is less than two percent of the national crop of South Vietnam in any one year, the most extensive crop destruction has been carried out in the central highlands, a food-scarce area with a population of about one million, mainly Montagnards. It is among these people that problems of malnutrition and starvation are most severe.

Birth abnormalities. According to a report released by the National Institutes of Health in the fall of 1969, 2,4,5-T (or an associated impurity, dioxin) was shown to produce significant increases in the incidence of fetus malformation in animals as early as 1965. Moreover, the Herbicide Assessment Commission team in Vietnam has found a suggestive correlation between years of peak defoliation in Tay Ninh province and an increase in stillbirths and birth deformities.

Malaria. Of the endemic diseases in Indochina, malaria is probably the most widespread; in the past it has been far more common in the upland regions than in the lowlands. Now, large numbers of bomb craters have filled with water. This stagnant water, present throughout Vietnam and parts of Laos and Cambodia, is an ideal breeding habitat for various species of mosquito, including those which are malaria vectors.

* * * * *

Americans have begun to become aware of the vast complexity of their environment, and of the unpredictable consequences that go with disturbing it. In Indochina, the environment has not merely been disturbed--there has been a deliberate and unprecedented onslaught on it, with chemicals, with explosives, and with fire. The short listing just given, incomplete and inconclusive as it is, by its very open-endedness points up the ominous results which may have been, and which may continue to be, provoked in Indochina.

CHAPTER 9

COSTS OF THE INDOCHINA WAR AND AIR WAR

Costs are often difficult to estimate with precision, or even to define. This is particularly true of the full costs of any large and complex publicly financed activity, and of the costs of war above all.[1] It is moreover true for both measurable and nonmeasurable costs, whether economic or noneconomic, though the latter raise especially obdurate problems. Evaluations of costs are therefore bound to differ, both in general and in detail. Where, as in the present case, a great deal of the relevant information is still classified, difficulties and uncertainties compound.

Nevertheless, official figures on the U.S. budgetary costs of the Indochina air war do provide a basic starting point. The picture becomes progressively less detailed and more subject to judgment as we move to a consideration of nonbudgetary and nonmeasurable economic costs, including those imposed on the South Vietnamese and other Indochinese peoples, and especially as we consider the political, social, cultural and other noneconomic costs, on whomever imposed. All these costs, though not necessarily quantifiable, must be taken into account in a full evaluation of the air war, especially since an unusually small share of the total cost of the Indochina war is actually borne by the major war-making power and strategist, the United States.[2]

We stress the non-American costs of the Indochina war because other chapters of this study show that they arise in large measure from the manner in which the war is fought, as exemplified particularly by the massive use

[1]For example, referring to the official Department of Defense estimates of war costs cited later in this chapter, the Assistant Secretary for Defense, Comptroller, Robert C. Moot, said: "It is necessary to emphasize, wherever Southeast Asia costs are discussed in any connection, that these figures are estimates. There are no accounting records to identify war costs, nor could there be. Moreover, even granting that war costs must be estimated, there is plenty of room for debate as to how particular items should be reflected. There is no one correct basis for stating the cost of the war." *Defense Hearings for 1971*, Committee on Appropriations, U.S. Senate; Part I, p. 358.

[2]The United States provides almost all of the materiel, munitions, and other logistical inputs utilized by Americans and their allies. Yet these American costs, though substantial, are far outweighed by the non-American costs which, in addition to demolition of structures and equipment, and damage to the environment, include: the infliction of large numbers of civilian casualties; massive movements of populations into unsanitary and overcrowded refugee camps or into cities swollen beyond humanly decent bounds; the loss of assured, customary, and defined means of livelihood; shattering of the webs of kinship and other social relationships; and sundering of the cultural heritage of the many indigenous religious, cultural, and ethnic groupings in Indochina. A few of these costs--such as destruction of manmade physical assets--can, and presumably in time will, be shifted from the Indochinese back to the United States, and perhaps to other industrialized nations, as they undertake to make good the damage. But most noneconomic costs cannot be shifted so easily, and human costs not at all.

of U.S. air power. A continuing air war, largely conducted and entirely supported by the U.S., could inflict ever-widening costs on the peoples of Indochina while incurring U.S. costs at little more than a normal peacetime readiness level, or at least a politically tolerable level for "permanent war." When one takes into account the future technological possibilities for warfare-from-a-distance[3] and when one considers the relative cheapness of this kind of mechanized war for the U.S.,[4] there emerge far-reaching implications for the possible future conduct of American foreign policy.

An attempt to evaluate the foregoing elements is made in Chapters 13 and 14, below. Here we limit ourselves to consideration of strictly economic costs borne by the U.S. alone:

A. We present and discuss the official Department of Defense (DoD) figures on the budgetary cost of the Indochina war as a whole for the six fiscal years from July 1, 1965 through June 30, 1971 (FY 66 through FY 71). We also present our own estimates for the cost of the air war alone; despite the paucity of official data we believe that a broadly accurate picture has been assembled.

B. Based largely on the work of others, we estimate the *total* American economic costs of the war and the air war, including:
   - -- goods and services forgone while the war is in progress (direct current costs);
   - -- goods and services expected to be sacrificed in the future as a direct consequence of the war (direct deferred costs);
   - -- present and future distributive inequities created by the economic impact of the war and of war-induced policies (indirect current and deferred costs).

C. We project the range within which costs seem likely to fall so long as the air war continues to play a significant role in the achievement of U.S. policy aims.

A. BUDGETARY COSTS OF THE INDOCHINA WAR AND AIR WAR

The Department of Defense has provided two sets of estimates for the budgeted costs of the war in Vietnam, Laos, and Cambodia. The first, called *full budgeted costs*, covers the amounts which must be appropriated by the

[3] These are described in Chap. 12.

[4] See Sec. 1-B.

Congress to cover the costs of all personnel, equipment, and supplies employed in the Southeast Asian theatre of war or in direct support of the war.[5] The second estimate, called *incremental costs*, is the excess of these full costs over estimated "normal" or "baseline" levels. That is, "incremental costs reflect the added costs of the war, over and above what would be spent in peacetime for the baseline units involved in the war. Of course, for non-baseline units in the war, the entire costs are shown as incremental."[6]

The full cost and incremental cost estimates of the DoD are given in Table 9-1. In view of both the greater accuracy of the full cost figures and the fact that they represent the actual outlays for the Vietnam war, a case can be made for using them as the costs of the war. Logically, however, the true cost of the war is only the increment over what would have been spent had there been no war; therefore, despite the difficulty of determining what the true baseline costs would have been, we accept the DoD estimates of *incremental* costs as the best available at present.[7] These estimates, it is safe to say, err on the conservative side, perhaps by a substantial margin.

Air War Portion of Incremental Budgetary Costs

The air war's share of costs is the estimated portion of incremental costs contributed by air combat activity. It represents the full activity costs of B-52 and fighter-bomber attacks on economic and interdiction targets, and of fighter-bomber and helicopter close-support and other combat operations, all of which are presumed to be incremental costs. Since few cost figures for these activities have been made public, it was necessary to synthesize estimates by putting together various bits of information. Among several possible methods, the least ambiguous and presumably most accurate is one based on (1) estimated average operating costs for each of the three major categories of combat aircraft (B-52s, fighter-bombers, and helicopters) multiplied by annual sortie or inventory data, plus (2) published official estimates of annual attrition due to both hostile action and accident for aircraft and helicopters. The figures, data sources, and estimating details are given in Table 9-2 and related appendices.

There are several reasons for believing that the figures for total dollar cost of the air war as estimated in Table 9-2 are somewhat understated, though otherwise correct to a fairly close approximation. A small degree of under-

[5]See letter from Secretary of Defense Laird to Senator Stennis, in *Defense Hearings for 1971, op. cit.*, pp. 179-180. See also pp. 180-181, 352-353, 363-370; and the statement of Asst. Sec. Moot in *The Military Budget and National Priorities,* Hearings, Subcommittee on Economy in Government, Joint Economic Committee, U.S. Congress, June 1969; Part I, pp. 295-376.

[6]Laird, letter, *op. cit.*

[7]See *ibid.*

TABLE 9-1

BUDGETARY OUTLAYS ON THE WAR IN SOUTHEAST ASIA

Fiscal Year	Full Costs	Incremental Costs
1965*	$ 0.1 billion	$ 0.1 billion
1966	5.8	6.0
1967	20.1	18.0
1968	26.5	23.0#
1969	28.8	22.0#
1970	23.1	17.0#
1971	15.3	12.0
1972##	13.0	10.0
Total, 1965-71	$132.7 billion	$108.1 billion

*Figures for 1965 clearly are too low in view of what we now know of the build-up in 1964-65, and of air activity both before and immediately after the Tonkin Gulf resolution of August 1964. There also should be figures before 1965. For example, information on total helicopter combat sorties, Jan. 1962-Jan. 1969 (*Defense Hearings for 1970*, House Appropriations Committee, Pt. 2, p. 257), and information obtained from interviews, indicate that helicopter combat sorties averaged around 1.7 million a year up to and including 1965 compared to 2.3 million in the three subsequent years. Helicopter sortie data are too erratic to be precise indicators of activity levels, but they do imply that war costs were incurred.

#These figures have apparently been revised from earlier estimates of $20.0 billion for FY 68, $21.5 billion for FY 69, and $17.4 billion for FY 70. See *Defense Hearings for FY 72*, House Appropriations Committee, Pt. 1, pp. 1163 and 1223.

##Our estimate of programmed expenditures for FY 72. See below.

SOURCES: *Impact of the Vietnam War*, prepared by the Congressional Research Service of the Library of Congress for the Committee on Foreign Relations, U.S. Senate (June 30, 1971), p. 2. Figures for 1970 and 1971 were furnished the Library of Congress by the office of the Assistant Secretary of Defense, Comptroller, Robert C. Moot. Figure for 1972 is our estimate of DoD programmed war expenditures. It is based on Mr. Moot's statement that "by June 1971, the costs of the war will be about half of the costs in fiscal year 1969 [*Defense Hearings, op. cit.*, p. 1222] and on the assumption that some further reduction from the June 1971 level of activity was expected when the budget was prepared. Using this evidence and assumption, we have projected $13 billion for full costs and $10 billion for incremental costs for FY 72. But see notes to Table 9-4 below.

TABLE 9-2: BUDGETARY DIRECT ACTIVITY COSTS OF THE INDOCHINA AIR WAR

(value figures in current dollars*)

	1	2	3		4	5	6	7	8	9	10	11	12	13
	Total Air-War Cost		Total Air Cost as % of Total Incremental		Total Attrition Cost			Total Operating Cost of Air War						
	Incl. Helicopters	Excl. Helicopters	Helicop's Incl	Helicop's Excl	Fixed-Wing & Helicopters	Fixed-Wing	Helicopters	Total operating cost	B-52s Sorties	B-52s Cost	Fighter-Bombers Sorties	Fighter-Bombers Cost	Helicopters Inventory	Helicopters Cost
Fiscal Year	$ billion	$ billion	(a)	(b)	$ billion	$ billion	$ billion	$ billion	Number thousand	$ billion	Number thousand	$ billion	Number	$ billion
1965	.46	.25	55%	30%	.04	neg'ble	.04	.42	neg'ble	neg'ble	30	.25	1483	.17
1966	2.83	2.51			.90	.84	.06	1.93	3.7	.12	184	1.55	2008	.26
1967	4.56	4.06	26	23	1.20	1.10	.10	3.36	7.4	.27	328	2.69	3041	.40
1968	5.99	5.30	26	23	1.70	1.46	.24	4.29	15.3	.58	366	3.26	3323	.45
1969	6.20	5.44	28	25	1.20	.95	.25	5.00	20.5	.85	375	3.64	3636	.51
1970	5.47	4.67	32	28	1.30	1.02	.28	4.17	19.8	.84	268	2.81	n.a.	.52
1971	3.51	2.93	29	24	.81	.60	.21	2.70	12.4	.55	153	1.78	n.a.	.37
Totals, 65-71	29.02	25.16	30	26	7.15	5.97	1.18	21.87	79.1	3.21	1704	15.98		2.68

*See footnote 12

Explanation and Sources

Column	
1	Column 4 plus Column 7. Estimate for FY 65 exceeds DoD war totals. See note on sources, Table 9-1.
2	Column 1 minus (Column 6 plus Column 13).
3a	Column 1 divided by Incremental Costs, Table 9-1.
3b	Column 2 divided by Incremental Costs, Table 9-1.
4	Official DoD estimate, except for FY 71. Cf. App. D-4.
5	Appendix D-4, Column 6.
6	Appendix D-4, Column 5.
7	Column 9 plus Column 11 plus Column 13.
8	Derived from DoD figures. See Chap. 13 and SS-6.
9	Column 8 times estimated average operating cost per B-52 sortie. See App. D-7.
10	Derived from DoD figures. See Chap. 13 and SS-5
11	Column 10 times the estimated average cost per fighter-bomber sortie. See App. D-7.
12	Official DoD figures, including the South Vietnamese Air Force.
13	Column 12 times annual direct operating cost per active helicopter, derived from figures furnished by DoD. The basic operating cost average is $150,000 for FY 70. See App. D-8. For other years this figure has been proportioned to "Non-munitions operating cost" for fighter-bombers as given in App. D-7. Figures for FY 70 and FY 71 = cost in FY 69 times ratio of helicopter combat sorties (from SS-2) to sorties in FY 69.

statement presumably results from failure of the figures to take adequate account of costs incurred to equip and support the Vietnamese Air Force. In addition, our activity cost data seem not to include either the cost of airfield and base construction in Southeast Asia, the increases in research, development, test, and evaluation (RDT&E) costs necessitated by the character of the Indochina air war, nor incremental training and basing costs in the United States.[8]

Except for these factors, there are several reasons to have confidence in the estimates in Table 9-2, taking them only for what they are, namely, incremental direct budgetary costs of the air war in Indochina. First, there is the fact that our unit costs of B-52 sorties for FY 68 and FY 69, which are the pivotal figures for our annual estimates, check out closely with data for total B-52 sorties, tons per sortie, and total B-52 costs as reported or estimated by DoD (see Appendices D-5 and D-7). Second, our method of estimating costs per sortie for fighter bombers, which uses data from the *Pentagon Papers* for FY 65 and FY 66 as a base, yields a close check with an officially reported figure for FY 69 (see Appendices D-6 and D-7). These correspondences suggest that our basic data are accurate and the method sound. Third, we know from the *Pentagon Papers* that the Air Force portion of the supplemental appropriation for FY 67 (excluding the air arms of the other three services) was 35 to 40 percent of the total. Since this was a period of rapid escalation in Air Force activity, it should be--as it was--larger than our independently derived estimates, but it is not out of sight. Fourth, the air portion of the full budget costs of total military deployments in all of Asia, excluding the incremental costs of the Indochina war, was around 35 percent in FY 71 and FY 72, as shown in Appendix D-3. If the share of airborne forces in baseline deployments in Asia is something over a third, it seems reasonable that their share in the Indochina war, with its heavy deployment of ground forces, should be somewhat less than a third, as our estimates suggest. Finally, we know that the operating cost per ton of munitions expended by B-52s is substantially less than for fighter bombers and our data consistently yield this result despite a slight increase in

[8]Cf. this statement by the Air Force: "Southeast Asia, like all wars, generated requirements in areas where we were deficient in capability. . . . Some of these are: improved navigation, bombing accuracy, ECM [electronic counter measures], radar homing and warning, missillery, survivability, rescue, communications, and, of course, gunships." *Defense Hearings for 1972,* House Committee on Appropriations, Part 5, p. 1080. Also consider the following exchange: "*Mr. Andrews:* The study also indicates . . . almost totally unprepared in electronic warfare . . . in 1965. . . . *Gen. Glasser:* . . . we have to return ourselves to the period just preceding the Southeast Asia conflict and realize that . . . we were primarily working on the approach to a nuclear war. . . ." [*ibid.,* p. 1095]. More specifically, RDT&E costs directly related to the air war in Southeast Asia were given by Gen. Goldsworthy as $593 million for FY 70 and $389 million for FY 71. [*Defense Hearings for 1971,* Part 6, House Appropriations Committee, p. 98.]

delivery cost per ton for B-52s over the war years and a rather substantial reduction in fighter bomber delivery costs per ton as average bomb loads increased.

Our estimates for the years of major war activity yield a reassuringly stable (though not invariant) percentage relationship to the DoD figures for the total incremental cost of the war, as shown in Table 9-2. As troops are withdrawn from South Vietnam but air forces are left to operate from carriers and from bases in Thailand, the air war share may be expected to increase (see Section C, below).

The estimates presented in Table 9-2 will probably be shown to be not far off the mark, though perhaps somewhat low, when the requisite data are declassified. As a rule of thumb, and making some allowance for the omitted factors mentioned earlier, we would be justified in saying that the share of the air war in the cost of the Vietnam war as a whole has been between a quarter and a third, or around 30 percent.[9] The percentage would probably not be very different for estimates based on full as opposed to incremental costs.[10]

B. ECONOMIC COSTS OF THE INDOCHINA WAR AND AIR WAR

Budgetary war costs represent estimates of actual government expenditures, compiled from the accounting records of the Department of Defense.[11] Since goods and services purchased by the government are necessarily diverted from other potential uses, and since their value in other uses would ordinarily be about the same as what the government pays, the budgetary estimates of war outlays are a proper initial measure of the goods and services foregone by the civil society in order to prosecute the war. They thus constitute a starting point for estimating the direct *economic* costs of the war.

Direct current costs. Budgetary figures are only a starting point, however, because some DoD expenditures do not accurately reflect the market value of goods and services denied to other uses. One necessary adjustment is for the failure of the Defense Department fully to maintain the "investment component" of baseline expenditures at the necessary levels. The investment component, consisting mainly of non-war-related procurement, re-

[9]Since helicopter costs are small relative to bomber costs, since there is some question whether or not to include them, and since the margin of error in the estimates could be several percentage points in any case, it seems reasonable to consider 30 percent as the air war share, in round figures, with or without helicopters.

[10]The full cost figures in Table 9-1 would thus yield around $40 billion as the cost of the air war alone through June 1971.

[11]But see footnote 1, above, on their approximate character.

search, development, test, and evaluation programs and military construction, was allowed to fall below normal, creating a backlog which is beginning to be made up in FY 72. We estimate that this shortfall, measured in constant dollars, amounted to about 50 percent of the FY 64 total.[12] Translated into prices of the years in which the DoD investment shortfall occurred, this amounts in round figures to $15 billion current dollars.[13]

A second adjustment is needed to take account of the fact that, because draftees have no choice, it is possible to pay them less than they could earn in private employment. Budgetary outlays for drafted servicemen are less than they would be if all service were voluntary. Because this represents a compulsory contribution of uncompensated services to the government, the President's Commission on an All-Volunteer Armed Force called it a *conscription tax*.[14] The value of uncompensated services is estimated by calculating the potential earnings of draftees, adding various nonbudgetary costs incident to the draft, and subtracting the military pay of the conscripts from the budget figure. The difference represents the extent to which budgeted military personnel costs understate the value of the potential goods and services lost by conscripting men from civil life. Using a revision of the method employed by Eisner,[15] which gives an estimate which is lower than his, we put the draft-cost adjustment at around $60 billion (current) over the six war years to June 1971.[16]

In addition to these adjustments it is necessary to take account of certain economic costs which are not reflected in the Department of Defense budget at all. One of these is the loss of output due to deaths and disablements. Men who die while in military service, or who are discharged as physically unfit, cease to be a charge against the DoD budget. The fact that their pro-

[12] Budget figures, which initially are expressed in *current dollars*, must for certain purposes be corrected for price changes, that is, expressed in *constant dollars*. Current dollars are recorded dollar values reflecting the prices of the period to which they apply. Thus, the budget outlays for FY 1966 reflect prices prevailing from July 1965 to June 1966, those for FY 1970 reflect prices in the twelve months ending June 1970, and so on. Current dollars are converted into constant dollars by dividing them by a price index with a given base year. That is, if prices in FY 1966 are expressed as a ratio to prices in FY 1970, and dollar values for FY 1966 are divided by this ratio (index), the effect is to revalue FY 1966 current dollars into FY 1970 base year dollars. If this is done for a series of years the result is a series of measurements in constant dollars of the base year. Note that, owing to the rise in prices over the war period, constant pre-war dollars (for example, 1964) would underestimate, and constant FY 1971 dollars would overestimate, real costs actually incurred. That is why we have expressed all value figures in current dollars.

[13] See App. D-9.

[14] *Report of the President's Commission on an All-Volunteer Armed Force* (USGPO, February, 1970).

[15] Robert Eisner, "The War and the Economy," in Sam Brown and Len Acklund, eds., *Why Are We Still in Vietnam?* (Random House, 1970). See especially p. 119 and the Appendix.

[16] See App. D-9.

ductive services have been lost to the economy, in whole or in part, thus ceases to be reflected in the budgeted costs of the war, but must be included in economic costs. The amount would not be large in relation to total GNP, but could be several billions. Finally, account must be taken of the fact that the war itself, and various economic policies designed either to facilitate its prosecution or to counteract its unfavorable economic effects (such as inflation and balance of payments difficulties), cause distortions and disruptions in economic activities. These lead to unemployment or inefficient production, causing losses of output which should be taken into account. A satisfactory methodology for estimating these costs has not yet emerged, despite efforts by Russet and, recently, by Hollenhorst and Ault;[17] our tentative calculations suggest that they could run into the tens of billions.

The costs we have been discussing are summarized in Table 9-3(A), below. They are the direct current costs--direct because they represent the goods and services which would have been available in the absence of war, current because they refer to the costs incurred during the war period itself.

Direct deferred costs. Wars also impose sacrifices on future generations, due either to war-induced reductions in productive capacity or to reductions in consumption imposed by the necessity of replacing the productive capacity lost as a result of the war. Just as the Department of Defense found it necessary to cut back on its "investment," creating a backlog to be made up in the future, so may other government departments and private industry have to do likewise.

To the extent that such cutbacks occur, total productive resources, public and private, material and human, will be less at the end of the war than they would have been in its absence. That is, we will end the war with impaired productive capacity, and for a certain future period the total GNP, especially its consumption component, will be reduced. In short, by "living off capital" in the present we are deferring costs to the future.[18]

[17] Bruce M. Russet, "The Price of War," *Trans-action,* October 1969. Reprinted in Seymour Melman, ed., *The War Economy of the United States* (St. Martin's Press, 1971); and Jerry Hollenhorst and Gary Ault, "An Alternative Answer to: Who Pays for Defense?," *American Political Science Review,* LXV, No. 3 (September 1971), pp. 760-763.

[18] The present value of deferred costs may be reckoned in either of two ways. If the amount of the shortfall in productive resources can be estimated directly, the value of the stream of future goods and servicss foregone for a finite number of years as a result of this shortfall can be estimated by employing the average rate of return that would have been earned by these assets, had they been available. The stream of future goods and services foregone then represents the deferred costs, and the amount of the directly estimated shortfall in productive assets is their present value. If, on the other hand, it is more feasible to estimate the value of goods and services to be foregone for a finite number of future years, the present value of these deferred costs can be estimated by discounting the cost in each future year at an appropriate interest rate (e.g., the average rate of return referred to above). The sum of these discounted deferred cost figures will be their present value.

TABLE 9-3

AGGREGATE DIRECT CURRENT AND DEFERRED ECONOMIC COSTS OF THE INDOCHINA WAR, FY 66 - FY 71

(in billions of current dollars)

	A. CURRENT DIRECT COSTS		
1.	Reported incremental budgetary costs [Table 9-1]		100
2.	Add: hidden or evaded budgetary costs		
	a. Backlog of deferred "baseline" costs	15	
	b. Excess of economic over budgeted cost of the draft	60	75
3.	Extra-budgetary costs		
	a. Output lost due to military deaths and disablements	?	
	b. Output lost to war-induced distortions and economic policies	?	??
	Total direct current costs		175 + ??
	B. DEFERRED DIRECT COSTS: PRESENT VALUE*		
4.	Shortfalls of investment in manmade, natural, and human resources		?
5.	Hostile destruction or impairment of productive capacity		
	a. Manmade and natural resources	nil	
	b. Labor force, due to casualties	20	20
	Total direct deferred costs		20 + ?
	C. INDIRECT COSTS		
6.	Current		?
7.	Deferred		?
	Total direct and indirect costs		195 + ???

*See footnote 18.

The phenomenon of living off capital in order to carry on a war without paying for it wholly in the present is one which may show up in measurable shortfalls of plant and equipment, structures, transport facilities, inventories, research and development, and such public services as education and health. The latter items adversely affect the rate of technical progress and the skill, strength, and motivation of the labor force.[19] However, it is even more difficult to estimate such shortfalls accurately than to esti-

[19] The following observations by Asst. Sec. Moot concerning the military importance of maintaining educational and health programs show that economizing on these services could indeed constitute a deferred cost: "If American educational efforts or health programs were seriously degraded, the military services would not be seriously affected next week or next year; in the long run, however, the impact upon our armed forces would be disastrous." *The*

mate the loss of potential GNP, so we include no figure, though it could be far from negligible.

A further category of deferred costs consists of those reflecting hostile destruction or impairment of productive capacity. For a country like the United States, which since 1812-14 has had to face no hostile forces within its boundaries except the Plains Indians, losses of resources from military action have not been a major factor, but overseas casualties have been important. Eisner has estimated that the present value of future output foregone because of reductions in the future labor force through deaths and disabilities caused by the Indochina War to the middle of 1970 was $23 billion (1970 dollars).[20] If we adjust this upward slightly for casualties in FY 71, and adjust it downward by about 10 percent to convert roughly from 1970 dollars to average dollars of the period FY 66-71, we arrive at an estimate of $20 billion.

Table 9-3(B) summarizes the costs due to impairment of future productive capacity in the United States. Only one figure is given, however, since the other deferred costs, as noted above, are either too difficult to estimate with suitable precision or have been unimportant.

Indirect economic costs. Beyond the direct costs are the redistributive, or indirect, economic costs.[21] These reflect the redistributions of real income which result from war-induced economic phenomena such as inflation, and from war-related fiscal, monetary, and other economic policies. New or increased taxes, higher interest rates, reduced government expenditures, and the overall or localized effects of these changes on employment and unemployment, affect the money incomes of different socio-economic groups differently, and the varied incidence of inflationary price rises causes real incomes to change differently from monetary incomes. The consequential redistribution of real incomes among various groups may sometimes favor those at the lower end of the income scale, but is far more likely to favor those near the top at the expense of those lower down. If the resulting redistribution is regarded as exacerbating pre-existing inequities and injustices, this must be counted an additional, though indirect and nonmeasur-

Military Budget and National Economic Priorities, op. cit., p. 309. If the contingency mentioned by Mr. Moot should arise it would also affect the skill and productivity of the civilian labor force, and reduce the future availability of goods and services. While deferred costs of this kind due to the Indochina War are certainly not large, their possible occurrence must not be overlooked.

[20] Eisner, *op. cit.*

[21] For a detailed discussion of the indirect costs of the war, including related data, see Douglass B. Lee, Jr. and John W. Dyckman, "Economic Impacts of the War in Indochina: A Primer," in Grant, Moss, and Unger, *Cambodia: The Widening War in Indochina* (Washington Square Press, 1971).

able, cost of the war. Since those who are more well-to-do generally have many ways of shifting the burden of adverse changes in their real incomes onto those who are less well off, while the reverse is seldom true, there is a presumption that the often substantial redistributive effects of war do cause new inequities and impose indirect economic costs.

To some extent these costs are borne only in the present, and may indeed be eliminated or compensated by reversal of current inequities in future years. The opportunities for such reversal are limited, however, by the fiscal necessity of meeting the long-continuing financial burdens of veterans' benefits and payment of interest on war-created public debt. James Clayton has estimated on the basis of past experience that veterans' benefits are likely to reach a cumulative total equal to between 100 and 300 percent of the initial budgetary cost of the Indochina War. Interest charges on war-related public debt will increase this total by 10 to 45 percent.[22] These transfer burdens, borne by the rest of society, may be a source of redistributive inequities. Veterans' benefits are not carefully adjusted either to the intensity of war service or the needs of the beneficiaries, and interest payments go mainly to the well-to-do.

Summary of economic costs. Estimated *direct* economic costs of the war, FY 66-71, including the present value of deferred direct costs, are summarized in Table 9-3. Since it is impossible to quantify the *indirect* redistributive costs of the Indochina war, whether current or future, they are shown in blank, and must be kept in mind as a possible addition to direct costs. Similarly, no estimates are presently available for some of the direct costs, and the corresponding spaces in the table are left blank.

In round figures, the aggregate incremental *direct* economic cost of the Indochina war to the United States, through the six fiscal years to mid-1971, has been around $200 billion--about double the budgetary incremental costs. This figure does not include unmeasured economic costs, noneconomic costs, or any non-American costs. Since the air war accounts for only 30 percent or so of the total cost of the Indochina war its direct impact on the American economy, considered in isolation from the rest of the war, is relatively small.[23] As emphasized earlier, this conclusion is based on a very parochial

[22]Statement by James L. Clayton in *The Military Budget and National Priorities, op. cit.*, pp. 143-150. Clayton finds that the peak of benefit payments to veterans, their survivors, and even some descendants is reached about 50 years after the end of the war to which they apply, and that the payments have typically continued, though at a decelerating rate, for over 100 years.

[23]Though the share of the air war in total economic costs may, as a first approximation, be assumed equal to its 30% share in budgetary costs, there are several factors which, on balance, suggest that a smaller proportion of strictly U.S. economic costs should be attributed to the air war. The accumulated baseline backlog of military "investment" is not distributed evenly among the services, and there is little direct evidence on whether the

conception of what constitutes the cost of a highly destructive and disruptive air war. However, it is presumably this parochial conception of costs, narrowed even further by ignoring nearly all except official budgetary costs, which enters into the Washington decision-making process.

C. COSTS OF A CONTINUING AIR WAR

The estimates in the preceding sections of this chapter relate to a war which is not yet ended, and in which the United States may remain involved for a considerable time. They constitute an interim report on the costs of that war. How soon a final report can be drafted and what it will reveal can only be guessed, but it is possible to establish some major probabilities with respect to the future.

Table 9-4 presents a series of projections of the costs of an air war which is almost certain to continue through FY 72 and possibly much longer. A projection is given for each of the items in Table 9-2, with the figures for FY 71 repeated for convenient comparison.

The most important projections in Table 9-4 are those for B-52 and fighter-bomber sorties. These, multiplied by the projected unit sortie cost estimates for FY 72 given in Appendix D-7, provide the figures of total operating costs for bombers. The Medium projection, which is geared to the 1971 figures in various ways, is the base from which the other projections are derived.

Sortie rates for B-52s are known to have been running at about 1,000 a month. We therefore selected this as the basis for our Medium projection. The other projections for B-52 sorties pivot on this figure. The Medium pro-

share of the airborne forces has been greater or less than for other branches. It could be considerably greater, however. According to a statement submitted by Asst. Sec. Moot, non-Indochina aircraft outlays for procurement, FY 1965-1970, were "far below what they would have been had we maintained a steady FY 1964 program level in constant dollars. The amount is in the neighborhood of $10 billion, in FY 1970 dollars." [*The Military Budget and National Priorities, op. cit.*, p. 366.] This is a large share of the investment shortfall as we have estimated it.

The conscription tax, on the other hand, is mostly chargeable against the Army, which relied on the draft more than the other services. Similarly, casualty costs, both current and future, are chargeable most heavily to the ground forces. Through 1970, deaths from aircraft losses have been about 8% of the total, due to hostile action, while deaths of air personnel from non-hostile causes were 29%. The combined ratio is only 11.5% [see B. F. Schemmer, *Armed Forces Journal,* January 18, 1971]. Similarly, the air war's share in future veterans' benefits will be less than its share in total costs. U.S. Air Force personnel in the Indochina theatre averaged only one-eighth of total military personnel; adding the personnel for the other airborne services may bring the total air fraction to about one-sixth.

Taking all factors into consideration, the proportionate economic cost of the air war in Indochina is less than its proportionate budgetary cost. A reasonable estimate would set the total economic cost at nearer 20 or 25 than 30%.

TABLE 9-4

PROJECTIONS OF DIRECT BUDGETARY COSTS OF THE AIR WAR FOR FY 72 AND BEYOND

	1	2	3		4	5	6	7	8	9	10	11	12	13
	Total Air-War Cost		Total Air Cost as % of Total Incremental		Total Attrition Cost			Total Operating Cost of Air War						
	Incl. Helicopters	Excl. Helicopters	Helicop's Incl	Helicop's Excl	Fixed-Wing & Helicopters	Fixed-Wing	Helicopters	Total operating cost	B-52s Sorties	B-52s Cost	Fighter-Bombers Sorties	Fighter-Bombers Cost	Helicopters Inventory	Helicopters Cost
	$ billion	$ billion	(a)	(b)	$ billion	$ billion	$ billion	$ billion	Number thousand	$ billion	Number thousand	$ billion	Number	$ billion
FY 71	3.51	2.93	29	24	.81	.60	.21	2.70	12.4	.55	153	1.78	n.a.	.37
ALTERNATIVE PROJECTIONS														
High #2 (Possible for FY 72)	4.25	3.60	38[a]	32[a]	1.10	.85	.25	3.15	13.5	.60	175	2.15	n.a.	.40
High #1 (Probable for FY 72)	3.80	3.25	35[a]	29[a]	.90	.70	.20	2.90	13.0	.60	160	1.95	n.a.	.35
Medium	3.10	2.70	31[b]	25[b]	.75	.60	.15	2.35	12.0	.55	125	1.55	n.a.	.25
Low	2.35	2.10	25[c]	21[c]	.60	.50	.10	1.75	11.0	.50	90	1.10	n.a.	.15

[a]If either of the high projections proves accurate, our estimate of $10 billion for the programmed level of incremental costs for FY 72 (Table 9-1) will be too low and the corresponding percentages will be too high. We have therefore increased the incremental cost figure by the excess of each high projection over the medium projection. This gives increases of $0.75 billion to $10.75 billion for high #1, and of $1.15 billion to $11.15 billion for high #2, and yields more accurate percentages. See note b.

[b]Based on total incremental cost of $10 billion for FY 72 (Table 9-1).

[c]Based on incremental cost total of $9.3 billion, a reduction of $0.7 billion in estimated FY programmed total. Cf. note a.

jection for fighter-bomber sorties, which also serves as the pivot for the other projections, is close to the initially programmed fighter-bomber sortie figure for FY 71. Since actual fighter-bomber sorties in FY 71 (153,000) exceeded the programmed total (120,000), it seemed reasonable to suppose that the programmed figure of 90,000 sorties for FY 72 also would be exceeded, even at substantially lower activity levels than in FY 71. We therefore chose to use 90,000 for our Low projection, and to use the higher programmed figure for FY 71 as the basis of our Medium projection.

Other data for the Medium projection are geared to the corresponding estimates for FY 71 through two assumptions. One is that the remaining U.S. forces in South Vietnam will be mainly concerned with assisting the South Vietnamese to carry out close support helicopter activity, and that neither operating cost nor attrition is likely to reach the FY 71 helicopter rates. The second assumption is that fixed-wing attrition cost will be somewhat higher than in FY 71, for any given level of sorties. This is assumed partly because the more sophisticated and concentrated anti-aircraft defenses along the Trail and in North Vietnam are likely to take a heavier toll, and partly because of the higher cost of planes equipped with advanced avionic equipment for attack and defense.[24]

If one could assume that military activity in general and the air war in particular were continuing to undergo the gradual winding down during FY 72 which they underwent in 1970 and 1971, our Medium projection would represent the most probable outcome for the current year, with the Low projection applying to FY 73 and beyond. Nothing less than the Low projection seems relevant, since it must be close to the minimum required for maintaining a stalemate in the absence of political settlement. Up to mid-December 1971, the assumptions and figures for the Medium projection might have seemed reasonable for FY 72 despite rather high activity levels in the summer and fall of 1971. Toward the end of December, however, the situation changed. There was an intensive escalation of air activity, allegedly aimed at new North Vietnamese anti-aircraft defenses, and this was followed in succeeding weeks by other intensive raids against special targets and by indications that strike levels against the Trail and other standard targets remained high. Early in February it was announced that a fourth carrier was to be dispatched to back up the three already at Yankee Station, and three squadrons of B-52s were to be flown to Guam, thus *doubling* our heavy bombing capability in the theatre. The contingency for which these preparations were being made was an anticipated Tet offensive. Stalemate, with low activity levels at least, thus seems not to be a likely prospect.

[24]Cf. footnote 8.

By the time this appears in print the first half of CY 1972 and the whole of FY 72 will be past history. Already, however, the #1 High projection in Table 9-4 seems more likely to hold for FY 72 than the Medium projection. And if the enlarged U.S. air forces are ordered into action, with or without a Tet offensive--we might, for example, decide once again to use air power in an attempt to force the North Vietnamese to negotiate--it is likely that our #2 High projection will be closer to actuality for FY 72. For the time being, therefore, the prospects that either the Medium or Low projection will be met, even in FY 73, must be regarded as slight.

As of this writing (February 1972) it appears that U.S. policy is to employ maximum diplomatic pressure to bring the war to an early close on terms acceptable to us, or, failing prompt success in this, to make continuation of the war so costly for the North Vietnamese and the NLF that our terms will eventually be acceptable to them.[25] The history of the air war in Indochina does not suggest that the latter policy is likely to succeed, but it does suggest that the policy may be tried, even to the point of resuming large scale bombing of the North, including the centers of its cities, its dikes, fields, forests, and roads. There have been Pentagon hints of this.[26] If large scale bombing of the North does occur, even our #2 High projection may be too low, both for FY 72 and for the future. How long such a one-sided escalation of the air war might continue seems less likely to depend on its eventual success or acknowledged failure, neither of which seems likely to occur soon, than on the willingness of the American people and the world to tolerate the compounding of past devastations, possibly even to the point of destroying North Vietnam as a society, or on the unwillingness of the communist world to let this happen without a fight.

In sum, the minimum incremental budgetary cost of the air war now seems likely to be at least $3.5 billion. It could easily be higher than this if the potential escalation, implicit in the announced enlargements of U.S. air forces deployed in the Indochina theatre, is realized. After FY 72 it seems likely that there will be either an end to air activity, reflecting the conclusion of a negotiated settlement, or an escalation of the air war and a further increase in its incremental budgetary costs even beyond the level indicated in our #2 High projection.[27]

[25]And, incidentally, more costly for the Laotians, Cambodians, and South Vietnamese as well.

[26]See, for example, *The New York Times*, February 11, 1972, p. 14.

[27]We do not undertake to estimate the *economic* costs associated with our projections. The assumptions which would have to be made would be surrounded by great uncertainy, and it is conceivable that the costs of the projected levels of activity could be largely handled by the U.S. baseline forces or absorbed by the slack in our economy, especially if there is continuing unemployment. In any case, the findings in the text that the direct economic costs of the war as a whole have been about double the budgetary costs would no longer apply, owing to the reductions in the numbers of draftees and American casualties.

CHAPTER 10

THE AMERICAN CONSTITUTION AND THE AIR WAR*

The bombing in North and South Vietnam, Laos and Cambodia described in previous chapters has taken place under the orders not of Congress but of the President of the United States. The President has stated that he acts as "Commander in Chief" of the armed forces in ordering the bombing. Currently, the main rationale for continuing the bombing is that it "protects the lives of American servicemen" whom the Chief Executive had previously sent to fight the undeclared war in Indochina.

Clearly, the constitutionality of the air war in Indochina is a part of the broader question whether the President had the power to involve this nation's armed forces in a war that had not been declared by Congress--though air warfare is presently in many ways a more dangerous and destabilizing aspect of power politics than the use of ground forces. Every bombardment could result in attacks on the perceived vital interests of other major powers. The threat of nuclear escalation in bombing missions is always present. Moreover, air warfare--by its very nature, as demonstrated in Indochina--tends to expand across boundaries more readily than ground warfare.

There is, indeed, a substantial question whether this air warfare, as conducted by the United States in Indochina, is in violation of international law--an issue which will be discussed in the next chapter. In any event, it is clear that the Executive's use of air warfare, on a scale that has already exceeded the total tonnage of bombs dropped in the Second World War and Korean War, raises an issue of profound importance under the United States constitution.

To examine this question of constitutionality, we should look at the words of the Constitution, the meaning that the Framers intended that the words should have, and the development of constitutional interpretation since 1789. But before examining the document itself, let us first consider the argument that apart from whatever the Framers intended, the Constitution has necessarily been changed and modified to meet the exigencies of the modern age. This argument is an interesting one in light of recent Supreme Court cases in the areas of civil rights, where the Court has often justified the expression of Constitutional protection in light of progressive societal demands and needs. One is tempted to say that in the modern world the President is the only efficient controller of foreign policy. Whatever his con-

*This chapter was contributed at our invitation by Anthony D'Amato, Associate Professor of Law, Northwestern University. He did not otherwise participate in the Study Group [Editors].

stitutional powers, he should be given the tools to deal with other nations flexibly and efficiently in the light of national interest as defined by him. An example that readily comes to mind is President Roosevelt's handling of preparations for the Second World War in the face of unenlightened Congressional demands for neutrality.

The problem with allowing one branch of the government to expand its Constitutional powers at the expense of another branch is not the same as the Courts' expansion of its judicial powers in the areas of civil rights and criminal justice. To say that we have a "living Constitution" may be perfectly satisfactory for the expansion of national powers at the expense of states in a Federal system--which is what has occurred in the civil rights and criminal area. But it is not sound with respect to the separation of powers and the equilibrium of checks and balances among the branches of the national government. If, for example, the courts were to allow the President to encroach upon Congressional powers by appeals through the mass media, we pretty soon would have a one-man government. The courts have indicated the precise opposite. In the famous Steel Seizure Case, the Supreme Court held during the undeclared Korean War that the President could not resort to "Emergency Powers" or to "Commander-in-Chief Powers" to validate executive seizure of the steel mills when the Congress had not explicitly granted its own legislative powers of seizure to the President.[1] In the course of that case the Justice Department contended, on behalf of President Truman, that a number of prior instances of "executive seizures" and other decisive "executive actions" during national emergencies had not been struck down by the courts; these prior acts thus amounted to precedents for Truman's seizures. The Justice Department argued that the Constitution had been, and was being, expanded by these assertions of Presidential powers and that by 1950 such actions were clearly constitutional. The Supreme Court, however, did not agree with this argument. Instead the Court indicated that no amount of "precedents" of this sort could amend the Constitution. In other words, a history of gradually increasing encroachments by one branch of the government upon another could not result in a permanent reallocation of constitutional powers. A case that challenged any of these encroachments, such as the Steel Seizure case, if upheld by the courts, would result in judicial restoration of the Constitution's balance among the branches of government.

Turning then to the question of the constitutionality of the undeclared war in Vietnam, let us ask first what argument can be made to support total Presidential authority to decide upon, and then to conduct, such a war.

The best case that can be made for the President is that he is Commander

[1] Youngstown Sheet & Tube Co. v. Sawyer, 343 U.S. 579 (1952).

in Chief, and can also (with Senate concurrence) make treaties and appoint ambassadors. Do these powers mean that the President can decide upon war? Alexander Hamilton, that staunch proponent of Executive power, wrote in *The Federalist* that the commander-in-chief role meant simply that the President was to be the top general of the army and the chief admiral of the navy.[2] And Abraham Lincoln, surely one of the outstanding proponents of the expansion of Presidential powers, wrote that

> Kings had always been involving and impoverishing their people in wars, pretending generally, if not always, that the good of the people was the object. This our Constitution understood to be the most oppressive of all kingly oppressions; and they resolved to so frame the Constitution that no one man should hold the power of bringing this oppression upon us.[3]

A study of the debates of the Constitutional Convention bears out these viewpoints.[4] The Framers, it must be remembered, modified but did not overthrow the setup that had obtained under the Articles of Confederation. Unlike the Articles, the Constitution gave more powers to the central government, particularly in the areas of commerce and national defense. But the pervading principle was one of representative, legislative government, for the Framers had been through a revolution against non-representation and "kingly" oppression; Congress was given vast powers over commerce and national defense. The new Constitution added a President as chief executive, but the powers of the President were carefully limited. The decision whether to go to war was given solely to the new Congress in the power "to declare war," a phrase taken from the Articles of Confederation which, too, had given to "the United States in Congress Assembled" the power to declare war.

That the intention of the Framers was to give only Congress the power to decide upon war--and not the President, who was only to be the top general and chief admiral--follows also from the various state constitutions at the time of the adoption of the national Constitution. A reading of the constitutions of the thirteen states reveals a consistent pattern of *legislative* determination of matters of military duty. Citizens of the pre-1789 sovereign states could volunteer for military duty, but if they were to be called in for such duty (as members of the state militia) an act of the legislature

[2] *The Federalist,* No. 69 (H. Lodge, ed., 1888), pp. 430-431. See also Joseph Story, 2 *Commentaries on the Constitution of the United States* 89-90 (2nd ed. 1851).

[3] See R. Basler, *The Collected Works of Abraham Lincoln* (1953), pp. 451-452. (It is noted at the same time that Lincoln as President set some of the precedents for Executive war-making powers which could be invoked in support of present Executive claims.) See generally L. Velvel, *Undeclared War and Civil Disobedience* (New York: Dunellen, 1970), pp. 11-89.

[4] See D'Amato, *et al.*, "Brief for Constitutional Lawyers' Committee on Undeclared War as Amicus Curiae, *Massachusetts v. Laird,"* 17 *Wayne Law Rev.* 122-141 (1971).

was the necessary prerequisite.[5] Again, one gets the sense of a pervading philosophy that the most important questions of life and death were to be handled by a representative, legislative government. The Framers, and with them all of the people, were not about to entrust matters of war and peace to a single governor or president but instead insisted that the legislature alone could make such decisions.

The Constitution as finally adopted clearly reflects this opinion. We have already seen how few foreign-affairs powers were actually given to the President. In contrast, Congress was given the power in Section 8 of Article I to tax to provide for the common defense, to define offenses against the law of nations, to declare war, to make rules concerning captures on land and water, to raise and support armies and provide a navy, and to call forth the militia when needed.

Clearly, if it were not for Korea and Vietnam, no reasonable man looking at the Constitution and at the intent of its Framers could conclude that the President, and not Congress, could lead this nation on his own initiative into a protracted foreign war, including bombing of the sort carried out in Indochina. At the very most, a President might order his troops to act in an emergency of brief duration, such as immediate self-defense, but only until Congress might have a chance to act. This "emergency" exception can easily be read into the Constitution without covering the cases of Korea and Vietnam, which were long wars with ample time for Congressional action. Indeed, the war in Indochina is the longest war in American history.

Some observers, however, insist upon focusing solely upon the Congressional power to "declare war." They argue as if this were the only power that Congress had in the war area--when, as we have just seen, there are many powers authorized--and they then proceed to give this one power an emasculated meaning. For example, some attorneys in the Department of Justice have claimed that the Congressional power to declare war means only that if a war is going on, Congress may or may not decide to declare that it really is a war.[6] They argue further that this is not an entirely meaningless gesture. Various insurance contracts that people may have on their lives or property might have escape clauses depending on whether a war is going on. Moreover, certain international treaty obligations that the United States may have, or other commitments under customary international law, may depend upon whether the U.S. is an official "belligerent" in an actual war.[7]

[5] *E.g.*, Mass. Const. Ch. II, Para. 1, Art. VII (1780). See generally Friedman, "Conscription and the Constitution: The Original Understanding," 67 *Michigan Law Rev.* 1423 (1969).

[6] See, *e.g.*, Brief for the Defendants, *Mitchell v. Laird,* U.S. District Ct. for District of Columbia, Civil Action No. 697-71.

[7] It may be noted that there have been many wars involving many nations since World War II

This argument gives to the term "declare war" such a trivial meaning as to rob it of the substance intended by the Framers in a way which no one would do to the terms "regulate commerce" or "coin money" (which are also found in the same section of the Constitution as the declaration-of-war clause). In its own terms, however, the argument is never actually supported. *Which* insurance policies depend upon a declaration of war by Congress? Insurance policies typically define "war" in terms other than whether or not Congress has declared it, and we even have some Federal cases arising after the Korean War that held it was a "war" for the purposes of insurance policies even though Congress had not declared it to be a war.[8] Also, *what* treaties and *what* rules of international law depend upon a Congressional declaration of war? No treaties have been cited; and as for customary international law, such law has never depended upon what a nation unilaterally decides are facts, such as a Congressional decision that a given situation is a "war."[9]

A different argument denigrating the effect of the declaration-of-war clause is that in this modern age, the President needs great flexibility to engage this nation in limited wars and other forms of limited military engagements. For Congress to come along and "declare war" would be to escalate the situation and perhaps make a total war out of a delicate limited war. According to this line of argument, the declaration-of-war clause is irrelevant to the needs of the modern age.[10]

It is interesting to look at the implications of this argument. Apparently if the United States is to engage in limited wars--of whatever duration and involving whatever number of casualties--Congress' power to declare war is anachronistic. On the other hand, if the United States were to engage in a total war of nuclear annihilation, then and only then would it be appropriate for Congress to declare war. No one explains in this argument how and under what conditions Congress could be called upon to deliberate and act in a total-war situation which, as we are told, could involve the destruction of

without a single instance of a formally "declared" war. Of course, as will be explained below, Congress may satisfy the requirements of the declaration-of-war clause simply by "authorizing" the President to initiate or maintain a war. This is necessary for internal U.S. Constitutional reasons; what the U.S. tells the outside world is an entirely different matter; whether the U.S. would want to proclaim a "declared" war to other nations, or even say nothing about it, is truly a political or diplomatic question.

8 See, *e.g., Carious v. New York Life Ins. Co.*, 124 F. Supp. 388 (S.D. Ill. 1954); *Weissman v. Metropolitan Life Ins. Co.*, 112 F. Supp. 420 (S.D. Cal. 1953). See generally D'Amato, Gould and Woods, "War Crimes and Vietnam: The 'Nuremberg Defense' and the Military Service Resister," 57 *California Law Review* 1055, 1060, 1060-61 (1969).

9 See Grob, *The Relativity of War and Peace* (1949), p. 288.

10 This argument is given in a judicial decision by Judge Charles E. Wyzanski. See *United States v. Sisson,* 294 F. Supp. 511, 513-515 (D.C. Mass. 1968). For a full discussion, see Tucker, Velvel, D'Amato, Vollen and Sanger, Brief in *Mitchell v. Nixon, Congressional Record-House,* H4333, H4346-47 (May 25, 1971).

the human race in a nuclear exchange that might last a couple of hours. The war itself could be irrevocably set off in fifteen minutes. Perhaps it is comforting to know that in the opinion of some learned jurists, Congress would truly have full power to declare total war, even if the circumstances make it unlikely that anyone at the time would be paying attention to what Congress might or might not be doing.

In this view, the Korean and Indochina wars are examples of limited, "Presidential" wars--the modern sort of wars that are irrelevant to Congress.[11] The Congressional role is thus reserved for World Wars I, II, and lastly, III. Is it reasonable to believe, knowing what we know about the background and language of the Constitution, that its Framers had only these total wars in mind when they gave Congress the power to declare war? Merely to state the question suggests its absurdity. To the Framers of our Constitution, limited wars were natural, plentiful, easily contemplated, and totally forseeable. In those days we engaged in a limited war against France, and soon later in a limited war against England. Moreover, the European countries were constantly involved in limited wars against each other. Total fight-to-the-death wars were rare, and of course the twentieth century's versions had not yet happened. Thus, contrary to the view propounded above, the Framers of the Constitution were dealing precisely with limited wars (such as those in Korea and Vietnam) when they gave Congress the power to declare war.

Finally, even in those days Congress did not always "declare war" in such terms. A limited war was "authorized" against France, for example.[12] The declaration-of-war clause does not require Congress to "declare" war as an all-out effort, but, sensibly, to "authorize" it in whatever language Congress deems appropriate. This is a point which the apologists for Presidential power conveniently overlook in their insistence that Congress can only "declare" war.

Some lawyers for the government are still heard to claim that Congress in fact declared war when it passed the Tonkin Gulf Resolution in 1964.[13]

[11] The question of responsibility is clouded by the fact that some Congressmen take a public position opposing such wars but vote for war appropriations, saying the war is the President's responsibility once it has been started. This permits them to stand politically with the "doves" and practically with the "hawks," vitiating their representative function vis-a-vis their constituencies. This is good reason why Congressmen should have to stand and be counted on the initial *authorization* of war--as the Framers intended they should.

[12] Act of July 7, 1798, 1 Stat. 578 (1798); "That the President of the United States shall be, and is hereby authorized to instruct the commanders of the public vessels which are, or which shall be employed in the service of the United States, to subdue, seize and take any armed French vessel, which shall be found within the jurisdiction limits of the United States, or elsewhere, on the high seas. . . ." See also the authorization of the Civil War, Act of Aug. 6, 1861, Ch. 63, Para. 3, 12 Stat. 326 (1861).

[13] S. J. Res. 189, 88th Cong. 2d Sess. (1964); H. R. J. Res. 1145, 88th Cong., 2d Sess. (1964).

But as a Congressional investigating committee later reported, that Resolution was obtained on the basis of Executive misrepresentations to Congress.[14] Additionally, the language of the Resolution is too broad and vague to be construed as a declaration of war.[15] In any case, the Gulf of Tonkin Resolution was repealed by both houses of Congress in 1971.[16]

What we have in Indochina is an undeclared war, a war initiated by the President (successive incumbents, actually) acting under his own authority under color of law. But nevertheless one might ask: has not Congress, by passing military appropriations and by renewing the Selective Service, in fact *consented* to the war? Declarations of war aside, this is in effect, according to such reasoning, as much a Congressional war as a Presidential war and hence it is indeed constitutional. If Congress does not like what is going on over Laos, it can cut off the funds and force the President to stop the bombing of that country. By its power of the purse, one might argue, Congress in fact controls the war-making power.

This line of reasoning has been upheld by the Federal court of appeals in New York in the case of *Orlando v. Laird* (1971)[17] The Supreme Court declined to review the *Orlando* case in October 1971, and hence it stands as an affirmation of the "appropriations" argument, which would bypass the declaration-of-war clause. In another case which is moving slowly through the Federal courts, thirteen United States Congressmen have challenged the appropriations argument, filing affidavits that the expenditure of monies for the war in Indochina is not at all equivalent to the power to decide upon war. This case of *Mitchell v. Laird*[18] is unique in that it is the first time in history that Congressmen have sued the executive branch of the government directly over an issue of Constitutional separation of powers and the rights of the legislative branch.

Attorneys for the Congressmen argue first of all that the decision to initiate war is far more important than any subsequent decision to consent to the war or to ratify it. Once the President gets the country into a war,

[14] *Hearings on the Gulf of Tonkin: The 1964 Incidents,* before the Senate Comm. on Foreign Relations, 90th Cong., 2d Sess. (1968); see M. Pusey, *The Way We Go to War* (1969), pp. 115-134.

[15] Couched in general terms, and on its face delegating to the President the power to decide whether or not to engage in military hostilities, the Resolution could not be a permissible delegation of power under the Constitution. Rather, such an attempted wholesale delegation of Congressional power would amount to an unauthorized and hence invalid amendment to the Constitution. Cf. *Greene v. McElroy*, 360 U.S. 474, 506-07 (1959).

[16] P.L. 91-672, Para. 12 (1971).

[17] U.S. Court of Appeals, Second Circuit, Docket No. 35535 (April 20, 1971).

[18] U.S. Dist. Ct., District of Columbia, Civil Action No. 697-71. For plaintiffs' brief and affidavits, see *Congressional Record-House*, H4333-67 (May 25, 1971).

the momentum changes; supporting the war becomes, for many legislators, a matter of national responsibility. In the first year or two of any war there is vast public support, however unreasoning, based simply on a conviction that the President must know what he is doing. It is vastly more difficult by cutting off funds to stop a war that has been started than to decline to go to war in the first place. There is little on the public record to suggest that a President could have gotten Congress to authorize war in Indochina; that is why the executive branch backed into the war or sneaked into it, depending upon how one interprets the *Pentagon Papers*.

Congressmen will appropriate funds for a war for reasons other than a sense of national responsibility. For humanitarian reasons they do not want to cut off support for troops in the field. Moreover, they will renew the Selective Service Act so that troops can be rotated out of combat. Many Congressmen, in voting for defense appropriations, have stated on the floor of Congress that they were opposed to the war but felt that they could not cut off funds for a war that had already been started.[19] Other Congressmen have stated that it is inappropriate, under Congressional procedures, to make substantive decisions in the debate to appropriate money. In other words, if the "power of the purse" were pushed to its limit, there would be no need for any committee in Congress other than the Finance and Appropriations Committees. Instead, long tradition has it that the appropriations process should be confined to questioning the dollar amount of appropriations and not the substantive policies for which the appropriations are allocated.[20]

Another fault with the "appropriations" argument is that military defense expenditures--due to the power of conservative leadership of appropriations committees--come in a lump sum. It is difficult, and in some cases impossible, to separate out those appropriations that are related to Indochina from the nongeographical categories that are used in the defense bills. Of course it is possible to put a rider on an appropriations bill cutting off the funds for Indochina--possible but not likely, since amendments are given very short shrift by the tight rules of the House of Representatives. But then the President could veto the entire bill and send it back, and one may be sure that Congress would not fail to appropriate the overall funds needed for national defense (missiles, submarines, troops all around the world, military pay, etc.). Thus the President effectively has a veto over any attempted fund cutoff, whereas he could have no veto over the *failure* of Congress to declare war in the first instance.

[19] See, *e.g.*, remarks of Congressman Fraser, 112 *Cong. Rec.* 4468 (1969); remarks of Senator McGovern, 112 *Cong. Rec.* 4409 (1966); remarks of Senator Gore, 111 *Cong. Rec.* 9497 (1965).

[20] See, *e.g.*, Affidavit of Congressman Benjamin S. Rosenthal, *Congressional Record-House*, H4354 (May 25, 1971).

As for renewals of the Selective Service Act, one of the Congressmen who is a plaintiff in *Mitchell v. Laird* points out in his affidavit that the Selective Service Act has been renewed continuously since 1940, in time of peace as well as war.[21]

But when all is said and done, the fact remains that Congress has certainly been implicated in the support of the war in Indochina. There may be many Congressmen now who are joining in the opposition to the war, as it has become unpopular with the public, but their public position four, six and eight years ago was one of acquiescence or even endorsement of the war. Even now, while many Congressmen are advocating "bringing the boys home," they are not talking about bringing the pilots home or halting the planes and helicopters flown continuously over Indochina. Should we conclude, therefore, that Congress "really" consented to the war even if Congress did not initiate it, and that it is therefore absurd to say that the war is unconstitutional?

On the contrary, the constitutional argument is fundamentally one of procedure. The Constitution *requires* that *Congress* declare or authorize a war. This requirement was built in because the Framers wanted to make sure that such a grave question would be decided in the glare of national debate by legislators who would have to stand up and be counted on the issue, justifying their position on the question to their constituents. The Framers specifically tried to avoid the kind of subterfuge that has in fact happened with respect to Vietnam, where a President takes the initiative and Congressmen "reluctantly" go along. The Framers were well aware of the British experience where kings got their nations into unwanted wars and Parliament came along after the fact and paid the bills. A mere copying of the appropriations "power of the purse" from Parliament to Congress surely would not correct the unenviable British experience. Thus the Framers put in a separate clause--that Congress must declare war.[22]

This *was* different from the unwritten British constitution and for good reason. It is historically, and constitutionally, unsound to argue that we can read the declaration-of-war clause out of the Constitution because Congress has the power of the purse. Rather, the Constitution as written *forced*

[21] *Ibid.*, at H4355: "This country has had a draft since 1940, in both times of war and times of peace. It obviously needs an army in peacetime, and this is aside from the fact that troops are fighting in Vietnam. Unless and until there is a volunteer army, the army must be raised by conscription. Thus, Congressmen felt it necessary to vote to extend Selective Service even though they would not have voted to authorize the war and were opposed to using American troops in the Indo-China war."

[22] See D'Amato, "Massachusetts in the Federal Courts: The Constitutionality of the Vietnam War." 4 *J. of Law Reform* 11 (1970).

Congress either to authorize war or to suffer the consequences of not going to war. In the words of a leading commentator on the Constitution, the Framers intended to make it difficult for this nation to get into war but easy to get out of war.[23] In the past two decades, for whatever reasons, this nation's government has effectively reversed the clear intent of the Framers and the manifest meaning of the Constitution. The characteristics of air war have reinforced this trend, since they make it easier to get into such a war than into one limited to ground forces.

One may then ask, if all this is so, why have not the courts declared the war to be unconstitutional? The simple answer is that the courts have been as reticent as Congress. Indeed, despite President Nixon's pronounced preference for "strict construction" of the Constitution, he has sought out appointees to the Supreme Court who would not consider reversing his war. In fact, before Chief Justice Burger was nominated, he joined in an opinion in the Federal court of appeals, where he was sitting as a judge, to the effect it was a "waste of judicial time" to hear arguments on the unconstitutionality of the Vietnam war.[24] In that opinion, the Court summarily dismissed a case of draft resisters challenging the war without even pausing to examine their arguments on the merits.

In fact, except for two lower-court cases, the courts have thrown out all cases involving the constitutionality of the war without going into the arguments--some observers believe, because the arguments are pretty much irrefutable. One exception has been mentioned--the court of appeals in New York, which held the war constitutional because of Congressional appropriations.[25] The other exception was a case tried by District Judge Sweigert on the West Coast, who actually held that the plaintiffs--three law students in the reserves--had made out a *prima facie* case that the war in fact *was* unconstitutional.[26] His decision, however, was immediately appealed by the Department of Justice, which then filed several motions in the court of appeals to delay the hearing of the case, with the result that only after a year had passed did the court of appeals hear oral arguments; apparently it is taking considerable time in studying the matter prior to announcing a decision.

Many years from now, historians will surely look back upon this war and note the great failure of the courts to uphold the plain meaning of the Constitution. They will also note the failure of Congress to assert its own

[23] Joseph Story, 2 *Commentaries on the Constitution of the United States* 89-90 (2nd ed. 1851).

[24] *Luftig v. McNamara*, 373 F. 2d 664 (1967), *cert. den.* 387 U.S. 945 (1967).

[25] See note 17 above.

[26] *Mottala v. Nixon*, 318 F. Supp. 538 (N.D. Cal. 1970).

powers in the face of Presidential monopolization of authority in foreign affairs. But this is of little significance at the present. What is important is that the courts' failure to rule upon the question of the constitutionality of the war not be taken to mean that the issue is a trivial one or that the war is *ipso facto* constitutional.

The question of constitutionality is a fundamental one, and the more Americans conclude for themselves that the war violates our Constitution, the less support there will be for its continuation. Even if the courts will not declare the war unconstitutional, the American people can do this in effect through political channels, giving a vote of confidence to the Constitution as written and not as amended *de facto* by the executive branch with the tacit consent of a diffident legislature[27] and an indifferent judiciary.[28]

[27] The Senate Foreign Relations Committee recently gave unanimous approval to legislation which would restrict the warmaking powers of the Presidency, thereby acknowledging what it sees as an imbalance of powers in this area. The bill provides that the President can use armed force to forestall an attack on the U.S. or its armed forces or to protect U.S. citizens while being evacuated from a foreign country, but requires Congressional approval for continuing hostilities more than 30 days. Also, unless Congress authorized it, the President would be prohibited from sending military advisors to a country engaged in hostilities. Sponsors of the bill range from Senator Jacob Javits (R.-N.Y.), a Senate liberal, to Senator John Stennis (D.-Miss.), a Senate conservative and chairman of the Armed Services Committee. Passage of some version of this bill by the full Senate seems assured. See *New York Times*, December 8, 1971, p. 14.

[28] The analysis of this chapter has not dealt explicitly with the doctrine of "political questions" which students of law recognize as a means whereby the Supreme Court has on numerous occasions declined to deal with certain types of cases because they involve questions of a highly delicate political nature best resolved by other branches of the government. Some people have argued that the Supreme Court has simply and impliedly applied the "political question" doctrine in ducking cases involving the Vietnam War. However, a study of this doctrine in constitutional law indicates its inapplicability to the Vietnam situation. In the first place, at issue in the various cases is the *constitutionality* of the President's actions. As the Supreme Court held in the recent case of *Powell v. McCormack*, 395 U.S. 486, 549 (1969), a *constitutional* determination by its very nature involves judicially manageable standards which a court can handle. Secondly, the question involves the President's powers vis-a-vis Congress, and thus for the courts to say that such an issue is non-justiciable would simply amount to saying that there is no "umpire" in such a conflict of powers. But the Supreme Court role is traditionally that of "umpire" in a case involving executive-legislative conflicts, as the Supreme Court pointed out in the Steel Seizure Case [*Youngstown Sheet & Tube Co. v. Sawyer*, 343 U.S. 579 (1952)]. No Supreme Court case has *ever been cited* applying the "political question" exception to matters of the division of power between Congress and the President. To the contrary, there are numerous cases throughout history, even involving "war" powers and coming up when the nation was at war, where the Supreme Court has handled the substantive issues and has not even seen fit to mention the "political question" doctrine. For a listing of many of these cases, see D'Amato *et al.*, *op. cit.* footnote 4 above, pp. 115-116.

CHAPTER 11

THE AIR WAR AND INTERNATIONAL LAW

In assessing the air war in Indochina according to the standards of international law, one should not assume that this law is as effective or definitive as domestic (municipal) law. In practice it usually is not. In principle, however, international law is as binding as domestic law, and indeed much international law has been incorporated by the United States into its own domestic law. The effect of international law, particularly in the area of warfare, stems by and large not so much from sanctions or adjudication as from education and the setting of standards for behavior in war. We think it worth evaluating the air war in terms of existing international law and the precedents being set. We consider also the issues of defining and fixing responsibility for illegal air warfare, and the need for international legal reform.

We shall work essentially from the traditional laws of war. No claim is made that war is anything but bloody and brutal, but there has been an expectation that nations willing to adhere to law can ameliorate the effects of war, particularly as these are visited upon the innocent--those not engaged in violent conflict but caught in its path. By setting standards and creating pressures for living up to them, it is expected that the excessive or superfluous costs of war can be reduced.

The fundamental moral premise underlying legal limitations upon warfare is the understanding by governments that "enemy forces and noncombatants are human beings possessing rights which must be respected even in the heat of war,"[1] and that the means employed in combat may not be unlimited. If this ethical presupposition is rejected, any rules governing warfare will be based only upon expediency or the dictates of superior military power.

Even while acknowledging an ethical basis for legal restraints in war, the significance of *reciprocity* in the establishment and maintenance of international law should be noted. Modes of warfare against which retaliation is relatively easy (such as poisoning of wells, dum-dum bullets, poison gas, bacteriological weapons) are more likely to be prohibited and remain unused than those which offer one side a clear advantage. The presence or absence of possibilities for retaliation surely condition--positively or negatively--the efficacy of legal strictures on conduct in warfare.

Generally, legal regulation of warfare has attempted to maintain a balance between competing considerations of military necessity and humanitarian-

[1]See William V. O'Brien, *War and/or Survival* (Garden City, N.Y.: Doubleday, 1969), p. 216.

ism.[2] This balance is made precarious by the weight which most decision-makers are likely to attach to the former. It has been necessary to place some emphasis in legal formulations on the latter in order that humanitarian requirements not be disregarded. The central function of international law has been to attempt to limit war's destructiveness, to establish a more humane political consciousness, and to achieve an understanding and common expectation that the savagery of war will be restrained.

Our analysis of the air war in the light of international legal standards carries no implication whatever that North Vietnamese and NLF forces should not be subject to the same searching review of military behavior. Indeed, our opinion is that both sides in the Indochina war have committed war crimes on a significant scale. However, given our responsibilities as American scholars we deal here with U.S. policies and the legal implications thereof. In any event, the air war in Indochina has been almost entirely an American activity. Whatever judgment is made on the actions of "the other side," this--according to long-standing legal tradition--does not absolve the U.S. of responsibility for its actions. At most it may be extenuating evidence in making an adverse judgment less harsh; it will not change the judgment.

We would note here that we do not address the question of the legal status of the air war per se. There is a body of law which deals with the right to *resort* to war--*jus ad bellum*. For several centuries, national claims to the right of sovereignty precluded judgments of whether war-making per se could be judged licit or illicit according to the standards of international law. At present it is clearly established--by conventions ratified following World War I, by the findings of the Nuremberg and Tokyo war crimes trials after World War II, and by the Charter of the United Nations which the world community has undertaken to uphold--that the right to make war is definitely circumscribed.

Application of this rule is difficult, however; being enforced usually against losers by victors. We have considered the arguments advanced by supporters of the Indochina war that U.S. military action in South Vietnam is sanctioned under international law, and find them tenuous at best. Still, we recognize that the issue is debatable and invariably shrouded in political judgments. We are prepared however, to argue strongly that the legal case for American bombing in the rest of Indochina is untenable.[3] Nevertheless,

[2] See generally, Morris Greenspan, *The Modern Law of Land Warfare* (University of California Press, 1959); Myres McDougal and Florentine Feliciano, *Law and Minimum World Public Order* (Yale University Press, 1961); Julius Stone, *Legal Controls of International Conflict* (Rinehart & Co., 1959).

[3] On the issue of the legal status of American bombing in Indochina, see generally Richard Falk, editor, *The Vietnam War and International Law*, Vols. I and II (Princeton University Press, 1968 and 1969).

we have chosen instead to concentrate on the legal status of the *conduct* of the air war. The body of law pertaining to this--*jus in bello*--is considerably clearer, and it is probably more useful to examine what lessons can be learned from the air war in Indochina thus far. In particular it becomes quite clear that detailed international law governing air warfare is sadly lacking or outdated, and thus that international efforts to develop such law are urgently needed.

A. RULES OF WAR AND AIR WARFARE

The law governing air warfare is without doubt the most underdeveloped and least significant part of the general body of rules regulating warfare generally. It is difficult to perceive any meaningful impact of law upon the air war in Indochina thus far. There are several factors that account for this, each of them important in the Indochina setting.

First, the technology of air war evolves very rapidly, leaving behind any detailed regulations. Indeed, to date there has apparently been insufficient time to develop *any* specific air-war rules of consequence. Even broad-based principles may be difficult if not impossible to apply when the weapons systems in use are undreamed of by those who earlier formulated the fundamental principles.

Second, since air warfare is extraordinarily powerful, and can be used in many instances instead of ground troops, the temptations to use it are naturally quite strong. Restrictions on its use are not likely to find easy acceptance by any nation of military significance. In fact, "military necessity" is very likely to be discerned in most situations where bombing and other means of air combat appear useful.

Third, air war is difficult to regulate by law since it normally tends to be indiscriminate. Target recognition and aiming accuracy are not as precise as in ground warfare, and air commanders thus often resort to area weapons, such as napalm, CBUs, or pattern bombing. This tends to diminish if not eliminate altogether the crucial distinction between combatant and non-combatant, and thus to weaken legal restraint. This factor is of obvious relevance in a guerrilla conflict in which the combatants and non-participants are deliberately mixed. In such conflicts one needs to be even more discriminating than in traditional warfare. Yet the difficulties encountered by ground troops in a guerrilla war often make air power appear the more attractive choice.

Fourth, air power requires advanced technology and large amounts of capital. In a war where the two sides are not symmetrical in terms of air power, reciprocity is eliminated, thus rendering it safe to violate any rule that might otherwise govern. This in turn further erodes the law.

Given these conditions, it is not surprising that international law has so little to say about the conduct of air war. A set of rules on the subject--the Hague draft Rules of Aerial Warfare[4]--was recommended by a group of international legal experts in 1923, but was not ratified by any country. Ever since, international lawyers have been hesitant to make another serious attempt to regulate air warfare, notwithstanding that it has become the most significant instrument of destruction in contemporary armed conflict.

In this situation, legal analysis of air warfare in general, and of the Indochina air war in particular, must rely heavily upon rules established for the regulation of land and naval combat. The most significant sources of these rules are several multilateral treaties in force among various major and minor powers, particularly conventions adopted at international conferences called to develop specific norms for the conduct of war. The most important, for our purposes, are the Hague Conventions of 1899 and 1907 and the Geneva Conventions of 1949.[5]

It is clear that the very few legal rules in these conventions devoted specifically to air warfare are outdated and unsatisfactory for any meaningful governance of contemporary conflict. Some writers have consequently questioned the existence of *any* definite rules of international law regulating air combat.[6] Our view is that some extrapolation from rules governing land and naval warfare can reasonably be made to air war and that such extensions should be regarded as presently valid international law. It would be preferable, however, for the organized international community, including the major military powers, to adopt and ratify a specific set of air rules.

In the absence of precise regulations governing air warfare, we have attempted here to work within the framework of the most fundamental principles underlying the law of land and naval combat, as they might properly be

[4]See M. W. Royse, *Aerial Bombardment and the International Regulation of Warfare* (Vinal, 1928); also *The American Journal of International Law,* Supplement Vol. 17 (1923), pp. 242-260. The text of the draft rules may be found in Greenspan, *op. cit.,* at pp. 650-667 and in the *American Journal* Supplement. The best and most complete analysis is in the Royse work.

[5]The basic texts are set out in Department of the Air Force, *Treaties Governing Land Warfare* (Washington, 1958). The most useful manual, presenting text and U.S. Army interpretations thereof, is Department of the Army, *The Law of Land Warfare* (Washington, 1956), FM 27-10, referred to subsequently as the Army *Field Manual.*

[6]See Hamilton Desaussure, "The Laws of Air Warfare: Are There Any?" *The International Lawyer,* Vol. 5, No. 3, July 1971, p. 529. One of the leading scholars on the law of warfare has written that "potentially decisive new weapons are the most intractable to regulation in the interests of chivalry or humanity; and air power is decisive in modern war. . . . In no sense but a rhetorical one can there still be said to have emerged a body of intelligible rules of air warfare comparable to the traditional rules of land and sea warfare." Stone, *op. cit.,* at p. 609.

applied to a legal analysis of the Indochina air war.

1. *Military Necessity and Proportionality.* Perhaps the single most important general requirement of law in warfare--clearly relevant to an appraisal of the air war--is that a reasonable proportionality exist between damage caused and the military gain sought or anticipated. Destruction not required by military necessity is prohibited and only legitimate military targets may be attacked. If destruction of such targets will cause incidental damage to non-military targets, that destruction is acceptable only under circumstances of compliance with the general rule of proportionality. The rule also requires that a military response be reasonably proportionate to the initial provocation.

2. *Prohibition of Direct Attacks on Non-Combatants and Non-Military Targets.* The rules of warfare prohibit direct attacks on enemy civilians, medical personnel and vehicles, and medical and other humanitarian installations. They prohibit attacks on churches, schools, historical monuments and other civilian buildings, and on "open cities"--undefended places that could be entered or occupied without the use of force.

3. *Prohibition of Weapons Causing Unnecessary Injury or Suffering.* The application of this principle to specific weapons systems is obviously a matter of subjective judgment. The Hague rules banned the use of poison or poisoned weapons, irregularly shaped bullets, and expanding (dum-dum) bullets. It is generally recognized today that the prohibition extends to barbed or other projectiles that cause pain beyond the requirements of disabling enemy troops. Debate on the subject of *which* contemporary weapons are or ought to be prohibited under international law is continuing.

The application of these three basic principles and the precise stipulations of law that give them meaning appear to present no particular problems in assessing the air war in North Vietnam. The absence of ground combat and guerrilla warfare in the North leaves legal analysis with the normal and traditional problem of judging proportionality and evaluating any attack on non-combatants and non-military targets. But guerrilla combat techniques in South Vietnam, Laos, and Cambodia have greatly complicated the task of the international lawyer who would judge whether American air combat practices are consistent with the applicable law. Guerrilla warfare renders the law itself extraordinarily difficult to apply, for the deliberate mixing of combatants and non-combatants and of military with non-military targets renders the required discrimination both onerous and vexing for military forces, and particularly for air forces.

Nevertheless, it is our view that the difficulties posed by guerrilla warfare do not relieve air commanders or pilots of the applicable legal requirements. Indeed, if the nature of the particular combat necessitates making even finer discrimination in order to comply with the law, then the desirable policy is to aim for that discrimination rather than to weaken or ignore the norms of behavior that incorporate unassailable policy bases. Further, the argument of "military necessity" is no defense against acts specifically forbidden by the laws of war. As the United States Government has itself emphasized, the prohibitions entailed in the laws of war have already "been developed and framed with consideration for the concept of military necessity."[7] If the various prohibitions are difficult for air forces to apply in the context of guerrilla combat, that cannot in itself be an argument for diminishing the vigor of the law.

There is one further technical issue of relevance here: the question whether the United States is legally bound in Indochina by all the provisions of treaty law governing warfare. There are legal problems of reciprocity involving the North Vietnamese and the NLF, as well as questions of crimes against civilians of friendly nations, such as South Vietnam or Cambodia. We think it unnecessary in this study to spell out in great detail a legal analysis of the issues posed in this regard. Suffice it to say that it appears most sound legally that the laws of war, whether treaty or customary, apply throughout Indochina. Hostile territory in all four states has been attacked and the areas should, in our opinion, be regarded as hostile territory within the meaning of traditional law. In any event, the United States has claimed no special exemption, but on the contrary has granted that the laws of war, both treaty and customary, are fully applicable throughout Indochina.[8]

B. A LEGAL ASSESSMENT OF AERIAL OPERATIONS IN INDOCHINA

1. *Proportionality*

While a substantial portion of the bombing in Indochina has been properly limited to purely military targets or known enemy troops concentrations, it seems clear that the bombing has generally failed to comply with the rule of proportionality. This is the central legal defect in the American air war throughout the four nations of the area. While judgments under the rule often necessitate difficult evaluations, it would appear that American destruction of non-military targets in Indochina and of objectives not having a purely military character has been grossly disproportionate and excessive in relation to the military gains. The tonnage figures alone depict the inordinate scope

[7] U.S. Army *Field Manual, op. cit.,* p. 4.

[8] See Telford Taylor, *Nuremberg and Vietnam: An American Tragedy* (Quadrangle Books, 1970), pp. 130-134. We note that the U.S., for example, has insisted that the DRV should conform to the provisions of the Geneva Convention regarding prisoners of *war* (our emphasis).

of the bombing, and the seriousness of the violation of law.[9]

The paucity of purely military targets in Indochina has resulted in frequent bombardment of objectives with a mixed military-civilian character, then largely civilian targets with some military import, and finally civilian targets where enemy units were thought to be (or to have been) located.[10] Thus by the end of 1967 some seventy percent of the villages in Quang Ngai province in South Vietnam had been destroyed, largely because of the actual or suspected presence at one time or another of enemy troops.[11] Pattern bombing and "free-strike" bombing have constituted serious violations of the proportionality rule. The destruction of entire towns and villages throughout Indochina indicates U.S. non-compliance with the law.

Further, the U.S. strategy of devastation of areas in South Vietnam and elsewhere to prevent enemy occupation is forbidden by the general rule of proportionality and by conventional law as well. As a matter of common international acceptance, and in accordance with the 1907 Hague Convention[12] and the views of writers,[13] devastation to prevent occupation is precluded by law except in cases of imperative military necessity. The emphasis has always been on the term "imperative" and measures of devastation are generally perceived as proper only in rare and exceptional cases. In Indochina, devastation of villages has become commonly accepted as a standard operating procedure when enemy military activity is indicated there.

In the case of devastation and "free-strike" zone policy, the illegality is clear not only under the customary legal rule of proportionality, but under precise treaty law as well. Hague Regulation 23(g) provides that it is "especially forbidden . . . to destroy or seize the enemy's property, unless such destruction or seizure be imperatively demanded by the necessities of war." This clause has been reinforced by the Charter of the International Military Tribunal at Nuremberg in which Article 6(b) specifies as war crimes, *inter alia*, "wanton destruction of cities, towns or villages, or devastation not justified by military necessity."[14] Article 147 of the 1949 Geneva Convention Relative to the Protection of Civilian Persons in Time of War pre-

[9] See Sec. 1-C.

[10] Henri Meyrowitz, "The Law of War in the Vietnamese Conflict," in Richard A. Falk, ed., *The Vietnam War and International Law*, Vol. II (Princeton University Press, 1968), p. 551.

[11] Erwin Knoll and Judith Nies McFadden, eds., *War Crimes and the American Conscience* (Holt, Rinehart and Winston, 1970), p. 63. See

[12] See formulation of Article 23(g) in the next paragraph; quoted from *Treaties Governing Land Warfare, op. cit.*, p. 12.

[13] See Greenspan, *op. cit.*, p. 285, and writers cited therein.

[14] On Nuremberg generally, see Robert K. Woetzel, *The Nuremberg Trials in International Law* (Praeger, 1962).

cludes "extensive destruction and appropriation of property, not justified by military necessity and carried out unlawfully and wantonly."[15]

It has never been held by a court trying war crimes that devastation of towns and villages to prevent reoccupation by enemy units, or as a reprisal measure, is legally justified. In the *High Command Case* at Nuremberg, it was clear that the defense of military necessity, while held good in that instance, is of no application to American tactics in Vietnam. "Defendants in this case were in many instances in retreat under arduous conditions wherein their commands were in serious danger of being cut off. Under such circumstances, a commander must necessarily make quick decisions to meet the particular situation of his command. A great deal of latitude must be accorded to him under such circumstances."[16] This analysis has no relevance to a well-thought out and carefully planned strategy in Indochina.

2. *Attacks on Non-Combatants and Non-Military Targets*

Like the rule of proportionality, the rule forbidding direct attacks on non-combatants and non-military targets is a vital part of customary international law and as such is binding without regard to particular treaty stipulations. There are important treaty clauses as well, including Article 23(g) of the Hague Regulations, prohibiting destruction or seizure of property unless "imperatively demanded by the necessities of war," and Article 25, which stipulates that "The attack or bombardment, by whatever means, of towns, villages, dwellings, or buildings which are undefended is prohibited."[17] Of particular relevance to the bombing of North Vietnam is Article 27:

> In sieges and bombardments all necessary measures must be taken to spare, as far as possible, buildings dedicated to religion, art, science, or charitable purposes, historic monuments, hospitals, and places where the sick and wounded are collected, provided they are not being used at the time for military purposes.
>
> It is the duty of the besieged to indicate the presence of such buildings or places by distinctive and visible signs, which shall be notified to the enemy beforehand.[18]

[15] *Treaties Governing Land Warfare, op. cit.*, pp. 183-184.

[16] *Trials of War Criminals Before the Nuremberg Military Tribunals* (USGPO, 1950), Vol. XI, p. 541.

[17] *Treaties Governing Land Warfare, op. cit.*, p. 13.

[18] *Ibid.* The detailed rules of engagement issued for the 1965 air attacks against POL storage facilities in North Vietnam, cited on p. 40, above, suggests that American planners are aware of this rule. The fact is, however, that such detailed restrictions are the exception rather than the rule. A recent dramatic illustration of this was provided by the December 1971 raids against North Vietnam, which were carried out in such adverse weather conditions that targets were totally obscured and little if any discrimination could be exercised. Cf. Sec. 13-3, Para. 3.

The evidence indicates that each of the treaty provisions cited and the general customary rule have all been violated by American bombing practices in Indochina, although official responsibility is clearer in some instances than in others. One of the clearest breaches is the bombing of villages, particularly in the South, on the basis of information that NLF forces had been harbored there or had been seen passing through.[19] This is certainly bombing of undefended places without the military necessity required by the Hague Regulations and customary law.

It is true, of course, that contemporary practice has accepted as lawful the aerial bombardment of undefended places containing or accommodating "legitimate military objectives." These are defined by law as including, according to the United States Army's 1956 *Field Manual*, "A place which is occupied by a combatant military force or through which such a force is passing."[20] Yet American bombs have destroyed villages empty of NLF and of no military value whatever, primarily for purposes of preventing later reoccupation by the enemy. At Nuremberg, such actions were held to be war crimes.[21]

Even conceding that undefended villages and towns containing proper military objectives may lawfully be bombed, American practice has frequently failed to meet this less rigid standard of the Army Field Manual. The Manual stipulates that "There is no prohibition of general application against bombardment from the air of combatant troops, defended places, or other legitimate military objectives."[22] The bombing of an open town or village with no military significance, simply to prevent its possible later use by enemy units, is a clear violation of the law.

The practice of bombing villages for purposes of collective penalty or reprisal[23] is also a violation of treaty law. The 1949 Geneva Convention Relative to the Protection of Civilian Persons in Time of War stipulates in Article 33 that

> No protected person may be punished for an offense he or she has not personally committed. Collective penalties and likewise all measures of intimidation or of terror-

[19] See Taylor, *op, cit.*, pp. 144-145.

[20] U.S. Army *Field Manual, op. cit.*, Para. 40, p. 19.

[21] Thus General Jodl was convicted of war crimes which included, in part, similar actions in Norway. The International Military Tribunal wrote: "By teletype of 28 October 1944 Jodl ordered the evacuation of all persons in northern Norway and burning of their houses so they could not help the Russians. Jodl says he was against this, but Hitler ordered it and it was not fully carried out. A document of the Norwegian Government says such an evacuation did take place in northern Norway and 30,000 houses were damaged." Jodl was convicted on on this charge. See *American Journal of International Law*, Vol. 41, No. 1 (January 1947), p. 316.

[22] U.S. Army *Field Manual, op. cit.*, para. 42, p. 20.

[23] See Taylor, *op. cit.*, p. 195.

> ism are prohibited. Pillage is prohibited. Reprisals against protected persons and their property are prohibited.[24]

As can be seen from leaflets cited in Section 4-A, violations of Article 33 have not been isolated cases or individual aberrations but rather a matter of official American policy.

The evidence, particularly in North Vietnam, also indicates several violations of Article 27 of the Hague Regulations, cited above, dealing with protected buildings, such as hospitals and museums. Our findings lead to the conclusion that bombing of legally protected buildings has not obviously been deliberate government policy set or approved at the highest levels, but that some of the bombings cannot be accurately characterized as accidental. Much of the reportorial literature points to deliberate bombing attacks on schools and hospitals, and only serious investigation will reveal the extent of official responsibility, and how far government policy is implicated. It is also true that destruction of protected buildings was often (certainly not always) incidental to attacks on legitimate military objectives.[25]

Finally, the several occurrences of "squirrel-hunting" for individuals in "free-strike" zones in South Vietnam is an obvious and striking violation of the law, as the practice involves a deliberate failure to make any distinction between combatant and non-combatant.[26] It is impossible to find government responsibility in these cases, and the many incidents are more likely cases of individual criminal actions than policy set at higher levels. Nevertheless, the practice is one of many violations of the law by American air forces in Indochina, and deserves mention here.

* * * * * *

While it is true that both the rules of proportionality and the prohibition of direct attack against non-combatants and non-military targets are part of customary law, and are binding on the world community without regard to conventional law, it is also the case that most of the precise treaty stipulations in both areas were written essentially for purposes of regulating land warfare. Yet their general applicability and the policy bases underlying

[24] *Treaties Governing Land Warfare, op. cit.*, p. 146. For the applicability of the Convention to the war in South Vietnam, see Taylor, *op. cit.*, p. 133.

[25] All visitors to North Vietnam report extremely widespread destruction of all types of permanent structure through the country, particularly outside Hanoi and Haiphong. Such destruction is often attributed to the need for bringing to bear suppressive fire against anti-aircraft installations (cf. Sec. 2-C); it is claimed that the North Vietnamese frequently placed their anti-aircraft guns near such buildings for cover. However, the munitions used for suppressive fire are typically CBUs and rockets, while much of the visible damage is due to high-explosive bombs, which are relatively ineffectual against anti-aircraft guns.

[26] See Taylor, *op. cit.*, p. 147.

their terms makes it imperative to utilize them in the context of the Indochina air war as well. The weakness of the law and the enormous destruction caused by bombing in the Second World War, Korean War and Indochina War make it essential to strengthen restraints on aerial bombardment and to develop the law as far as possible.

While this must eventually be done in systematic fashion, current efforts are perforce restricted to legal provisions of general applicability. The generality of their formulation may weaken legal principles and diminish their persuasiveness and impact in contemporary conflict, but their relevance is not eliminated. The policy bases and even terminology of such principles are suggestive of the more precise efforts that must be undertaken to fashion meaningful rules of law governing air warfare. In any event they are all the world community possesses at present. It is not sufficient; but the law, old and imprecise as it is, must be emphasized if the aims of saving lives and educating decision-makers and the public are to be achieved.

3. *Use of Weapons of Questionable Legality*

There are four types of weapons used in aerial operations by the United States that have raised serious legal questions: tear gases, herbicides, napalm, and anti-personnel fragmentation bombs. Each is discussed here in terms of its international legal status.

a. In the case of tear gases (and herbicides), the legal controversy centers around the meaning of the 1925 Geneva Protocol, i.e., whether it was intended at the time to ban tear gases, and whether its terminology is sufficiently broad to include a ban on herbicides and defoliants. The Protocol, which has been formally ratified or accepted by 85 nations, including every major power except the United States, prohibits "the use in war of asphyxiating, poisonous or other gases, and of all analogous liquids, materials or devices." The world community, through the United Nations, has taken the position that the Geneva Protocol includes tear gases and herbicides in its ban.[27] The vote on this--80 to 3--was however not conclusive; there were 36 abstentions, and the negative votes were cast by Australia, Portugal, and the United States.

The United States insists that use of tear gases and herbicides in war is not inconsistent with the Protocol, which in any event it has not ratified. In the years since 1925 most nations have supported the liberal

[27] For comprehensive analyses, see Ann Van Wynen Thomas and A. J. Thomas, Jr., *Legal Limits on the Use of Chemical and Biological Weapons* (Southern Methodist University Press, 1970), and R. R. Baxter and Thomas Buergenthal, "Legal Aspects of the Geneva Protocol of 1925" in *The Control of Chemical and Biological Weapons*, published by the Carnegie Endowment for International Peace in 1971.

construction of the Protocol and no state has ratified the instrument with a reservation for tear gases or any other type of chemical weapon.[28] In 1970 the Protocol was submitted to the United States Senate for its advice and consent to ratification. However, the Senate Foreign Relations Committee has refused to act favorably, maintaining that the advantages of ratification would be lost by the strict construction contended for by the President.[29] Given the U.S. position and the great number of abstentions in the UN, it is impossible to conclude that American use of tear gas in Indochina is *ipso facto* a violation of law. The law is still in the process of development, and while the final outcome is likely to be a ban on tear gas, the current legal regulation is indeterminate.

b. The question of herbicides is also open at the present time. The Geneva Protocol forbids in addition to gases "all analogous liquids, materials or devices." In 1925 the draftsmen of the Protocol were unaware of chemicals used in warfare for destroying crops or defoliating jungles, although the wording is obviously broad enough to cover herbicides and defoliants, and the majority of the world community has so interpreted it. But again, the U.S. position and the number of abstentions in the UN has left the matter unsettled.[30]

The central issue of American use of herbicides in Vietnam, however, may not be the weapon itself (even though such chemicals appear on the way to legal exclusion) so much as the use to which it is put. The targets have been principally rice paddies and jungle canopies. Article 23(a) of the Hague Regulations provides that "It is especially forbidden . . . to employ poison or poisoned weapons." The U.S. Army Field Manual stipulates that this rule does not prohibit the destruction of crops by chemical or bacterial agents harmless to man *provided* that the crops are "intended *solely* for consumption by the armed forces (if that fact can be determined)."[31]

It is apparent that American practice is not consistent with our own interpretation of the Hague Regulation, for in areas of South Vietnam occupied by NLF forces it is frequently impossible to determine whether rice crops are "intended solely for consumption by the armed forces." In most instances, indeed, it is obvious that the rice must in great part be intended

[28] The 1922 Treaty on the Use of Submarine and Gas Warfare, which never entered into force but which the U.S. did ratify, contained a similar ban and also the phrase "or other gases." In neither case does the legislative history reveal a precise answer to the question whether tear gases were intended at the time for inclusion in the ban.

[29] See Desaussure, *op. cit.*, p. 541 and *The Washington Post*, March 23, 1971.

[30] The U.S. construction contends that herbicides are exempted partly on the grounds that their use is licit in the U.S. As in the case of tear gas, the fact that a chemical is used domestically does not necessarily render its use in warfare legal.

[31] U.S. Army *Field Manual*, *op. cit.*, para. 37, p. 18 (emphasis added).

for the civilian inhabitants of the area.

The defoliation of jungle canopies presents no traditional legal problem. But it has been argued, primarily by biologist Arthur Galston, that use of herbicidal chemicals, as in Vietnam, whether or not in violation of the 1925 Geneva Protocol, should be banned in an effort to preserve the ecology of the country. Galston maintains that it is "quite clear that some long-range ecological defects have occurred" and that "at best we will have produced a massive alteration of the vegetational complex of Vietnam. At worst we may have produced permanent damage (mangroves might never recover, soil might be laterized) and we may have been responsible for inducing some abnormal births."[32] He proposes an international convention to ban what he characterizes as the crime of *ecocide*.

c. Napalm is another weapon in use in Southeast Asia that has evoked great controversy, with serious questions raised about its legality as a weapon of war. Fire weapons generally are both extraordinarily cruel when used against human beings and unusually efficient as weapons whether used against persons or objects. They have been utilized frequently in the large-scale wars of this century, although there has been some recent effort to ban them altogether.

The only clear conventional rule relevant to the use of fire as a weapon is the 1868 Declaration of St. Petersburg, which in its intent renders illegal the use of fire to kill or injure persons; it forbids land or naval forces from using any projectile of less than 400 grams which is charged with fulminating or inflammable substances.[33] Fire weapons, including napalm, may also violate Article 23(e) of the Hague Regulations, which enjoins the use of "arms, projectiles, or material calculated to cause unnecessary suffering." It might be argued that fire weapons are barred by the 1925 Geneva Protocol, particularly if they are used to kill through extensive bodily damage (as do certain war gases) or through asphyxiation. Yet the repeated use of incendiaries, both through flamethrowers and aerial bombs, has destroyed any incipient rule of law barring their use, whether through interpretation of convention or customary law. Certainly the Allied use of aerial incendiaries in the Second World War, both in the destruction of German industrial centers and of Japanese cities after March 1945, and the sanctioned use of flamethrowers by United Nations forces during the Korean War has established the legitimacy of incendiaries as such.

[32] See Knoll and McFadden, *op. cit.*, pp. 70-71. These effects were considered in Chapter 8 and their biological and geological bases are examined in App. E.

[33] The text may be found in James Brown Scott, *Documents Relating to the Program of the First Hague Peace Conference* (New York, 1921), p. 30. Given the possibility of large incendiary weapons, this established a principle rather than a rule of contemporary warfare.

Once again the central problem in terms of legal regulation may well be the use to which napalm and incendiaries are put. The precise question put by contemporary writers[34] and by the UN Secretary-General[35] is not whether such weapons should be banned altogether, but whether their use against human beings should be prohibited. There seems to be general agreement that no rule of law restrains their use against non-human objectives, and to this extent American aerial bombing with incendiaries has been viewed as legally justified. Concerning use against persons, the American position, supported by some writers, is that use against combatants is proper provided there is compliance with the "unnecessary suffering" rule of Article 23(e) of the Hague Regulations. The Army *Field Manual* stipulates:

> The use of weapons which employ fire, such as tracer ammunition, flamethrowers, napalm and other incendiary agents, against targets requiring their use is not violative of international law. They should not, however, be employed in such a way as to cause unnecessary suffering to individuals.[36]

This assumes, rather than states clearly, that incendiaries can legally be employed against individuals. It is our view that any use of fire weapons against human beings causes unnecessary suffering. Given the intensity of public interest in the matter, and the current indeterminacy of the law, the issue could well benefit from regulation by international convention. The efficiency of incendiaries makes it impossible to ban their use altogether, but a comprehensive rule enjoining employment against human targets is far preferable to the present state of the law.

d. Still another issue is the use of antipersonnel bombs by American air crews. Particular attention has been drawn to the use of cluster bombs, which upon impact will fragment into hundreds of thousands of steel projectiles and are intended for use against human beings. This is a relatively new weapon and there is no extensive discussion in the literature of its legal status.

It may be argued that antipersonnel bombs fall within the ban of the "unnecessary suffering" rule of the Hague Regulations, or, as suggested by Meyrowitz,[37] that they should be treated analogously to dum-dum bullets, which were expressly forbidden by the Third Hague Declaration of 1899.[38]

[34] See Greenspan, *op. cit.*, pp. 360-361; Thomas and Thomas, *op. cit.*, pp. 238-240; McDougal and Feliciano, *op. cit.*, pp. 620-622. McDougal and Feliciano hold that "the nature and situation of the target would seem the factors of decisive significance." They support the use of napalm against combatants.

[35] United Nations Doc. A/7720, 20 November 1969, paras. 196-201, pp. 62-63.

[36] U.S. Army *Field Manual, op. cit.*, para. 36, p. 18.

[37] See Meyrowitz, *op. cit.*, p. 553.

[38] The United States was not a party to this Declaration, but its provisions are binding as

The Army *Field Manual*, in its interpretation of the "unnecessary suffering" rule, provides a listing of weapons that might include the new anti-personnel bombs.[39] The larger question remains whether use of these weapons should be rendered illegal by specific international agreement, since the general proscription of Article 23(e) has not been accepted by the U.S. as binding for antipersonnel bombs.

C. FIXING RESPONSIBILITY FOR ILLEGAL AIR WARFARE

Given the conclusion that much of the American bombing in Indochina has been and remains in violation of the laws of warfare, it becomes important to focus on the issue of responsibility, both civilian and military, for the war crimes committed. Notwithstanding the unusually poor record of the armed forces in uncovering and punishing criminal behavior in Indochina, it is our view that there should be some official attempt to determine the extent of international law violations resulting from the air war and to fix responsibility for the transgressions. This is a task which may be separated from specific prosecutions for war crimes. In this section, we address first the problem of assessing legal responsibility, and second, a reasonable course of official action.

International law, particularly since the Nuremberg and Tokyo trials, has had a good deal to say about responsibility for war crimes, and much of the law has been absorbed into the field manuals of national armed forces, including those of the United States. The basic principles may be summarized as follows.[40] First, the fact that a nation's domestic law may not hold a particular act criminal when international law does is no defense. International law is at once higher than municipal law, and in the case of the United States, frequently part of American law as well. Second, the fact that criminal acts were committed by responsible government officials or even by the head of a state is equally irrelevant. Any person, civilian or military, may be responsible for war crimes. Third, superior orders constitute

customary international law.

[39]The *Field Manual* stipulates:

> What weapons cause 'unnecessary injury' can only be determined in light of the practice of States refraining from the use of a given weapon because it is believed to have that effect. The prohibition certainly does not extend to the use of explosives contained in artillery projectiles, mines, rockets, or hand grenades. Usage has, however, established the illegality of the use of lances with barbed heads, irregular-shaped bullets, and projectiles filled with glass, the use of any substance on bullets that would tend unnecessarily to inflame a wound inflicted by them, and the scoring of the surface or filing off the ends of the hard cases of bullets." (para. 34, p. 18.)

[40]The "Nuremberg Principles" were formulated by the International Law Commission of the United Nations in 1950 at the request of the UN General Assembly. The wording was patterned after that used in the Judgment of the International Military Tribunal.

no defense, unless the defendant "did not know and could not reasonably have been expected to know that the act ordered was unlawful."[41] Superior orders may, however, be considered as a factor justifying mitigation of punishment.

The central issue in the context of Indochina, however, is not the application of the fundamental Nuremberg rules, but rather the "chain of command" question--that is, in assessing the legal responsibility for aerial warfare crimes, how far up the chain of command should that responsibility be taken? The question turns essentially on whether responsible high-level officials, military and civilian, had knowledge that war crimes were being committed in the execution of the bombing. In light of the fundamental importance of the issue, the degree of public interest, and the widespread discussion of the key cases in the area, we here set forth in some detail our understanding of the crucial problems posed.

The most famous case dealing with this issue is *In Re Yamashita*, 327 U.S. 1 (1946), a case originally tried before an American military commission in the Philippines. The validity of the proceedings of the commission were eventually upheld by the U.S. Supreme Court.[42] The defendant, General Tomayuki Yamashita, was commander of the Japanese forces in the Philippines during the last months of the war, and under the stresses of a rapidly degenerating military position and overall collapse of military discipline, his troops committed numerous crimes against prisoners, civilians, and property. No charges were made that General Yamashita ordered the commission of criminal actions or approved of them. Indeed, it was inferred more than demonstrated that he even knew of the violations; there was no proof of knowledge beyond an assumption that he must have known something of the crimes simply because of their extent. The military commission nevertheless found him guilty of war crimes for "failing to provide effective control of his troops as required by the circumstances" and sentenced him to death. The sentence was upheld by the area commander, by General Douglas MacArthur, and finally by the Supreme Court.

A central issue, stressed by both supporters and opponents of the Supreme Court decision, was the responsibility of a commander for crimes committed by his troops *even* when the commander had no knowledge of the un-

[41]This formulation is the U.S. position, as set out in the 1956 U.S. Army *Field Manual* at para. 509, p. 182. The difference in wording from the "moral choice" formula of the Nuremberg Judgment and Principles is not significant in its effect. Principle IV of the Judgment provides as follows: "The fact that a person acted pursuant to order of his Government or of a superior does not relieve him from responsibility under international law, provided a moral choice was in fact possible to him."

[42]For a highly critical account of the *Yamashita* case, see A. Frank Reel, *The Case of General Yamashita* (University of Chicago Press, 1949). Reel was one of Yamashita's defense attorneys.

lawful acts.[43] "Command responsibility" is purported to be the central meaning of *Yamashita*, and the issue is then whether it should not be applied to the entire chain of command responsible for alleged American war crimes in Indochina.

Our view is that the *Yamashita* decision does not carry the weight assigned to it by ardent supporters or critics. At no point did the military commission or the Supreme Court hold that knowledge was irrelevant. It is true that the original decision by the commission did not make a specific finding of knowledge, but it did quote from and apparently accept prosecution evidence "to show that the crimes were so extensive and widespread, both as to time and area, that they must either have been willfully permitted by the accused, or secretly ordered by the accused."[44]

The Supreme Court's approach was extremely circumspect. It emphasized its very limited review powers over judgments of military tribunals, and held that its own power was effectively limited to deciding whether the charge made against the defendant was such as to authorize the commission to hear and decide the case. The Court also refused to deal with the evidence on which General Yamashita was convicted, and did not deal with the question of knowledge one way or the other.

The Court did decide that the precise substantive question before it was whether the laws of war imposed on a military commander an obligation to take "such appropriate measures as are within his power to control the troops under his command" for the prevention of war crimes.[45] The Court cited several provisions of conventional law (the Hague Conventions and the 1929 Geneva Convention) to demonstrate the existence of an international legal obligation for the defendant amounting to "an affirmative duty to take such measures as were within his power and appropriate in the circumstances to protect prisoners of war and the civilian population."[46]

The proposition of law which General Yamashita was held to have violated was thus formulated in a rather elliptical manner that avoided the element of knowledge while leaving it as a variable for consideration by the court of first instance. Given the significance of the issue and the punishment of death, it is regrettable that the Supreme Court did not present a full-scale analysis of the legal significance of a commander's knowledge, or

[43] See Richard A. Falk, Gabriel Kolko & Robert Jay Lifton, editors, *Crimes of War* (Vintage, 1971), 224-225; Taylor, *op. cit.*, pp. 91-92, 181-182; generally, Reel, *op. cit.*

[44] Reel, *op. cit.*, p. 169.

[45] *In Re Yamashita*, 327 U.S. 1 (1946) at 15. The Court also said "We consider here only the lawful power of the commission to try the petitioner for the offense charged." (at p. 8.)

[46] *Ibid.*, p. 16.

lack of knowledge, of war crimes committed by his troops. But the unsatisfactory nature of the Court's opinion in 1946 is certainly not to be taken as a clear statement that there is command responsibility for crimes of which a commander has *no* knowledge.

Another case of great importance in this context is *The High Command Case*, in which fourteen high Nazi military leaders were tried at Nuremberg subsequent to the main Nuremberg trials.[47] The defendants were charged with the planning and waging of aggressive war, war crimes against enemy belligerents, prisoners, and civilians, and crimes against humanity. The *High Command* tribunal argued that a commander cannot be completely informed of the details of military operations of his subordinates and "has the right to assume that details entrusted to responsible subordinates will be legally executed."[48] The tribunal asserted that criminal acts committed by American military forces could not in themselves be charged to the President of the United States simply because he is the commander-in-chief of the armed forces. And the same was held true for other high level officers in the chain of command.

> Criminality does not attach to every individual in this chain of command from that fact alone. There must be a personal dereliction. That can occur only where the act is directly traceable to him or where his failure to properly supervise his subordinates constitutes criminal negligence on his part. In the latter case it must be a personal neglect amounting to a wanton, immoral disregard of the action of his subordinates amounting to acquiescence. Any other interpretation of international law would go far beyond the basic principles of criminal law as known to civilized nations.[49]

We think the *High Command Case* is far preferable to the *Yamashita* holding, because it deals clearly with a crucial issue--knowledge--rather than avoiding it, and because the doctrine it evokes appears to be more equitable and better law. Further, as an expression by an international tribunal rendering judgment in one of a large series of war-crimes trials, its legal weight is probably greater than a judgement even of the U.S. Supreme Court, at least in terms of formulating rules of international law. And, ironically, it is far more likely than the Supreme Court ruling to win acceptance in the United States, among lawyers, the public, and government and military decision-makers. Investigation is more likely to be initiated and maintained if *High Command* is accepted as the relevant law rather than *Yamashita*. It is

[47]See *Trials of War Criminals Before the Nuremberg Military Tribunals* (USGPO, 1950), Vols. X and XI.

[48]*Ibid.*, Vol. XI, p. 544.

[49]*Ibid.*

important to note here that the U.S. Army *Field Manual* accepts the *High Command* test in stipulating that the commander is responsible "if he has actual knowledge, or should have knowledge" that his troops are about to commit or have committed a war crime and "he fails to take the necessary and reasonable steps to insure compliance with the law of war or to punish violators thereof."[50]

Only full-scale investigation will reveal which key officials, civilian and military, were aware of bombing policies that included unjustified devastation, reprisals, collective penalties, and grave breaches of the proportionality rule, as well as widespread destruction of food crops. The burden is particularly heavy for military commanders in Vietnam who, as many have noted, have had excellent communications and transportation facilities and little excuse for not knowing of criminal behavior.[51]

To date, while very limited inquiry has begun into crimes connected with ground actions--mostly those in connection with My Lai--there has been no comparable official investigation of crimes committed by means of aerial bombardment, and certainly no inquiry into high-level responsibility.

Whether high-level policy makers charged with war crimes should be punished or not if found guilty poses a troubling question for the U.S. and the world community. We are inclined to believe it should be answered in the negative. Domestic and international efforts along these lines are foreseeably futile, even assuming a general measure of agreement can be reached on the applicable law and the responsible persons. There is, moreover, substantial doubt whether punishment would result in any meaningful deterrence of subsequent criminal behavior. International law governing warfare has saved lives because the great majority of decision-makers and members of the armed forces have become imbued with its principles: but criminal activity has apparently not been deterred by past punishments. The essential purpose of focusing on international law, and elaborating the criteria of war crimes and individual responsibility, is not so much to punish as to educate, to create a constant awareness of broadly supported and sanctioned limitations on behavior even in war, and to establish a political and ethical consciousness more likely to minimize the cruelty and suffering resulting from armed conflict, especially as improvements in air war technology increasingly magnify the destructive capabilities of war.[52]

It may be argued that war crimes trials are themselves most responsible

[50] U.S. Army *Field Manual, op. cit.,* para. 501, pp. 178-179.

[51] Taylor, *op. cit.,* p. 181.

[52] See Falk, Kolko & Lifton, eds., *op. cit.,* pp. 3-10.

for generating a new political consciousness, or at least new laws of war, much as the Nuremberg and Tokyo trials did after World War II. Perhaps so, although high-level Congressional and international investigations, even without powers of punishment are likely to have as much effect. We would probably prefer such investigations to formal trials.

The clearest need in terms of legal regulation, however, is for a Hague-model, world-wide intergovernmental conference charged with drafting a convention on the laws of warfare, including aerial warfare, to establish more relevant and precise norms than the law currently in force. Preparatory work for such a conference has been undertaken by the International Committee for the Red Cross and meetings of government representatives have been held. The law has been permitted to lag for far too long, and the air war in Indochina has demonstrated anew how clear is the need for international law-making in an area of increasing importance.

D. THE NEED FOR INTERNATIONAL LEGAL REFORM CONCERNING AIR WARFARE

There has been a good deal of effort recently, particularly within the United Nations Human Rights Division[53] and in the International Committee of the Red Cross,[54] to formulate rules of warfare (including air warfare) more relevant to contemporary conflict than the Hague Regulations and the 1949 Geneva Conventions.

The weakness of current law on air combat stems not only from the generality of existing formulations and their obvious obsolescence, but also from the failure of the Big Four at Nuremberg and Tokyo to bring criminal charges in the context of air warfare. Neither the Nuremberg Judgment itself, the several Nuremberg cases that followed, nor the Tokyo Judgment have anything to say on the subject of aerial bombardment crimes. The reason seems clear enough. Serious questions of legality were raised by Allied target-area bombing in Germany, by the destruction of Dresden, and by the explosion of atomic bombs over Hiroshima and Nagasaki.

It appeared wiser to the Allies in the immediate aftermath of World War II to avoid these questions altogether, and no charges of criminal air bombardment were brought against anyone. Similarly, the Korean War produced no new law. The result has been quite damaging. The 1949 efforts to update the laws of war followed the Nuremberg lead and ignored air war. Moreover, the

[53]See United Nations Documents A/7720 of 20 November 1969 and A/8052 of 18 September 1970, both entitled "Respect for Human Rights in Armed Conflicts," Report of the Secretary-General.

[54]See International Committee of the Red Cross, Report of Experts, presented to the 21st International Conference of the Red Cross, Istanbul, Turkey, September 1969.

law was set back as questionable precedents were permitted to stand unchallenged. This weakened the notion that international law set any limits on aerial bombardment, which is important because the international legal system is particularly dependent upon the impact of precedent and world community acceptance of behavior patterns by nation-states.

Official efforts to regulate air operations in wartime have so far been remarkably few and almost totally ineffective.[55] The most ambitious attempt to devise a comprehensive code culminated in the publication of draft Rules of Aerial Warfare in 1923, a set of rules recommended by a commission of jurists who were given this task by an authorizing resolution passed at the 1921 Conference on the Limitation of Armaments. The draft was never ratified, however, and thus did not become binding international law. According to some writers, however, the rules suggested still possess "a strong persuasive authority, as the chief existing guide to the rules of air warfare."[56]

The 1923 draft code purports to regulate all aspects of air warfare, but for our purposes the key provision is Article 24 which lists the permissible targets for aerial bombardment. Article 24 drops the "open city" test of the 1907 Hague Regulations in favor of the criterion of "military objective," which is defined narrowly in the insistence that bombardment is legitimate only when directed at the following military targets:

> military forces; military works; military establishments or depots; factories constituting important and well-known centres engaged in the manufacture of arms, ammunition, or distinctly military supplies; lines of communication or transportation used for military purposes. (Article 24, para. 3)

This definition of military objective precludes destruction of industrial facilities of many kinds, such as oil and petroleum installations or chemical works, that can be of crucial importance in wartime. There is no chance whatever that important military powers can be persuaded to accept such restraints within a legally binding framework. Certainly, since it was written, this

[55] See Desaussure, *op. cit.*, p. 530. The initial provisions to govern aerial warfare were adopted at the First Hague Peace Conference in 1899 and stipulated that "The Contracting Powers agree to prohibit, for a term of five years, the launching of projectiles and explosives from balloons or by other new methods of a similar nature." The declaration was renewed in 1907 at the Second Hague Peace Conference and the intent was to keep it in force until the end of the Third Conference, scheduled for 1915 but never called. The declaration was intended to be in force in conflicts among contracting parties only; and since France, Russia and Spain never ratified--and Germany did so only on the condition that all other parties at the Conference ratify--its impact was nil. The only other officially adopted provision designed for regulating air warfare was Article 25 of the 1907 Hague Regulations, which banned attacks on an "open [undefended] city." This provision was subsequently weakened by emphasis on what constituted a "military objective," such a target being considered legitimate whether defended or not.

[56] See sources cited in footnote 4 above.

provision has been ignored in every war in which bombing played an important part.

The draft code was also found unacceptable by major military powers because of a provision prohibiting the bombardment of inhabited places or dwellings "not in the immediate neighborhood of the operations of land forces." Further it was stipulated that where legitimate military objectives could not be bombarded "without the indiscriminate bombardment of the civilian population, the aircraft must abstain from bombardment."[57] The major powers were not happy with either provision. There are many legitimate targets not in the immediate neighborhood of military operations on land, and this clause was therefore deemed clearly unacceptable. Abstention from bombing of legitimate targets to avoid "indiscriminate" bombings of civilians is in principle clearly meritorious. But target-area bombing has been accepted since World War II, and this fact probably precludes general acceptance of a similar prohibition today.

The code also stipulated that bombardment in the immediate neighborhood of land force operations is legitimate "provided that there exists a reasonable presumption that the military concentration is sufficiently important to justify such bombardment, having regard to the danger thus caused to the civilian population."[58] In general terms, the code also banned bombardment for terror purposes, or to destroy private property not of a military character, or to injure noncombatants.[59] There were also provisions for protected buildings, in the Hague Regulation fashion, and for immunity zones around such buildings.

Much of the code was considered realistic by the major powers, but the crucial provisions on legitimate military objectives and bombings only in the neighborhood of land operations were perceived as too confining to serve as an accepted code of law. Failure to ratify was not followed by renewed effort to reach agreement, and the draft rules were ignored during World War II.

The 1954 Hague Convention for the Protection of Cultural Property provides a more liberal definition by equating "military objectives" with "large industrial centers"(safety zones for movable cultural property must be an adequate distance from either in order to secure immunity from bombardment), and by listing as examples of legitimate military objectives targets such as ports, railway stations, broadcasting stations, etc. The 1954

[57] Article 24, para. 3.

[58] Article 24, para. 4.

[59] Article 22.

Convention was in force among 58 states as of 1970.[60]

While a legal rule prohibiting target area bombing *per se* is unlikely to receive approval by important military powers, the Red Cross and the UN Secretary-General have touched on the problem of bombings of civilians. The Secretary-General's Report calls for

> The prohibition of attacks directed against the civilian population, as such, whether with the objective of terrorizing it or for any other reason, and the consequential prohibition of attacks against dwellings, installations or means of transport, which are for the exclusive use of, and occupied by, the civilian population; in this connection, consideration might be given to the specific prohibition of the use of 'saturation' bombing as a means of intimidating, demoralizing and terrorizing civilians by inflicting indiscriminate destruction upon densely populated areas.[61]

While the wording is imprecise because there is no reference to legitimate military objectives that may be located in densely populated areas, the intent is reasonably clear--the preclusion of target-area bombardment. The Red Cross stipulates that to "attack without distinction, as a single objective, an area including several military objectives at a distance from one another [would be] forbidden whenever elements of the civilian population or dwellings, are situated in between."[62]

While target-area bombing during the Second World War was questioned, it came to be accepted as legally justifiable, largely because of the military significance of industrial concentrations such as that in the Ruhr valley, where population was mixed with industry and the targets were well concealed and very heavily defended. In defense of target-area bombing, Greenspan notes that it is "selective to the extent that the target is confined to a particular area; and the purpose of the bombing is the destruction of a military objective, all other damage being incidental," and he argues that

> Any legal justification of target-area bombing must be based on two factors. The first must be the fact that the area is so preponderantly used for war industry as to impress that character on the whole of the neighborhood, making it essentially an indivisible whole. The second factor must be that the area is so heavily defended from air attack that the selection of specific

[60] See *United Nations Treaty Series*, Vol. 249 (1956), No. 3511.

[61] United Nations Doc. A/8052, *op. cit.*, p. 17. The Secretary-General recommends a rule obligating the person responsible for ordering or launching an attack "to ensure that the objective to be attacked is not the civilian population or the dwellings, installations or means of transport, which are occupied by or for the exclusive use of civilians." *(Ibid.)*

[62] See Desaussure, *op. cit.*, p. 537.

targets within the area is impracticable.[63]

Quite clearly, this kind of analysis and legal justification are in no way applicable to much of the American bombing in Indochina. None of the tests cited above are met by "free-strike" zones or devastation policies. It is one thing to cause civilian deaths and property damage in the bombing of Ruhr industrial centers; it is quite another matter to bombard a village because an NLF unit was seen passing through the day before. In this sense, the ICRC and Secretary-General's conception of target-area bombing points to the Indochina experience rather than the Second World War. The impropriety of much of the American bombing throughout Indochina has been due to the absence in so many cases of a military objective important enough to justify destruction of entire towns and villages, and the motivation and purposes have frequently been legally untenable.

There is no doubt that military commanders will not relinquish the option of target-area bombing if they perceive it as helpful. In our view, however, the practice may be justified *only* if the conditions specified above are met. If they are not, the ICRC rule should merit the most serious consideration as the preferred policy. The Ruhr case is perhaps the justified exception to the preferred ICRC rule; but it is an exception, we feel, that should be very narrowly construed and applied. We would strongly support international law-making along these lines.

Another idea that has received considerable attention and support recently is that of civilian refugees or sanctuaries--areas for the protection of people and property that would be legally immune from bombardment. A substantial segment of the Secretary-General's Report of 18 September 1970 details recommendations for safety zones, somewhat after the 1949 Geneva Convention pattern of hospital and safety zones or otherwise neutralized areas. The Secretary-General outlines his notion of the conditions and obligations to be observed in the establishment and operation of civilian sanctuaries, their markings and insignia, and the essential control and verification required.[64] The Secretary-General wants to shelter "as large a part of the civilian population as possible, especially women, children, the elderly, the sick and those who do not participate in the armed conflict, nor contribute in any way to the pursuit of military operations."[65]

While we can agree with the purpose of such a proposal, the practical difficulties in implementing it would be immense, even aside from getting the

[63] Greenspan, *op. cit.*, p. 336.

[64] United Nations Doc. A/8052, *op. cit.*, paras. 45-87, pp. 18-30.

[65] United Nations Doc. A/7720, *op. cit.*, para. 145, p. 49.

parties involved to agree to it in principle. In guerrilla warfare, a crucial tactic is the deliberate mixing of military targets and combat units with the general population, and this creates an enormous obstacle to legal regulation of bombing. Moreover, in the implementation of such a scheme, there would occur the kind of dislocation of population currently resulting from bombardment, and devastation of areas outside the safety zones might actually be increased. In our view, more basic remedies need to be sought.

* * * * * *

Clearly air warfare has been left almost totally unregulated, and air commanders and crews have been left with only general customary law and rules of land warfare as sources of guidance. The need for new and precise law is evident. While the United Nations could help shape the law through its own interpretations, it is far preferable to regulate air war through well-drafted treaties and conventions that permit detailed applications of restraining rules and precise coverage. The need for general principles will certainly remain, particularly as technology continues to provide an ever more rapid proliferation of sophisticated and devastating air weaponry. But there is a clear need for more precise and contemporary regulation of bombing practices and weapons systems.

The great law-making efforts of 1899 and 1907 have not been repeated for nearly three-quarters of a century. We feel strongly that the world community should undertake another such effort. One possible positive consequence of the air war in Indochina could be a concerted international movement to curb at least the most devastating and wanton effects of air warfare for civilian populations. Certainly it is worth a serious attempt to ensure that continuing advances in weapons technology do not produce sophisticated barbarism on an ever increasing scale.

CHAPTER 12

COMBAT BY PROXY: THE EVOLUTION OF AIR WAR TECHNOLOGY*

> We have sensors that listen to sounds, detect the footsteps of people walking, smell the presence of human beings, and radars that detect trucks; we have MTI's [moving target indicators] on aircraft, we have coherent and noncoherent side-looking radars. We have infrared scanners, image converters, and infrared superheterodynes. We can use all of these sensors in remote-control and remote-reporting systems that we call the "instrumented battlefield."[1]

Since the Battle of Agincourt, where the English long-bow was decisive, warfare has become increasingly depersonalized. The distance between the combatants has become progressively greater, and each man has been given a growing offensive capability that permits him to kill many others with a single effort. The massive use of air power in World War II and in Korea contributed to this trend of increasing the physical and psychological separation between combatants and of minimizing the emotional interaction between them. The most recent developments in the instrumentation of warfare in Indochina have accelerated this trend considerably.[2] In this chapter, we will look at the development of this new technology and at some of its practical and ethical implications.

A. DEVELOPMENTS IN THE INDOCHINA AIR WAR

Many weapons of American aerial warfare in use in Indochina, such as helicopter gunships, B-52s, fragmentation antipersonnel weapons, napalm, and herbicides, are familiar to the public. Less widely known, however, are other recently developed systems for detecting and destroying vehicles and

*We would like to acknowledge the contributions of Carl Sagan and Robert Tolz to the first two sections of this chapter.

[1] E. Fubini, former IBM and DoD official, in *Impact of New Technologies on the Arms Race: A Pugwash Monograph*, B. T. Feld et al., ed. (M.I.T. Press, 1971), p. 153.

[2] A RAND Corporation report describes the trend in this way: "We have in hand the ability to develop systems that are manned, but *remotely manned* rather than with the man 'up front' in the vehicle. A remotely manned system is one in which the man controls the system in real time from a separate ground or airborne station, with his senses (typically vision) remoted to the vehicle. . . . In the remotely manned system the man does the tasks he is best equipped to do: recognize, discriminate, decide, adapt in real time. The machine does what it can do best: fly, track assigned targets, and so forth." Terrell E. Greene, *Some Design Possibilities for Tactical Aircraft in the Decade Ahead*, P-4362, (RAND Corporation, 1970).

people. Some of these systems have been field-tested extensively in Indochina while others are just reaching operational status.

The basic impetus for a majority of these systems has come from the need to improve the ability to interdict the movement of supplies and men, especially at night or in poor weather. When this movement is over well-organized route networks such as railroads or highways, air interdiction is relatively effective, provided the interdicting aircraft have access to the air space involved. In Indochina, the air environment has indeed been relatively "permissive," with U.S. planes having general air superiority, but the transportation targets by contrast are highly elusive. Supplies move over a network of jungle trails, much of it covered by dense tropical vegetation. These trails are hard to spot from the air. Even when they are bombed extensively, they can readily be repaired by men with shovels or with simple earth-moving equipment. Consequently, an effective interdiction campaign requires not only attacks on the supply routes and associated stationary targets such as storage areas, but also the destruction of the vehicles themselves and their cargo. Interdiction in Indochina, then, is a problem quite different from that of destroying a railroad marshalling yard or a multilane highway bridge.

The cover of vegetation can be removed, at least over certain segments of the trails, by defoliation or by direct bombing. The trucks and their attackers are then effectively eye-to-eye: in daylight hours, this situation favors the attacker who, by flying armed reconnaissance patrols over the region, can take an unacceptably high toll of any traffic moving below. The only recourse for the defenders would be to bring in enough anti-aircraft artillery to deny the aircraft ready access to the region. The rough jungle terrain, however, makes this difficult.

In response to this problem the movement of traffic has shifted to the night hours. People on the ground can still orient themselves at night by adapting to the low residual light level, by their sense of touch, or by ear. To a pilot none of these is any help; just blind-flying his plane is already a challenge. Of course he could turn night into day by dropping flares. But the Washbowl Effect and other shortcomings of illumination by flares have made this method of night interdiction ineffective.[3]

One of the tasks, then, has been to find a "replacement" for the human eye. A second task is to improve the accuracy of weapons delivery: improved accuracy not only increases the amount of destruction that can be inflicted,

[3] A pilot flying over a landscape illuminated only by flares gets the illusion that the terrain curves up around him on all sides, like a giant washbowl. This is a disorienting experience. Moreover, flares do not last very long and tend to show up the aircraft, making them excellent targets for gunners below.

but also lessens the number of sorties needed to achieve that level of destruction, thus reducing the cost in terms of pilot lives and aircraft lost. A third task is to increase the distance from the target at which the aircraft can release its weapons effectively; this permits the attacking aircraft to avoid the ground defenses, an advantage technically known as *standoff capability*.

Achieving these goals entails a series of technical problems which can be grouped under the headings (1) navigation; (2) target detection and identification; (3) aiming of weapons with precision through instrumentation on the aircraft or on the weapon itself; and (4) achieving standoff capability. These are the challenges which led to the development of what has come to be called the *electronic battlefield*.[4] In describing the various systems that have been developed, it is hard to avoid giving a somewhat technical account which may be of little interest to the general reader. Some jargon will inevitably find its way into the descriptions which follow, but we will concentrate on the general principles rather than on particulars.[5]

1. *Navigation*

Standard navigation instruments are adequate to guide a pilot into a desired region and to help him avoid flying into mountains; but if the navigational instruments are to determine also where the bombs should be dropped, much higher accuracy is required. Precision of navigation has been greatly improved recently through a combination of inertial guidance devices, such as are used on spacecraft, with Loran radio beacons.[6] Loran tells a pilot his position with respect to fixed, known radio transmitters, of which there are now three or four in Southeast Asia. Precise, extensive mapping of Indo-

[4]Much of the impetus for this development originated with ground combat objectives. We are, however, concerned primarily with its implications for air warfare. For a discussion of the "McNamara Line," which was to erect a ground barrier across the narrow part of Vietnam, just south of the DMZ, to be equipped with extensive sensor networks for detecting the movement of infiltrators, see *The Senator Gravel Edition, The Pentagon Papers* (Beacon, 1971), Vol. 4, pp. 112 ff. The line would have required many ground troops for patrols and enforcement, a major reason why it was not implemented. Such equipment integrated with air weapons, however, would be in large part "labor-saving."

Important organizational developments associated with the electronic battlefield include the Tactical Air Warfare Center, set up by the Tactical Air Command of the Air Force in 1963, and the Defense Communications Planning Group (whose misleading title has now been changed to Defense Special Projects Group), organized in September 1966. The latter group, with a priority on funds and manpower, was responsible for the development, within two years of its founding, of the IGLOO WHITE program for Trail interdiction over Laos.

[5]An extensive list of the components is given in "The Components and Manufacturers of the Electronic Battlefield," August 1, 1971, a preliminary summary compiled by Gene Massey for NARMIC (National Action/Research on the Military-Industrial Complex), American Friends Service Committee, Philadelphia, Pa. See also the *Electronic Battlefield Hearings* (1970). (For a key to abbreviated titles of hearings, see App. A.)

[6]*Aviation Week and Space Technology (AW&ST)*, July 13, 1970, p. 57.

china has been carried out to take advantage of this navigational capacity. A system recently introduced into Indochina to establish a blind-bombing capability is called PAVE PHANTOM. It is automated to the extent that the pilot need merely punch Loran data on the desired target position into his computer's keyboard, together with information about his chosen weapon, and the computer will steer the aircraft over the target and release the weapon. Blind bombing is not directed against individual trucks, but it can serve to attack area targets such as truck parks and supply depots, or it can be used to block choke points in the trails by actual modification of the terrain.[7]

2. *Target Detection and Identification*

a. *Airborne devices.* Even the most sophisticated machines have so far been unable to match the human eye's remarkable ability for recognizing subtle distinctions. A photograph is still the best way of identifying a person, and even such a simple problem as recognizing numerals on a bank check requires special printing in a distinctive style for the machine's benefit. So the most direct approach to target detection is an airborne device that projects an image of the ground scene on a screen for the pilot to examine. The simplest such system is Low Light-Level Television (LLLTV), which uses very sensitive TV cameras to view the nighttime scene in the residual light. This system fails if the night is very dark or if visibility is hindered by clouds. Under such conditions the ground may be scanned by radar signals, which are unaffected by weather but yield less clarity of detail.

Images may also be formed with infrared radiation, emitted by all objects according to their temperature. A recently perfected device called Forward Looking Infrared (FLIR) picks out objects which are warmer than their surroundings. Aimed from the front of the aircraft, it can detect men, cooking fires, recently stopped vehicles, or foxholes. In all of these systems the pilot obtains a less realistic view, of course, and his ability to pick out and identify the desired targets is correspondingly impaired.[8]

There have been many attempts to design more specific target detection devices. These make their selection by keying on individual items of information which are deemed to be characteristic of the targets but not of their surroundings. Moving vehicles may be spotted by means of the electrical interference signals generated by their ignition systems. Smoke from engines or fires can be picked up by a device which detects particulate matter in the

[7] The American bombing technique of making roads unusable by causing rockslides across them from adjacent hillsides is described by Henry Kamm, *New York Times,* April 11, 1971.

[8] For information on LLLTV, FLIR, and other airborne systems, see *AW&ST*, November 3, 1969, p. 63; May 3, 1971, p. 48; May 10, 1971, p. 75; June 22, 1970, p. 155.

air.[9] The Moving Target Indicator (MTI) distinguishes objects in motion relative to their background by applying sophisticated electronic techniques to the processing of radar signals.[10] A very ambitious device, the Augmented Target Screening Subsystem (ATSS), is being developed to recognize targets in categories selected by the pilot by means of the special patterns of the infrared radiation emitted from them.[11]

All these devices share a common limitation: they attempt to identify a target by means of one or two characteristic features, rather than by an overall process of recognition. Not only is such one-sided identification quite fallible, but it naturally invites the use of *decoys*, some of them very simple. Warm objects can be proliferated on the ground at little cost, electrical signals can be generated in profusion, and radar images can be falsified. As a result of this depersonalized and formalized target search, unintended targets may be struck or fire may be diverted by the enemy toward harmless decoys.

b. *Ground-implanted sensor devices.* Instead of gathering information from the air, devices for target detection may also be implanted in the ground or suspended in the foliage. Such devices may be scattered by aircraft over the regions to be monitored; being battery-operated, they may have useful lives of several months.[12] The sensors can detect vibrations from trucks or people; they can listen to sounds; they may be sensitive to metallic objects, to heat radiation, or to chemical emanations from human beings.[13] As one commentator has put it, "We wired the Ho Chi Minh trail like a drugstore pinball machine, and we plug it in every night."[14]

The information is transmitted by high-frequency radio to receivers which must be in the line of sight--on exposed mountain tops or in continu-

[9] Such a device can be used in a helicopter, for example, to pick up the smoke "plume" from a distant camp fire in the forest. The helicopter can then weave its way in along the plume, guided by the particle detector, until it finds the location of the fire.

[10] Looking down on the ground from a plane with radar, one obtains reflected signals from all parts of the terrain. These signals "clutter up" the display and obscure the tiny blips which might correspond to the desired targets. Electronic filtering techniques can be used to separate those radar signals which come from moving objects, permitting a much less cluttered display.

[11] Pattern recognition by machines is still in its infancy. These devices rely for their target criteria on the sharp contour edges presented by man-made objects, or on extensive areas with uniform surface properties.

[12] For more information on ground sensors, see "Igloo White," *Air Force*, June 1971; and *Electronic Battlefield Hearings* (1970), pp. 109 ff.

[13] For example, "urine sniffers" detect the ammonia molecules present in human and animal urine.

[14] "Battle for Control of the Ho Chi Minh Trail, *Armed Forces Journal*, February 15, 1971, p. 19.

ously airborne communications aircraft.[15] The signals are then relayed to a central processing post where the responses of the various sensors are correlated, conversations may be monitored, and the decision to strike a certain region is finalized. Any delay involved in this processing chain is a handicap; immediate action (*real time* response, in current jargon) is the aim of COMMANDO BOLT, a computerized system which displays sensor responses directly on a map of the region and produces target coordinates which allow strike aircraft to proceed to their targets automatically, guided by their on-board computers.[16]

3. *Weapons Delivery*

The accuracy with which munitions can be directed against a chosen spot on the ground is measured in terms of the *circular error probable* (CEP).[17] Just how small the CEP must be to achieve the desired effectiveness depends

[15] Initially, large transport planes were used, loaded with enough equipment to process the data and to direct fighter planes to the attack. But such manned aircraft are expensive to operate and very vulnerable to ground fire, so small commercial planes under the code name PAVE EAGLE have been replacing the transports, relaying the signals to a ground station for processing. These planes can act as drones, circling unmanned under the control of a UNIVAC microwave command guidance system, eliminating all risk to American pilots, and reducing the risk to expensive equipment. See "Igloo White," *op. cit.*, p. 51; also *DMS Market Intelligence Reports* (McGraw Hill Publications), February 1971.

[16] "Battle for Control of the Ho Chi Minh Trail," *op. cit.*, p. 22. The procedure is described by George L. Weiss as follows:

> When the sensors have provided enough information to the computer the action shifts to another room in the ISC [Infiltration Surveillance Center] known as COMMANDO BOLT, a term which refers to one of the most sophisticated combat control functions in the Air Force. The decision can also be made to switch the scene of the action to an Airborne Battlefield Command and Control Center . . .
>
> The function is usually retained at the ISC if the situation does not appear to require airborne assessment. In that event the computer switches the sensor-acquired information to the ground-based Assessment Officer [AO] in the building who will direct the air attack.
>
> A TV-type screen provides the Assessment Officer a map of the section of Laos under his control. Each of the roads used by the North Vietnamese in his area is etched on his screen. As the seismic and acoustic sensors pick up the truck movements their locations appear as an illuminated line of light, called 'the worm,' that crawls across his screen, following a road that sometimes is several hundreds of miles away.
>
> From there the battle becomes academic. The Assessment Officer and the computer confer on probable times the convoy or convoys will reach a pre-selected point on the map. This point is a 'box' selected by the Igloo White team of experts at the ISC. Airborne at the moment are gunships and fighters. A decision is made as to the type of ordnance best suited for the area.
>
> If the trucks are moving under jungle canopy, it is likely the AO will select fighters armed with CBU type weapons and attack the convoy with them. If the convoy can be caught in an open area, then gunships will be waiting for them. "The Air Force's Secret Electronic War," *Military Aircraft*, 1971. Reprinted in *Indochina Chronicle*, October 15, 1971, p. 6. See footnote 32 below for a discussion by two AOs of their mode of operation in practice.

[17] The CEP is the radius of a circle centered on the aiming point such that, on the average, half the bombs dropped strike within it. See Sec. 2-B, p. 24.

on several factors: the size and vulnerability of the target (vulnerable targets are called *soft*, more resistant ones are *hard*); the precision with which the location is known; and, above all, the power and radius of destruction of the weapon itself.

In the 1950's, when nuclear weapons were considered the mainstay of U.S. aerospace armaments, no great emphasis was placed on improving bombing accuracy.[18] In a limited war fought with conventional munitions, however, accurate delivery becomes more important. Through recognition of this fact in Indochina, performance criteria in research and development have been changing: less emphasis is placed on maximizing the weight of munitions expended and more on reducing the cost of destroying the target and the number of sorties required. According to an analyst close to the military, "the institutional bias against better CEPs is being eroded by realities of modern limited war and the effects of inflation."[19]

One approach through which planners have attempted to increase delivery accuracies is through improvements in the aircraft itself, by automating the weapons release process; an on-board computer is utilized to carry out ballistic calculations, directing the aircraft's approach run as well as releasing the munitions at the appropriate moment. The incorporation of such systems into recently introduced aircraft such as the A-6E and the A-7D/E has resulted in improved CEP performance.[20]

However, the most important development in weapons delivery has probably been the evolution of *smart* bombs or rockets, i.e., those which during flight can home in on their intended targets.[21] A system in extensive use works as follows: the target is designated by shining an intense beam of laser light on it; the bomb detects the reflected light and follows it to the target. The laser designator can be operated from the ground, from a FAC plane, or from the strike aircraft itself. An airborne designator may be pointed at the target once and then set to hold its direction automatically despite the motion of the aircraft.

Conventional high explosive bombs are commonly used, modified by the addition of a laser guidance kit. On the nose there is a sensor to pick up the laser radiation from the target spot; on the tail there are movable fins which steer the bomb in the required flight path. Such bombs can be released from about 20,000 feet altitude and still score direct hits in as many as

[18] *Tactical Air Hearings* (1968), p. 129.

[19] Barry Miller, *AW&ST*, May 3, 1971, p. 49.

[20] *AW&ST*, May 3, 1971, p. 51, and January 9, 1969, p. 93.

[21] *Electronic Battlefield Hearings* (1970), p. 146; *AW&ST*, May 3, 1971, p. 48; January 19, 1970, p. 55; June 22, 1970, p. 155; and July 13, 1970, p. 55.

80 percent of the cases.[22] They are effective against stationary interdiction targets such as bridges and cave entrances; against moving trucks their use is limited by the target's mobility and by the relatively high cost of of the guidance outfit.[23] Of course the whole system can be used only when the laser designator is unobstructed by clouds or other obstacles.

The BULLPUP, an early type of guided bomb, was steered via radio control by the pilot, who visually tracked it to its target. The WALLEYE carries a TV camera and can be set, at release, to home in automatically on a selected visual feature. These smart bombs, like the laser-guided versions, can be used only under conditions of good visibility.

There is also a guidance kit for bombs which steers them automatically in response to Loran navigational signals. Such bombs are directed to predetermined map coordinates and need no attention after release. However, Loran accuracy is not high enough to achieve anything like pin-point bombing accuracy, so these bombs are useful only against fixed targets and using "area munitions" whose destructive effects extend over a wide area.

4. *Standoff Capability*

Improved standoff capability is achieved through increasing the distance from the target at which weapons can be released with the desired accuracy. Some standoff capability results from the use of guided bombs, since they can be released from very high altitudes and the aircraft can stay out of the most effective range of ground defenses. Even greater separation between the plane and its target is provided by self-propelled air-to-ground missiles, whose range may be many miles and whose accuracy is augmented by guidance or homing during flight. For example, the MAVERICK and the CONDOR can be launched from a distance, with their optical tracking systems set to seek out a distinguishing feature of the chosen target (such as the dark mouth of a cave). Such weapons are as yet limited in their versatility. Continuing research and development are, however, being devoted to them to further automate the conduct of air warfare.

B. A FORWARD LOOK AT TECHNOLOGICAL DEVELOPMENT

With this outline of the technical developments which contribute toward the implementation of the *electronic battlefield* we turn to a consideration of its progress thus far and its implications for the future.

[22] *AW&ST*, June 22, 1970, p. 167; also "Igloo White," *op. cit.*

[23] An assembled guided bomb costs about four to five times as much as a conventional "iron" bomb. For 1971 smart bombs reportedly accounted for less than one percent of the total weight of munitions dropped in Indochina. *Ithaca Journal (AP)*, January 15, 1972.

So far, advances in navigation and computerized weapons release have had their greatest impact on interdiction attacks by fixed-wing aircraft against stationary, soft targets; some degree of blind bombing capability has been achieved. Ground sensors are used primarily for accumulating intelligence for pre-planned strikes on stationary targets, though they are utilized for immediate strikes against trucks in COMMANDO BOLT. The airborne sensor devices, on the other hand, have found their most important use in the truck interdiction campaign over the Ho Chi Minh trail, about which the Air Force has recently made such impressive claims. The U.S. night interdiction capability there rests on fixed-wing gunships, first deployed in 1968, that carry various combinations of the night viewing and other target detection devices described above. Armed with large-caliber, rapid-firing cannon, the gunships are able to operate from altitudes of 5,000 to 10,000 feet.[24]

The enormous U.S. industrial and scientific research base has made possible these rapid advances in weapons technology, but the demand for new military capabilities plus the availability of a combat testing ground in Indochina has been a major contributing factor to these developments. The results portend significant changes in the mode of operation of U.S. tactical air power for the future, particularly in counterinsurgency operations. Military enthusiasm for these systems obviously centers on their technical performance, on their cost savings, and their increased effectiveness.[25] Spokesmen have claimed that electronic battlefield developments have significantly reduced a "long recognized deficiency of tactical airpower--its lack of a high-confidence, all-weather interdiction capability."[26] The Air

[24] *AW&ST*, May 10, 1971, p. 76. For a more detailed discussion of the recent AC-130 gunships, see "AC-130 Gunships Destroy Trucks and Cargo," *Air Force*, September 1971, p. 18. In the latest models, 40-mm cannon firing up to 6,000 shells per minute are used. The larger calibers have been added recently in an attempt to destroy the cargo more effectively as well as disabling the truck itself. They also enable the aircraft to operate from altitudes of about 10,000 feet, above the effective range of much of the smaller AAA fire.

[25] Senator Barry Goldwater has described these developments as having "the possibility of being one of the greatest steps forward in warfare since gunpowder." [*Electronic Battlefield Hearings* (1970), p. 3.] Estimates of the cost of the Electronic Battlefield run from $3.25 billion to $20 billion. [*Congressional Record,* July 13, 1970, S11104.] According to the *DMS Market Intelligence Report,* $1.7 billion has been spent in the last five years, "and the predominant verdict in military and political circles is that 'it is worth every cent.'" [*Op. cit.*] George L. Weiss writes: "When you balance it out in dollars it may not be the cheapest way to fight a war. When you balance it out in [our] lives lost it certainly is. Every bullet destroyed on the Ho Chi Minh trail is one less that will be fired at an American or a Vietnamese villager." [*Op. cit.*, p. 6.] (This argument ignores the possibility that extra bullets may be shipped to replace those destroyed so that the number "getting through" is not substantially reduced.)

[26] As quoted in "Battle for Control of the Ho Chi Minh Trail," *op. cit.; Armed Forces Journal,* May 3, 1971; and in "Igloo White," *op. cit.* Officials claim that IGLOO WHITE technology has enabled the U.S. to improve substantially the efficiency of its interdiction campaign in the Laotian panhandle. For the most recent figures, see *Air Force,* September 1971, p. 42; cf. also Sec. 5-B.

Force has begun a modest program for the integration of IGLOO WHITE technology into its world-wide operational capability, and the success of the gunship packages has resulted in a follow-on program, the goal of which is "a fully operational force of such weapon systems to be used mainly in a nighttime close air support and interdiction role."[27]

What tends to be forgotten or minized are the limitations inherent in the system. Sensors are vulnerable to decoys and countermeasures, and the possibilities for false responses abound.[28] The battle between men and machines is not as one-sided as the machine designers claim. Highly motivated men are amazingly resourceful, and, as mentioned previously, automated detectors are an open invitation to human ingenuity.

Beyond practical limitations there lies a fundamental problem. When friend and foe are intermingled, how can electronic sensing and controlling devices discriminate between them? This remains a basic problem under any conditions. A seismic detector cannot tell the difference between a truck full of arms and a school bus; a urine sniffer cannot tell a military shelter from a woodcutter's shack.[29] The further the U.S. goes down the road to automation, and the greater its capital investment becomes relative to its investment in manpower, the more deeply will it become committed to this blind form of warfare.[30]

[27] *Electronic Battlefield Hearings* (1970), pp. 154-155 and 162; and *Air University Review*, XX (1969), No. 4, p. 80. The USAF took over management responsibility for IGLOO WHITE from the Defense Communications Planning Group on January 1, 1971. [*Aerospace Daily*, January 21, 1971.]

[28] The term "false alarm" has been stricken from the vocabulary; one refers now to a *nontargetable activation*. *Electronic Battlefield Hearings* (1970), p. 96.

[29] The following exchange bearing on this problem occurred during the Electronic Battlefield Hearings:

> *Mr. Gilleas*. There is a lot of interest in the ability of sensors to discriminate between enemy forces and friendly civilians who are out in remote areas. I wonder if you would comment on the role of the military commander and his judgment, and whether he does or does not bring firepower to bear. The question is, how do we prevent sensors from killing innocent people versus enemy troops?
> *Maj. Gen. John R. Deane, Jr., USA*. You say the sensors won't tell you. And the sensors might give you an indication if over an acoustic sensor you heard voices and determined from the conversation that they were enemy, that is the only way I would know you could be able to tell. Now when you get into that kind of problem, you have to bring to bear your knowledge of where your friendly forces are, where it is likely friendly people are civilians and use your best judgment. I think the commanders that I have known, if they had any doubts they would not fire.
> *Senator Goldwater*. Could you tell by a formation count?
> *Maj. Gen. Deane*. I think that would be an indication, sir, but, you know, you could have in Vietnam, for example, a group of woodcutters coming back down the trail that may look like a squad of them [Vietcong]; you could make a mistake, I think. [*Op. cit.*, p. 33]

[30] Gen. William Westmoreland, Army Chief of Staff, has stated: "On the battlefield of the future, enemy forces will be located, tracked, and targeted almost instantaneously through the use of data links, computer assisted intelligence evaluation, and automated fire control. . . . I am confident the American people expect this country to take full advantage

Air Force spokesmen frequently point out that the data from electronic target detection and acquisition machinery are never used without collation with other inputs, and that no counteraction is ever ordered without the intervention of the "essential element of trained human judgment."[31] The human operator, however, is terribly remote from the consequences of his actions; he is most likely to be sitting in an air-conditioned trailer, hundreds of miles from the area of battle; from there he assesses "target signatures," evaluates ambiguities in the various sensor systems, collates their reports, and determines the tactical necessity for various forms of action which are then implemented automatically.[32] For him, the radar blip and flashing lights no more represent human beings than the tokens in a board-type war game. War and war games become much the same.[33]

Moreover, an explicit goal of research and development programs is an improved "real-time" response, in all conditions of weather and visibility, to the information provided by the detection apparatus. The present bottleneck in the automated response process, as perceived by the Air Force, lies in the analysis of this information. According to the head of the Air Force

of its technology--to welcome and applaud the developments that will replace wherever possible the man with the machine." [*Congressional Record,* July 13, 1970, S11104]

[31]"Investigation into Electronic Battlefield Program," Report of the Electronic Battlefield Subcommittee of the Preparedness Investigating Subcommittee of the Committee on Armed Services, U.S. Senate (USGPO, 1971), p. 5.

[32]Two Assessment Officers commented on their experience in Indochina, in an interview with Bob Schieffer, as follows:

> *John Smith.* In order to break up the boredom and to get good credit on your record, to show everyone else that your equipment is working well, that you're doing a good job, you want to fire right away, and you're not as interested in discriminating because you're not looking at what you're firing at, and you don't have to go up there and clean it up. You don't have to look and see whether it's men, women or children. You're essentially going to fire, and then--and try to stop the [blip].
>
> *Gregory Hayward.* My experience has been that on--when you use an airborne electronic device, sensor device of any kind, that there's no checking as to who you're firing on because the curfew covers our conscience on that. We have the curfew which says nobody, no civilian is allowed out in the countryside at night, and if you pick up somebody moving at night, that's it. There's no checking. [*CBS Evening News,* June 26, 1971]

[33]An account provided us by a retired General further illustrates this potential for depersonalization. He reported that when he was a student at the National War College he began to sense a regularity in the responses of the student officers to the various war game scenarios endemic to such places of higher military learning. When faced with situations requiring either a diplomatic or a military response to a given crisis, experienced Navy PT-boat commanders tended to favor diplomatic solutions, while Polaris submarine commanders preferred tactical or strategic military responses. Similar distinctions were observed between Army infantry and artillery commanders, and between Air Force Tactical Air Command and Strategic Air Command officers. He concluded that those officers who were confronted directly with the consequences of their actions in the form of human lives lost, whether adversary, neutral, or allied, were more reluctant to resort to military solutions. Those officers whose weapons systems delivered death remotely were much more willing to call awesome amounts of firepower into play.

Systems Command Laboratories the "big problem" facing the labs today is how to analyze and correlate this input data for immediate response: "Microelectronics, coupled with new storage devices, offers some hope of dealing effectively with the data manipulation problem . . ."[34] But, to the extent that this problem in data manipulation is solved, the contribution from human judgment in the target selection process is likely to decline.

Automated warfare has certain "advantages," however, apart from its technical features. Instruments do not defect. They are not known to take consciousness-expanding drugs, nor to have ethical qualms about coincidental killing of civilians. They do more or less what they are told, and represent a powerful, mechanized, mercenary army. Ultimately we can have the machines fighting the "target signatures" with no human beings involved on either side! As two commentators have put it, the Electronic Battlefield

> . . . eliminates a constant problem of Vietnam and other wars--that some men must go and fight while others watch on television. With the truly automated system, everybody, including the soldiers, will watch the war on televisions--the only difference between the Army and the American Legion being the placement of the viewing screen.[35]

The very existence of such an advanced technology produces pressures for its use; it will be hard to resist deploying these powerful weapons and gadgets for "countering insurgency" wherever found. Such a movement may have indirect consequences of considerable import. For example, the channeling of scientific and engineering effort into destructive applications of this sort may well encourage the currently emerging disaffection with technology *per se*, when in fact technology may be needed for extracting mankind from a wide range of ecological disasters. This disaffection in the U.S. is fueled by the recognition that American scientists and engineers--civilians as well as those working for the Department of Defense--have been deeply involved in the development of the electronic battlefield.[36]

[34] Brig. Gen. Raymond Gilbert, "The AFSC Laboratories," *Air University Review*, XX (1969), No. 2, pp. 17 and 19.

[35] Paul Dickson and John Rothchild, "The Electronic Battlefield: Wiring Down the War," *The Washington Monthly*, May 1971.

[36] For example, at the 30th Anniversary Research Conference on Instrumentation Science, sponsored by the Instrument Society of America, there was a full-day session [July 27, 1971] on "Problems in Military Sensors," chaired by Dr. Marvin E. Lasser, Department of the Army. The papers included: "Introduction to Battlefield Sensors and Related Computer Systems," Dr. Marvin E. Lasser; "Unattended Ground Sensors," Mr. Manfred Gale, Department of the Army; "Attended Ground Sensors," Dr. Paul Kruse, Honeywell, Inc.; "Airborne Sensors," Dr. Richard Legault, Willow Run Laboratories, University of Michigan; "Airborne Readout of Ground Sensors," Mr. Victor L. Friedrich, Department of the Army; "Control of Air Space," Dr. Richard L. Haley, Department of the Army. There is little doubt that popular disaffection with science and scientists, engineers and technology is accelerated when professional organizations lend themselves, with little or no discussion of the larger human consequences, to such activities.

C. AIR WAR TECHNOLOGY AND THE PROBLEM OF RESTRAINT IN WARFARE

The difference between war and a competitive sport has always been clear. A game of tennis cannot be won by blasting one's opponent clear off the court: the concept of "winning" is, by definition, tied to the rules of the game. Not so in war. Here the explicit objective is to reduce the opponent to a state of helplessness or willingness to capitulate. Anything that furthers this aim is part of the effort; there is no umpire who might invalidate a victory that was won by breaking the rules. Of course there are moral reasons for not going to excess with the destructive process of war--indiscriminate killing and devastation are repugnant to the individual, and few governments would subscribe to them as a matter of avowed policy. However, the exercise of moral restraint in practice comes under constant pressure from the practical calculations of the moment. If the advantages gained by transgressing a moral limitation appear great enough, the limitation is likely to give way. The practical calculations must of course take into account the possibility that the opponent, or one of his allies, will retaliate in like manner. This is a major factor inhibiting the unrestrained quest for immediate advantage; by comparison, moral rectitude exerts a very limited leverage. History abounds with examples of ruthless warfare, to say nothing of gratuitous brutality and wholesale massacre, in cases where one of the adversaries was free from the fear of retaliation.

Modern warfare poses new problems not because of a decline in morals as such, but because its impact has increased so dramatically through the evolution of the weapons of war. At one time, war's ruthlessness was to some degree discriminating: a distinction between soldiers and noncombatants was possible. Fighters were a specialized breed, and to kill civilians was an act not justified by military necessity, but motivated by religious or ideological fervor, by passion or sadism. With the growing organizational and industrial capacities of modern nations, the definition of a *combatant* grew broader. The requirement of massive mobilization of national resources made civilian society an integral part of the war-making machine, radically altering the concepts of "combatant" and "front line." The airplane and other long-range weapons then permitted the belligerents to cross the old front lines and get at the new.

This was a signal feature of World War II, when strategic bombing missions encompassed civilians as well as strictly military targets. Indiscriminate "terror" bombing of population centers was adopted by the British air force with the avowed objective of breaking German morale.[37] As the

[37]During the fall of 1940, British planners "began to speculate that German morale might be

Allies acquired air superiority, there were not only increased attacks against industrial targets of direct military significance, but also an increase in the scale of less discriminate bombing.[38] Similarly, in the air war against Japan when the U.S. forces had complete control of the air and could have been highly selective, 80 percent of the high-explosive and fire bombs dropped by B-29s were directed against urban areas, with devastating effect on the populations of Tokyo and other central cities.[39] The two nuclear bombs were dropped on cities at least one of which (Nagasaki) was of such limited economic and military significance that previously it had remained virtually unscathed.[40]

The subsequent major conflicts, in Korea and in Indochina, have been marked by a continuing emphasis on strategic bombing missions. Particularly in counterinsurgency warfare, such strategic missions tend to be lacking in discrimination and to be directed against the civilian population and the structure of society at large. A highly industrialized nation has many obvious targets of military significance which are fixed at known locations; in counterinsurgency operations, by contrast, targets are small and generally elusive, and most are highly mobile. Specific strikes on such targets are usually beyond the technical capabilities of air warfare; the category of strategic targets is then broadened to justify the more indiscriminate patterns of bombing.[41]

Rather than renounce the use of weapons which have been the subject of so much theorizing, research, development, and investment, the military effectiveness of strategic air power is vigorously extolled. Exaggerated claims are made about the results of such bombing, and consideration of ancillary damage is minimized. Shattering the enemy's morale and breaking his will to resist become military objectives, and damage or terror against civilians within enemy territory, whether intentional or not, is considered acceptable.[42]

a key target, . . . [a conclusion which] stemmed partially from the disappointing inaccuracies shown in missions against precise targets." These speculations were operationalized in February 1942, when the RAF Bomber Command was ordered "to embark on a new offensive, of which the primary target would now be the morale of the German people." George Quester, "Bargaining and Bombing During World War II in Europe," *World Politics*, April 1963, pp. 417-437. See App. B-I.

[38] See App. B, Table B-1.

[39] See App. B, Table B-2.

[40] *United States Strategic Bombing Survey: Summary Report (Pacific War)* (USGPO, 1946), p. 24.

[41] This kind of strategic thinking is presented by Kipp in "Counterinsurgency from 30,000 Feet: The B-52 in Vietnam," *Air University Review*, January-February 1968, pp. 13-20. It parallels British military thinking reported in footnote 37 above.

[42] For statements on current U.S. doctrine concerning the uses of strategic air power, see the following articles in the *Air University Review*: "Psychological Operations and Air

Such a broadening of the concept of military necessity implies that, in a conflict between equals, war will rapidly escalate to the stage of *total* warfare. If the adversaries are grossly unequal in their command of capital and technology, it implies that destruction will be inflicted unilaterally by the stronger on the weaker. The weaker nation's inability to retaliate leaves the stronger free to act with impunity. What restraints are there then remaining to limit the amount of devastation which can be unleashed? We have seen, in Chapter 11, that the rules of war have not been able to keep up with the explosive developments of the technology of warfare. Moreover, in the observance of what rules there are, the chief consideration has not been moral restraint so much as expediency.[43] Moral judgments would ideally be called upon to limit the destruction to the strict minimum justifiable by self-defense. Such restraint becomes ever more necessary as new technologies augment the power deployed by the weapons of war; and it becomes the only hope for limiting destruction of life and land when the contestants are so mismatched as to permit one of them to operate without fear of retaliation.

Unfortunately, the effectiveness of moral restraints in practice has never been great; and there are factors in the new technologies which serve to undermine the foundations on which such restraints rely in large measure. The change in attitude is already profound in the normal exercise of strategic air power. It becomes particularly marked, however, with the evolution of the electronic battlefield and of automated warfare, the full development of which has far-reaching implications.

Remote-controlled warfare reduces the need for the public to confront the consequences of military action abroad. The cost of a fully automated war can be reckoned in dollars and machinery--a small price compared to a harvest of casualties. No longer must the leaders of a nation first establish widespread support for the policies which require fighting a war. Wars

Power," March-April 1971, pp. 34-36; "Interdiction--A Dying Mission?" Jan.-Feb. 1971, pp. 56-59; "Power, Strategy, and Will," *ibid.*, pp. 19-26; "History, Vietnam, and the Concept of Deterrence," Sept.-Oct. 1969, pp. 51-57; "Gradualism--A Flexible Response," May-June 1969, pp. 63-68; "U.S. Policy in Asia," March-April 1969, pp. 93-96; "Whose side is God on?" *ibid.*, pp. 97-101; "What is Security in S.E. Asia?" Nov.-Dec. 1968, pp. 103-112; "Korea in Retrospect," *ibid.*, pp. 113-117; "SAC: An Instrument of National Policy," Jan.-Feb. 1968, pp. 2-9. On the military effectiveness of strategic bombing in Indochina, see *Defense Hearings for 1970*, House Appropriations Committee, Pt. 3, pp. 1074-75 and Pt. 7, pp. 394-95, 412, 428; also *ibid*. for 1971, Pt. 5, p. 713; and *ibid*. for 1972, Pt. 1, pp. 818, 872.

[43] For example, according to the former commander of U.S. forces in Vietnam, Lt. Gen. Samuel T. Williams, his recommendation to bomb the "dikes and dams on the Red River, north and west of Hanoi . . . to put Hanoi under a couple of feet of water . . . and hurt them badly" was rejected by superiors because of its "political naivete," not because of moral scruples. [See Interview in *Oakland Tribune*, August 20, 1965.] Similarly, Gen. Maxwell Taylor stated his grounds for opposing the bombing of the city of Hanoi itself: "I wouldn't think we would want to bomb Hanoi. I think that we need the leadership in Hanoi to be intact to make those essential decisions we hope they will make sometime." [*New York Times*, November 23, 1965.]

can be entered quickly, if need be even in a clandestine manner, and fought with minimum repercussions at home.[44] Indeed, an automated war might soon fade from the public consciousness and become *institutionalized*. Modern air capabilities make realistic Orwell's vision of *1984*.

Remote-controlled warfare also reduces the need for emotional conditioning of the armed forces so that they can engage in face-to-face killing. With automated war the combatants are *technicians*. Their powers of destruction are enormous, but their emotional involvement can be small. The use of complex gadgetry and the acquisition of the skills to operate it successfully can endow the entire destructive process with the characteristics of a game. The mere manipulation of the machinery is absorbing and pleasurable, like playing with a super-sophisticated pinball machine. The effects or merits of the actions are not considered; if such questions arise at all, they are dismissed as matters for high-level decision of no legitimate concern to those who execute the commands.[45]

At work, too, is the psychological principle derived from Milgram's experiments, that one's sense of responsibility is weakened toward persons he cannot see.[46] Through its isolation of the military actor from his target, automated warfare diminishes the inhibitions which could formerly be expected on the individual level in the exercise of warfare. With calm detachment, and without even being aware of it, persons can participate in the kind of indiscriminate destruction and killing which, in the context of conventional

[44]For example, American participation in the war in Laos was not acknowledged publicly until several years after it had begun in earnest; cf. Chap. 6. This war involved Americans principally through the use of air power. Contrast this with the war in Vietnam, which involved the deployment of a large number of U.S. ground troops. There was much effort at public justification of the American involvement, in political *and* moral terms. American troops are now being withdrawn from Vietnam, largely in response to pressure from the public; but the air war continues.

[45]Various reports from the theater of war support these conclusions. For example, a B-52 pilot in Indochina told a CBS reporter: "I think anyone who dwells on what he does over here in any long term sense, he's probably going nuts. . . . I don't dwell on it. . . . I don't think anybody else in the crew could. . . . The entire scope of things is just too big for us to understand." [*CBS News with Walter Cronkite*, December 21, 1971.] Cf. also the reports of interviews with carrier-based pilots aboard the *Coral Sea* [*New York Times*, January 9, 1972, and the account given in footnote 32, above.

[46]In a now-classic experiment, Stanley Milgram tested the conditions under which persons would obey or disobey commands to hurt another person. As part of a "learning experiment," subjects were told to give the "learner" increasingly strong shocks as "punishment" for making mistakes. The dial showed shocks ranging from 30 volts ("Slight shock") to 450 volts ("Danger: Severe shock"). The victim did not actually receive the shocks but was cued to act convincingly as though he did.

Four different relationships between subjects and the victim were tested: (a) where the subject and victim were in different rooms and the former could not see or hear the latter; (b) where they were in different rooms but the victim's voice (protests and finally screams) could be heard over a loudspeaker; (c) where both were in the same room; and (d) where the subject had to hold the victim's hand on a metal plate in order to administer the shock.

ground warfare, has so far been classified as a war crime.[47]

This brief discussion outlines a rather somber view of the consequences of technological developments in warfare, particularly those involving progress toward a greater degree of automation and remote control. This is by no means a look into the distant future: though not yet fully developed, the electronic battlefield is a reality, and the strong pressures for its further refinement and free deployment cannot be ignored.[48] What possibility is there, then, for restoring the balance in favor of restraint in warfare, on both the policy-making level and that of the individual combatant?

This is too broad and difficult a question to answer here. One can suggest certain ways, however, of creating or reinforcing such restraint. Increased awareness of the destructive power of modern air war with its burgeoning technology could make more people question the use of such destructive power to support limited policy aims. Indicidual in positions of responsibility might become more willing to oppose decisions which violate the principle of proportionality and other well-founded rules of warfare. Still, it is no easy task to create greater public awareness of these matters, and to inculcate a greater sense of personal moral responsibility would require an all-out educational effort.

Such an effort would initially be handicapped by the progressive erosion of legal and moral restraints which has accompanied the development and use of strategic air power. Basic concepts like "military necessity," though applicable in principle to air warfare, have become nearly meaningless in practice. A concerted international effort to review and evaluate the juridical status of air warfare is vitally needed as suggested at the end of the previous chapter. Big-power agreement to a treaty limiting the use of air power could be a major achievement.

No one familiar with military developments over the last thirty years can believe that such agreement will be reached easily. An absolute prohibition of strategic bombing would probably be more practicable and effective

With no penalty for disobeying the order (contrary to what would be the case in military service), one-quarter of the subjects gave the maximum shock of 450 volts when they had to hold the victim's hand onto the metal plate. This proportion went up to *three-fifths* when the subjects were in a different room from the victim and even higher when subjects could not hear the victim.

Milgram says that the subjects were not sadistic, but rather quite ordinary persons who "under the demands of authority [would] perform actions that were callous and severe." It was clear that callousness and severity increased in proportion to the distance between subject and victim. See "Some Conditions of Obedience and Disobedience to Authority," *Human Relations*, February 1965, pp. 57-75.

[47]Automated warfare *can* reduce one class of war crimes--that committed by combatants exposed to personal danger.

[48]Cf. page 157, above.

than attempting to define which targets could be attacked at all, or only under specified conditions. Another possibility would be specifically to define air-war crimes in connection with an affirmation or reformulation of the Nuremberg principles, thus helping to institutionalize restraint at all levels. As a further internal restraint it would be well to curb the power of the executive to withhold information from the public. There is also the constitutional issue raised in Chapter 10 of restoring Congressional control over war-making activities. Apart from the direct effects of international or domestic actions restraining the use of modern air power, the process of working out measures should itself have major educational value.

No one of the measures we have discussed--except possibly the absolute prohibition of strategic bombing--could effectively prevent the widely destructive use of air power, but all taken together possibly could. There doubtless are many other steps which could be taken. What is needed is a package of many mutually reinforcing measures. The design and creation of such a package is an urgent task, requiring imagination and leadership of the highest order.[49]

[49]A first step of this kind has already been suggested with respect to the ground war. Telford Taylor, chief U.S. prosecutor at the Nuremberg trials and now professor of law at Columbia University, recently criticized the government's response to the Mylai disclosures and proposed among other actions the "creation of a national commission of inquiry, vested with power to compel testimony and grant immunity, in accordance with the recent recommendations of the Association of the Bar of the City of New York. The commission's range of investigation should include at a minimum the military operational directives in force in Southeast Asia, the standards of training and discipline with regard to observance of the laws of war, and the process of military justice in dealing with war crimes. Only by treating the end of the courts-martial as the beginning of serious efforts to confront the facts and learn from experience can the failure of the judicial process be redeemed, and the stain of Mylai lightened." [*New York Times,* February 2, 1972, "Op-Ed" page.] Such an action would seem appropriate concerning the air war in Indochina.

CHAPTER 13

PRESENT TRENDS IN THE AIR WAR

A. U.S. AIR ACTIVITY

U.S. air activity in Indochina as a whole has declined substantially in the years since 1968-69, when the air war reached its greatest intensity. There has been a concurrent change in the geographical distribution, in the kinds of targets hit, and in some of the munitions used; these factors must be considered before the present trends in the air war can be assessed properly.

To provide a measure for the overall volume of air activity, the monthly tonnage of aerial munitions dropped on Indochina since 1965 is shown in Figure 13-1. This curve represents the official Department of Defense figures which include munitions dropped by all Allied air forces; however, the U.S. share of this total is well over 90 percent, so that the curve can be read with little error as an indicator of U.S. activity. There are great fluctuations in the bombing level from month to month. These reflect seasonal variations, such as the dry-season intensification of the interdiction activity over the Trail, and they also indicate the effects of individual ground actions which

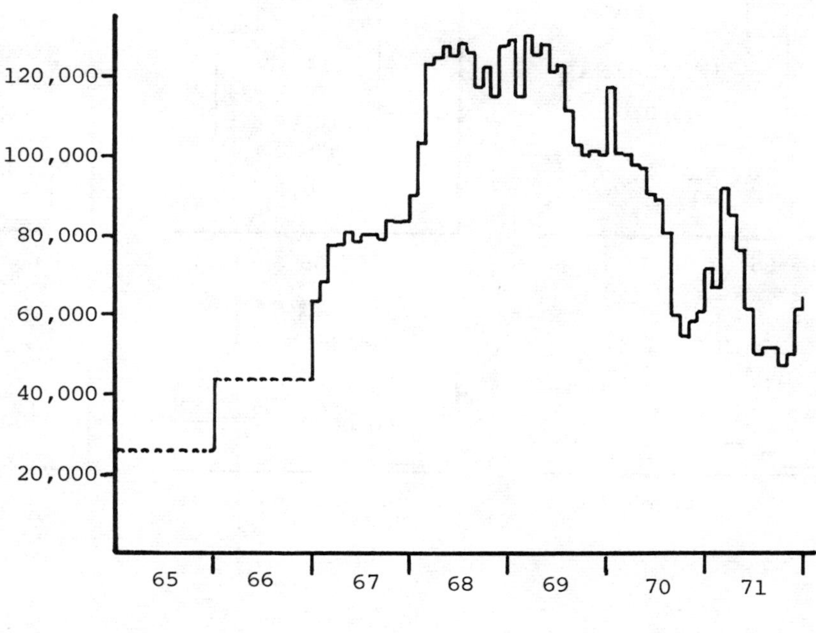

Figure 13-1

INDOCHINA: MONTHLY TONNAGE OR AERIAL MUNITIONS*

*Cf. Statistical Summary, Sec. SS-8.

elicited heavy air support.

To eliminate some of these fluctuations, the same data are presented on a yearly basis in the upper left-hand graph of Figure 13-2. They show that if total tonnage is used as an indicator, the pace of the U.S. war in 1971 (764,000 tons) was about 53 percent of the maximum (1,432,000 tons) achieved in 1968. Thus the air war continues to be waged on a very intense scale, despite the decline from the maximum rate established previously. Moreover, the downward trend shows signs of levelling off. The decrease in 1971 was less steep than that of the previous year, and in February 1972 a significant re-escalation of the bombing level took place.

We have estimated how this bomb tonnage was distributed among the var-

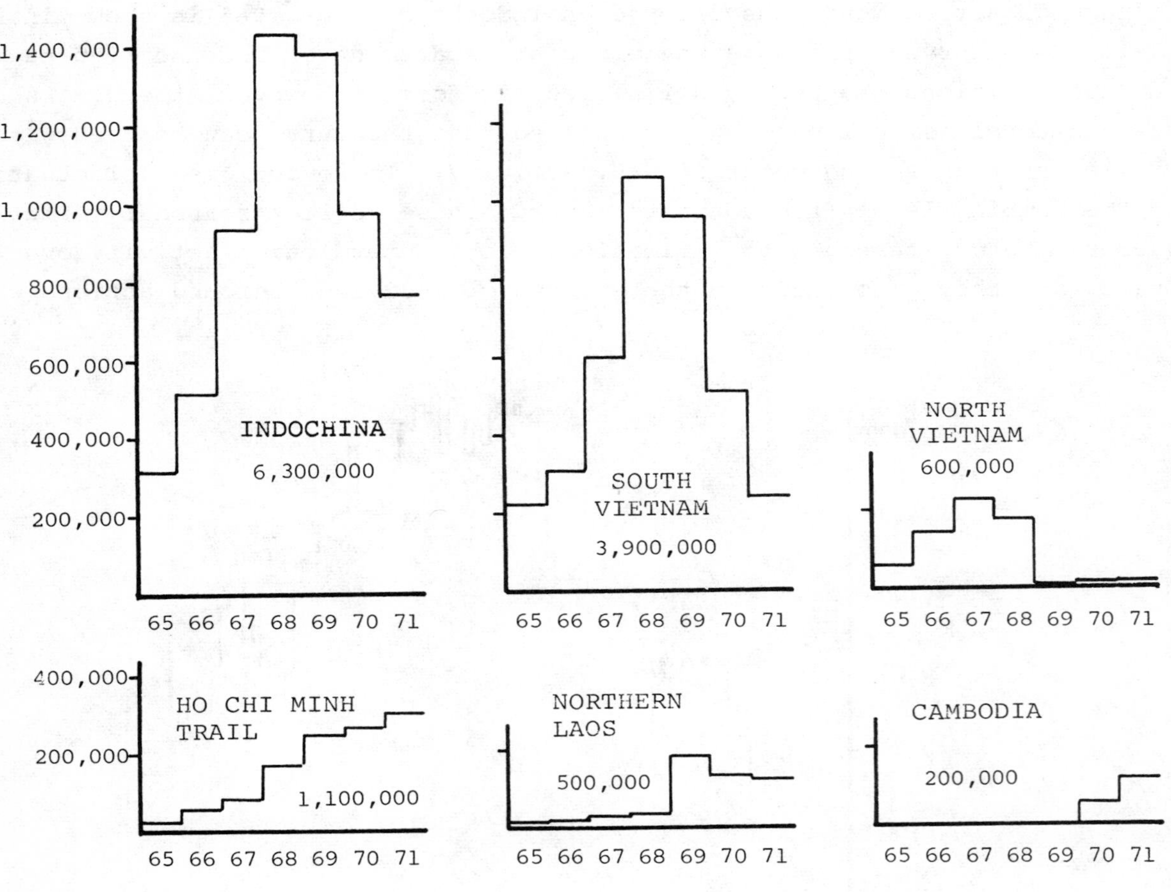

Figure 13-2

ANNUAL TONNAGE OF AERIAL MUNITIONS*

*Cf. Statistical Summary, Sec. SS-8. 1965-1971 totals are rounded to nearest 100,000 tons.

ious theaters of action; the calculations are based on the relative sortie rates and should be regarded as approximate only.[1] These estimates were shown previously in Figure 1-1 and are reproduced here in Figure 13-2. It is immediately apparent that there have been major changes in emphasis, and implicitly in objectives, for the deployment of U.S. air power.

The air war against *North Vietnam*, officially brought to a halt in November 1968, has continued since that time with sporadic attacks on a smaller scale. Though these attacks are not yet heavy in terms of total tonnage, their dramatic escalation in December 1971 has a special significance to which we return below in Section C.

Within *South Vietnam*, U.S. air action has declined sharply. However, a major resurgence took place in February 1972, resulting in a return to a bombing level not far below that for earlier years. (This renewed activity does not, of course, show on the graphs of this report, which stop at the completed calendar year 1971.)

In *northern Laos*, too, U.S. air action has declined relative to the 1969 peak of activity. By contrast, bombing of the *Trail* has shown a constant trend of escalation. Activity in *Cambodia* is not officially documented; since the invasion of April 1970 it apparently continues at an approximately constant rate.

The overall picture confirms the officially announced concentration of U.S. air power on interdiction of the Ho Chi Minh trail, but it also illustrates dramatically how the conflict, which prior to 1969 was confined mostly to Vietnam, has since that time widened to cover the whole of Indochina. U.S. air support for allied forces in the regions of heaviest fighting (Laos and Cambodia) continues at a high level.

Annual sortie rates for U.S. fighter-bombers in the various theaters are shown in Figure 13-3. Corresponding data for B-52s are not available in such detail; Figure 13-4 shows the total B-52 sorties for all of Indochina, with the dotted line indicating an estimate for the portion directed against South Vietnam.[2]

Overall, fighter-bomber sorties at the end of 1971 had declined to about 40 percent of their maximum rate; B-52 sorties were at about 60 percent of their maximum. The downward trend was sharply reversed during February 1972, however, and it is now no longer possible to work with earlier projections

[1] Details are given in the Statistical Summary, Sec. SS-8.

[2] This estimate is derived from published figures for B-52 *missions* in South Vietnam; cf. Statistical Summary, Sec. SS-6.

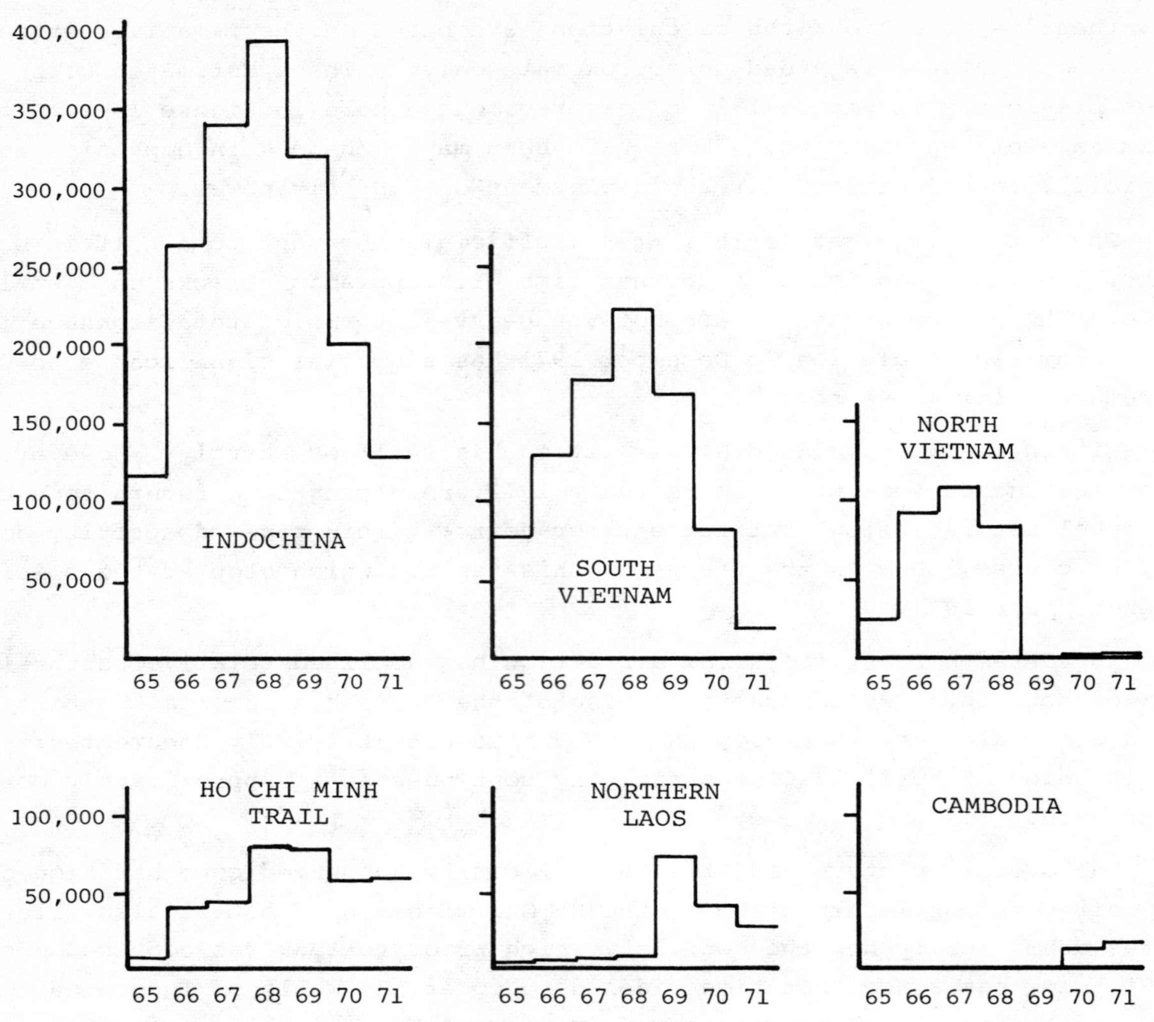

Figure 13-3

ANNUAL FIGHTER-BOMBER SORTIES*

*Cf. Statistical Summary, Sec. SS-5

for the air war, which predicted a further gradual decline of activity.[3]

The tonnage per sortie has increased steadily during the war, partly because of changes in the aircraft and partly through changes in the patterns of activity. The estimated weights of munitions delivered by B-52s and by smaller aircraft are compared in Figure 13-5, which indicates that the fraction of the air-war effort being carried by strategic bombers is increasing. A significant change in the way B-52s are used was reported recently; they

[3] *Associated Press* dispatch, April 27, 1971. Cf. also news conference of Air Force Secretary Robert C. Seamans, Jr., December 16, 1971.

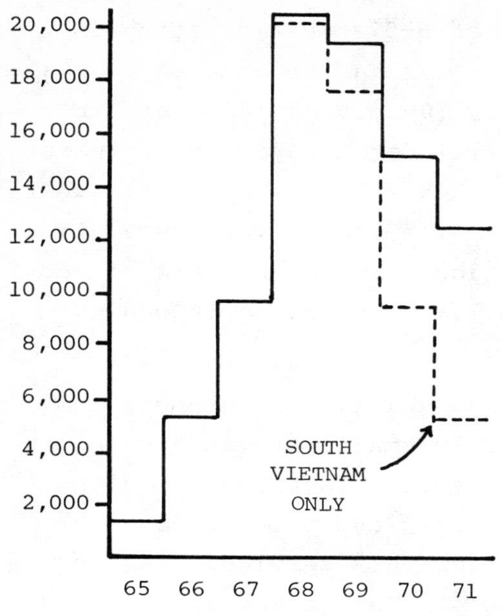

Figure 13-4

INDOCHINA: ANNUAL B-52 SORTIES*

*Cf. Statistical Summary, Sec. SS-6

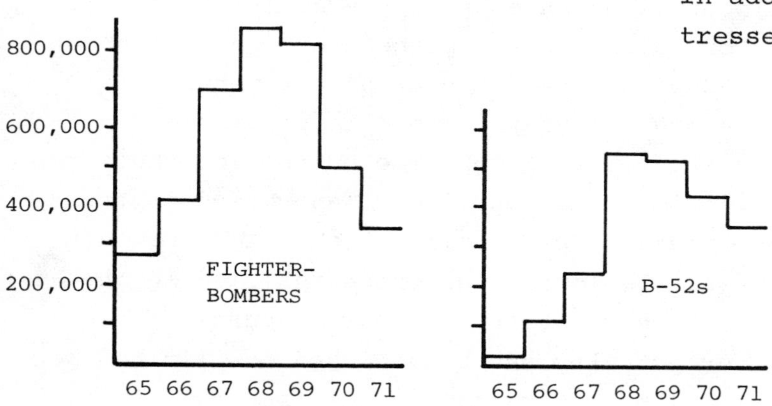

Figure 13-5

INDOCHINA: YEARLY TONNAGE OF MUNITIONS DELIVERED BY FIGHTER-BOMBERS AND B-52s*

*Cf. Statistical Summary, Sec. SS-8

can now carry cluster-bomb units (CBUs) which, delivered in a dense pattern, constitute an extremely deadly weapon against personnel and against trucks.

The number of U.S. tactical aircraft deployed in Southeast Asia is shown in Figure 13-6. Withdrawal has been most rapid for aircraft based within South Vietnam. It has been reported that all U.S. bases there will be closed or transferred to VNAF by the middle of 1972, though some U.S. operations other than attack missions may continue at these bases beyond that time.[5] After 1972, U.S. attack aircraft in the theater will be based only in Thailand and on carriers in the South China Sea. In addition to the B-52 Stratofortresses discussed below, there will remain about 400 fighter-bombers in Thailand and 225 on carriers.[6]

This basing of U.S. aircraft on the periphery of the area of conflict represents a significant evolution. Together with the development of the automated battlefield it emphasizes the remote-control aspect of U.S. warfare in Indochina.

4 *Arkansas Gazette* (AP), February 6, 1972. The load capacity, when CBUs are carried, is reduced slightly--to about 25 tons from the normal figure of 30 tons.

5 *New York Times*, January 27, 1971. By February 1972, U.S. fighter-bombers in South Vietnam operated mainly from Danang air base.

6 Craig Whitney, *New York Times*, February 14, 1972. The aircraft carriers *Constellation*, *Coral Sea*, and *Hancock* were on duty at Yankee Station at this time; the *Kitty Hawk* was being prepared for Indochina duty.

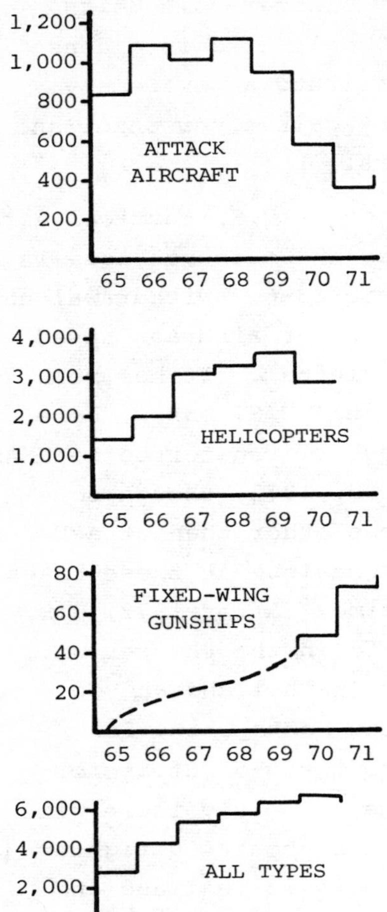

Figure 13-6

SOUTHEAST ASIA:
U.S. AIRCRAFT DEPLOYMENT*

*Cf. Statistical Summary, Sec. SS-3

The number of B-52s participating in the Indochina air war has fluctuated from a peak of just over 100 planes (70 based in Thailand, the remainder in Guam and Okinawa) to a low of about 45 (all in Thailand) at the end of 1971. The February re-escalation brought 12 additional B-52s to Thailand and 30 to Guam, the latter entering Indochina service directly.[7]

Fixed-wing gunships, though their numbers are relatively small, are in a category of growing importance. Technical developments have been rapid and more planes are being outfitted for this service. The more advanced gunships are all based in Thailand and will not be affected by Vietnamization.

The schedule of aircraft deployments corresponds well with that for sortie rates, suggesting that U.S. aircraft in Indochina operate on an essentially full-time basis. For carrier-based planes this rate is about 1,500 sorties per carrier per month, or 54,000 per year for the three carriers presently on station. The balance of the sorties must be handled by land-based fighter-bombers. These utilization rates are only a little lower than those realized in the peak years of the air war. Spurts of heavier activity can be achieved for limited periods, but sustained action is tied fairly closely to the number of aircraft available.

Redeployment of planes can be carried out at very short notice, however, as demonstrated in February 1972. An additional carrier was sent to Yankee Station, the number of B-52s in service was almost doubled, and an extra squadron of F-4s from the Philippines was made available--all in a matter of days.[8] The fighter-bomber sortie rate indicated by the February 1972 in-

[7] *Washington Post*, February 10, 1972; *New York Times*, February 14, 1972; *Ithaca Journal*, February 15, 1972.

[8] Talk of stationing an aircraft carrier in the Gulf of Siam, off the western coast of Cambodia, was reported from Phnom Penh by Iver Peterson in the *New York Times*, November 27, 1971.

ventory of aircraft in Southeast Asia is about 200,000 per year, which represents a return to a level above that for the year 1970.[9]

B. THE SOUTH VIETNAMESE AIR FORCE

The South Vietnamese Air Force (VNAF) was created in July 1955 from 32 planes inherited from the French. As the level of combat increased, the U.S. began supplying aircraft of all types: Figure 13-7 sketches VNAF's approximate inventory since 1962 for attack planes, helicopters, and aircraft of all types, indicating also the projections for the near future.

Initially, the only strike aircraft in VNAF were propeller-driven A-1s. The first jets, a squadron of F-5 Freedom Fighters, entered the inventory in 1967, and in 1968 the first A-37 light attack jets were turned over from the U.S. Air Force. The major goals in 1971 included a speed-up in the rate at which helicopter units are turned over to VNAF, and the addition of a squadron of C-123 Providers to improve its airlift capabilities.[10] VNAF's AC-47 gunships, the original "Spookies," will be replaced by the more effective AC-119s sometime in 1972 to help fill a gap in VNAF's ability to operate at night.[11]

The Vietnamization schedule calls for an eventual total of 50 squadrons (about 1,200 aircraft) in VNAF.[12] Of these, about 500 or 600 will be helicopters.[13] Fixed-wing strike aircraft, of the types previously discussed, will number between 300 and 400. Present indications are that VNAF strength will approach these figures by the end of 1972. VNAF's personnel in 1968 was less than 20,000; by the end of 1971 its strength was reported at about 50,000.

VNAF attack sorties, shown in Figure 13-8, have been increasing only slowly--from about 2,000 per month in 1968 to about 3,000 per month at the end of 1971. Sorties within South Vietnam dropped sharply when air activity in Cambodia began in April 1970; this suggests that VNAF was operating at

[9] This estimate is based on 54,000 sorties per year by carrier-based planes, and about three times that number by the 400 Thai-based and 50 South Vietnam-based fighter bombers.

[10] For a history of VNAF, see "Vietnamization's Impact on the Air War," *Vietnam Feature Service* (TCB-089), January 1971.

[11] John L. Frisbee, "USAF's Changing Role in Vietnam," *Air Force*, September 1971, p. 44. The new gunships will reportedly be the AC-119G "Shadow" aircraft, which contain some of the new sensors but are less sophisticated than the AC-119K "Stinger" or the newer AC-130 gunships.

[12] William Beecher, *New York Times*, January 26, 1971; Craig Whitney, *New York Times*, May 20, 1971. Figures reported by A. Shuster in the *New York Times*, November 26, 1971, fit well into these projections.

[13] In contrast to the U.S. practice of assigning combat helicopter units directly to the Army, South Vietnamese helicopters will be flown by VNAF.

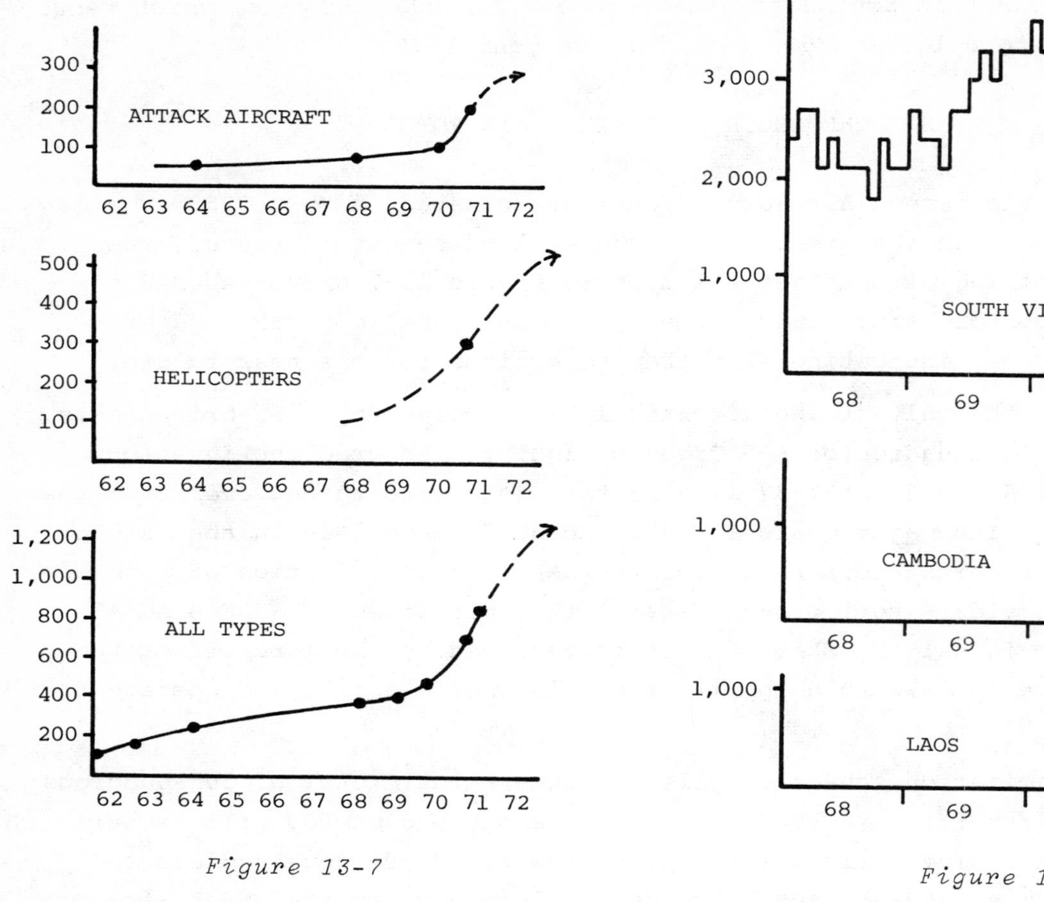

Figure 13-7

VNAF AIRCRAFT INVENTORY*

*Cf. Statistical Summary, Sec. SS-4

Figure 13-8

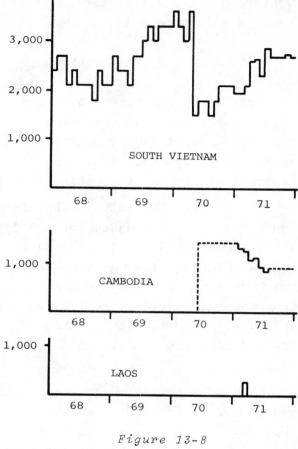

VIETNAMESE AIR FORCE:
MONTHLY FIXED-WING ATTACK SORTIES*

*Cf. Statistical Summary, Sec. SS-5

close to its maximum capability then. Similarly, the VNAF sortie rate remained unchanged at the time of the February 1972 escalation by U.S. fighter-bombers in South Vietnam.[14] Thus, though inventory of aircraft is being augmented rapidly, there is no suggestion that VNAF will be able to take over all the functions performed by U.S. air power in Indochina in the next few years.

At times of very low U.S. activity, VNAF flies most of the fighter-bomber attack sorties within South Vietnam. In November 1971, for example, VNAF flew 2,745 such sorties while U.S. aircraft flew only 218.[15] One should not infer from this type of statistics, however, that the Vietnamization

[14] *Washington Post*, February 11, 1972.

[15] *Ithaca Journal* (AP), December 8, 1971. (The DoD figure for U.S. sorties that month was actually 366.)

of the air war is progressing at anything like the rate for Vietnamization on the ground. These figures apply to South Vietnam at a time when ground fighting there was at a low ebb; moreover, they take no account of the activity of B-52 bombers, for which VNAF has no equivalent.

The role envisaged for VNAF by U.S. policy makers is circumscribed by several considerations. Though VNAF pilots are very effective in daylight bombing (many have been flying in combat for ten years, while for U.S. pilots the tour of duty is often as short as a year), their night-time and all-weather capabilities are lagging. A recent training program in radar bombing, "Combat Skyspot," has attempted to overcome this deficiency, but maintenance of the more sophisticated avionics required is a problem.

The jet aircraft delivered to VNAF--the A-37, developed specifically for counterinsurgency use, and the F-5, developed for Third World air forces--are devoid of much of the complex instrumentation that makes maintenance such a formidable task. They lack the capability for suppressing surface-to-air missiles and for instituting sophisticated electronic countermeasures. Because of this, and because of their modest maximum speed, they are not suited for operation in areas of significant anti-aircraft defenses. Their tonnage capacity and range are moreover relatively low. Thus VNAF is being prepared primarily for in-country activity in support of troops in combat. It is unlikely that it will be able to conduct any significant long-range strategic operations or to offer close support to troops far from the borders of South Vietnam.

With A-1s, A-37s, and gunships it is possible to carry out interdiction within South Vietnam and on sections of the Ho Chi Minh trail bordering on South Vietnam, provided the ground defenses there remain minimal. Some token participation in the bombing of the Trail was announced late in 1971:

> The Vietnamese Air Force will be flying over the more benign area down near the southern panhandle. They'll be flying with us, using AC-47s and AC-119s and maybe a few fighter-bombers too. . . . But they will never be able to build up the capability to do all that the United States Air Force has been doing in Laos.[16]

Since VNAF is being geared to fight an air war in which complete air superiority is assumed, this superiority will have to be maintained by U.S. aircraft, presumably operating from Thai and carrier bases.[17] VNAF's limited air-to-air combat capability rests on a squadron of F-5 Freedom Fighters (about 25 planes) to be supplemented after 1973 by the new F-5E.

[16] Secretary of the Air Force Robert C. Seamans, Jr., quoted by Craig R. Whitney, *New York Times*, December 12, 1971.

[17] Kenneth Sams, 7th Air Force Historian in Vietnam, "How the Vietnamese Are Taking Over Their Own Air War," *Air Force*, April 1971, p. 30.

In this category of jet fighters and interceptors, VNAF is more than matched by the North Vietnamese Air Force, whose inventory reportedly includes 91 MIG-21s and 166 MIG-17s and MIG-19s.[18]

According to one military spokesman, "austerity was the name of the game in Vietnamization."[19] The necessity of tailoring force levels to the South Vietnamese economy and to their maintenance and supply capabilities makes it unlikely that VNAF will be able to substitute to a significant extent for U.S. air power in Indochina in the next few years.

C. A LOOK AHEAD

As we have seen, U.S. air activity in Indochina continues at a high rate, despite the relative decline since the peak years. 1971 appears to have marked a low point, with a rapid escalation early in 1972 making predictions for the future very uncertain. In rough terms, the annual total tonnage rates remain more than half the peak rates, and thus more than the average annual tonnage rate realized by U.S. forces in all theaters of the Second World War. Moreover, the part to be played by VNAF is likely to remain relatively minor.[20] It will be instructive to examine the aims and effects of this continued presence of U.S. air power in Southeast Asia.

1. *Interdiction.* The interdiction of supplies and reinforcements has become the most important mission in recent years, and continued emphasis is likely to center on that mission:

> Barring two unlikely developments--an internal breakdown of the South Vietnamese government, or a large-scale sustained attack from the North--the USAF mission will continue to be focused on interdiction.[21]

Official pronouncements have singled out the interdiction objective, coupling it to the needs resulting from U.S. withdrawal of ground forces:

> As we reduce the number of our forces, it is particularly important for us to continue our air strikes. . . . If we see any substantial step-up in infiltration . . . we have to not only continue our air strikes; we will have to step them up.[22]

[18] William Beecher, *New York Times,* January 26, 1971. Cf. also *Washington Post,* December 23, 1971.

[19] "How the Vietnamese Are Taking Over," *op. cit.,* p. 29.

[20] The Laotian and Thai air forces are also involved, but because of their still smaller size, they will not be considered separately here. (The Lao air force is reported to have about 70 aircraft, including 40 T-28s, 10 helicopters, and some AC-47 gunships. *Far Eastern Economic Review,* November 13, 1971.)

[21] "USAF's Changing Role," *op. cit.*

[22] President Nixon in press conference, November 12, 1971.

Not only is a large fraction of U.S. air power being devoted to interdiction, but there is also an intense and continuing effort to develop new, automated weapons which will permit this interdiction to be performed without the close involvement of U.S. men at the scene of battle. An outline of this technical effort was presented in Chapter 12; assuming, for the sake of argument, that the new methods will meet with increasing success, what other developments in the use of air power are they likely to entail?

When aerial interdiction becomes sufficiently effective and begins to inflict heavy costs on the enemy, he can be expected to concentrate on instituting countermeasures. The most obvious such measure is an improvement in anti-aircraft and missile defenses around the contested Trail regions. This improvement is already under way, with repeated reports of SAM firings at American aircraft near the North Vietnamese borders.[23] As ground defenses are strenthened, the amount of suppressive fire which must be directed against them must also increase. This accounts, in part, for the growing number of "protective reaction" strikes being flown against North Vietnam. It also implies that the elements of the automated battlefield will not be able to operate unmolested, but will require substantial escorts from sophisticated U.S. fighter-bombers.

Another countermeasure is the strengthening of air-to-air defenses, again a process which has recently been set in motion. In December 1971 it was reported that "the American air war in Indochina has entered a new phase with direct confrontations between American and North Vietnamese planes."[24] MIGs have been encountered repeatedly by U.S. planes operating over Laos. The Secretary of the Air Force, Mr. Seamans, said of this MIG activity:

> We are concerned about it, but it is too early to know now how intensive it is likely to become.[25]

In any event it is clear that U.S. interdiction activity is predicated on the maintenance of total air superiority. If this is seriously challenged, major escalation of air attacks outside the Trail region itself must follow; the airfields from which the MIGs operate have already been bombed on several occasions.[26]

Thus, while it is tempting at first sight to consider interdiction of the Trail as a self-contained problem which can be tackled with automated

[23] UPI reported [*Washington Post,* April 27, 1971] that the North Vietnamese were receiving an advanced defensive missile, the SA-3, from the Soviets. In the Trail regions, "Hanoi's anti-aircraft power has doubled since this time last year." [*Christian Science Monitor,* December 28, 1971.] See also *Washington Post,* December 23, 1971.

[24] *New York Times,* December 20, 1971.

[25] *New York Times,* December 12, 1971.

[26] *Ibid.; New York Times,* December 31, 1971.

weapons in a localized, surgical manner, the actual situation is quite different. The enemy cannot be compelled to hold still while the operation is being performed on him. His defensive reactions necessitate, on the part of the U.S., a much wider range of supportive air activity. The resulting escalation is likely to have an important impact on the surrounding regions, including in particular North Vietnam itself. This in turn bears on the prisoner-of-war issue and, more generally, on the conduct of negotiations for the settlement of the conflict.[27] It also bears on the course of international diplomacy as a whole.[28]

2. *Support of Ground Troops.* A substantial amount of U.S. air activity is devoted to the support of friendly ground troops, directly or through close interdiction strikes. In South Vietnam itself this activity has declined, at least for considerable periods of time. However, major attacks are carried out by B-52s wherever the need arises; these planes are readily diverted to trouble spots from their normal standby mission of bombing the Trail. Thus, in August 1971, when North Vietnamese attacks against South Vietnamese fire bases near the demilitarized zone had the South Vietnamese marines "near collapse," half of the B-52 force in Southeast Asia was devoted to a series of raids in that region.[29] In January 1972 B-52s were diverted to the central highlands of South Vietnam in response to reported NLF/NVA preparations for an offensive in that region.[30] Similarly, it was reported that B-52s dropped almost 1,000 tons of bombs on Cambodia in an action near the town of Krek.[31] B-52 raids are equally common in northern Laos.

American fighter-bombers play the major role in close ground support, however, and since the scene of most intense fighting has recently been in Laos and Cambodia, it is here that this support is most important. From Cambodia it is reported that

> . . . it was still American air power that played a crucial role in recent major battles. The substantial South Vietnamese losses would have been greater if it had not been for the American planes.[32]

[27]It is worth noting that more than half of the American prisoners in North Vietnamese hands are in fact airmen.

[28]Michael Morrow reports from Vientiane that there was official speculation about some form of bombing halt in Laos to coincide with President Nixon's planned trip to Peking early in 1972. Cessation of U.S. bombing, not only over northern Laos but also over the Trail region, is seen there as a precondition for fruitful negotiations on a possible cease-fire in Laos. [*Dispatch News Service*, October 11, 1971.]

[29]*New York Times*, August 19, 1971.

[30]*New York Times*, January 20, 1972.

[31]*Washington Post*, October 10, 1971.

[32]*New York Times*, November 26, 1971.

> The U.S. sources said the Cambodians had been getting substantially more American air support in the last ten days than previously. "They asked the U.S. for more air support because they were in a pinch," one source said.[33]

Secretary of State Rogers has declared that U.S. warplanes would continue their strikes against enemy positions in Laos and Cambodia during 1972 to blunt the new North Vietnamese offensives in those areas.[34] There is no indication, however, that the enemy will be forced to reduce his pressure as a result of these attacks. Actually, in Laos, the enemy has launched his annual dry-season offensive "from a position of greater strength than in any past year."[35] In Cambodia, he is now said to control 80 percent of the country.[36] Even in South Vietnam there are reports that the buildup of Communist forces and supplies in the central highlands has reached "historic" proportions, indicating NLF/NVA intentions to launch a major offensive in 1972.[37] Militarily, therefore, the need for U.S. close air support is likely to remain acute, and American air power seems destined to continue playing an important role in all the theaters of the Indochina conflict.

3. *"Protective Reaction" Strikes against North Vietnam.* The continuation of sporadic raids against North Vietnam, partly in response to attacks or threatened attacks on U.S. planes, and partly against "military objectives" in general, has been described previously in Chapter 3. Of interest here are the motivations for such raids and the likely trend they will follow in the near future.

The North Vietnamese posture vis-a-vis the continued use of U.S. air power in Indochina has been hardening since the 1970-1971 incursions into Cambodia and Laos; ground defenses have been strengthened considerably and MIGs have occasionally challenged U.S. aircraft. A dramatic illustration was provided in December 1971 when four American F-4s were downed in action over northern Laos.[38] Immediately thereafter, the U.S. staged a five-day series of maximum-effort raids against North Vietnam, utilizing "every aircraft that the U.S. could spare in Indochina."[39] These raids, which averaged over 200 sorties a day, were directed against airfields, anti-aircraft installations, supply depots, and "military targets" in general. The raids came under the official classification of "reinforced protective reaction,"

[33] *New York Times*, November 19, 1971.

[34] *New York Times*, December 24, 1971.

[35] *Washington Post*, November 28, 1971.

[36] *Associated Press* dispatch, carried in *Ithaca Journal*, December 12, 1971.

[37] *Washington Post*, January 4, 1972.

[38] *New York Times*, December 27, 1971.

[39] *Ibid.*

to distinguish them from attacks on anti-aircraft installations directly threatening U.S. aircraft. However, the coining of new terminology does not shed new light on the underlying motivation. As a senior Pentagon official was quoted,

> Look, these so-called reinforced protective reaction strikes amount to a limited, selective resumption of the bombing [of North Vietnam].[40]

Militarily, there are two main motivations behind the resumed bombing of the North: first, to suppress North Vietnam's air defenses and attack the MIG airfields; second, to seize an opportunity for destroying supplies stockpiled in North Vietnam prior to their entry into the Ho Chi Minh trail system. These supplies could of course be partially destroyed in transit by interdiction raids on the Trail itself, but an overall interdiction campaign is more efficient if attacks can be directed against the system at all levels.

The timing and manner of execution of these raids indicate, however, that they had an important *political* function which overshadowed these military objectives. The bombings were carried out almost entirely in bad weather, the pilots unable to see their targets:

> "It was sheer insanity," said a Phantom navigator who did not want to give his name. "The clouds were so solid we couldn't see the ground, but the SAMs could still see us."
>
> Other pilots reflected the widely held view that the bombing was not successful because of poor timing and bad weather. "It was a farce," one of them remarked.[41]

If the strikes had been motivated by purely military considerations, they could not have taken place under these circumstances, but rather at another time. This would have sharpened the military effectiveness of the bombing and reduced the extent of any contingent civilian casualties and other damage. However, the U.S. is evidently intent on demonstrating, first, that it will brook no interference with the exercise of its air power in Indochina and, second, that it is prepared to re-escalate the war by bombing the North if the flow of supplies south threatens the Vietnamization program, as apparently is the case.

While such demonstrations are calculated to lend credibility to the American deterrent during a time of withdrawal, there is presently no reason or evidence to believe that Hanoi's posture on the war has been influenced in the direction desired by Washington. Actually, resumed bombing of the

[40] *New York Times*, December 28, 1971.

[41] *New York Times*, January 9, 1972; see also *New York Times*, January 3, 1972. We have found no reports indicating a contrary opinion of the conditions prevailing during these raids; nevertheless, the raids were described by President Nixon as "very successful."

North commits the U.S. to a future "high risk" course of military action in order to preserve this credibility; yet the opportunities to challenge or test the remaining U.S. deterrent are to a great extent controlled by the options of the other side.

Having served notice of intent in the clearest possible manner, how can the U.S. avoid a major re-escalation of the air war should Hanoi fail to be deterred by the warning? To re-escalate the air war in any important manner, the U.S. would have to consider a range of dangerous actions (such as the bombing of major North Vietnamese cities or the mining of Haiphong harbor) whose implications might be more far-reaching than anything so far encountered in the Indochina conflict.[42] In other words, a commitment to enforce its policies from the air, without the use of American ground forces, may shortly lead the U.S. to a very difficult position in its Indochina involvement.

[42] Jack Anderson, "The New Secrets," *Washington Post,* June 21, 1971. "These top-secret [contingency] plans, . . . transmitted to the Pentagon on October 17 [1970], offer options for a three-day, seven-day, or ten-day aerial offensive. The[y] . . . include detailed plans for the bombing and mining of Haiphong harbor."

CHAPTER 14

CONCLUSIONS

The facts outlined in Chapter 13 confirm what, in the light of repeated official pronouncements, is projected U.S. policy:

> U.S. ships and warplanes will remain on duty in Southeast Asia after the last American soldier leaves Vietnam. . . . [They will form part of the] realistic deterrent which we will maintain in Asia.[1]

> I am not going to place any limitations on the use of air power.[2]

This projected American air and naval combat role in Indochina extends far beyond the interdiction mission so often emphasized. It involves fighting on all fronts, commits the U.S. to responding to threats both on the ground and in the air, and continues the heavy toll levied by the bombing on the peoples engulfed by the conflict. To characterize such a policy as "withdrawal" or "disengagement" is grossly misleading. Rather, the policy seems to be a direct extension of the previous American efforts in Indochina, but using Asian instead of American ground forces. The major objective and a major instrument of U.S. policy in Indochina thus appear to have been reaffirmed, not rejected, by the present Administration. Only the *form* of the U.S. involvement has changed.

This policy raises many questions which we are not qualified to answer unequivocally. In looking back over the history of the Indochina conflict, we have tried--admittedly in a rather arbitrary way--to separate issues specifically relevant to the air war from the more general questions concerning U.S. policy as a whole. As we turn to the trends for the future, however, the dominant role being played by air power makes such a separation less meaningful. The whole of U.S. policy in Indochina is becoming a function of the capabilities and limitations of air power. It thus seems relevant, in this concluding discussion, to widen the topic somewhat and to attempt an evaluation of this relationship.

First, we will briefly recapitulate some of the general aspects of air power in Indochina which emerge from the evidence and analysis presented in the earlier chapters of this report; second, we ask whether air power is likely to be adequate for the tasks it is asked to perform; and, last, we examine some of the reasons commonly given for continuing the use of American air power in Indochina.

[1] Secretary of Defense Melvin Laird; *Washington Post,* April 14, 1971.

[2] President Richard Nixon; *New York Times,* February 18, 1971.

A. SOME GENERALIZATIONS

1. *By narrow military criteria, air power is effective*

Once a target has been selected and identified, the existing technology virtually guarantees that the mission can ultimately achieve its immediate objective. Industries in North Vietnam *were* knocked out, trucks along the Ho Chi Minh trail *are* destroyed, enemy troop concentrations *are* dispersed. Of course the accuracy of an air operation is often rather low. Repeated strikes must be carried out against certain targets to ensure their destruction; but this merely raises the scale for the required effort. With respect to the material and technical results, air power can be counted on to perform its missions successfully.[3]

It is tempting to jump from this observation to the conclusion that air power is "effective" in a more general sense. This however overlooks the collateral impact of air power--its often indiscriminate devastation, its psychological and political connotations--and it assumes that the objectives achieved were indeed those which would advance overall American policy aims. These questions are not as readily quantifiable as are truck kills and secondary explosions, but the answers to them are as vital as are the truck kills themselves.

2. *Air power is economical, flexible, and unobtrusive*

In this capsule statement are contained many of the aspects of air power which make its use so attractive. The direct costs of delivering a ton of ordnance by air are lower than for other methods; as outlined in Chapter 9, the air war (which delivered about the same tonnage of munitions as the ground war) accounts for no more than one-third of the total dollar costs of the Indochina war. More importantly, the number of American lives lost in the air is less than ten percent of the total.[4]

The deployment of air power is flexible and can be very unobtrusive. Aircraft can be based far from the scene of action. They need not take war correspondents or television crews with them on their missions, their destinations may remain obscure, their targets unpublicized. Air power can be turned on and off quickly and quietly: no trumpets or fanfares, no mobilization or draft calls need disturb the peace of the voters.

[3]This presupposes air superiority and sufficient technological dominance to overcome ground-based anti-aircraft defenses. In Indochina both these conditions are satisfied, though the effort to overcome the ground defenses has been costly.

[4]By the end of 1970, the number of airmen killed through enemy action was 3,559; the total deaths for all services were 44,241. Benjamin F. Schemmer, *Armed Forces Journal*, January 18, 1971, p. 29.

These are all advantages to which the U.S. electorate is highly responsive. Above all, the public is sensitive to the cost of war in terms of American lives. Military and civilian policy makers, aware of this, are quick to point out the advantages of air war in these terms. This favorable evaluation rests, however, on two contestable premises: that the effectiveness can be evaluated through counting successes in military operational terms alone, and that only the direct costs in American lives and dollars need be considered, not the costs borne by others.

3. *Air war is costly to the people of Indochina*

The relative lack of discrimination of air operations has been described in several sections of this study. It derives from the technical limitations of air warfare and from its effects on the men who participate in it. The damage includes civilian dead and wounded, civilian refugees, villages and crops destroyed, cultural treasures lost, and ecological damage to the countryside; it also extends to the very structure of society, to Indochinese culture and traditions. The impact of air warfare is as severe psychologically as it is physically, especially in a predominantly rural society many of whose people are suddenly forced to move into cities and refugee camps.[5]

4. *The costs of air war accumulate, but its successes do not*

It is a commonplace that one can win a battle, even many battles, and yet lose the war. This dictum applies with special force to the use of air power in Indochina. The ultimate goal of the struggle there is political, not military.[6] Yet air power is far from being an instrument of political persuasion. It can force people to move, even remove them from the scene literally, but win allegiance from them or establish the legitimacy of a regime it cannot. Even as an instrument of coercion it is deficient, because its effects are *intermittent*. It can disrupt economic, social, and political activity, but it cannot enforce desired behavior in the way that ground forces can. Once the planes have passed, the survivors are free to act as they choose--unless they are incapacitated or totally demoralized. The will to resist the government can even be strengthened by the aerial assault. So the military gains which may be obtained through the use of air power are difficult to translate into political objectives. A succession of "successes"

[5] Cf. Chap. 4-C.

[6] Admiral U.S.G. Sharp, Commander-in-Chief, Pacific wrote: "In coordination with our military operations, the task of nation building in South Vietnam, the ultimate goal of our struggle, received its full share of attention." *Report on the War in Vietnam* (USGPO, 1968), p. 9.

does not necessarily add up to accomplishment of one's aims.

The penalties inflicted by the air war, on the other hand, are cumulative. The costs accruing to the recipients *and* to the makers of the war mount as the war grinds on. Unless eventually there is some dramatic achievement resulting from the air war, the ratio of its cost to its effectiveness becomes progressively less favorable. It is possible to envisage the day when the devastation of Indochina and the disruption of its societies will have progressed to the point where a victory declared by either side will have become an empty concept.

5. *Escalation is an easy, even attractive course of action*

Because air power is remote and indirect in its application, and because it is relatively economical and painless to the side doing the bombing, it appears reasonable to apply more air power in the event that "success" is elusive, or failure threatens. If the ultimate objectives remain out of reach, and other courses of action are unattractive, policy-makers are likely to escalate the air war, applying "more of the same medicine."

Escalation is easier when, as in Indochina, there is no fear of retaliation in kind by the other side. It is almost unthinkable for the North Vietnamese to be bombing ARVN positions with napalm, strafing villages held by pro-Western forces, or interdicting the movement of allied traffic[7]--to say nothing of their bombing the American homeland. So, in the use of air power against a weaker nation, there need be no thought of possible retribution. It is exactly this fear of retribution, however, which has proved to be the most powerful factor disciplining the use of weapons of war.[8]

B. OBJECTIVES AND PERFORMANCE IN INDOCHINA

The withdrawal of American ground forces from Indochina leaves air power as the only active military element for enforcing U.S. objectives in the area. The manner in which this is evolving has been described in Section 13-C. Here we enquire whether air power is in fact likely to be able to perform the tasks allotted to it.

[7]There are occasional reports of North Vietnamese MIGs giving close support to troops, but they represent rare exceptions in view of U.S. air superiority over the whole of Indochina. See *New York Times,* January 5, 1972.

[8]This is argued in Chap. 11 and in Sec. 12-C above.

1. *Inhibiting enemy escalation to large-scale warfare*

The presence of American air power in Indochina does indeed exert a strong inhibiting influence on the other side's military choices. We have seen that air power is not particularly effective against an adversary operating with small units in a dispersed and flexible manner. Whenever the conflict involves more conventional, set-piece battles, however, air power becomes a powerful and often decisive tool. Doubtless, the NVA and its local allies are aware that, were they to mass their forces for a decisive onslaught, they would expose themselves to crippling punishment from U.S. aircraft. It is thus likely that, once the enemy has gained the initiative on the ground, air power helps to slow his progress significantly. This effect should not be underestimated; but it can be achieved only when the enemy already has the initiative and is in effect "winning." If he were on the defensive, he would not be massing his troops; rather, he would be keeping the "low profile" characteristic of guerrilla warfare and offering few targets for effective bombardment.

2. *Gaining time to achieve stabilization*

The military rationale implicit in the Nixon Doctrine rests on the assumption that U.S. air power (and other technical and economic assistance) supporting indigenous ground forces can effectively keep the present Saigon, Phnom Penh, and Vientiane regimes in power against determined attacks by their enemies.[9] The military forces of the latter two regimes, however, have shown little indication of achieving substantial strength, and even the ARVN has yet to demonstrate extended self-sufficiency in combat with its enemy's best forces. The official American hope is that enough time can be gained to permit these armies to be consolidated into effective fighting forces. It is assumed that "Vietnamization" can succeed in South Vietnam, and that a similar transformation can be effected in Cambodia and Laos, if military disaster can be staved off sufficiently long.

Even in South Vietnam, however, Vietnamization has been a slow and often faltering process. Elsewhere in Indochina it may be even slower and less promising. The ARVN's rebuilding program was made possible by the protection U.S. ground forces offered between 1965 and 1970. This situation will not, in all likelihood, be repeated in Cambodia and Laos, where the local armies have compiled a very poor performance record vis-a-vis their opponents. Thus, even if the deployment of U.S. air power slows down the enemy's progress,

[9]Cf. Sir Robert Thompson's concept of achieving a "stable war." *U.S. News & World Report*, November 1, 1971.

these armies still remain under constant pressure.

In Laos the indications are that pro-government forces are becoming weaker, not stronger. With the essential decimation of Vang Pao's forces of CIA-trained Meo tribesmen, and with their base at Long Tieng effectively put out of action for the forseeable future,[10] Thai mercenaries and regulars have been increasingly brought into Laos in an effort to shore up the deteriorating military situation. The Cambodian army, too, has been unable to fend off its attackers, much less take the offensive, without intervention of ARVN units and U.S. air strikes.[11] As more U.S. ground troops leave South Vietnam, fewer ARVN forces will be available to keep Lon Nol's army in the field. Thus the timetable of "Asianization" may be overtaken by the onrush of events.

3. *Aerial interdiction*

One cannot assess the success or failure of an interdiction campaign in short-run terms. To be effective it must have an impact over long periods, and its influence on the balance of power is often manifested in subtle ways. U.S. aerial interdiction efforts have been pursued with maximum pressure for several years now, so that some general indication of their effectiveness should be apparent. The results so far have not been impressive. Communist forces in Laos and Cambodia continue to demonstrate considerable offensive powers. At the same time, while there has been an extended lull in the ground fighting within South Vietnam, a supply buildup of "historic" proportions is reportedly taking place there, indicating that the NLF/NVA still have substantial logistic capabilities in that theater despite the overall interdiction pressure on their supplies.[12]

One of the results of interdiction is, of course, that the infiltrators are obliged to expend much greater effort, and provide a much larger initial amount of materiel, in order to obtain the required output from the supply lines. With respect to materiel, the North Vietnamese appear to be favorably situated, however, since they receive support from the U.S.S.R. and from China, and such support cannot be interdicted "at source" without the gravest of consequences. With respect to manpower, the North Vietnamese have always

[10] *New York Times,* January 20, 1972.

[11] Cf. *New York Times,* January 6, 10, and 13, 1972.

[12] *Washington Post,* January 4, 1972; *Aviation Week & Space Technology,* January 10, 1972. Air Force Secretary Robert C. Seamans, Jr. at his December 16, 1971, news conference quoted figures which indicate that the volume of supplies *started* down the Ho Chi Minh trail changed very little during the years 1969-1971. This might be read as an indication that the communists were not, in fact, feeling the interdiction pressure very badly. According to one source, the Ho Chi Minh trail network is reported to be working better this year than in the past. [Jean-Claude Pomonti, *Le Monde,* December 31, 1971].

been thought to have an ample supply of labor,[13] and it is well to remember that they have so far not committed the main forces of their army to the conflict at all.[14] One possible military advantage that could accrue from interdiction bombing of the infiltration routes is that troops may arrive at their destinations with diminished energy and with lowered morale due to the constant pressure of the bombing. Interviews with captured or defecting NVA troops suggest that this is so.[15] The sample available for such interviews is, to be sure, not a representative one.

4. *Deterrent effects*

American policy makers attribute an important deterrent effect to air power, a deterrent that acts on the political plane as much as in direct military terms. This thinking parallels that of global nuclear strategy, in which air and missile power are thought to deter hostile nations from advancing their interests by force. However, it has not been demonstrated--in Indochina or elsewhere--that conventional air power can exert controlling leverage in limited wars. Past attempts at deterrence, most directly exemplified by the air war against North Vietnam, have been signally unsuccessful.[16] The North Vietnamese on that occasion were willing to take rather severe punishment, in the process inflicting heavy losses on the attacking U.S. planes. Their defenses have since been strengthened considerably; they are now rated third best in the world, after those of the U.S.S.R. and Israel.[17] This indicates that North Vietnam anticipates future air attacks, and, far from being deterred, is prepared to face them. American threats to resume major bombing of North Vietnam therefore appear unlikely to inhibit Hanoi's actions.[18]

[13] Cf. *Air War Hearings* (1967), Part 4, pp. 324-325 *inter alia*.

[14] Regular armed forces in North Vietnam (PAVN) total approximately 480,000 men, of which 205,000 are estimated to be deployed outside the North: 90,000 in South Vietnam, 75,000 in Laos, and 40,000 in Cambodia. This means that about 275,000 regular troops are uncommitted and could be deployed. Backing up this force are frontier and public security units totalling about 20,000 men and an estimated 425,000 men in regional militias. The latter force provides a pool of trained manpower that can be integrated readily into regular PAVN units. Thus the reserve forces of North Vietnam are over 700,000 men. See *The Military Balance, 1971-72* (International Institute for Strategic Studies, 1971), pp. 51-52.

[15] This was stressed in a private communication from Gen. Harold B. Chase, USMCR, who has served in MR I of South Vietnam.

[16] Cf. Sec. 3-B for a discussion of how political considerations in a limited war circumscribe the use of air power for deterrent effect.

[17] *Aviation Week and Space Technology*, January 10, 1972.

[18] The *Aviation Week and Space Technology* analyst just quoted suggests that it is the "long record of basic misuse of U.S. air power over North Vietnam" which has undermined its credibility as a deterrent. (He believes previous attacks on North Vietnam to have been far too restrained.)

The further the U.S. becomes committed to following through on these threats, the more likely an armed confrontation becomes in which, once again, America will have to start pounding away at a smaller nation while being compelled to circumscribe its actions for fear of a Russian and Chinese military response. This is the road that has been travelled before; there does not seem to be any basis for expecting greater success this time.[19]

The deterrent effect of air power may be intended to apply not only to North Vietnam but also to the local regions over which it is routinely deployed. Throughout Indochina, wherever there are areas clearly under "enemy" control, sustained bombing has resulted in general devastation. We are not in a position to determine whether this represents an explicit policy aim or is only the incidental cumulative outcome of a military strategy, but the results present a clear picture. Recurrent reports from Cambodia, for instance, indicate that

> villages have been seized [by the communist forces] in the full awareness that they would then be levelled by air strikes.[20]

In the words of the former Ambassador to Laos, William H. Sullivan, "most Lao civilians learn very quickly that bombing necessarily follows the North Vietnamese."[21] American policy thus confronts the advancing troops and their local supporters with a painful choice. We are inclined to doubt that this local deterrence greatly affects the military choices made by the communist forces; at the same time, such a "scorched-earth" policy can hardly strengthen the foundations of the U.S. position in Indochina or those of the governments it supports.

C. COMMENTS ON THE CASE FOR CONTINUING THE AIR WAR

In the preceding section, we discussed the major objectives of U.S. air power in Indochina: inhibiting enemy escalation, gaining time for consolidation, interdiction, and direct deterrence. The analysis suggests that the bombing in general is not in fact likely to perform these tasks very well. Though it has an undoubted marginal utility in the conflict, air power appears to be mismatched to the problems being tackled.

Utility is of course not the only criterion by which the continued deployment of U.S. air power in Indochina should be judged. As explained at the end of Chapter 1, however, we have (with the exception of Section 12-C)

[19] Any possible diplomatic accommodation with China in this regard is likely to be a goad to the Soviet Union.

[20] *Ithaca Journal,* December 17, 1971.

[21] *Refugee Hearings (1971),* Part II, p. 40.

abstained from interposing ethical issues which, it should be agreed, need to be weighed in any final judgment on the air war. Our intent has been to deal with utilitarian arguments about the air war on their own ground so that once the actual utility of the bombing is assessed in realistic terms, a more comprehensive and satisfactory evaluation of the air war policy can be made.

To conclude this discussion, then, we examine in summary form the arguments most frequently advanced as justification for the continued deployment of American air power in Indochina. As will have become clear to the reader by now, we have reached the conclusion that, in view of the undeniably heavy costs of the air war, the burden of proof for justifying its continuation should lie with those who advocate it. The questions raised will have to be answered by the American government more convincingly than heretofore if prolonged American involvement in Indochina on the present basis is to appear defensible.

1. *Mechanized firepower is America's greatest strength, and therefore should be used*

The observation that mechanized firepower--and, in particular, air power--is America's outstanding strength is no doubt correct, if by "strength" is meant military strength alone, and if by "greatest" is meant "capable of inflicting the most destruction." Thus defined, however, the assertion loses much of its appeal; a wrestler's great strength may be useless to a watchmaker. The question is whether air power is in fact *appropriate* to the tasks confronting the U.S. in Indochina. The material presented in this study suggests that all too often it is not. We are not suggesting that the U.S. should voluntarily handicap itself in the Indochina conflict. Rather, to continue the metaphor, we suggest that if a watchmaker is not available, the wrestler should not be given the job by default. If the task were recognized by public consensus as being truly worth doing, the right craftsman could be found or trained.[22]

2. *The reliability of American commitments must be demonstrated*

Notwithstanding the pessimistic outlook for the military situation in much of Indochina, it is often argued that the U.S. must exert itself to the

[22] This is doubtless what the developers of the *electronic battlefield* have in mind--making air power more specific in its counterinsurgency capabilities. However, the primary assumption--that an insurgency can be tackled remotely by the deployment of firepower--remains unchallenged. It appears to us that the step toward automated warfare is in this context a step backward, not forward.

utmost degree possible to stave off a military defeat of its allies, since not to do so would cast doubt on the value of its commitments around the world. This argument is sometimes phrased in terms of the danger of "losing face." This is seen as casting doubt on the "great-power status" of the U.S. in the world arena--an erosion of prestige which might adversely affect the global power balance. As long ago as 1966, Assistant Secretary of Defense John T. McNaughton was writing,

> *The present U.S. objective in Vietnam is to avoid humiliation.* The reasons why we *went into* Vietnam to the present depth are varied; but they are now largely academic. Why we have *not withdrawn* from Vietnam is, by all odds, *one* reason: to preserve our reputation as guarantor, and thus to preserve our effectiveness in the rest of the world. . . . At each decision point we have gambled; at each point, to avoid the damage to our effectiveness of defaulting on our commitment, we have upped the ante.[23]

The amount of face lost is, however, related to the amount of effort made previously to succeed in the venture--related, that is, to the *ante*, in the words of McNaughton's memorandum. A calculated accommodation may thus serve to save face in the long run, despite the momentary setback it entails. It would even appear at present that, having already lost face by not defeating a small, weak nation, the U.S. is violating the "face" argument by continuing policies which appear no more likely to be successful in the future.

In any event, the whole line of reasoning raises two prior questions: first, does a demonstration of commitment justify the costs that it entails; and, second, will the results on balance be in the direction desired?

The political polarization within Indochinese countries brought about by the continued bombing may ultimately consolidate, rather than weaken, the hold of unfriendly governments over the contested areas. The overall escalation is likely to drive the peoples involved more firmly into alignment with the communists, or at least alienate them enough from the U.S. that the much-desired increase in support for friendly governments in Indochina is vitiated. This effect can be discerned through the whole course of the Indochina conflict; the most striking recent example is that of Cambodia, where the neutralist leader, Prince Norodom Sihanouk, was driven into the arms of Peking by a Western-backed coup, and within a short time most of his countrymen were in a rapidly expanding communist zone.

On the detailed operating level, too, the demonstration of commitment

[23] *The Pentagon Papers* (Bantam, 1971), pp. 491-492 [emphasis in original]. Secretary McNaughton was arguing in this memorandum that the U.S. should consider coming to terms in Vietnam.

may entail counterproductive results. The heavy raids against North Vietnam at the end of 1971, for example, brought about a prompt increase in the aid given to Hanoi by Moscow.[24] Thus the domino theory, which holds that every communist success entails further successes unless massively opposed, can become a self-fulfilling prophesy.

3. *The bombing is America's best bargaining counter*

No matter what the chances of success for American military policy in Indochina, it seems evident that a cessation of U.S. air activity would bring about a fairly quick collapse of the pro-Western forces there. Those who have strong convictions about the immorality of American bombing may well insist that it should be discontinued unilaterally nonetheless. In this study we have not based conclusions on ethical premises, leaving these judgments to the reader, and thus we do not argue such a position. It is clear, however, that U.S. air power does represent an important bargaining counter in any negotiations for an end to hostilities on mutually acceptable terms.

The important point about this bargaining counter, however, is that its value is not necessarily lasting. While at one time it may be possible to obtain important negotiating concessions in return for a bombing cessation, the enemy may in due course accommodate to an indefinite prolongation of the air war. If the military situation for pro-Western forces in Indochina deteriorates, and the relative ineffectiveness of bombing as a stabilizing factor becomes more apparent, the value of a stop to bombing decreases. If this should come to pass, the bargaining counter will have been wasted and there will remain, all too literally, only the ashes of destruction.[25]

4. *Successive U.S. Administrations cannot have been simply wrongheaded*

When the wisdom of the American involvement in Indochina is called into question, and a total disengagement is advocated, it is certainly tempting to say in rejoinder that this involvement represents the decisions and judgments of several U.S. administrations (the thread can be traced back to the early post-World War II period), and that surely all these men cannot have

[24] *New York Times*, December 31, 1971.

[25] Another consideration in weighing whether or not continuing use of air power represents an effective bargaining counter is how the other side views it in strategic terms. Roger Hilsman maintains: "The fact of the matter was that Asians tended to interpret the use of air power *alone* as a weak response, even though they feared air power. The United States has so often flirted with the idea of 'immaculate' war in Asia, war fought in the air above the muck and blood of jungle fighting, that Asians thought of air power alone as a bluff." *To Move a Nation* (Delta, 1967), p. 533.

been fools or knaves. This observation does not, of course, prove the involvement to have been wise; but it would indeed be surprising and more than a little disquieting to find that American policy makers over such an extended period were uniformly incompetent or had concealed motives. We do not believe it is necessary to make such an assertion to conclude that American policy has been misguided and in many respects self-defeating.

We put forward the view, instead, that a crucial failure occurred in a different domain: it can perhaps best be described as a *failure of the imagination.*

Decision makers in Washington remain isolated, both geographically and imaginatively, from the effects of their decisions; military commanders are similarly separated from the consequences of their actions. The culture and traditions of Indochina remain strange and remote, as does the historical and political background of the present conflict. The people there are pictured as pawns who count their own lives cheaply and respond like marionettes to manipulation from Peking or Moscow.

The reasons for such a collective failure of the American imagination are manifold, but two seem particularly relevant to the use of air power. First, the U.S. has never suffered aerial bombardment. Suppose the North Vietnamese had been in a position to carry out occasional air attacks in retaliation for the bombing of their country, say against Seattle. Who can doubt that the tenor of the bombing discussions would have changed radically? The question to bomb or not to bomb would quickly have taken on an added dimension of tangibility.

Second, the very availability of an advanced technology tends to inhibit the imagination.[26] If powerful tools are at hand, it is almost a reflex to reach for them first: and how much greater the temptation to do so if the cost is relatively low. The Nixon Doctrine, Vietnamization, and the evolution of the electronic battlefield and automated warfare, all place growing emphasis on the technology of air warfare as a handmaiden to a set of policy aims which, with lesser though still awesomely powerful means of implementation, have shown themselves elusive and costly. The experience with air warfare in Indochina suggests that a reassessment of American policy there is long overdue.

[26] From reading *The Pentagon Papers* and the reports of participants in Vietnam policy-making, one senses how the confidence American policy-makers had in the technology at hand kept them from looking more for non-technological factors. There was a "can do" attitude taken toward the machines and equipment that had been developed with America's brains and wealth; if they didn't achieve results, it was seen as a matter of getting more and better machines. For specific references, see Townsend Hoopes, *The Limits of Intervention* (McKay, 1969), pp. 18-19, 70, and 79-80.

APPENDIX A

GLOSSARY OF ABBREVIATIONS

AA	Anti-aircraft
AAA	Anti-aircraft artillery
ARVN	Army of the Republic of (South) Vietnam
BARREL ROLL	Code name for air operations in central and northern Laos
BG	*Bataillons Guerriers*, pro-Government irregular forces in Laos
CBU	Cluster-bomb unit, an anti-personnel weapon
CEP	Circular error probable, distance from aiming point within which half the bombs or projectiles are expected to strike
CIA	(U.S.) Central Intelligence Agency
DMZ	Demilitarized Zone, region near 17°N separating North and South Vietnam
DRV	Democratic Republic of (North) Vietnam
FAC	Forward air controller
FFZ	Free-fire zone
FUNK	*Front Uni National Kampuchea*, National United Front of Kampuchea (Cambodia)
GVN	Government of (South) Vietnam
IGLOO WHITE	Code name of program for developing electronic battlefield
JCS	Joint Chiefs of Staff, U.S. Defense Department
LOC	Lines of communication
Loran	Radio navigation aid
MIG	Soviet fighter-bomber
MIG cap	Fighter escort to protect an air mission from hostile fighters
MR	Military Region
NLF	National Liberation Front (for South Vietnam)
NVA	North Vietnamese Army
PARVELA	Partially validated area, for bombing in Laos
PL	Pathet Lao, anti-Government forces in Laos
POL	Petroleum, oil, and lubricants
Psyops	Psychological operations, e.g., leaflet drops
RDT&E	Research, Development, Test & Evaluation
Real Time	A computer operates in real time if it absorbs and processes information as received, providing an essentially instantaneous output
RLAF	Royal Laotian Air Force
RLG	Royal Laotian Government
ROLLING THUNDER	Code name for air operations against North Vietnam
SAM	Surface-to-air missile
SEA	Southeast Asia

SOLOA Specially validated area, for bombing in Laos
SSZ Specified Strike Zone, official name for free-fire zone
STEEL TIGER Code name for interdiction campaign over the Ho Chi Minh trail

TOA Total Obligational Authority
Trail Ho Chi Minh trail, network of supply routes from North Vietnam to South Vietnam and Cambodia

VC Viet Cong
VNAF (South) Vietnamese Air Force

Key to Abbreviated Titles for Congressional Hearings

AIR WAR HEARINGS (1967). *Air War Against North Vietnam*, Hearings before the Preparedness Investigating Subcommittee (Chairman: Sen. J. Stennis) of the Committee on Armed Services, U.S. Senate, 90th Congress, 1st Session, August 1967.

CLOSE AIR SUPPORT HEARINGS (1965). *Close Air Support*, Hearings before the Special Subcommittee on Tactical Air Support (Chairman: Rep. O. G. Pike) of the Committee on Armed Services, U.S. House of Representatives, 89th Congress, 1st Session, September-October 1965.

ELECTRONIC BATTLEFIELD HEARINGS (1970). *Investigation into Electronic Battlefield Program*, Hearings before the Electronic Battlefield Subcommittee (Chairman: Sen. H. W. Cannon) of the Preparedness Investigating Subcommittee of the Committee on Armed Services, U.S. Senate, 91st Congress, 2nd Session, November 1970.

REFUGEE HEARINGS (1970). *Refugee and Civilian War Casualty Problems in Laos and Cambodia*, Hearings before the Subcommittee to Investigate Problems Connected with Refugees and Escapees (Chairman: Sen E. M. Kennedy) of the Committee on the Judiciary, U.S. Senate, 91st Congress, 2nd Session, May 1970.

REFUGEE HEARINGS (1971). *War-Related Civilian Problems in Indochina*, Hearings before the Subcommittee to Investigate Problems Connected with Refugees and Escapees (Chairman: Sen. E. M. Kennedy) of the Committee on the Judiciary, U.S. Senate, 92nd Congress, 1st Session, April 1971.

SECURITY AGREEMENT HEARINGS (1969). *United States Security Agreements and Commitments Abroad*, Hearings before the Subcommittee on U.S. Security Agreements and Commitments Abroad (Chairman: Sen. S. Symington) of the Committee on Foreign Relations, U.S. Senate, 91st Congress; Parts 2 & 3, October-November 1969.

TACTICAL AIR HEARINGS (1968). *U.S. Tactical Air Power Program*, Hearings before the Preparedness Investigating Subcommittee (Chairman: Sen. J. Stennis) of the Committee on Armed Services, U.S. Senate, 90th Congress, 2nd Session, May-June 1968.

APPENDIX B

HISTORICAL NOTES ON AIR WARFARE FROM WORLD WAR II TO INDOCHINA

Air warfare did not begin in Indochina nor is it at all likely to end with Indochina. To provide some historical perspective from which to view the air war in Indochina, this appendix reviews the outstanding features of other air offensives and makes certain comparisons which may be helpful in understanding the dynamics and difficulties of the Indochina campaigns. The first significant military uses of air power were in the First World War, where air planes were a quite unconventional weapon used in a quite conventional war.[1] Because the technology of air warfare was then so different from what it is now, however, we have restricted our survey to the more modern era.[2]

In looking first at the use of air power in World War II, we examine how and with what effect it was used in a large-scale war having mostly "conventional" features: front lines, set-piece battles, and developed systems of production, transportation and communication on both sides. Then, in the Korean War, we find air power used where such systems are more primitive on one side, though the other features hold. Finally, we consider the use of airpower in counterinsurgency efforts in Malaya, the Philippines and Algeria, where most of the conventional features are absent.

While the circumstances of the offensives under review varied widely, making each a special case, familiarity with each provides insights into the potentials and limitations of the use of air power under differing conditions and with different objectives.

I. THE AIR WAR IN EUROPE, 1940-1945[3]

The air war in Europe is almost entirely a story of the German, British and American air forces (the *Luftwaffe*, RAF and USAF). Activities by other countries and by other branches of the armed forces of these three countries were so unimportant that details of their operations can be ignored. The German air force, moreover, had been planned to provide close support to the *Wehrmacht* on the ground. Hence, except for the abortive attack on Britain in 1940-1941, it was used almost exclusively as a tactical and defensive arm. The *Luftwaffe* thus played a role primarily of delaying and partially frustrating the launching of the massive Allied air offensive against Germany. The RAF and the USAF were the principal actors.

[1] For an analysis of air warfare prior to World War II, see George Quester, *Deterrence Before Hiroshima: The Airpower Background of Modern Strategy* (Wiley, 1966).

[2] Use of air power in counterinsurgency efforts has some dim antecedents prior to 1940. The first record of threats to use air power against guerrillas was in Mexico, where the Carranza government threatened to use it against the agrarian movement of Emilio Zapata. See *El Democrata* (Mexico City), February 1, 1916, cited by John Womack in *Zapata and the Mexican Revolution* (Vintage, 1968), p. 250. There is no record of actual use. It has been suggested that Great Britain was reluctant to place limitations on the use of air power between the two World Wars because "[t]he threat of bombing unadvanced peoples, such as the Afghans in 1919, the Somalis in 1920, and the Iraqis in 1921-22 proved to be a much less costly means of controlling these areas than the use of conventional troops." See Quester, *op. cit.*, p. 60.

[3] For statistics and documentation in this section, we rely primarily on the *U.S. Strategic Bombing Survey* [*USSBS*] dealing with Europe. For a treatment of more of the policy and political factors involved, see Quester, *op. cit.*, and his article, "Bargaining and Bombing During World War II in Europe," *World Politics* (April 1963), pp. 417-437.

We shall concentrate on the Allied efforts to bomb Germany into submission. This was attempted by missions (1) to destroy civilian morale and the will to fight, (2) to reduce Germany's capacity to produce selected military items of crucial necessity, and (3) to bring military and economic activity to a state of collapse once the transportation system had been reduced to chaos. The first was the primary aim of the RAF's night-time "area raids" against German cities; the second was the central task of the USAF's daylight "precision raids"; and the third became the main objective of the combined Allied air forces as the war drew to a close in the winter of 1944-1945.

Area raids by the RAF began on a small scale in 1940 when it was found that the strong German anti-aircraft and fighter defenses made daylight bombing of specific industrial plants impossible. The scale of the raids was increased somewhat in 1941, but they did not become massive until early in 1942 following a build-up of RAF heavy bomber strength and the appointment of Sir Arthur Harris as Chief of the Bomber Command. Harris, according to the *USSBS*, "regarded area bombing not as a temporary expedient but as the most promising method of aerial attack."[4] He and his staff were allegedly skeptical of economic target systems, partly because of their belief in Germany's powers of industrial recuperation, and therefore "doubted that her war potential could be significantly lowered by bombing. At the same time, they had a strong faith in the morale effects of bombing and thought that Germany's will to fight could be destroyed by the destruction of German cities."[5] British area raids were expanded under Harris and continued to be the major British contribution to the air war until about the time of the Normandy invasion (June 1944). The distinction between area raids and attacks on industrial areas and railway marshaling yards then became fuzzy.

Some 30 percent of all British and American tonnage dropped on Europe during the war, and perhaps 55 percent of the tonnage of bombs dropped on Germany, was accounted for by area raids. The percentages prior to D-Day were very much higher. High explosive, incendiary, and (to a smaller extent) fragmentation bombs were all used. (See Table B-1 for statistics on bombing tonnages.)

The mission of the USAF was based on the assumption that precision bombing of specific targets was possible. At the Roosevelt-Churchill conference in Casablanca (January 1943), a directive was issued to the Allied air forces which stated that the primary object of the strategic bombing offensive was "the progressive destruction and dislocation of the German military, industrial, and economic system, and the undermining of the morale of the German people to a point where their capacity for armed resistance is fatally weakened."[6] The concluding portion of this directive was presumably for the RAF. The first part, designed to guide the American 8th and 15th air forces (based in Britain and Italy), was based on the doctrine that the initial objective must be to defeat the enemy air force and achieve air superiority as a precondition for carrying out the main strategic mission.

Reflecting this doctrine, the directive later specified five priority target systems, in the following order: (1) submarine yards (since trans-Atlantic logistics were even more basic than control of the air), (2) the aircraft industry, (3) transportation, (4) oil, and (5) other war industry targets. Soon, however, owing to successful attacks on submarines by naval planes at sea, the German fighter aircraft industry was made the target of first priority, with submarines, other aircraft targets, ball bearings, and oil as further primary targets.

The considerations behind the new directive were (a) the recognized need

[4] *U.S. Strategic Bombing Survey: Europe*, Volume 3: *Economic Effects* (USGPO, 1947), p. 2.

[5] *Ibid.*

[6] *Ibid.*

TABLE B-1

STRATEGIC BOMBING OF AXIS EUROPE IN WORLD WAR II, 1940-1945 (000 tons)[a]

	Area Raids	Trans-portation[b]	Oil production & storage[c]	Aircraft & anti-friction bearings[d]	Submarine facilities & airfields[e]	Miscel-laneous[f]	All Target Systems
Jan. 1940- Dec. 1942	55 (5)	11 (1)	-	-	4 (*)	32 (3)	102 (9)
Jan. 1943- Mar. 1944	177 (35)	31 (6)	* (*)	16 (3)	20 (4)	77 (15)	321 (64)
Apr. 1944- Apr. 1945	376 (88)	488 (114)	216 (50)	22 (5)	110 (26)	355 (83)	1567 (365)
Total	608	530	216	38	134	464	1990

*Less than 500 tons.

[a]Tonnages of bombs of all kinds (high explosive, incendiary, fragmentation) dropped on Axis Europe by the British RAF Bomber Command and the U.S. 8th and 15th Air Forces. (Figures in parentheses represent average tons per quarter.) Total tonnage including that deployed by non-strategic, naval and marine air forces was 2,700,000 tons (*USSBS:E*, 2: *Overall Report*, Chart 1).

[b]Includes railroad facilities, railroad equipment manufacturing, and roundhouses.

[c]Includes nitrogen and other chemicals for explosives produced in synthetic oil plants.

[d]Of this total, 5,000 tons were used against anti-friction bearings production, concentrated during the four quarters ending June 1944.

[e]Submarine facilities only through end of 1943; airfields only thereafter.

[f]Includes rubber products in 1943, and selected armament factories and naval targets in 1944-45.

Source: *USSBS:E*, 3, *Economic Effects*, pp. 2-5.

to achieve air superiority before precision targets could be successfully attacked, (b) a desire to concentrate on targets which would affect frontline strength fairly quickly and thus render maximum assistance for the eventual ground offensive on the Continent, and (c) a decision to exclude targets whose effective reduction was deemed to be beyond the capabilities of the air force.[7] "Effective reduction" meant a degree of destruction of a militarily crucial industry's productive capacity sufficient (i) to eliminate the "cushion" of inessential uses, reserve stocks, normal inventories, pipeline supplies, recuperative possibilities, and potential substitutes, and then (ii) to cut so deeply into the remaining "essential" capacity that shortages of operationally necessary supplies would measurably reduce front-line fighting power.

The fighter aircraft industry was regarded as meeting the foregoing criteria better than any other in the early stages of the stepped-up air war. The industry cushion was thought to be rather thin, and fighters were a major obstacle to Allied control of the air. For over a year after Casablanca, however, the USAF could mount only sporadic and limited attacks. Two of the most successful sets of attacks, operationally speaking, were those against aircraft and antifriction bearings, which were carried out in August and October 1943. Production of both aircraft and bearings declined after these

[7]*Ibid.*, pp. 6-7.

attacks, but a more important consequence was to alert the Germans to the need to take defensive measures, including dispersal and preparations for rapid recovery from attack, which they did promptly.[8]

The economic and morale effects of the strategic air offensive up to the end of 1943 were too small to cause a visible diminution in German front-line fighting power. The expanded scale and increased rate of RAF area raids in 1942 and 1943, augmented by the initiation of USAF attacks, shown in Table B-1, had caused appreciable damage to buildings and delayed production locally through the diversion of labor to repair work and debris clearance, and by causing absenteeism and local disorganization. The *Strategic Bombing Survey* concluded, however, that "the total loss of German armament output from air raids in 1943 cannot be put higher than about 2 to 5 per cent."[9] Aircraft and bearings losses were probably somewhat higher than this, but not enough to hurt.

By early 1944, the German planners had been alerted to the potential seriousness of their situation and had formulated plans for a rapid increase in armament production; at the same time they took defensive measures, including dispersal and the construction of underground plants in crucial industries. Meanwhile, however, the capabilities of the USAF had been greatly augmented. Toward the end of February, following a long wait for favorable weather conditions, USAF launched a week-long attack on fighter assembly plants. The raids were highly successful in an immediate sense, causing a timely and perhaps important dip in production. Nevertheless, output rose to a new high in the third quarter of 1944 before it finally began to diminish.

The rise in German aircraft production was largely the result of carrying out and accelerating plans made earlier. For similar reasons, total German production of major armament items reached a peak in July which was 45 percent higher than in December 1943. But this level, as in the case of aircraft, could not be maintained in the closing months of 1944. By the third quarter, as the result of several convergent influences, both the RAF and the USAF had achieved the capability of flying over Germany in daylight virtually at will. The most important factor contributing to this result was the build-up in numbers of U.S. bombers and long-range fighter escorts which made possible attacks like that against the aircraft industry in February.

In view of the impending June landing in Normandy, it was decided in early March 1944 that railway bottlenecks of major importance to the defenders would have first priority for bombing. Hence, the weight of attack on transportation rose rapidly to a peak in the second quarter (see Table B-1). Second priority was given to synthetic oil, especially the hydrogenation plants which produced virtually all German aviation gasoline, and a strong series of attacks on this system was initiated early in May. About the same time, the increased rate of attrition imposed on the *Luftwaffe* by the massive Allied offensive, and a shortage of skilled pilots stemming from training difficulties which had become manifest as early as 1942 (owing to a chronic shortage of aviation gasoline), began to affect German fighter defenses adversely. Also, for various reasons, the higher output of German defender aircraft in the 2nd and 3rd quarters was not translated into increased combat strength. By early summer these factors, together with the rapidly accumulating effects of fuel shortages and logistical problems, had

[8]The effort to cut through the antifriction bearings cushion and into essential production might have been successful if the attacks could have been continued. However, the center of the bearings industry (at Schweinfurt) was deep inside Germany, so that bombers could be given fighter escorts only part way. In the two attacks, by 183 and 228 B-17s respectively, about a quarter of the attacking planes and crews were lost. This was too great a loss to bear. By the time the attacks were resumed in the following year, after long-range fighter escort became technically feasible, the Germans had dispersed production and taken other defensive measures.

[9]*USSBS:E*, Volume 2: *Over-all Report* (USGPO, 1947), pp. 36-37.

combined to give the Allies virtually complete control of the air over the German *Reich*.

From mid-1944 on, the shrinkage of output of key industries, and the drying up of economic activity in general, proceeded with gathering speed. In the thirteen months from April 1944 to April 1945, for example, the total tonnage of bombs dropped on Europe, of which more than two-thirds fell on Germany alone, jumped to an average of 365,000 tons a quarter, compared with 65,000 tons in the preceding 15 months. Before the end of the year, German output of aviation gasoline and nitrogen had fallen 90 percent and that of other fuels was cut in half. Carloadings were reduced by 75 percent and steel production in the Ruhr fell by 80 percent as the result of the heavy attacks on railway facilities and cities, especially in the outlying industrial areas, all of which could now be attacked in daylight. In addition, 20 percent of the nonagricultural labor force had been tied down for some time in clearance of debris, reconstruction and dispersal of important facilities, and other types of repair activity. Casualties over the course of the war reduced the labor force by perhaps an additional 2 percent.

Notwithstanding these and other consequences of the bombing, the index of armament production in the fourth quarter of 1944 was only 10 percent less than its high in the third quarter. This is interpreted as only a superficial sign of strength, however, by the *USSBS*:

> The index of armaments production fails to reflect the serious damage done in 1944 to specific segments of the German economy--oil, steel, and transportation. This illustrates that the Allies did not attempt to destroy the German economy as a whole, or even the war economy as a whole. The bombing offensive sought rather to stop it from operating at key points.[10]

Whether or not this judgment was justified, it seems to be true that the destruction and incapacitation of productive facilities reached advanced levels only in those few key sectors of the economy which had been selected as priority targets. The *Strategic Bombing Survey* concluded, for example, that damage to the civilian economic sectors, taken as a whole, was not great enough to have been of itself a contributing proximate cause of Germany's final military collapse. "The most that can be said is that bombing destroyed a substantial part of the consumer-goods cushion and thereby prevented further conversion to war production during 1944."[11]

This economic judgment, however, touches on only a minor aspect of the intentional, incidental, and indirect effects of bombing on the civilian population. In the aggregate, according to the *Survey*, over 25,000,000 German civilians were subjected to Allied bombing.[12] The direct civilian effects, most of which were almost certainly the result of area raids and other attacks in which nonmilitary objectives had a high priority, were estimated by the *Survey* staff to be as follows (the figures are higher than the official German estimates):

Civilian casualties:	305,000 killed
	780,000 wounded

[10] *Ibid.*, p. 37.

[11] *Ibid.*, p. 38.

[12] This figure excludes the civilian populations which were subjected to bombing in other European countries, especially Italy, where there was an explicit intent to destroy morale. The total number of civilians subjected to bombing would also include the British population exposed to German air attacks in 1940-41.

Other civilian effects: 18-20,000,000 deprived of essential services (gas, water, electricity)
5,000,000 evacuated because of bombing (3,600,000 dwellings destroyed or seriously damaged--20 per cent of the German total)

The human significance of these figures, when translated into their implications for daily life--and not the relatively small impairment of German capacity to produce civilian goods and services--is what underlies the judgment of the *Survey* that "bombing appreciably affected the German will to resist." The main psychological effects, the *Survey* continues, were defeatism, fear, hopelessness, fatalism, and apathy. "War weariness, willingness to surrender, loss of hope in a German victory, distrust of leaders, feelings of disunity, and demoralizing fear were all more common among bombed than among unbombed people. . . . By the beginning of 1944, three-fourths of the German people regarded the war as lost."[13]

Even so, recalling that armament production increased to its war-time high in the third quarter of 1944 and only began to decline thereafter,the *Survey* notes that while Allied bombing had "widely and seriously depressed German civilian morale," it was nevertheless true that "depressed and discouraged workers were not necessarily unproductive workers."[14] The final judgment of the *USSBS* morale evaluation team was that "a minor, but not negligible, portion of this drop [in munitions production after the middle of 1944] was the result of the cumulative effects of lowered morale."[15]

The entire German economy gradually ground to a halt in the opening months of 1945. The cumulative effect of the air offensive, together with the territorial and other losses inflicted on the *Wehrmacht* by the Allied forces on the ground, caused an increasingly severe strangulation of the flow of coal, basic raw materials, and components to and among all economic sectors, and of logistical supplies to the fighting units. Though much plant and equipment remained operational, it could not operate. Realizing what was happening, Speer, the then Minister of Armament Production, reported to Hitler on March 15, 1945, that "the German economy was heading for an inevitable collapse within 4-8 weeks."[16] Of the correctness of this judgment there can be no doubt. An economy of the sort Germany relied on, once completely vulnerable to aerial attack, could not be sustained so as to support a vast conventional army in the field. Whether Hitler's forces could have been defeated without Allied offensive bombing cannot be known, but certainly the war could not have been brought to an end as soon as it was without the massive use of air power.[17]

II. THE AIR WAR IN THE PACIFIC, 1941-1945

The war in the Pacific, and the air war in particular, were fundamentally different from the war in Europe. Excluding the atom bombs (which are a special case and are treated separately below), total tonnage of bombs

[13] *Ibid.*, pp. 95-96.

[14] *Ibid.*, pp. 97-98.

[15] *Ibid.*, p. 98.

[16] *Ibid.*, p. 38.

[17] For other considerations of the air war over Germany and its effects, see: B. H. Liddell Hart, *The Revolution in Warfare* (Faber & Faber, 1946); Denis Richards and Hilary St. G. Saunders, *The Royal Air Force, 1939-1945*, Vols. I-III (HMSO, 1953-54); Charles Webster and Noble Frankland, *The Strategic Air Offensive Against Germany, 1939-1945* (HMSO, 1961).

dropped by Allied planes in the Pacific war was only 656,400, or less than a quarter of the European tonnage. Of this total, only 160,800 tons were dropped on the Japanese home islands, compared with 1,360,000 tons dropped on Germany--a ratio of 1 to 8. The strategic offense against Japan did not begin until late November 1944, and did not become intense until the following March. The bulk of the physical destruction was achieved in the six months ending in mid-August, yet it approximated that suffered by Germany, and the aggregate economic and morale effects were substantially greater owing both to Japan's greater vulnerability and her failure to take early and effective defensive measures against massive air attack.[18]

By far the greater share of the air power in the Far East was devoted to support of naval and ground forces in their advance across the Pacific, beginning with the battles of the Coral Sea and Midway in May and June 1942. From then until the end of the war, three-fourths of the total bomb tonnage was employed in supporting amphibious landings, providing cover for the advances of ground forces, attacking outlying Japanese bases and airfields, and destroying naval vessels, transports, and merchant shipping. Much of this action was carried out by carrier-based aircraft, and the attacks on naval and merchant ships were greatly assisted by submarines. In the end, the aggregate effects of the losses inflicted on Japan, including the almost complete interdiction of a large number of crucial raw material imports and the resulting exhaustion of stockpiles, were so nearly catastrophic in themselves that the authors of the *Strategic Bombing Survey* were led to express the opinion that "even without direct air attack on her cities and industries, the over-all level of Japanese war production would have declined [by August 1945] below the peak levels of 1944 by 40 to 50 percent solely as a result of interdiction of overseas imports."[19]

The strategic air offensive could not begin until the capture of the Mariana Islands in the summer of 1944 had provided suitably close and readily supplied bases for the main force of B-29s.[20] Of the total tonnage dropped on Japan the island-based B-29s accounted for over 147,000 tons, with the rest being dropped by other Army aircraft and carrier-based Navy aircraft.

From the beginning of the strategic offensive to March 9, 1945 a total of only 7,180 tons was dropped on Japan, though the amounts increased monthly. The most exclusive target was the aircraft industry, especially engines. The B-29s bombed from about 30,000 feet and only about 10 per cent of the bombs hit the target areas. Nevertheless, the effects were substantial, and induced the Japanese to initiate a wholesale and hasty dispersal program, with seriously adverse consequences for production (which was already suffering from shortages of special steels requiring imported and stockpiled ferro-alloys).

Beginning in March 1945, the method of attack was fundamentally revised. Cities became the main targets, with incendiaries dropped from 7,000 feet instead of high explosive bombs from 30,000 feet. Tokyo and three other cities were the targets of a series of ten raids beginning on March 9 in which some 1,600 sorties delivered nearly 9,400 tons of bombs and destroyed 30 square miles at the cost of 22 planes. Thereafter, urban area raids against 66 cities alternated with precision attacks on selected industrial and military targets, and an extensive program of sowing minefields in channels and harbors. Bombing altitudes were lower in daytime as well as at night than they had been previously. Accuracy increased substantially, averaging 35 to 40 percent of

[18] See *U.S. Strategic Bombing Survey: Pacific,* Volume 1: *Summary Report* (USGPO, 1947), p. 17.

[19] *Ibid.,* p. 19.

[20] Some 800 tons of bombs were dropped on Japan proper by China-based B-29s in the period from June 1944 to January 1945, but the raids produced no significant effects.

TABLE B-2

BOMBING OF MAJOR TARGET SYSTEMS IN JAPAN IN WORLD WAR II, 1942-1945 (tons)[a]

U.S. Army aircraft		
B-29 bombers		147,031[b]
Urban areas	113,373[c]	
Aircraft factories	14,150	
Oil refineries	10,600	
Arsenals	4,708	
Miscellaneous industrial targets	3,500	
Mines sown	700[d]	
Other Army aircraft (target systems unspecified)		7,000
U.S. Navy carrier-based aircraft		6,740
Airfields, warships, and other military targets	5,040[e]	
Merchant shipping and other economic targets	1,700[e]	
Total tonnage dropped on Japanese islands		160,771[f]

[a]Breakdown partially estimated according to following footnotes.

[b]In addition, 8,115 tons were dropped on airfields and seaplane bases in connection with the invasion of Okinawa.

[c]Of this, 9,373 tons were dropped in March 1945.

[d]Approximate figure, chosen for consistency with given tonnage figures; number of mines sown was 12,054.

[e]Approximate figure, based on statement that three-quarters of the total of 6,740 tons was directed at military targets and one-quarter against the others.

[f]Figure consistent with reported round total of 160,800 tons.

bombs within 1,000 feet of the aiming point in daylight attacks from 20,000 feet or lower.

The maximum monthly tonnage, reached in July, was 42,700, far below the rate of well over 100,000 tons a month sustained against Germany from the 2nd quarter of 1944 to the end of the war. Had the war continued, plans called for escalation to 115,000 tons a month, which was still below the figure planned for Germany.

Despite the far lower intensity of attack, the physical destruction in Japan was about equal to that in Germany, as noted above, and the economic, human and morale effects were considerably more severe. To a great extent these effects were due to the success of attacks against merchant shipping, which effectively isolated the Japanese island economy from its essential sources of supply of critical raw materials and needed food. At the beginning of the war, Japan had some 6,000,000 tons of merchant shipping capacity, and built another 4,100,000 tons during the war. Of this total, almost 9,000,000 tons were sunk or so seriously damaged as to be out of action when the war ended. Over half of this damage was inflicted by submarines; the rest was caused by carrier-based planes, land-based planes, mines (largely dropped from B-29s), and incidental causes.

Perhaps because of these successes, the Japanese railroad system was left almost undamaged. In the opinion of the *Strategic Bombing Survey*, however, this was a mistake. The island of Honshu had few main lines, and these traversed bridges of high vulnerability. A successful attack on one major rail ferry, one series of tunnels and only 19 bridges and vulnerable line sections "would have virtually eliminated further coal movements, would have immobilized the remainder of the rail system through lack of coal, and completed the strangulation of Japan's economy. *This strangulation would have more effectively and efficiently destroyed the economic structure of the country than individually destroying Japan's cities and factories.*"[21]

The extent of the physical damage in Japan was partly due to the greater concentration of the attack in time, which inhibited effective protective and recuperative measures, and partly to the fact that the target areas were smaller and more vulnerable. In the aggregate, some 40 percent of the built-up area was destroyed in the 66 cities subjected to attack, and approximately 30 percent of the entire urban population lost their homes and many possessions. The physical destruction of industrial plants subjected to high explosive attack was correspondingly great. B-29s carried larger bomb loads than the B-17s and B-24s used in Europe, and somewhat heavier bombs were used. Hence the damage tended to be more complete than in Germany. Reductions in physical productive capacity in major industries, including the losses due to attempted dispersal, were as follows:[22]

Oil refineries	83%	Army ordnance plants	30%
Aircraft engine plants	75%	Naval ordnance plants	28%
Air-frame plants	60%	Merchant and naval shipyards	15%
Electronics and communications equipment plants	70%	Light metals	35%
		Ingot steel	15%
		Chemicals	10%

The destruction just described forced the Japanese people and economy to operate on progressively diminishing rations of food and other essentials. Undernourishment was widespread. In addition, during the nine months of direct attack on the home islands, there were over 800,000 civilian casualties, of which about 330,000 were deaths. (The latter figure exceeded the number of German deaths.) Consequently, in the period of the strategic air offensive, there was a rapid weakening of morale, already undermined by news of the defeats of Japanese forces at one point after another in the Pacific. Whereas in June 1944 only about 2 percent of the population had believed that Japanese defeat was probable, 10 percent believed victory impossible by December, 46 percent by June 1945, and 68 percent just prior to surrender. Over half of these persons attributed their belief principally to air attacks *other than atomic*, and about a third to Japanese military defeats.

Hiroshima and Nagasaki. To describe in detail the particularly horrible character of an atomic blast, or its biological and physical effects, should be unnecessary here. Television and the testimony of atomic scientists have made us as familiar as we need to be with the nature of nuclear holocaust. We therefore present only a brief summary of the impact of the two atomic bombs as formulated by the authors of the *Strategic Bombing Survey*.[23]

The bombs were dropped on Hiroshima and Nagasaki on August 6 and 9, 1945. They killed at least 100,000 people and caused injury to approximately an equal number. This was 40 percent or more of the (then subnormal) populations of the cities. Six square miles, or over 50 percent of the built-up areas, were destroyed.

> . . . the primary reaction of the populace to the bomb was

[21] *USSBS:P*, Volume 2, p. 19 (italics added).

[22] *Ibid.*, pp. 17-18.

[23] Details are included in the *USSBS:P*. For other considerations on this subject, see: Robert Batchelder, *The Irreversible Decision, 1939-1950* (Houghton, Mifflin, 1962); Edwin Fogelman, ed., *Hiroshima: The Decision to Use the A-Bomb* (Scribner, 1964); Herbert Feis, *The Atomic Bomb and the End of World War II* (Princeton, 1966); and Robert Batchelder, "Changing Ethics and the Crucible of War," in Paul R. Baker, ed., *The Atomic Bomb: The Great Decision* (Rinehart & Winston, 1968).

fear, uncontrolled terror, strengthened by the sheer horror of the destruction and suffering witnessed and experienced by the survivors. Prior to the dropping of the atomic bombs, the people of the two cities had fewer misgivings about the war than people in other cities and their morale held up after it better than might have been expected. . . .

Based on a detailed investigation of all the facts, and supported by the testimony of the surviving leaders involved, it is the Survey's opinion that certainly prior to 31 December 1945, and in all probability prior to 1 November 1945, Japan would have surrendered even if the atomic bombs had not been dropped, even if Russia had not entered the war, and even if no invasion had been planned or contemplated.[24]

III. THE AIR WAR IN KOREA, 1950-1953

Like World War II, the Korean conflict is described as a conventional war since the ground war was characterized by traditional strategies and clearly defined front lines. A set of maps arranged in chronological order with the front line drawn across the Korean peninsula would give a clear picture of the movements of armies and consequent course of the war from 1950 to 1953. Nevertheless, the use of air power in Korea was by comparison not so conventional.

This war--the first in which jet aircraft figured prominently--was directed against a much less industrialized enemy than the Axis powers of World War II. This posed problems of strategy unfamiliar to the U.S. Air Force, which believed on the basis of its earlier experience that the most effective use of air power was against enemy war capacity through strategic bombing of production sources.[25] In this case, however, the sources of production supporting the North Korean war effort were located in China and could not be attacked for political reasons.

Moreover, air interdiction did not prove as successful in Korea as it had in the Second World War. Based on the success in isolating the German Normandy front from its lines of communication in 1944, by destruction of bridges and railroad junctions linking the front line to its base of support, the USAF sought to isolate the North Korean and Chinese forces at the front during the course of the war. Although the flow of supplies to the front lines was cut by 90 percent, it was not reduced below the critical level required by the enemy infantry.[26]

Thus, while the ground war in Korea was conventional, the air war seems almost to presage the Indochina air war. Although able to work in conditions of almost complete air superiority, the USAF in Korea chafed under the "limitations on the use of airpower," the political restrictions on bombing sources of war supplies in China[27] and on the use of the ultimate nuclear weapon. Also in Korea as later in Indochina, the American military were frustrated by the enemy's ability to move the necessary amount of supplies to their soldiers despite strenuous air interdiction; ". . . the enemy forces proved to be highly

[24] *USSBS: P,* Volume 1, pp. 25-26.

[25] Robert Frank Futrell, Brig. Gen. Lawson S. Mosely, and Albert F. Simpson, *The United States Air Force in Korea 1950-1953* (Duell, Sloan and Pearce, 1961), p. 653.

[26] David Rees, *Korea: The Limited War* (St. Martin's Press, 1964), pp. 374-375; also the RAND study by Gregory Carter, "Some Historical Notes on Air Interdiction in Korea," in *Air War Hearings* (1967), p. 376.

[27] Air University Quarterly Review Staff Brief: "Korea--An Opportunity Lost," *Air University Review,* IX:2 (Spring, 1957), p. 22.

elusive and their communications lines did not prove to be highly vulnerable to this form of attack."[28]

During the first year of war in Korea, during which the two armies moved back and forth across the peninsula and three rapid military reversals took place, the demands of ground strategy dictated how air power would be used.[29] The first phase of the Korean War began with the North Korean invasion on June 25, 1950. At the earliest stages of the invasion, despite initial hopes in Washington that the invasion force could be stopped by air and naval action alone, ground forces had to be committed. The first two companies of American infantry were landed at Pusan on July 1st, a matter of days after the invasion. The first phase lasted until September 1950, when United Nations forces stopped the North Korean People's Army (NKPA) from occupying the entire country by successfully defending the Pusan Perimeter, a small rectangular area on the southeastern edge of Korea.

For the first three weeks of July, the most important missions for the USAF's Far East Air Force (FEAF) and for the other UN air forces (which included units from the U.S. Marines, U.S. Navy, British, Australian, South African, Greek, South Korean, and Thai air forces) were provision of tactical air support for ground forces attempting to maintain their precarious foothold on the peninsula, and air superiority operations. Although controversy over the best use of air power accompanied the entire Korean War, the American infantry commanders during the Pusan perimeter defense period were certain that close air support made it possible for UN infantry to survive in Korea.[30] The close air support provided during July often acted as a substitute for the army's lack of sufficient artillery support during the first weeks of war.

At the same time FEAF conducted a series of air raids against North Korean airfields, destroying most North Korean aircraft on the ground. By the end of July, after only one month of war, FEAF had attained complete air superiority over North and South Korea, leaving perhaps only 18 enemy aircraft serviceable. "From then until the armistice was signed, the air attack by the NKAF [North Korean Air Force] could be considered strictly of a nuisance variety."[31] By August, interdiction missions could begin on supply routes behind the front lines. FEAF claims to have reduced the flow of supplies reaching the front from 206 tons per day in early July to 21.5 per day during the most crucial period of the perimeter defense in August.[32] In spite of the Allies' achievement of complete air superiority, heavy close air support, and interdiction, the North Korean high command was able to maintain its armies along a front deep in the South.

On September 15, 1950 the second phase of the war began with the simultaneous Inchon landing behind enemy lines and the beginning of a drive out of the Pusan Perimeter in an attempt to encircle and capture the NKPA. There is no question that this strategy proved to be very successful, but it is difficult to assess the importance of the role played by close air support

[28] Gen. S. L. A. Marshall, *The Military History of the Korean War* (Franklin Watts, 1963), p. 73.

[29] Gen. Otto P. Weyland, "The Air Campaign in Korea," *Air University Review,* VI:3 (Fall, 1953), pp. 3-28; and Rees, *op. cit.*

[30] Rees, *op. cit.*, p. 51.

[31] Weyland, *op. cit.*, p. 5.

[32] *Ibid.* At the request of UN Commander MacArthur, FEAF conducted a carpet bombing mission on the 16th of August on an enemy assembly area (3.5 miles wide and 7.5 miles long) near the defense line. Ninety-eight B-29s dropped close to a thousand tons of bombs in 26 minutes in carrying out this order, the biggest use of air power in support of ground troops since the Normandy invasion, "but no evidence was ever produced that this mission killed a single NK soldier, and the Communist pressure on the . . . front remained unaltered." Rees, *op. cit.*, pp. 46-48.

and air interdiction in this campaign.[33]

The success of the Inchon landing and push out of the Pusan Perimeter coincided with an end to the nearly completed bombing of military and logistic targets in North Korea which had been underway since the end of July. Because of the heavy losses sustained by the NKPA, and clear UN victories on the ground, it appeared that North Korea was now open to occupation by UN forces. Correspondingly, plans for air operations in the North shifted to industrial targets so as to disrupt the economy.[34] FEAF even had a plan for hitting an industry that provided the USSR with a chemical used in its atomic-energy program, thereby striking a blow in the Cold War.[35]

The use of incendiary bombs was considered in the planning stages.[36] However, the attacks on factories, ports, marshalling yards, communication centers, and supply areas were carried out without the use of incendiary bombs after all, because "Washington was hesitant about any air action which might be exploited by Communist propaganda and desired no unnecessary civilian casualties which might result from fire raids." The Air Force was further directed to drop warning leaflets in industrial areas before bombing raids.[37]

By October 2, the few industrial targets in the North lay in rubble and further raids on facilities of long-term significance were discontinued. As UN forces moved north toward the Yalu River border with Manchuria, medium bombers ran out of targets.[38]

At the height of UN military successes, the Chinese Communist Forces (CCF) entered the war on November 26, 1950. By the spring of 1951, the UN forces were forced to retreat below the 38th parallel. Close air support of ground troops again assumed primary importance while, at the same time, FEAF was forced to prepare for a new fight to maintain air superiority. Chinese MIG-15 fighters were committed to combat in November along with CCF troops. FEAF close air support and interdiction missions were successful enough to force the CCF and NKPA troops to move only at night. CCF reinforcing units needed two-and-a half to four months to travel to the front from the Yalu because of harassment of supply lines. On the other hand, the MIGs control-

[33] Much of the literature, both military and non-military, on the Korean War is filled with the debates between the USAF and other services over which factors were actually decisive. The most vigorous debate surrounds this campaign, with many seeing the Inchon landing as the decisive tactic, while Air Force men claim that the success of breaking out of the Pusan Perimeter was due to the devastation caused behind enemy lines by interdiction bombing.

[34] "If North Korea was to be occupied, FEAF wanted to neutralize the industrial targets; if North Korea would not be occupied, FEAF wanted to destroy its industrial potential . . ." Futrell, *et al.*, *op. cit.*, p. 184.

[35] *Ibid.*, p. 177.

[36] General O'Donnell hoped that "we would be able to get out there and to cash in our psychological advantage . . . by putting a very severe blow on the North Koreans, with an advance warning, perhaps, telling them that they had gone too far . . . and go to work burning five major cities in North Korea to the ground, and to destroy completely every one of about 18 major strategic targets." *Ibid.*

[37] *Ibid.*, pp. 178-179. Incendiary bombs were used later, after China entered the war.

[38] "Because of the lack of targets for medium bombers, General Weyland on 10 October instructed Bomber Command to reduce its sorties to 25 per day, a figure which would increase Bomber Command's aircraft serviceability in case it was needed for all-out ground support. But the ground forces needed no [such support]. . . . Finding nothing better to bomb, one 92nd Group crew recorded that it chased an enemy soldier on a motorcycle down the road, dropping bombs until one hit the hapless fellow. . . . [In late October] General Stratemeyer stood down the whole B-29 command: only three of the bridge targets assigned to Bomber Command for destruction were still usable and it had begun to look as if these bridges might be of more value to United Nations forces than to the defeated Reds." *Ibid.*, p. 195.

TABLE B-3

SORTIES FLOWN BY U.N. FORCES AND BOMBING TONNAGE IN KOREAN WAR, 1950-1953

	Counterair Sorties	Interdiction Sorties	Close Air Support	Cargo Sorties	Misc. Sorties[a]	Total Sorties	Bombing Tonnage[b]
FEAF	66,997	192,581	57,665	181,659	222,078	720,980	476,000
U.S. Navy	-	-	-	-		167,552[c]	120,000
U.S. Marines	2,096	47,873	32,482	-	24,852	107,303	82,000
Other UN	3,025	15,359	6,063	6,578	13,848	44,873	20,000
Total	72,118	255,813	96,210	188,237	260,778	1,040,708	698,000[d]

[a]Includes reconnaissance, air control and training missions.

[b]Breakdown of tonnage by target categories not found in literature.

[c]Not classified by mission.

[d]Breakdown by type of ordnance includes: 386,037 tons of bombs, 32,357 tons of napalm, 313,600 rockets, 55,797 smoke rockets, 166,853,100 rounds of machine-gun ammunition.

Source: Futrell *et al., The United States Air Force in Korea, 1950-1953, op. cit.*, p. 645.

led the northwestern area of North Korea, or "MIG Alley," along the common Korean-Manchurian border.[39] In the new battle for air superiority over the northernmost part of North Korea, FEAF pilots flying Sabre jets were able to down 10 MIGs for every FEAF plane lost. Even so, by October 1951, the Chinese Communist Air Force had done something in the Korean context which the *Luftwaffe* had been unable to do. It had stopped precision daylight bombing by the USAF over an important part of enemy territory.[40]

Coordinated with the air war between fighter planes over northwestern Korea were new attacks on North Korean airfields. After the entry of Chinese infantry and airmen into the war, an unwritten understanding governed the use of air space and "sancturies." Because the UN air forces did not bomb airfields and other targets in Manchuria, the Chinese airmen did not strike UN facilities in the South. However, the effective use of North Korean and Chinese air forces in close support and other attack missions depended on the operability of airfields in North Korea. Since FEAF had already established its air superiority over most of the North and lost some control only over MIG Alley, the airfields were bombed by FEAF as quickly as they were repaired, and the attempt to put North Korean airfields back into use was finally completely abandoned.[41]

On July 10, 1951 the last phase of the Korean War began with the start of Armistice talks. Both sides gave up plans for the unification of Korea by force, and the negotiations centered around the new border to be drawn between the two Koreas and arrangements for release of prisoners. UN ground strategy therefore was limited to defensive measures along a stabilized front somewhat north of the 38th parallel. Close air support accounted for 30 percent of all FEAF sorties after July, and was often used as a substitute

[39]Weyland, *op. cit.*, pp. 10-11; Futrell, *op. cit.*, p. 269.

[40]Futrell, *op. cit.*, p. 651.

[41]*Ibid.*, pp. 275-284.

for artillery,[42] but the emphasis in the use of air power centered on interdiction missions to bring maximum pressure for a settlement favorable to the UN forces. Throughout the Korean War, interdiction sorties accounted for 48 percent of all combat sorties, making it the major mission flown.[43]

According to a study sponsored by the RAND Corporation, the USAF interdiction program in Korea "all seemed to follow the same cycle: initial success and then defeat by enemy countermeasures."[44] The limitations which were experienced on the effectiveness of interdiction campaigns were traced to the low supply requirements of NKPA and CCF troops. "A Chinese Communist or North Korean division of 10,000 men required only 48 tons of supplies per day, allowing for 'some' stockpiling. . . . This may be compared with the 500 tons per day needed to support a 16,000-man U.S. division."[45] The low requirements of NKPA and CCF forces depended, of course, on obtaining food from local sources and on using captured weaponry. Aside from the variety of countermeasures employed by the NKPA and CCF, such as night travel, multiple parallel bridges, underwater bridges, removeable bridge spans, etc., it is generally agreed that the "single most effective technique, and the one that is generally credited with keeping the Chicom supplies moving, was their ability to repair bomb damage in minimum time."[46]

Although the results of special-purpose interdiction were disappointing, the Bomber Command continued to look for new targets which would prove decisive militarily and bring about a truce agreement. A new campaign against strategic target systems in North Korea was therefore begun in June 1952, with a combined strike by 500 Air Force, Navy and Marine planes against North Korea's hydroelectric system which supplied most of the North's electricity as well as 10 percent of the electricity used by the Manchurian industrial complex. Attacks on factories, barracks, and airfields followed and 23,000 gallons of napalm were dropped on the North Korean capital in July. All industrial plants in northeast Korea were destroyed, even the most remote. In January 1953, 54 percent of all FEAF sorties were devoted to a new interdiction effort on the northwestern Korean railroad network, but six days after the operation a limited supply started moving again.

Finally, in May 1953, bombers struck the irrigation dam system, flooding the main road and rail communication system north of the capital of Pyongyang. Additional strikes on dams did not cause flooding, due to emergency action by the North Koreans, who lowered the water level. Fifteen remaining North Korean dams were not struck.[47] The potential threat of flooding may have influenced the North Korean agreement to sign an armistice on July 27, 1953, establishing a boundary between North and South Korea quite near where it was when the war had begun.

The effectiveness of close air support was never seriously in dispute: but the results of interdiction and strategic bombing disappointed the military. Destruction by air never isolated the front lines, nor did it bring a speedy signing of the armistice, though it was apparent that the NKPA and CCF forces were weakened and the war might otherwise have dragged on even longer. One thing is clear: the bombing did bring enormous destruction to Korea. In supporting a claim that Air Force bombardment had been responsible for bringing the enemy to terms at the armistice table, General Zimmerman, FEAF Deputy for Intelligence, said:

[42] Rees, *op. cit.*, p. 371.

[43] Carter, *op. cit.*, p. 377.

[44] See *ibid.*, pp. 378-379.

[45] *Ibid.*, p. 376.

[46] *Ibid.*, p. 379.

[47] Rees, *op. cit.*, pp. 378-382.

> We established a pattern of destruction by air which was unacceptable to the enemy. The degree of destruction suffered by North Korea, in relation to its resources, was greater than that which the Japanese islands suffered in World War II.[48]

The estimated number of civilian casualties in the North was 1,000,000, approximately twice the number of military casualties suffered by the NKPA. In addition, 1,000,000 civilians in the South became casualties of war, approximately three times the number of military casualties incurred by the South Korean armed forces.[49] This was the price of restoring the *status quo ante bellum.*

IV. COUNTERINSURGENCY AIR WARFARE DURING THE 1950s

During the 1950s air power was used in counterinsurgency operations in Malaya, the Philippines, and Algeria. Though the individual circumstances of course differ for each conflict, and direct inferences cannot be drawn for the Indochina context, nevertheless there are lessons to be learned from these earlier operations.[50]

1. *The Malayan Emergency*

British colonial authorities in Malaya declared an "Emergency" in 1948 after the Malayan Races Liberation Army launched a wave of murders against rubber planters. The insurgency reached its peak of activity around 1951, though it did not die out until the end of the decade. As in Indochina, the insurgents drew on previous guerrilla warfare experience against the Japanese.[51] With organizational roots in the Chinese community within Malaya, the "CTs" (Communist terrorists) were for a while able to make road travel hazardous throughout Malaya and to demonstrate enough strength that the population would not expose or oppose their activity.

By 1951 the insurgents were successful enough that the British undertook serious countermeasures. Chief among these was the formation of an integrated command effort, with the British High Commissioner becoming also Director

[48] Quoted in Futrell, *op. cit.*, p. 643. A more graphic description is presented by Rees in *Korea: The Limited War*. "The total effect of the war had been to turn most of Korea into a desert. The cumulative result of the ground fighting, naval gunfire, the bombing, and the close support strikes with the ferocious all-destroying napalm with its 2,000°F heat, the elimination of even individual shacks which gave shelter to the Communist forces in the winter fighting, all made the havoc caused before the Chinese intervention seem as nothing. Even atomic bombing could hardly have pulverised man and his property more thoroughly than this ultimate of conventional warfare." [*Op. cit.*, p. 194.] Certainly only some part of the total damage was the result of aerial bombardment, but the military intention of inflicting such damage through bombing is stated by General Zimmerman.

[49] Statistics from Rees, *ibid.*, pp. 410-411.

[50] Relatively little attention appears to have been paid to these lessons, except for a symposium organized by the RAND Corporation in January 1963 on "The Role of Airpower in Counterinsurgency and Unconventional Warfare." As documentation is otherwise sparse, we rely heavily upon the proceedings of this Symposium, which is referred to below simply as "The RAND Symposium."

[51] The Malayan Peoples' Anti-Japanese Army, led largely by the Communists, was aided by the British in its resistance activities against the Japanese occupation forces. It drew on the Communist supply organization, the Min Yuen, which was submerged among the Chinese population, collecting supplies, information and recruits for the guerrilla units. For background, see Sir Robert Thompson, *Defeating Communist Insurgency* (Praeger, 1966).

of Operations. At all times the military campaign was directed by civilians and subordinated to political objectives. These were to show British determination and to gain (or regain) the people's confidence. There were as many as 22,000 British soldiers serving in Malaya in addition to the Malay Army and Police. Also, half a million Chinese squatters living in rural areas were resettled to secure them from coercion by the insurgents or to prevent them from giving voluntary assistance. However, as the commander of the No. 1 Bomber Squadron in Malaya at the time has stated, the campaign "was run basically as a civilian operation by the civilian power."[52]

The basic strategy was to separate the guerrilla forces from the population. This was made easier by the fact that most insurgents were of Chinese extraction while most of the rural population was Malay. There was no independent role assigned to air power; rather, it was almost always used in close coordination with ground forces. Offensive air support was found to be of limited effectiveness: so, instead of trying to kill insurgents from the air, the effort was directed at keeping them on the move, with ground forces assigned the actual task of eliminating the guerrilla units. Planes and helicopters gave invaluable logistic support, making the army units mobile in otherwise inaccessible terrain, ferrying them in and out of the jungles, and keeping them supplied. Aircraft were also used for reconnaissance and intelligence purposes, and for psychological operations. But the offensive air effort was very limited, as shown by the small amount of air-dropped munitions deployed. During almost ten years of warfare, the total of munitions dropped reached only 33,000 tons.[53]

All air operations were cleared with the local police in order to keep civilian casualties to an absolute minimum. As a planning staff officer for the Director of Operations put it:

> If you kill a few civilians from the villages or the aborigine tribes, particularly if they are children, you do more harm than all the good you may do by killing a few CTs. You have made those people, villagers or tribes, enemies for good. Quick air strikes, also indiscriminate bombing, became very unpopular toward the end.[54]

Also, special attention was paid to avoiding destruction of private property; rather than destroy a house in the target area, a raid was likely to be aborted, so strict were the rules of engagement.[55]

Direct aerial attacks on the guerrillas were found to be counterproductive; few casualties were inflicted on them, and incidental civilian damage was deemed very costly.[56] At the same time, when the guerrillas could be

[52] Air Commodore A. D. J. Garrisson, in *RAND Symposium: The Malayan Emergency,* Memorandum RM-3651-PR (RAND Corporation, 1963), p. 13. This series of publications was edited by A. H. Peterson, G. C. Reinhardt and E. E. Conger.

[53] *Ibid.*, p. 49. On objectives and evaluation of effectiveness, see pp. 7-10 and 70-78.

[54] Col. R. L. Clutterbuck, *ibid.*, pp. 56-57. Air Commodore P. E. Warcup, who commanded the Royal Air Force in Malaya, 1957-59, stated categorically in his concluding remarks, "If you let the military--I always use the word 'military' in its broadest sense--if you let the military run riot, so to speak, you will probably do more harm than good by getting the local populace against you, and so increasing their unwillingness to give you information, which is vital to your success." *Ibid.*, p. 70.

[55] See *ibid.*, p. 58. Squadron Leader J. C. Hartley reported that air crews were even threatened with court martial if they hit rubber trees as unbriefed targets.

[56] Between 1950-58, one air squadron dropped 17,500 tons of bombs and was credited with only 16 guerrillas killed. [*Ibid.*, p. 60.] This surprisingly low figure was supported in the Symposium by Brig. Gen. Russell W. Volckmann, USA (Ret.), who organized and led Philippine guerrilla forces against the Japanese in Northern Luzon between 1942 and 1945. "Of course,

harassed by air with no risk of civilian casualties, this proved useful by keeping them on the move and lowering their morale as they became more and more isolated in the hills. During the course of the war, less and less offensive air activity was undertaken, with the air forces concentrating increasingly on reconnaissance, transport and psychological operations. In these roles, in support of ground activity, air power was found to be valuable, even indispensable.[57]

Certainly the requirements for successful counterinsurgent warfare were less demanding in Malaya than in South Vietnam. In the former, there was no neighboring country that could easily support the insurgency with men and materiel, nor could the insurgents readily blend into the rural population to escape government forces. However, part of the reason for success in Malaya appears to have been the consistent recognition, on the part of the military, of the political basis of the war. The contribution of air power to the government effort was positive to the extent that it gave logistic and intelligence support and refrained from massive bombing of the countryside.[58]

2. *The Philippine Campaign against the Hukbalahap*

The insurgency in the Philippines after World War II had similar origins to that in Malaya. The Hukbalahap movement had opposed the Japanese occupying forces in the Philippines during the War and had the military experience necessary to mount a serious guerrilla effort after being barred from parliamentary participation.[59] Between 1946 and 1950 the Huks expanded their control from their four base provinces in central Luzon to include all of central Luzon and most of southern Luzon, starting efforts even in northern Luzon and in the southern islands. The Philippine Constabulary, which was supposed to eliminate the Huk movement, proved quite incapable of accomplishing this, lacking numbers and integrity. At this point, Ramon Magsaysay was appointed Secretary of Defense and launched a concerted and integrated military-socio-

being on the receiving end of these air strikes in the Philippines," he remarked, "I can't remember ever suffering one casualty in three years from an air strike. . . . As a matter of fact, the air strikes put on us helped us more than they did the Japanese. They brought more people to our side because they killed the civilians." Commodore Warcup underscored this remark: "There you are. I don't think that can be said too often in this kind of war." *Ibid.*, p. 77.

[57]See statement by Col. Clutterbuck, *ibid.*, p. 77, and Commodore Garrisson, *ibid.*, p. 74. Note that the contribution of *jet* aircraft to the air effort was judged relatively inefficient. *Ibid.*, pp. 79-83.

[58]See statements by Commodore Warcup: "I am quite sure in my own mind that we, the military, won because the political background was right and because the political and military aims were convergent. . . . A war like this is a lengthy business. I do not believe there are any shortcuts. Certainly, quick military victories cannot be expected. Patience and careful joint planning between the civil and military authorities are essential. Air support has to adapt itself to the over-all requirement. I repeat, perhaps to the point of boredom, that we won because the political aim was right, because the Malayan people were won over. [*Ibid.*, pp. 1 and 9.] See also Sir Robert Thompson's statement on the role of air power in this kind of insurgency, *op. cit.*, pp. 106-108.

[59]The movement's name is a Tagalog acronym for the People's Anti-Japanese Army. After 1948, its name was changed to the People's Army of Liberation, but the old name remained in common usage. During World War II, U.S. forces working with Filipino anti-Japanese guerrillas had some cooperation with the Huks, though never close collaboration. See *RAND Symposium: Allied Resistance to the Japanese on Luzon, World War II,* Memorandum RM-3655 PR (RAND Corporation, 1963). After the War, the Huks mobilized on both the military and political fronts to end American involvement in the Philippines as well as to oust Filipino leadership sympathetic to the Americans. Six candidates supporting their program, including the Huk leader Taruc, were elected to the Philippine Congress in 1946 but were denied seats by the majority.

economic-political effort to counter Huk influence. There is no need to discuss his strategy or measures here, but only to note that he succeeded in forcing the Huk leader to surrender by 1954 and in ending the insurgency by 1956.[60]

The Philippine Air Force had little combat role in the campaign, guerrilla targets not being concentrated or easily identified. Ground forces had the major responsibility for dealing with guerrilla forces. Air power was used primarily for reconnaissance and air supply, though also for communication, inspection and psychological operations.[61] The effectiveness of air power, it was felt, depended heavily on ground intelligence, and numerous examples are given showing that successful harassment of guerrillas from the air depended on local informants. For this reason, air power had to be used very carefully in order not to alienate the people and dry up sources of information.[62]

In general, the use of air power in the Philippines appears to have been quite similar to that in Malaya, and to have been part of a similarly successful effort. Offensive aerial operations were sharply circumscribed, with great care taken to avoid civilian casualties. The primary contribution of air power was in transport and reconnaissance activities, not separate from but rather in support of ground operations.

3. *The Algerian War*

The war over Algerian independence turned into a larger-scale conflict than that in Malaya or the Philippines, and it was ultimately successful for the insurgents. In a number of respects it was more like the war in Indochina than were the other two conflicts, though in the critical matter of terrain it was altogether different. It is worth giving somewhat more attention to the details of this war, as air power was used more extensively against the insurgents.

Algerian forces seeking independence from France launched a small rebellion on V-E Day in May 1945, but this was quickly put down by French forces. Thereafter, several groups began organizing politically and militarily to oppose the French, and in November 1954 nationalists resumed the armed struggle, under the aegis of the *Front de la Liberation Nationale* (FLN). It is reported that French aircraft were used in combination with ground troops

[60] For a detailed discussion of Magsaysay's campaign against the Huks see Col Napolean D. Valeriano and Lt. Col. Charles T. R. Bohannan, *Counter-Guerrilla Operations* (Praeger, 1962). Insurgent activity, it should be noted, has revived in the last few years.

[61] Maj. Gen. Edward Lansdale, who served as an American advisor to Magsaysay, suggests that perhaps the most important contribution of the air force was getting Magsaysay, "the real commander of the Philippine Armed Forces, . . . around very quickly to visit the troops who were in combat. His presence there, his leadership, his inspection and the swift follow-through of the staffs in getting the troops what they needed were most important." *RAND Symposium: The Philippine Huk Campaign,* Memorandum RM-3652-PR (RAND Corporation, 1963), p. 53; also pp. 47-48 and 58.

[62] See pp. 39-43 for discussion of the importance of reliable intelligence. Gen. Lansdale reports: "Magsaysay had a very clear understanding of the war's objective, to win the people away from the other side over to the Philippine government's side. You don't do that by killing people's innocent relatives. You don't make war where it will hurt the people you are trying to win over; you try to strike an identified enemy." [*Ibid.,* p. 57.] This statement was evoked by a discussion of Magsaysay's restrictions placed on the use of napalm. "Magsaysay was afraid that napalm might be used in populated areas and kill innocent bystanders." Landsdale reported that Magsaysay was quite prepared to use napalm when the target was "a long way from villages or the civilian population." It may be noted that Commodore Warcup stated with respect to the air war in Malaya that napalm "was not part of our normal armory." *Op. cit.,* p. 49.

from the very outset of the war.[63]

Initially the FLN forces numbered only about 6,000 uniformed men, but despite military pressure they grew to about 18,000 within a year and a half. An FLN offensive launched in the spring of 1956 was met by a French counter-offensive in which good intelligence and air support brought the weight of modern firepower against the insurgent forces, cutting their number by about one third. Nevertheless, FLN troops continued to increase, reaching their peak of about 40,000 by 1957.[64]

The French armed forces in Algeria in 1954 totaled 50,000 men plus two squadrons of fighter-bombers (about 50 planes); by 1959 they had increased to 400,000 men, backed by 1,000 aircraft including helicopters, and assisted by several hundred thousand *harkis* (Algerian forces, mostly veterans of military service with the French).[65] French casualties in the first five years of the war were 13,000 killed, out of 1.4 million who had served in Algeria during this period; by comparison, the FLN lost 120,000 men and had 60,000 captured.[66]

The French Air Force, augmented by Army Aviation and Navy planes, played a major role in the counterinsurgency effort, flying as many as 10,000 sorties per month by 1958.[67] Every type of fire mission was flown, though most sorties operated in conjunction with ground forces rather than on independent offensive actions, and the primary task was reconnaissance.[68] Helicopters were widely used for transport, reconnaissance and liaison, and also for medical evacuation. As reported in *El Moudjahid*, a newspaper sympathetic to the FLN: "Every time one of the French units is in trouble, numerous air detachments fly immediately to its aid at the request of the local headquarters."[69]

[63] Edgar O'Ballance, *The Algerian Insurrection, 1954-62* (Archon, 1967), p. 50. O'Ballance has also written on unconventional warfare in Indochina, Greece, Malaya, and the Sinai Peninsula.

[64] *Ibid.*, pp. 65 and 88. The 40,000 were supported by 80,000 or more irregular forces and local militia. Reportedly, 30,000 rebel troops were killed and 13,000 captured during the first three years of the war. O'Ballance says the FLN army was "wiped out" but persisted. [*Ibid.*, p. 92.] This phenomenon is documented by Brig. Gen. A. Giroult, who commanded French forces in the mountainous Kabylia region. His 2500 men faced 600 guerrillas who were, however, "moving among 120,000 friendly Kabyles who provided much information and support. I had poor information on my side." After two years, in which 750 guerrillas were killed and another 1,000 captured, their activity was reduced but still not eliminated. Gen. Giroult attributed the relative success in his sector as much to medical and educational activities of the Army as to its military action. See *RAND Symposium: The Algerian War*, Memorandum RM-3653-PR (RAND Corporation, 1963), pp. 48-51.

[65] These are the figures given by French officers in the RAND Symposium, *ibid.*, pp. 7 and 13. George Armstrong Kelly puts the figure at 450,000 in *Lost Soldiers: The French Army and Empire in Crisis 1947-1962* (M.I.T. Press, 1965), p. 169; however Peter Pavet cites the number of French forces in 1959 as 800,000, in *French Revolutionary Warfare from Indochina to Algeria* (Praeger, 1964), p. 96.

[66] General Charles deGaulle gave these figures in a press conference, November 10, 1959; cited by O'Ballance, *op. cit.*, p. 141.

[67] *Revue de la Défense Nationale* reports a sharp increase in sortie rates, 1,500 in January 1956 to nearly 10,000 in March 1957; see issue for August-September 1957, p. 1393, cited in Hafid Keramane, *La Pacification: Livre Noir de Six Années de Guerre en Algérie* (La Cité Editeur, 1960), p. 230. Edward Behr, in *The Algerian Problem* (Norton, 1961), says that any number of witnesses will testify to the constant activity of rocket- and occasionally napalm-carrying French Air Force planes between 1956 and 1960 [p. 248].

[68] See discussion in *RAND Symposium*, *op. cit.*, pp. 22 and 27; also pp. 61-62.

[69] 15 mars 1958, cited in Keramane, *op. cit.*, p. 232. An account of largely ineffective offensive air action is given by Herb Greer, an American who fought with the FLN, in his book,

During the course of the war, between 1.5 and 2 million Algerians were relocated from their villages and homes, most of them into compounds commonly surrounded by barbed wire, watchtowers and guardposts. Whether this "regroupment" program--similar to the "pacification" program in South Vietnam and the "strategic hamlet" program in Malaya--was intended to protect the indigenous population from marauding rebels or to prevent the population from aiding the rebels, it failed to provide satisfactory living conditions for most of the refugees. The FLN claimed to have been able, despite French measures, to infiltrate and gain security and supplies in these compounds.[70]

Integrally linked with the regroupment strategy was the creation of forbidden zones--*zones interdites*--similar to the "free fire zones" established in South Vietnam. Assuming that all innocent persons had been removed from the area, planes and troops were free to shoot on sight.[71] As in Vietnam leaflets were dropped, warning villagers that "disaster" would befall them. But still it is reported that threats of bombardment had to be carried out to get the population to move in many cases, and that people got used to the daily raids, posting lookouts and taking shelter when necessary, concentrating most of their activity during the nighttime.[72]

The "quadrillage" strategy of securing specified areas against FLN activity--a form of "zone defense" where Algerians were either in "pacified" areas or liable to air or ground attack--met with considerable success when coupled with practically sealed borders with Tunisia and Morocco. The borders were fenced with electrified barbed wire, vulnerable only to tanks and rockets, and patrolled continuously by radar-equipped bombers to prevent even these from breaching the barrier.[73] Though the patrol activity tied up 80,000 French forces, it kept 30 FLN battalions formed in Tunisia and Morocco (about 20,000 men) from reinforcing the rebel army. Perhaps more significant, the barrier greatly reduced the supply of arms and ammunition available to the rebels. It should be stressed that the terrain in Algeria, much of it flat and most of it without foliage, was relatively favorable to the construction of border barriers and to the discovery and pursuit of rebel forces by air or ground.

By 1959, the FLN army had been reduced to about 10,000 to 12,000 regulars. What this meant in military terms is not agreed. Paret sees it as a standoff, in which the French forces could only contain but could not roll back the FLN army.[74] The French military, on the other hand, noting that they had reduced the scale of conflict, so that the FLN could no longer operate with company units but rather only with platoons, felt that they had achieved a significant measure of victory.[75] In any case, the FLN was

A Scattering of Dust (Hutchinson, 1966).

[70] Behr says as many as 1.5 million civilians were rounded up in regroupment centers by the end of 1960 [*op. cit.*, p. 250]; according to O'Ballance, 1.8 million were uprooted from their homes [*op. cit.*, pp. 200-201], and Paret gives the higher figure of 2 million [*op. cit.*, p. 45], neither specifying that all were interned in camps. The FLN claim is in *El Moudjahid*, 1 février 1958; cited in Keramane, *op. cit.*, p. 245.

[71] See Behr, *op. cit.*, pp. 250 ff.

[72] One leaflet quoted in *El Moudjahid* stated: "the moment of choice has come . . . you must decide between France and the rebels . . . you have 8 days to go to the camps listed, otherwise terrible machines will attack you"; another warned of "God's anger," followed by napalm and other weapons. See discussion in Keramane, *op. cit.*, pp. 233-234 and 241-246. In the *RAND Symposium*, it was reported that napalm was "pretty much standard" against entrenched FLN troops, though there is no report of use against civilian populations. *Op. cit.*, p. 41.

[73] See description of the "barrage" in the *RAND Symposium*, *op. cit.*, pp. 63-65.

[74] *French Revolutionary Warfare from Indochina to Algeria*, *op. cit.*, p. 96.

[75] Gen. Ezanno: "The war was over in Algeria as far as the military aspect was concerned. I am not talking about the political side. I am talking about the military aspect." *RAND*

successful in its objective, separating Algeria from France and winning national independence. The use of air power in this guerrilla war gave a decided advantage to the government forces, but it did not get translated into achievement of France's political goal. Even though battles were won in military terms, for France the war was still lost.

Symposium, op. cit., p. 8; also p. 74. Kelly confirms that FLN companies had been reduced and isolated so that they could engage only in terrorism and small skirmishes. Nevertheless, the French "superior force did not, for all its skill, crush the rebellion or demoralize it beyond repair, for as the latter was losing on the battlefield, its political credit was soaring in the chancelleries of the world aided by Western hesitations and by the skill of its external leadership." *Op. cit.*, p. 176.

APPENDIX C

TECHNICAL NOTES

1. AIRCRAFT

The air war is prosecuted with many types of aircraft, ranging from the Cessna 0-1 light observation plane to the giant B-52 Stratofortress. A detailed familiarity with all these planes is not needed to understand the main aspects of air warfare; a brief outline will suffice to place the various families of aircraft in perspective. (Table C-1 summarizes some of the relevant technical data.)

Observation Planes (Prefix O): These are used primarily by forward air controllers (FACs) who spot likely targets from the air, establish liaison with ground forces, and direct the strike aircraft to the scene. A FAC cruises low and slow to get a clear and leisurely view of the ground. He is vulnerable to ground fire and so does not venture into heavily defended areas. Most planes for this duty are derived from civilian craft for private use, e.g., the 0-1 Bird Dog, a modified Cessna 170.

Reconnaissance Planes (R): Photography, electronic spying, and sophisticated detection devices are involved here; the planes are often adapted from other types by adding special equipment.

Electronic Warfare and Tactical Air Control Planes (E): These act as airborne control centers for communications and navigation, and they may institute electronic countermeasures against the enemy's detection and tracking systems.

Cargo Planes (C): The rapid movement of men and supplies is an important function of air power in modern warfare. The aircraft used cover the whole spectrum of size and performance, including helicopters.

Attack missions in Indochina are flown by fighter-bombers, attack bombers, strategic bombers, and gunships.

Fighter-Bombers (F): The fighter's function is air-to-air combat, for which it needs speed, maneuverability, and specialized armament. Supersonic flight capability is important, but such flight consumes large amounts of fuel, especially at low altitude. Normal cruising is subsonic. Examples: the F-100 Supersabre, important in South Vietnam in the early years of the air war; the F-105 Thunderchief, the principal aircraft used against the heavily defended areas of the Red River delta in North Vietnam; and the F-4 Phantom, now the U.S. workhorse in this category. A lighter plane is the F-5 Freedom Fighter, the only jet fighter given to the Vietnamese Air Force (VNAF). These fighters double in the role of attack bomber. Usually they carry bomb loads on exterior racks, but while doing so cannot fly supersonically. The weight of ordnance carried varies from two tons for the F-8 to eight tons for the F-4, but depends on the amount of fuel needed and the armaments employed. Fighter-bombers cannot loiter for extended times; they can be refuelled in the air, however, if they can reach a spot where that maneuver will not be harrassed by the enemy.

Attack Planes, Bombers (A or B): Supersonic flight is helpful if a heavily defended air space must be penetrated. Otherwise, a subsonic plane is likely to have better bombing accuracy, greater maneuverability for evading ground fire, and longer range and loiter time. In a permissive environment even a training plane can serve as a bomber: the Royal Laotian Air Force flies T-28s,

TABLE C-1a: SOME STRIKE AIRCRAFT DEPLOYED IN INDOCHINA[a]

Aircraft	Service	Ordnance Capacity (tons)	Fixed Armaments	Speed[b] (mph)
A-1	AF,VNAF	4	4 20mm cannon	280
A-4	N,MC	5	2 20mm cannon	675
A-6	N,MC	9	5" rockets, BULLPUP	620
A-7	N	6.5	1 20mm cannon	700
A-37	AF,VNAF	2	1 7.62mm minigun	478
AC-47	AF,VNAF		3 7.62mm miniguns	230
AC-119G	AF		4 7.62mm miniguns	250
AC-119K	AF		4 miniguns, 2 20mm c.	250
AC-123[c]	AF		Area munitions	230
AC-130	AF		20mm & 40mm cannon[d]	315
B-52	AF	30[e]		650
B-57G	AF	2.5	20mm cannon, .50 cal.	600+
F-4	N,MC,AF	8	some have 20mm cannon	1600+
F-5	VNAF	3	20mm cannon	1000
F-8	N	2	4 20mm cannon	1000
F-100	AF	3	4 20mm cannon	800+
F-105	AF	6	1 20mm cannon	1400
T-28D		below 1	2 .50 cal.	350

[a]Not included are the F-111 which flew briefly before being grounded, the B-57 and F-104 which flew some missions early in the war, and the helicopter gunships which are flown by all four services in Indochina.

[b]The speed of sound is about 700 mph, depending on temperature.

[c]Another conversion of the C-123 Provider, the UC-123, has carried out defoliation missions in Indochina.

[d]A 105mm howitzer is reportedly being installed on at least one AC-130.

[e]See Statistical Summary, Sec. SS-6, for average bomb tonnages achieved in service in Indochina.

which in origin are slow, light, piston-engined trainers. Common attack bombers in Indochina include the A-1 Skyraider, A-4 Skyhawk, and A-6 Intruder. The A-6, a recent design, can carry up to nine tons of bombs and is equipped with highly sophisticated electronic "black boxes" for all-weather navigation and computer-controlled bomb delivery.

The B-52 Stratofortress is in a class by itself. Originally designed to deliver nuclear weapons, it was adapted for conventional munitions early during the Indochina war and has since been in very extensive use there, including some activity in each of the five theaters. A B-52 can carry 108 500-pound bombs and will release them rapidly to lay down a saturation pattern of explosives on the ground. It flies subsonically, usually at altitudes

TABLE C-1b: SOME OTHER AIRCRAFT OPERATING IN INDOCHINA

Mission	Aircraft
Observation, FAC	O-1, O-2, OV-10A
Electronic Warfare	EA-6, EB-66, EC-121, EC-47
Reconnaissance	RA-5C, RB-57, RB-66, RF-101, RF-4
Airlift	C-47, C-123, C-7A, C-54, C-118, C-130

Sources: *All the World's Aircraft* (Janes)

Aviation Week & Space Technology, May 10, 1971.

Fact Sheets, Directorate of Information, Headquarters 7th Air Force, Tan Son Nhut Air Base, Saigon.

Frank Harvey, *Air War--Vietnam* (Bantam, 1967).

Press reports.

above 20,000 feet. It is vulnerable to surface-to-air missiles (SAMs) and has generally avoided those areas, such as North Vietnam, where they are deployed.

Gunships: As implied by the name, the chief armaments for these craft are rapid-firing guns or cannon. Their purpose is to give close air support to troops in battle, or to stalk mobile targets. Helicopter gunships, though restricted by short loiter times, have the hovering ability to give precise local support. Fixed-wing gunships can remain airborne for long periods, which enables them to maintain uninterrupted patrols against such elusive targets as trucks on jungle trails. Most such gunships are adapted from transport planes; the first example was the AC-47 (nicknamed "Puff the Magic Dragon" and "Spooky"), a C-47 cargo plane equipped with three 7.62-millimeter rapid-firing machine guns, each discharging up to 6,000 bullets per minute. Indochina has been the laboratory for developing gunship technology. Not only is their armament becoming heavier, so as to ensure destruction of a truck's cargo as well as putting the truck out of commission, but also their on-board devices for finding and tracking targets at night are steadily becoming more sophisticated.

2. ORGANIZATION

Aircraft of the Air Force, Navy, Marine Corps, and Army have participated in the air war in Indochina. Operational control over the whole theater is exercised by the Commander in Chief, Pacific (CINCPAC), through the Commanders in Chief of the Pacific Fleet and the Pacific Air Forces, and the Commander, U.S. Military Assistance Command, Vietnam (COMUSMACV). The 7th Air Force, with headquarters at Tan Son Nhut Air Base outside Saigon, acts as coordinating mechanism for strikes by all the services through its Tactical Air Control Center in Saigon.

Air Force: 7th Air Force planes operate from bases within South Vietnam.[1]

[1]Some of the major air bases in South Vietnam are Bien Hoa, Binh Thuy, Cam Ranh Bay, Da Nang, Phan Rang, Phu Cat, Chu Lai, Tan Son Nhut, and Tuy Hoa.

Planes from Thai bases are serviced and supported by the 13th Air Force, whose headquarters are at Clark Air Force Base in the Philippines; the aircraft themselves remain under the control of the 7th Air Force, so that the combination in Thailand is known as the 7/13th Air Force.[2] B-52 bombers are flown by the Strategic Air Command, mainly from U-Tapao base in Thailand. B-52s based in Guam and Okinawa have also flown missions over Indochina.

Marines: The First Marine Air Wing was based at Da Nang and Chu Lai in South Vietnam.[3]

Navy: Apart from some riverine patrol planes based in South Vietnam, Navy aircraft operate from carriers stationed in the South China Sea. In the early years of the war, planes operated over South Vietnam from one to four carriers at Dixie Station, off the Mekong delta. For strikes against North Vietnam and Laos, planes come from carriers at Yankee Station, about 100 miles northeast of Da Nang.

3. MUNITIONS

A systematic description of all the types of aerial munitions is difficult; they can be classified according to many different headings. We will briefly enumerate some of these classifications, and then present a short discussion of some munitions which are typical of the kinds used most extensively in Indochina. Data on the relative amounts of each kind actually used in the conflict are not commonly released, and we have been unable to make a systematic effort at uncovering this information.

Method of delivery: Free drop (this is the usual bomb or canister ordnance; it is carried in bomb bays or on external pylons below the aircraft); free drop with guidance (steerable fins control the trajectory of the bomb and permit it to be directed with improved accuracy to its target, even when released from a greater altitude); cluster units (containers carrying many bomblets, bursting above ground level to distribute the bomblets over a large area); projectiles (from guns or cannon which are usually capable of firing at a high rate, and mounted in a fixed position within the aircraft); self-propelled projectiles (rockets: these increase the lateral range of the munitions); guided rockets.

Armament: Blast effect from high explosive; fragments or other projectiles (e.g., flechettes, pellets) driven by an explosive; incendiary action; chemical action.

Intended targets: Fixed or mobile; "point" or "area" targets; "hard" or "soft" (depending on the blast overpressure required for destruction, or impact velocity of projectiles needed for penetration); flammable or nonflammable, or explosive; personnel or materiel.

Fuzing: Detonation on impact; penetration (short delay, sometimes mounted on tail of bomb); advance (on nose probe to detonate before impact); time delay (seconds to days, to provide long-time interdiction of area covered); external stimulus (mines: sensitive to pressure from personnel or vehicles, vibration, magnetic metals).

Some common examples will serve as illustration:

General-purpose high-explosive bombs ("Iron bombs"): These account for the greatest fraction of the total weight of aerial munitions used; they are carried by fighter-bombers, attack bombers, and high-flying strategic bombers (B-52s), and delivered by free fall. Special streamlined models have

[2] Active bases in Thailand include Khorat, Nakhon Phanom, Ubon, Udorn, and U-Tapao.

[3] All Marine aircraft were withdrawn from Vietnam in 1971.

been developed to minimize interference with aircraft flight performance when carried externally. If delivery is to be from low altitude, high-drag fins may be fitted to slow the bomb down and ensure that it strikes the ground well behind the position of the plane itself. Weight ranges from 100 pounds to 3000 pounds; most common range is 500-1000 pounds; about 50 percent of weight is explosive. The bomb works mostly by blast effect, although shrapnel from the casing is also important. The bigger bombs are needed where strong targets must be knocked down (e.g., ferro-concrete buildings, or--more commonly in Indochina--deep bunkers). The crater from a 500-lb. bomb with impact fuze (e.g., MK 82) is typically 30 feet in diameter and 15 feet deep (this obviously varies greatly with the terrain). Shrapnel is important over a zone about 200 feet in diameter. Simple shelters (sandbags, earthworks, even bamboo) protect against all but close hits. To be effective, the bomb must be aimed precisely, often within tens of feet of its target; making the bomb bigger does not increase its effective radius of action proportionately.

Fragmentation bombs: Similar to general-purpose bombs, except only about 14 percent of weight is explosive, the remainder being metal in the casing (often a wire wrapping) intended to increase the amount of shrapnel. Intended for use against personnel concentrations or fragile equipment (trucks, radars, storage vessels).

Cluster bombs: Single, large bombs do not achieve a uniform coverage over large areas; making them bigger does not help much. The cluster-bomb unit (e.g., CBU-24, the "guava" bomb) solves the problem by packaging many smaller bomblets in a single container. The casing is blown open (by compressed gas) above ground level (typically 500-foot altitude), distributing the bomblets over an area several hundred feet on a side. The CBU-24 contains about 600 bomblets, each of which has a charge of about 2 ounces of explosive and carries in its casing some 300 steel pellets--which become the effective weapons (180,000 projectiles in all). The bomblets may be fused to explode on impact, or they may have time-delays of varying lengths. The CBU is essentially an area weapon and does not need to be delivered with great accuracy. It is effective against personnel and vulnerable equipment. Some of the many bomblets may be expected to drop into enclosed, fortified areas such as gun emplacements; thus CBUs have proven particularly effective in suppressing the use of crew-attended weapons (anti-aircraft artillery). They are also used in area denial against personnel, especially if provided with random time delay fuses; and against vulnerable, extended equipment such as radar antennas.

Napalm: Delivered by free fall in thin containers which tumble during flight, hence should be dropped from low altitude for accuracy. The active agent (250-1000 pounds) is gasoline jellied by mixing it with a soap powder (aluminum soaps of coconut oil). A later type, napalm B, consists of 50 percent polystyrene, 25 percent gasoline and 25 percent benzene, yielding a longer-burning fire and greater stickiness. On impact, a burster core surrounded by white phosphorus is detonated, scattering the napalm (with particles of phosphorus embedded throughout) over distances up to 100 feet. The phosphorus ignites spontaneously, and the napalm burns with a hot flame (up to 2,000°F) for several minutes. Napalm is sticky and cannot be readily removed from surfaces against which it has been splattered; attempts to brush it off result in further spreading. It is also quite mobile and can penetrate through openings into areas which are otherwise sheltered. A canister of napalm achieves excellent area coverage. Napalm is extremely effective as an antipersonnel weapon. It inflicts deep burns which, if not fatal, heal slowly and leave characteristic disfigurement. Its flame also has an asphyxiating action (by using up much oxygen, and producing carbon monoxide). Its area coverage, and the fact that it starts fires in many places simultaneously, also makes it an effective fire weapon against combustible targets.

Rockets: The most common size is 2.75" diameter, delivered singly or in bursts from tubes mounted under the aircraft. Accuracy of delivery is generally higher than for free-fall weapons. Warheads include fragmentation (flechette), high explosive (including shaped charge against armored vehicles), and incendiary action (most white phosphorus or plasticized white phosphorus, PWP). Phosphorus may be used as anti-personnel weapon, but also serves to generate white smoke (often for target designation for further strikes). Guided rockets include special devices (e.g., SHRIKE) that home on enemy radar signals.

Guns, Cannon: These range from the 7.62-mm "minigun" to 40-mm cannon (with explosive or incendiary shells). Most types can fire up to 6,000 projectiles per minute. In fixed-wing aircraft, guns and cannon are in stationary mounts within the plane and must be aimed by pointing the plane as a whole. Cannon are often used in strafing fire, producing a linear coverage on the ground. Gunships, with guns pointing out of the side of the fuselage, may be fitted with devices enabling them to circle their targets and keep the guns aimed at a fixed spot on the ground. Miniguns produce, by their volume of fire and the motion of the aircraft, an area coverage effective in close air support, area interdiction, and reconnaissance by fire (previous to ground penetration by troops). Cannon are effective in armed reconnaissance missions along lines of communication; they also serve for ground-fire suppression. The larger calibers (40 mm) were introduced to augment the destructive capacity of cannon fire against trucks and their cargo.

The "*Daisy Cutter*" (BLU-82/B general-purpose bomb) is the heaviest conventional weapon delivered by air. Of the total weight (15,000 pounds), 12,600 pounds are high explosive. The bomb is intended to work mostly by blast effect. It is delivered from slow-flying cargo planes by parachute; a probe detonates it just above ground level, and there is only minimal cratering The intensive blast zone is about 300 feet in diameter, clearing trees and other obstructions (instant helicopter landing zone). Also effective against troop concentrations and clustered installations such as anti-aircraft emplacements.

Guided bombs ("smart bombs") are discussed in greater detail in Chap. 12.

Mines: Various anti-personnel and anti-vehicle mines can be laid by aircraft. An example would be the *Gravel Mine*, a small explosive charge (in canvas cover) which explodes when stepped on; it maims but does not kill. Gravel mines are sown in high density to provide area interdiction against ground movement. Smaller mines, the size of an aspirin tablet, can be scattered to give audible warning as persons pass; larger mines (e.g., the *Claymore*) deliver a deadly blast of steel pellets in a concentrated pattern just above ground level.

Sources

1. *Status of Ammunition and Air Munitions*, Hearings, Preparedness Investigating Subcommittee, Committee on Armed Services, 89th Congress, 2nd Session, March 1966.

2. Army Technical Manual TM9-1325-200, *Bombs and Bomb Components* (April 1966).

3. *Aircraft Weaponization* (September 1970), U.S. Army Materiel Command Publication.

4. *The Components and Manufacturers of the Electronic Battlefield*, preliminary summary compiled by Gene Massey (August 1, 1971), NARMIC, American Friends Service Committee, 160 North 15th Street, Philadelphia, Pa. 19102.

5. *Weapons for Counterinsurgency*, Arthur Kanegis *et. al.* (January 15, 1970). NARMIC.

6. Arthur H. Westing, "The Big Bomb," *Environment* (November 1971).

7. J. B. Neilands, "Napalm Survey," in *The Wasted Nations* (Harper & Row, to be published).

APPENDIX D

NOTES ON ECONOMIC CALCULATIONS

Contents

D-1

DEPARTMENT OF DEFENSE ESTIMATES OF THE BUDGETARY COSTS OF THE INDOCHINA WAR METHODS AND DATA, FY 66 - FY 70

Extracts from: House Appropriations Committee, Defense Hearings for 1970, *Part 6, pp. 296-300*

COST OF SOUTHEAST ASIA CONFLICT

General Comments

1. There are two general approaches to describing the cost of the Southeast Asia conflict, the incremental cost approach and the full, or prorated, cost approach.

2. Incremental costs are the Southeast Asia-related costs over and above the normal costs of the Defense Establishment. These "normal" costs are assumed to be the annual costs as they existed at the end of fiscal year 1965, adjusted for any known changes in activity not related to Southeast Asia. For making management decisions within the Defense Department, estimating the impact of the Southeast Asia conflict on our economy, and estimating our resource requirements for the Southeast Asia conflict, the relevant consideration is the estimate of the incremental costs associated with Southeast Asia.

3. The full, or prorated, cost of the Southeast Asia conflict to the Defense Department includes a proration of the normal cost of the Defense Establishment. This estimate is not used for any management purpose and is included here only because it has been requested.

4. Estimates of prorated costs for a given period can vary over a wide range depending upon the assumptions used to make the proration. The two methods shown below, for example, which are equally defensible, produce estimates which are $1.9 billion apart. Any number of different figures could be computed simply by using other methods.

INCREMENTAL COSTS

Approach

1. To estimate military personnel costs, we first estimated the military personnel strength which was associated with Southeast Asia by taking the difference between the total personnel strength in a year and the strength for fiscal year 1965, adjusted for changes in strength not associated with Southeast Asia. The strength figure was then multiplied by the worldwide average cost per man, and to this was added special Southeast Asia cost items, such as hostile fire pay.

2. We estimated other operating costs by assuming that annual operations and maintenance total obligational authority above the fiscal year 1965 base, adjusted for known changes and pure financial changes, was equal to such costs.

3. For ammunition, we assumed that consumption costs were the current replacement cost of actual/planned consumption. The cost of aircraft and helicopter attrition was estimated by multiplying actual/estimated losses by original costs. We estimated equipment and spares by assuming that the net of all new equipment and spares delivered, plus inventory drawdowns, less increases of equipment in use, was used to replace Southeast Asia-related losses and was the cost for the year.

ESTIMATE

(in billions of dollars)

	Fiscal Year				
	1966	1967	1968	1969	1970
Military personnel costs	1.6	4.4	5.5	5.9	5.8
Other operating costs	3.0	6.6	7.3	8.1	7.2
Subtotal, operations	4.6	11.0	12.8	14.0	13.0
Ammunition consumption	2.0	3.7	5.8	6.9	5.9
Aircraft and helicopter attrition	.9	1.2	1.7	1.2	1.3
Equipment and spares consumption	1.2	2.4	3.1	3.5	3.0
Construction	.6	.9	.8	.5	.2
Research and development	.1	.2	.6	.6	.4
Total, incremental costs	9.4	19.4	24.8	26.7	23.8

Reconciliation of current estimate of fiscal year 1969 incremental costs with estimate furnished in the testimony on the fiscal year 1969 budget (in billions of dollars)

Fiscal year 1969 Southeast Asia incremental costs, per fiscal year 1969 budget testimony	25.2
Differences:	
1. Military personnel costs:	
Pay raise	+0.2
Other differences	-0.1
Total increase, military personnel costs	+0.1
2. Other operating costs:	
Price increases	+0.3
Pay raise	+0.1
Other differences, net	-0.2
Total increase, other operating cost	+0.2
3. Ammunition consumption: Net increase in consumption	+1.1
4. Aircraft & Helicopter attrition: Net reduction	-0.6
5. Equipment & spares consumption: Net increase	+0.1
6. Construction: Net increase	+0.2
7. Research and development: Revised estimate of requirements	+0.4
Total difference	+1.5
Fiscal year 1969 Southeast Asia incremental costs, current estimate	26.7

PRORATED COSTS

Two of the many possible ways of estimating prorated costs are given below.

METHOD A: ESTIMATE OF PRORATED COST FROM DEFENSE APPROPRIATION DATA ASSUMPTIONS

1. Operating costs not directly identified with Southeast Asia conflict are prorated in proportion to military strength to estimate the full, or prorated, operating cost of the Southeast Asia conflict. For fiscal year 1970, we estimate that the Southeast Asia-related average military strength is approximately 840,000 or 24.2% of the worldwide average military strength of 3,466,000.

2. Total worldwide operating costs are equal to new obligational authority (military personnel and operations and maintenance appropriations) for the year.

3. All other costs (ammunition consumption, aircraft attrition, construction, etc.) directly identified with Southeast Asia conflict are equal to full cost without any proration.

ESTIMATE, FISCAL YEAR 1970
(In billions of dollars)

	Total NOA (1)	SEA direct (2)	Other (Col. 1 minus 2 equals col. 3) (3)	SEA proration (24.2 percent times col. 3 equals col. 4 (4)	Total SEA (Col. 2 plus col. 4 equals col. 5) (5)
Military personnel, Active Forces	21.6	5.8	15.8	3.8	9.6
Operations and maintenance	21.8	7.2	14.6	3.5	10.7
Total operations	43.4	13.0	30.4	7.3	20.3
Ammunition consumption		5.9			5.9
Aircraft and helicopter attrition		1.3			1.3
Equipment and spares consumption		3.0			3.0
Construction		.2			.2
Research and development		.4			.4
Total		23.8			31.1

METHOD B: ESTIMATE OF PRORATED COST FROM DEFENSE BUDGET PROGRAM DATA ESTIMATE, FISCAL YEAR 1970

(In billions of dollars)

	TOA	SEA direct	Other direct	Common (col.4 equals col. 1 minus col. 2 plus col.3)	SEA proration[1] (col.5 equals f times col.4)	Total, SEA (col.6 equals col.2 plus col.4)
	(1)	(2)	(3)	(4)	(5)	(6)
1. Strategic Forces	8.0	0.6	7.4			0.6
2. General Purpose Forces	30.9	12.9		18.0	4.4	17.3
Operations[2]		(3.9)				
Procurement		(9.0)				
3. Intelligence and communications	6.1			6.1	1.5	1.5
4. Airlift and sealift	2.1			2.1	.7	.7
5. Guard and Reserve Forces	2.9		2.9			
6. Research and development	5.6	.4	5.2			.4
7. Central supply and maintenance	9.6			9.6	4.0	4.0
8. Training, medical, etc.	10.5			10.5	2.5	2.5
9. Administration and associated activities	1.5			1.5	.4	.4
10. Military assistance program	3.2	1.8	1.4			1.8
Total	80.4	15.7	16.9	47.8	13.5	29.2

[1]Factors (f) are as follows:

$$\text{General purposes} = \frac{\text{SEA-related military strength}}{\text{Total military strength}} = 0.242.$$

Intelligence and communications = same as General Purpose = 0.242.

$$\text{Airlift and sealift} = \frac{1}{2}\,\frac{(\text{SEA strength}}{(\text{Total strength}} + \frac{\text{SEA procurement})}{\text{Total procurement})} = 0.331.$$

$$\text{Central supply and maintenance} = \frac{\text{SEA procurement}}{\text{Total procurement}} = .420.$$

Training, medical, etc. = same as General Purpose = 0.242.
Administration and associated activities = same as General Purpose = 0.242.

[2]SEA direct operating costs are estimated as follows: Assume that the SEA proration for programs 3, 4, 7, 8, and 9 is essentially pure operating costs. Then, to estimate SEA direct operating costs, General Purpose Forces, deduct the sum of the proration from estimate of total SEA direct operating costs of $13.0 billion, i.e.:

	Billions
SEA direct operating costs	$13.0
Less:	
Intelligence and communications	-1.5
Airlift and sealift	- .7
Central supply and maintenace	-4.0
Training, medical, etc.	-2.5
Administration and associated activities	- .4
SEA direct operating costs, General Purpose Forces	3.9

D-2. BASIC ECONOMIC DATA, 1960-1971

	1960	1961	1962	1963	1964	1965	1966	1967	1968	1969	1970	1971
GNP, billions of 1958 $	488	497	530	551	580	614	658	675	707	727	724	740[p]
GNP, billions of current $	504	520	560	591	632	681	743	790	865	931	977	1047[p]
Consumer price index (1967 = 100)	88.7	89.6	90.6	91.7	92.9	94.5	97.2	100	104	110	116	121[p]
GNP Expenditure deflators (1958 = 100)												
For total GNP	103	105	106	107	109	110	114	118	122	128	135	142[p]
For Federal gov't. purchases	104	105	106	108	112	116	119	129	135	144	157	157[p]
Employment, in millions	65.8	65.7	66.7	67.8	69.3	71.1	72.9	74.4	75.9	77.9	78.6	79.0[p]
Unemployment percent	5.5	6.7	5.5	5.7	5.2	4.5	3.8	3.8	3.6	3.5	4.9	6.0[p]
Industrial production	66	67	72	77	82	89	98	100	106	111[p]	107[p]	107[p]

p = Preliminary

Sources: *Economic Report of the President*, February 1971. Washington, D.C.: USGPO, 1971, except as below.

Survey of Current Business, Jan. 1972 for all 1971 data; for GNP deflators, 1960-70, *ibid.* for July 1971, 1969, 1968 and *National Income and Product Accounts of the U.S.*, 1929-65, all published by U.S. Office of Business Economics, Department of Commerce.

ALLOCATION OF COSTS OF GENERAL-PURPOSE FORCES IN EUROPE AND ASIA, FY 71 AND FY 72 (PROPOSED) EXCLUDING INCREMENTAL COSTS OF INDOCHINA WAR

	Europe				Asia			
	$ billions			Percent of	$ billions			Percent of
	FY71 +	FY72 =	Sum	FY71 + FY72	FY71 +	FY72 =	Sum	FY71 + FY 72
Active divisions (Army and Marine Corps)[a]	6.4	9.3	15.7	35	6.4	4.6	11.0	34
National Guard and Reserve Divisions	2.0	2.1	4.1	9	-	-	-	
Navy attack carrier task forces) main air combat forces[b]	1.9	2.6	4.5	10) 35[b]	2.8	4.0	6.8	21) 35[b]
Air force tactical air wings) main air combat forces[b]	4.6	6.4	11.0	25)	2.3	2.0	4.3	13)
ASW and AAW forces	2.5	3.3	5.8	13	2.5	3.3	5.8	18
Amphibious and other forces	0.7	1.1	1.8	4	1.3	1.1	2.4	8
Airlift and sealift forces	1.0	0.6	1.6	4	1.0	0.6	1.6	5
Research and development	-	-	-	-	-	-	-	-
Total	19.1	25.4	44.5	100	16.3	15.6	31.9	

[a]Includes Marine air wings of unspecified deployment, estimated at $0.9 billion in FY72. Also presumably includes Army airborne units.

[b]Includes none of forces specified in note a.

Source: The Brookings Institution, *Setting National Priorities: The 1971 Budget*, p. 44; *1972 Budget*, p. 55. Washington, D.C., 1970 and 1971.

D-4

DOLLAR VALUE OF AIRCRAFT AND HELICOPTER ATTRITION, INCLUDING LOSSES DUE TO NON-HOSTILE CAUSES ESTIMATED BREAKDOWN OF OFFICIAL AGGREGATES

	(1)	(2)	(3)	(4)	(5)	(6)	(7)	(8)	(9)
	Aircraft and Helicopter Attrition		Helicopters			Fixed Wing Aircraft			
Fiscal Year	$ Value	Losses	Losses	Unit Cost	Total Value of Losses	Derived Value of Losses	Losses	Derived Unit Cost	Estimated Unit Cost
	$ 10^9	Number	Number	$ 10^6	$ 10^9	$ 10^9	Number	$ 10^6	$ 10^6
1966	0.9	764	257	0.23	.059	0.84	507	1.66	
7	1.2	1054	406	0.24	.097	1.10	648	1.70	
8	1.7	1737	942	0.25	.236	1.46	795	1.84	
9	1.2	1472	996	0.25	.249	0.95	476	2.00	2.97
70	1.3	1423	1027	0.27	.277	1.02	396	2.58	3.77
71[a]	0.8	950	750	0.28	.207	0.60	200	3.00	3.01

[a] Our estimate. See explanation below.

Explanation and Sources

Col. 1: Except for FY 71, DoD figures from App. D-1. Col. 1 = col. 5 + col. 6 for all years, including FY 71.

Col. 2: Except for FY 71, DoD figures of losses in SVN and NVN only. See SS-2. Col. 2 = Col. 3 + col. 7 for all years, including FY 71.

Col. 3: Same as col. 2 except that the DoD figures for FY 71 has been increased by about 10% to allow for Laos, etc.

Col. 4: Figures for FY 68 and FY 69 estimated from procurement data published in various Congressional hearings. Other years derived by using weighted mean of DoD B and C deflators, App. D-7.

Col. 5: Col. 3 times col. 4.

Col. 6: Col. 1 minus col. 5, except for FY 71, which is product of Col. 7 and col. 8.

Col. 7: Same as col. 2, except for FY 71, which has been taken as 50% of FY 70, owing to Laos, etc., instead of 139 as reported for SVN and NVN only.

Col. 8: Col. 6 divided by col. 7, except for FY 71, which is rough extrapolation of preceding trend.

Col. 9: Estimated from published procurement data, as for col. 4, and shown for comparison with col. 8.

D-5
B-52 OPERATING COSTS PER SORTIE IN INDOCHINA WAR

The following data are from the House Appropriations Committee, *Defense Hearings for 1970*, Part 2, pp. 749-50.

B-52 Munitions and Operating Costs
(in millions of dollars)

Appropriation	FY 68[a]	FY 69[b]
Operation and maintenance	$166.0	$325.7
Other procurement, munitions	330.2	486.0
Aircraft procurement, spares	51.9	21.8
Military personnel	33.3	59.9
Total	$581.4	$893.4

B-52 Average Costs per Sortie

Aircraft POL		$ 3,397
Depot maintenance		4,424
Transportation		3,468
Military sea transport service	2,312	
Stevedoring	626	
Commercial surface	530	
Systems support supplies		1,349
Base operating support		1,270
KC-135 support (refueling)		1,368
Munitions		22,500
Aircraft spares		872
Military personnel		2,773
Total average cost per sortie		$41,376[c]

In oral testimony [*ibid.*, p. 749] it was said that the average munitions drop was 27 tons. This gives cost price per ton of $833.

[a]These appear to be actual expenditures for FY 68.

[b]These appear to be programmed expenditures for FY 69.

[c]This figure is incorrect. Correct total is $41,421.

D-6

FIGHTER-BOMBER OPERATING COSTS PER SORTIE IN INDOCHINA WAR

Data on fighter-bomber (F/B) operating costs are less precise or less inclusive than those for B-52s. Figures in the *Pentagon Papers* for the ROLLING THUNDER campaign of 1965 set the number of F/B sorties at 55,000 and direct cost of the campaign at $460 million, or $8,400 per sortie. The same sortie cost is shown by the figures for the 1966 campaign, with 148,000 sorties and a direct cost of $1,247 million. These programming figures can be presumed to be lower than the average for the war period as a whole owing to the inflation of later years. Hence they have been adjusted for price change. See App. D-7.

A staff report to the Refugee Committee[1] sets the per sortie F/B cost excluding military personnel and the cost of aircraft spares, at $7,400 for flights into Laos from the Udorn base in Thailand, presumably for FY 69. Average cost per sortie for all fighter-bombers would be substantially higher than this for several reasons. Flights from Udorn would be relatively short and inexpensive. Carrier-based sorties cost considerably more than land based for the same distance covered. And, finally, inclusion of the costs of military personnel and aircraft spares would increase the FY 69 average by perhaps $2,000.

[1] *Refugee and Civilian War Casualty Problems in Indochina*, Staff Report to Subcommittee on Problems of Refugees and Escapees, Senate Judiciary Committee, 91st Congress, 2d Session, September 28, 1970, p. 27.

D-7

FISCAL YEAR ESTIMATES, FY 65 - FY 72, OF AVERAGE OPERATING COSTS PER SORTIE

	B-52s and Fighter Bombers										DoD Expenditure Deflators (FY 64 = 100)			
	B-52s					Fighter Bombers					A	B	C	D
			Munitions					Munitions						
	Ave. total cost per sortie	Average non-munitions cost	Cost per sortie	Tons per sortie	Cost price per ton	Ave. total cost per sortie	Average non-munitions cost	Cost per sortie	Tons per sortie	Cost price per ton	Mili-tary basic pay	Class-ified civilian salaries	Non-comp-sation component of USDC Fed.Gov't Deflator	B + C weighted mean
	1	2	3	4	5	6	7	8	9	10	11	12	13	14
	$000	$000	$000	tons	$	$000	$000	$000	tons	$	index numbers			
FY 64	--	--	--	--	--	--	--	--	--	--	100	100	100	100
5	--	--	--	--	--	8.4	6.2	2.2	2.75	800	106	106	102	103
6	31.4	16.2	15.2	19	800	8.4	6.9	1.5	1.83	800	117	109	104	105
7	35.9	16.7	19.2	24	800	8.2	6.9	1.4	1.63	832	120	113	107	108
8	38.0	16.4	21.6	25.9	833	8.9	7.1	1.8	2.15	856	125	117	110	112
9	41.4	18.9	22.5	27	833	9.7	7.4	2.2	2.50	896	136	124	114	116
70	42.3	19.4	22.9	27	850	10.5	8.0	2.5	2.60	952	159	140	119	124
71	44.2	20.4	23.8	28	850	11.6	8.4	3.2	3.25	992	172	148	123	129
Percent change FY 66-FY 71	+41%	+26%	+57%	+47%	+6%	+38%	+22%	+113%	+78%	+24%	+47%	+36%	+18%	+23%
Projection for FY 72 and beyond	$000	$000	$000	tons	$	$000	$000	$000	tons	$	index numbers			
	45.2	21.4	23.8	28	850	12.3	8.8	3.6	3.45	1032	185	157	128	135

Explanation and Sources on next page

NOTES TO TABLE D-7

B-52s

Col. 1: Sum of col. 2 and col. 3, except FY 68 and FY69 derived or taken from App. D-5.

Col. 2: Non-Munitions cost comprises "operation and maintenance" (around 3/4 of N-M cost), "aircraft spares," and "military personnel." From DoD data (App. D-5) and total sorties (col. 8, Table 9-2) we computed averages for all items in FY 68. For FY 69 full details are provided in App. D-5. To get estimates for other years, the two-year averages of these "benchmark breakdowns" were taken as a base and adjusted as follows, using the deflators (with base-year transformation) given in columns 11-14, above:

Deflator A for military personnel
" C " aircraft spares
" D " operation and maintenance (see *Sources*, below for deflator information)

Col. 3: Col. 4 times col.5. FY 68 and FY 69 are benchmark figures, derived independently from App. D-5.

Col. 4: Based on data in Congressional hearings and other sources (see below) on B-52 modification schedules and reported maximum capacities (or actual loadings, which always average less than the maximum) at various dates. Maxima were adjusted downward and curve through benchmark points was smoothed. Benchmark figure for FY 69 from App. D-5.

Col. 5: Figure for FY 69 (and consistency test for FY 68) from App. D-5. Since B-52s carry mostly conventional "iron" bombs, a standardized and mass-produced product, little adjustment was deemed necessary for the effects of inflation or increasing technical sophistication on costs per ton. The two adjustments were therefore based on hunch.

Fighter-Bombers

Col. 6: Sum of col. 7 and col. 8, except FY 65 and FY 66 from *Pentagon Papers* (see App. D-6).

Col. 7: Same definition as for B-52s, but no details available. We therefore computed munitions cost (columns 8-10) and subtracted from benchmark figures for FY 65 and FY 66 to get col. 7 for these years; subdivided this in proportion to breakdowns for B-52, and adjusted for price change by same method.

Col. 8: Col. 9 times col. 10.

Col. 9: Derived by subtracting total B-52 tons (col. 8, Table 9-2, times col. 4 above) from total air tonnage (SS-8) and dividing by F-B sorties (col. 10, Table 9-2).

Col. 10: Assumed that F-Bs used mainly "iron" bombs in FY 65 and FY 66, at same unit cost as for B-52s. Employment of increasingly selective and sophisticated ordnance--cluster bombs and "smart" bombs--presumably began to raise the average cost of F-B munitions soon thereafter. For example, the *Armed Forces Journal* (May 3, 1971) quotes figures from Sec. Packard which show that smart bombs cost about twice as much *per sortie* as conventional bombs. This might be an underestimate since laser guidance kits cost about $4000 each, and electro-optical kits cost $16,000 each. (Infrared guidance abandoned as insufficiently selective.) However, the overall average cost per ton would not have increased as much as any of these figures indicate, because less than half of the cost of total ordnance bought is for smart or sophisticated bombs. (*Defense Hearings for 1972*, Part 5, House Appropriations Committee, p. 1215.) Instead of trying to guess the changing mix of conventional bombs and various types of sophisticated bombs over the years, we chose to inflate the basic unit cost ($800 a ton) by deflator D (see *Sources*, below). The result seems highly conservative.

SOURCES FOR TABLE D-7

Data for cols. 1-10 (and helpful for Tables 9-2 and 9-4) on bomb capacities, actual average loads, ordnance technology and costs, sortie rates, losses, etc.:

Air University Review, Jan.-Feb., 1968
"Counterinsurgency from 30,000 Feet: The B-52 in Vietnam" by Robert M. Kipp.

Ibid., Nov.-Dec., 1968
"Khe Sanh: Keeping an Outpost Alive" by Maj. Gen. Burl W. McLaughlin

Ibid., May-June 1969
"Air Power in Limited War" by Dr. Harold Brown, former Sec. of the Air Force

Aviation Week and Space Technology, 5/13/68, 7/15/68, 7/22/68, 8/12/68, 8/26/68
Articles by Cecil Brownlow, datelined Saigon

Defense Hearings, House Appropriations Committee
-for 1967, Part 1: pp. 281-2, 525, 541-2
ibid., Part 3: pp. 481-2, 498, 503
ibid., Part 4: pp. 292, 327, 347
ibid., Part 5: p. 385
-for *1968, Part 2:* pp. 91, 237, 589-9, 601-3, 610-12, 620, 627-32, 726, 801, 808-9
-for *1969, Part 2:* p. 137
ibid., Part 4: pp. 999-1001
ibid., Part 5: pp. 231-4, 269-72, 440-46
-for *1970, Part 2:* pp. 748-51
ibid., Part 3: pp. 1074-5
ibid., Part 7: pp. 368-9, 394-5, 412, 428
-for *1971, Part 5:* pp. 711-13, 814, 835, 878, 907, 939-41
ibid., Part 6: pp. 98, 829
-for *1972, Part 1:* pp. 732, 766, 817, 819, 864, 872-3
ibid., Part 5: pp. 779-84, 902-05, 1071-82, 1085-89, 1167-72, 1175, 1182-88, 1213-15, 1217, 1219, 1226-30

Sources of deflator indexes (cols. 11-14)

Defense Hearings for 1972, Part 1, House Appropriations Committee, Table 5, p. 1158. Columns 11 and 12 are DoD indexes. Col. 13 is the U.S. Dept. of Commerce deflator for Federal Gov't. purchases of GNP (see App. D-2), adjusted by DoD to remove the influence of Federal expenditures on wages and salaries. It is thus a "goods only" index. Col. 14 is a weighted average of columns 11 and 12, with weights of 1 and 3 respectively. For additional information, see *ibid.*, p. 1136.

D-8. HELICOPTER OPERATING COSTS

Helicopter operating costs are estimated on the basis of annual operating costs per active helicopter because sortie data are operationally erratic. A sortie is defined as "from take-off to landing." While this works well for fixed wing aircraft, with sortie times usually measured in hours, it does not work for helicopters, with sorties which frequently last only 25-30 minutes, often less.

The following table shows annual operating costs per helicopter in FY 70 for the major types of ships. Direct operating costs cover the crew, maintenance personnel, maintenance of all kinds including depot maintenance, POL, munitions, but probably not transport to theatre (cf. App. D-5). Indirect costs include aliquot share of backup personnel and headquarters outlays (information obtained by interview).

Annual Average Operating Costs of Helicopters
Official DoD Figures as of FY 70

Type	Total per unit	Direct per unit	Indirect per unit
Combat and Observation	10^3	10^3	10^3
AH-1G	$244	$161	$ 83
UH-1B/C (utility role)	257	152	105
" (gunship role)	277	147	130
UH-1D/H	260	153	107
LOH	84	51	33
Cargo			
CH 47	639	486	153
CH 54	618	439	179

Average Operating Cost, Col. 13, Table 9-2

The simple mean of direct operating costs for combat and observation planes = $\frac{664}{5}$ = 135. This rounded up to $150,000 is the average cost used to derive figures in Col. 13, Table 9-2, FY 65 to FY 69.

The figures in Col. 13 for FY 70 and FY 71 are 95 percent and 63 percent of the FY 69 figure, these being the ratios of SVN combat helicopter sorties in the two fiscal years to those in fiscal 69. The actual figures are as follows (see SS-2 for underlying data):

FY	Combat Sorties July-Dec	+ Jan-June	= July-June	Combat Sorties Number	Percent of
	10^3	10^3		10^3	FY 69
1968	1771				
1969	1723	1816	→ FY 69	3587	100
1970	1286	1671	→ FY 70	3394	95
1971		961[a]	→ FY 71	2247	63

[a]June taken as equal to May.

D-9. ESTIMATED BUDGETARY UNDERVALUATIONS OF INDOCHINA WAR COSTS

Official budgetary estimates of war costs are too low for two major reasons. One reason is that the Department of Defense has failed to maintain "investment component" of baseline expenditures at the estimated level required for normal peacetime operations. Since it is the estimated required level of baseline expenditures which is subtracted from actual budget expenditures to get incremental war costs, and not the lower level of actual expenditures, use of the former figure instead of the latter results in an understatement of war costs.

A second understatement occurs because men who are drafted into military service can be and are paid less than their true economic worth as measured by what they could earn (and produce) in private employment. The excess of economic over budgetary costs for the draftees inducted because of the war must be added to the official figures to obtain a proper figure of the incremental cost of military personnel used in the war.

The methods employed for estimating the magnitudes of these two adjustments are described below.

a. *Undervaluation of Investment Component of Baseline Costs*

The so-called investment component of baseline expenditures includes a large part, or all, of the following appropriation categories:[1]

Procurement
RDT&E (research, development, test, and evaluation)
Military construction

Our estimate of the backlog of baseline investment accumulated because of wartime deferments of expenditures is 14 billion current dollars. The estimate is based on official data from cited sources. The data and derived estimates are shown below. Estimated shortfalls, year by year and for the war period as a whole, are given in line 11 of the table. All estimates and derivations are explained in the notes on the following page.

DoD BASELINE INVESTMENT EXPENDITURES

	FY64	FY66 thru FY71	FY66	FY67	FY68	FY69	FY70	FY71
	Billions of Current Dollars							
1. Procurement	15.1	n.a.	n.a.	n.a.	14.6	15.8	16.1	n.a.
2. RDT&E	7.0	n.a.	n.a.	n.a.	7.1	7.6	7.4	n.a.
3. Military construction	1.0	n.a.	n.a.	n.a.	1.2	1.0	1.0	n.a.
4. Totals	23.2	141.5	23.1	23.0	22.9	24.4	24.5	25.1
	Billions of FY72 Dollars							
5. Procurement	19.5	n.a.	n.a.	n.a.	17.2	17.9	17.4	n.a.
6. RDT&E	9.3	n.a.	n.a.	n.a.	8.5	8.8	8.0	n.a.
7. Military construction	1.3	n.a.	n.a.	n.a.	1.4	1.1	1.1	n.a.
8. Totals	30.1	164.5	29.1	28.1	27.1	27.8	26.5	25.9
9. Index of baseline quantity	100		97	93	90	92	88	86
10. Baseline quantity in current $	23.1	155.6	23.8	24.7	25.4	26.5	27.8	29.2
11. Quant. shortfall in current $		14.4	.7	1.7	2.5	2.1	3.3	4.1

[1] House Appropriations Committee, *Defense Hearings for 1972*, Part 1, pp. 1140-41 and 1164-65.

Explanation and Sources for table on previous page

Lines 1-8: FY64 and FY68-FY70 from House Approp. Comm., *Defense Hearings for 1972*, Part 1, pp. 1164 and 1165.

Lines 4, 8: FY66 and FY67 interpolated. FY71, line 8, estimated on basis of statement [*ibid.*, p. 1140] that investment total for that year, *excluding war costs*, was roughly 14% less than 1964 in FY72 dollars; conversion to current dollars in line 4 effected by applying ratio (.97) of total investment plus operating costs in current dollars for FY71 (26.5) to the corresponding sum in FY72 dollars (27.5).

Line 9: From line 8, FY66 through FY71 divided by FY64, and summed.

Line 10: Line 4 divided by line 9.

Line 11: Line 10 minus line 4.

Though the DoD figures given above relate to Total Obligational Authority (TOA) rather than actual outlays, there was little difference between the two in 1964, and the differences in later years would tend to wash out over time. The 1964 total outlay for the three investment items was $22.6 billion, current [see *ibid.*, p. 1160], vs. $23.2 billion for TOA, given above. Baseline investment outlays not available for later years.

b. *Undervaluation of Military Personnel Costs of the War*

Our estimate of the budgetary undervaluation of the true economic costs of conscripts required because of the Indochina war is a revised and adjusted version of an estimate by Robert Eisner.[1] His method and calculations, which are fully described in the appendix noted in the footnote, have been modified in the following respects:

1. We fitted our own equation to the data used by Eisner and came up with somewhat lower coefficients. The two equations are as follows:

Ours: $$ACC = (-26.21) + (38.32)(AF) - (18.00)(AF)^2 + (2.88)(AF)^3$$

Eisner's: $$ACC = (-52.93) + (71.12)(AF) - (31.24)(AF)^2 + (4.64)(AF)^3$$

where ACC stands for Added Costs of Conscription in billions of dollars and AF stands for total military personnel in millions.

2. Because of our lower coefficients, our subtrahend for the baseline costs of conscription for a standing peacetime force of 2,500,000 which would have been maintained in the absence of war is $4.21 billion instead of Eisner's $4.24 billion.

3. We used the actual figure of 3,161,000 for AF in 1970, whereas Eisner used the planned figure of 3,456,000.

4. We carried our estimate through FY 71, using a planned figure of 2,908,000 for AF, whereas Eisner's estimate stopped with FY 70.

[1]"The War and the Economy," in S. Brown and L. Acklund, *Why are We Still in Vietnam?* (Random House, 1970). See pp. 117-121 and Appendix on Added Conscriptive Costs.

APPENDIX E

NOTES ON THE ECOLOGY OF INDOCHINA AND THE IMPACT OF THE AIR WAR*

Ecological damage resulting from the air war in Indochina has caused considerable concern both in the United States and elsewhere. Much of this concern arises from biologists who, unlike the public at large, are aware of the staggering complexity of interactions involved in the continued function of natural ecosystems and of the extreme delicacy, and therefore vulnerability, of tropical ecosystems in particular. They are conscious, also, of the ease with which chain reactions of ever increasing magnitude may be triggered by perturbations which in themselves seem relatively minor. They are disturbed, finally, that what has become an all-out environmental onslaught in Indochina has been authorized in almost total ignorance and with an apparent lack of concern as to the potential ecological consequences to the land and its population.

In Chapter 8, we summarized some of the more obvious ecological effects of the air war which, for the most part, have relatively direct effects on man, his agriculture and his health. In this Appendix, we elaborate on some possible consequences to the natural ecosystems themselves. Since man's welfare is intimately and totally dependent on that of his environment, many of these consequences will also have effects on human life, though their manifestations are presently less predictable. After reviewing the nature of the herbicide agents used and presenting a geographical sketch of Indochina, we outline what is known about the possible effects of the air war on the soil, flora and fauna. Much more extensive discussion of these topics may be found in the cited literature, especially in the publications of the Herbicide Assessment Commission of the American Association for the Advancement of Science [1].** Any current assessment of the ecological effects of the war in Indochina must of necessity be based on a hopelessly inadequate collection of facts and a heritage of ignorance about tropical ecosystems in general.

*A brief outline covering much of the material collected here is given in Chap 8.

**An extensive review of much of the available literature may also be found in the recent book *Ecology of Devastation: Indochina* by J. Lewallen [2]. References identified by bracketed numerals are listed at the end of this Appendix.

I. CHEMICAL HERBICIDES

(1) *Agent Orange* is an undiluted 1:1 mixture of the n-butyl esters of 2,4-dichlorophenoxyacetic acid and 2,4,5-trichlorophenoxyacetic acid, known generally as 2,4-D and 2,4,5-T. The oily droplets of this most widely used herbicide combination penetrate the waxy leaf surfaces and are absorbed systemically into the plant; the compounds act as plant growth regulators, distorting the growth processes of the tissues. The main cause of death following systemic poisoning through the leaves or roots is apparently unbalanced tissue growth, particularly in the phloem, resulting in blockage of nutrient flow and formation of lesions which are vulnerable to microbial infection [1, 3]. In tropical hardwood forests, leaf fall occurs within 3 to 6 weeks, with surviving branches and trees refoliating within a year [1, 3]. A single spraying of hardwood forests with agent Orange causes a modest kill of the tall canopy trees, which intercept most of the spray droplets and afford partial protection to lower vegetation. Further spraying may then cause a heavy kill of all woody plants, no longer protected by the upper canopy [2, 4, 5, 6].

Agent Orange persists only for a few weeks in ground water or soil (2,4,5-T being rather longer lived than 2,4-D), though its disappearance depends upon microorganisms requiring specific conditions, including abundant oxygen [7, 8]. Orange accounted for 58% of total herbicide usage in Vietnam, where it has been used primarily for general defoliation against forests, brush and broad-leafed crops [1, 2].

(2) *Agent White* is a 25% solution in water of a 4:1 mixture by weight of the triisopropanolamine salts of 2,4-D and picloram (4-amino-3,5,6-trichloropicolinic acid) together with surfactants and a rust inhibitor [1]. Picloram is one of the most potent herbicides known, and unlike 2,4-D and 2,4,5-T, it is remarkably persistent [7, 9]. In a California test site, less than 20% of the picloram applied had disappeared from the soil after 467 days; in clay soils, the figure was less than 3.5%. Tropical test plots in Puerto Rico were still bare of leaves two years after defoliation by picloram [10]. First introduced in quantity in 1967, agent White has accounted for 31% of total herbicide usage in Vietnam; it is used mainly for forest defoliation and brush suppression [1, 2].

(3) *Agent Blue* is an aqueous solution of a 6:1 mixture of sodium dimethyl arsenate and dimethyl arsenic acid (cacodylic acid). Unlike the other herbicides, this compound does not act to distort the growth of plant tissues but acts instead as a desiccant, drying out the vegetation with which it comes into contact. It acts more rapidly and effectively on grasses than do Orange or White, withering the vegetation within a few days [1, 6]. Ac-

counting for 11% of total herbicide usage in Vietnam, its prime use has been for rapid defoliation of grassy plants and especially for rice destruction [1].

(4) *Area of application.* The total area sprayed one or more times in South Vietnam (about 21,000 km^2) represents approximately one seventh of the country's land area [1]. Probably the majority of the affected areas have received only one application of herbicide. Many areas, though, including roadsides and riverbanks, are regularly treated and at least 20-25% of the sprayed forests in South Vietnam have probably been sprayed twice or more [11]. Herbicides have also been used in Laos and Cambodia, for example along the Ho Chi Minh trail and Sihanouk trail systems, but the extent of use is not known [2]. Extensive damage is known to have occurred to Cambodian rubber plantations near the South Vietnam border in 1969, apparently as a result of direct spraying [9].

(5) *Cost of application.* Costs of defoliation are difficult to calculate with precision, though the scale can be judged from a cited figure of $70.8 million for 1968 alone [12]. In 1967, a single C-123 plane-load of herbicide (about 4,000 pounds) apparently cost about $5,000 [2].

(6) *Restrictions on use.* In April 1970, the Department of Defense ordered the suspension of the use of 2,4,5-T in Vietnam as a result of studies implicating this compound as a teratogen. The Army admitted continued use of this material, however, at least until August 1970 [10]. In December 1970, the White House announced that an "orderly yet rapid phase-out" of all herbicide operations in Vietnam had commenced. In March 1971, the Secretary of State informed Congress that chemical crop destruction had been stopped. In May 1971 the U.S. military use of herbicides in Indochina ended,although such use is apparently being continued at a very low level by the South Vietnamese [13].

II. NATURAL REGIONS OF INDOCHINA

Indochina can be divided into nine reasonably distinct geographic regions (Figure 1) [14, 15, 16]. These are as follows:

1. *The Mekong Delta.*--Approximately 67,368 km^2 of low-lying, mostly flat alluvial plain, largely built up by the five main distributary channels of the Mekong River. Lying mostly within South Vietnam, it also extends into Cambodia as far as Phnom Penh. Deposition of sediment is so heavy that parts of the shoreline are extended by up to 250 feet per year.

2. *The Mekong Plain.*--A large, gently rolling lowland with a few small upland areas, extending over three-fourths of Cambodia. The lower areas are flood plains of the Mekong River.

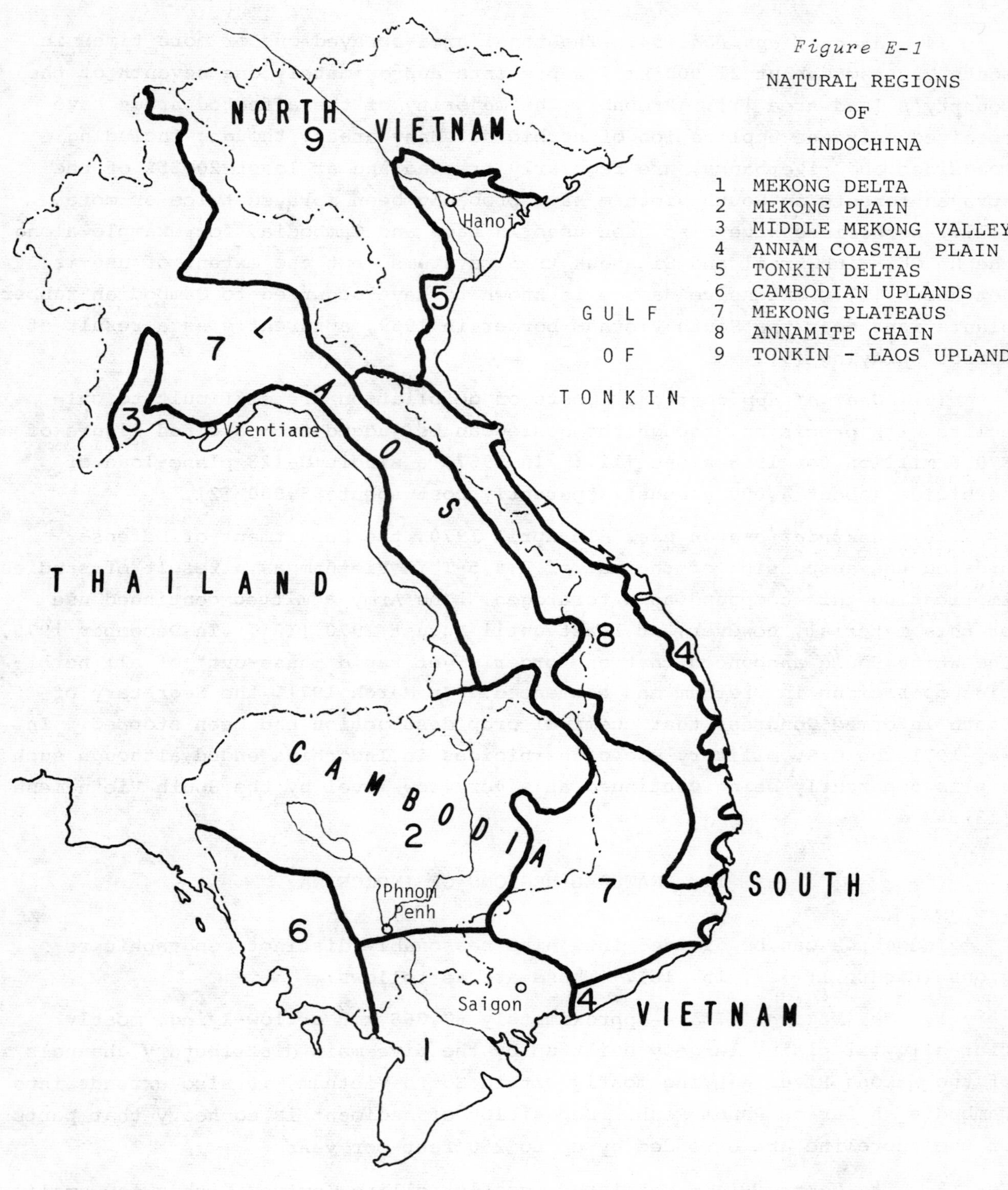

Figure E-1

NATURAL REGIONS OF INDOCHINA

3. *The Middle Mekong Valley*.--The alluvial valley of the middle part of the Mekong River, and the lower parts of its tributaries, extending from approximately the Cambodia-Laos border in the south to slightly north of Vientiane.

4. *The Annam Coastal Plain*.--The narrow and sometimes discontinuous series of low plains and relatively small deltas extending along the coast of South Vietnam north of the Mekong Delta and along the coast of North Vietnam up to the Tonkin Deltas.

5. *The Tonkin Deltas*.--A contiguous area of deltas along most of the coast of North Vietnam.

6. *The Cambodian Uplands*.--The hilly region along the southwest coast of Cambodia, comprised mainly of the Cardamom and the Elephant mountain ranges.

7. *The Mekong Plateaus*.--A large, frequently rugged upland area, composed of a series of plateaus and mountain ranges, extending from northern Laos to the Mekong Delta, bordering for much of its extent the Mekong plains on the west and the Annamite Chain on the east.

8. *The Annamite Chain*.--The range of mountains extending along much of the coasts of North Vietnam and South Vietnam to the west of the coastal plains and deltas.

9. *The Tonkin-Laos Uplands*.--The area of frequently abrupt mountains and plateaus which cover approximately 85% of North Vietnam and much of northern Laos.

III. ECOLOGICAL EFFECTS OF THE AIR WAR

A. *SOILS*

The soils of Indochina are very diverse and their properties are rather poorly understood, especially outside South Vietnam.* In common with many tropical soils, however, they are generally low in organic matter [19]; chemical weathering and organic decomposition proceed rapidly and under certain conditions accelerated loss of nutrients may be brought about by rapid leaching.

Alluvial soils are characteristic of the Mekong and Tonkin Deltas and the Middle Mekong Valley; they also make up much of the Cambodian Plain and some of Annam Coastal Plains. Continued natural fertility of some of these

*Several different classifications have been used in describing Indochina soils. Consideration of Moormann [17], Dudal and Moormann [18], and Tung [16] has led to the broad groupings used here.

soils is dependent on the periodic deposition of nutrient-rich silt, carried downstream by the rivers. Especially suitable for agriculture, alluvial soils support much of Indochina's rice cultivation. Agricultural productivity depends on careful control of freshwater distribution, yet influx of salt water in delta areas (a threat in the dry season) must be prevented. Over the years an intricate system of irrigation canals and dikes has been constructed to manage the cultivation of rice [15].

Less fertile, older *humic gley soils*, sometimes with subsurface laterite, are found on the higher terraces along the Mekong River. The *grey podzolic soils* dominate the terraces of the Mekong in Laos, Cambodia and South Vietnam. They have low fertility, are acidic, and contain laterite as concretions or layers. Where the water table does not fluctuate greatly, the laterite is usually soft and capable of being quarried. Where the water table has dropped, as by erosion, the laterite is usually hardened. *Red-yellow podzolic soils*, quite low in nutrients and often containing laterite as concretions or as continuous layers, cover large areas of many kinds of terrain. These soils, covering about half of Vietnam, are very susceptible to erosion.

Dark red and reddish brown *latasols* occur over extensive upland areas of South Vietnam, Laos and eastern Cambodia. They are granular and not particularly fertile, though relatively resistant to erosion. They respond well to fertilizers and are extensively used for upland cultivation. *Organic soils* have developed in some wet coastal regions of the Mekong Delta; they require carefully controlled drainage for agricultural use.

The widespread presence of *laterite* deserves further comment. It occurs in many of the soil types of Indochina, existing either as a fossil deposit from a time when conditions were suitable for its formation or as an 'active', frequently soft formation. Laterite is formed in soil that is saturated with water and it remains soft while wet. When dried, it may harden irreversibly, like concrete, and can then be used for construction of roads, buildings, etc. If near or at the surface, it renders the land almost useless for agriculture and restricts most other forms of revegetation. However, soil containing laterite which has not so hardened is not necessarily infertile or otherwise unsuitable for agriculture. Parent material and the type of lateriate are important in determining the ability of lateritic soils to support vegetation.

Over large areas of Indochina, soil conditions have been altered by herbicide spraying and by bombing. Cratering and the loss of vegetation have brought about reduced fertility, increased erosion, problems related to water balance and a greatly increased risk of widespread and irreversible hardening of laterite. We will consider these problems in turn.

1. *Reduced Fertility Following Loss of Vegetation*

Nutrient cycling is a vital process in the functioning of any ecosystem [20]. Inorganic nutrients such as nitrate and phosphate are absorbed from the soil through the roots of the plants and are incorporated into their tissues along with carbohydrates formed by photosynthesis. Dead plant material is broken down by an array of different kinds of decomposer organisms into inorganic forms which are then available for other plants, and so on [21, 22]. The original supply of these nutrients comes from the painstakingly slow weathering of bedrock and from the gradual accumulation of tiny amounts of materials deposited from the atmosphere by rainfall or 'fixed' from the atmosphere by certain microorganisms. In tropical rain forests, almost all plants nutrients in the ecosystem are in the vegetation itself, unlike many temperate systems where much is stored in the soil [19]. Many thousands of years may be necessary to build up the nutrient stocks of a forest and yet almost all can be lost in a short period following severe defoliation. Removal of foliage exposes the organic humus layer to full sunlight; decay is rapid and yet few living plants remain to trap the nutrients as they are released from the dead vegetation. Instead, they are quickly removed from the system by leaching and surface run-off as a result of the heavy rains [1, 10, 23, 24, 32]. The soil infertility resulting from such loss of nutrients may prevent forest regeneration for hundreds of years, condemning the area to occupation by relatively impoverished thickets of bamboo and other grasses. We discuss this further in the later section on Flora.

As a consequence of habitat alteration following even partial defoliation, loss of soil fertility may result also from changes in the composition of the soil microfauna and microflora itself.* Relatively little is known about the resilience of decomposers to environmental change, especially in the tropics.

2. *Erosion*

Increased soil erosion, especially in hilly areas with red-yellow podzolic soils, can be expected as a consequence of defoliation, whether by herbicides or by bombing. The soil is exposed to the direct force of heavy rains and also is no longer held together by live root systems. Approximately half the rain falling on terrestrial ecosystems is normally returned to the

*It does not appear that herbicides are directly toxic to such microorganisms, though this is not known for certain [4, 10]. Phenolic substances which are toxic to plants may be produced by the action of microorganisms on 2,4-D and 2,4,5-T. It is also possible that 2,4-D will affect the nitrogen-fixing activity of nodules on legumes, having consequences for soil fertility, and that 2,4-D and 2,4,5-T may induce chromosomal aberrations in plants, affecting their environmental fitness [26].

atmosphere by transpiration through the vegetation [22]. Loss of vegetation thus greatly increases water run-off, augmenting erosion further and causing an increased danger of flooding after heavy storms. Loss of organic matter due to decomposition and leaching of humus might also alter the soil structure and make it more vulnerable to erosion. Cratering is likely to disrupt soil stability and structure, upset local drainage patterns, and cause extensive erosion of terraced hillsides by destruction of terrace and water control structures. Increased erosion will result in added silt deposition elsewhere, with as yet unknown effects [15, 26, 27, 28]. A great danger of coastal erosion by the sea now exists in some areas as a consequence of mangrove destruction.

3. *Salinity*

The water content of soils is particularly important in relation to problems of salinity and laterization. Some areas of the Mekong Delta are invaded seasonably by salt water as the level of the Mekong river drops during the dry season. Damage to water control structures built to prevent this could lead to high salt build-up in the soil, with damaging consequences to local agriculture. Mangrove destruction further augments the risk of salinization. Salt must be flushed from some of the soils with large quantities of fresh water; this is made more difficult by destruction of water control systems [27].

4. *Laterization*

Irreversible hardening of lateritic soils could conceivably be caused by changes in the water table and exposure to weathering following bombing and, possibly, multiple herbicidal treatment of forests. An estimated 30-50% of Vietnamese soils have the potential for laterization. Significant areas of lateritic soils are found, for example, on the Bolovens Plateau in Laos, where bombing of the Ho Chi Minh trail has been escalating [18, 26]. Hardened laterite can make land unusable for agriculture and, when near or at the surface, reduce vegetation markedly.

Exposure of a lateritic subsurface pan by cratering, exposure of the soil surface by loss of vegetation (resulting in higher temperatures and in erosion which may uncover the lateritic pan) and a lowering of the water table following erosion, can all initiate or accelerate the hardening of laterite. Furthermore, any disruption of water balance that results either in drying of soils that were previously wet or in alternate wetting and drying of soils, creates appropriate conditions for hard laterite formation. Much of the lateritic soil which underlies 4% of the Mekong Delta, for example, would probably harden if denuded of vegetation and dried. Destruction of irrigation systems might very easily bring about suitable conditions for laterization in some rice-growing regions [4, 16, 18, 24, 29]. The magnitude of the danger of laterization in Indochina, is, however, very difficult to estimate. Though the major features of the laterization process are fairly well known, the actual outcome in any particular area depends on subtleties which are poorly understood.

5. *Bomb Craters*

More than 10 million craters have now been created in South Vietnam alone, mostly by 500 lb. and 750 lb. bombs dropped by B-52 aircraft [11]. This is equivalent to an area of as much as 650 km^2 and to the excavation of some 2.5 billion cubic yards of soil [11]. Substantial areas of Indochina are now so pockmarked with craters that they resemble the surface of the moon. Craters persist for many years, as evidenced by the continued presence in New Guinea jungles of bomb craters from World War II. Cratering has rendered useless much agricultural land; filling in even a single crater (as much as 15 to 30 feet deep and 30 to 45 feet in diameter) is a difficult task for farmers who do not have mechanized equipment. The task of land reclamation is made especially hazardous by the widespread occurrence of unexploded munitions buried in the soil [11]. Cratering also has the effect of altering the soil structure, bringing infertile subsoil to the surface, creating severe local relief and erosion, and affecting drainage patterns. Craters which have filled with water provide breeding grounds for malaria-carrying mosquitos. The full impact of large-scale cratering has not been studied. Beneficial effects are unlikely; any postulated mixing of useful nutrients from deep in the soil would have only short-lived effects. In the absence of vegetation, the nutrients would be leached away rapidly, leaving sterile subsoil at the surface [10, 11].

6. *Bulldozing*

Air warfare is also partly responsible for much of another kind of land destruction, the bulldozing of more than 3,035 km^2 of forests and fields by the Army Corps of Engineers in South Vietnam since 1965. Much of this land clearing is done to remove cover in which enemy troops could hide and to expose their movements to aerial observation.

Bulldozing is more effective at removing cover than is spraying with herbicides. The teams of huge armored D-7E and D-9 caterpillar tractors, equipped with sharpened Rome plow blades which cut off or push over all vegetation just above the ground, leave nothing standing. Strips up to 1000-2000 feet wide along the roads, large blocks of forests,and agricultural lands are bulldozed. Sometimes the ground is scraped down to the infertile subsoil; in farming areas, dikes and other water control structures are flattened. Bulldozing is apparently continuing at a rate of about 4 km^2 per day [2, 24, 25].

The most obvious ecological consequences of this vegetation and soil destruction include prevention of forest regrowth, invasion of cleared areas by grasses, erosion on slopes, and rapid run-off of rain water with consequent risk of flooding.

B. *FLORA*

Indochina was once almost entirely covered with forests which have since been greatly modified by human activities.* Much of the lowlands has been cleared for rice paddies; in the highlands most of the original 'primary' forest has been cut or burned at one time or another and the land cultivated or grazed, under systems of nomadic agriculture. When abandoned, such areas commonly undergo succession, leading over a period of years from initial grass and weed stages to 'secondary' forest, composed mostly of fast-growing softwood species. Over many centuries, if left undisturbed, the softwoods may be replaced by the hardwoods characteristic of the original primary 'climax' forest.** Where soils have been exhausted by heavy and extended cultivation, overgrazing, or burning, however, or where there has been considerable erosion, the former forest may never regenerate itself and succession can be permanently 'deflected' to an impoverished flora of savannah grasses.

At least nine main types of natural vegetation are recognized as occurring in Indochina. These 'formations', as they are called, are determined by various physical and chemical features of an area but more especially by the seasonal variations in temperature and rainfall[21]. The major formations of Indochina are as follows:

1. *Evergreen rain forest* characteristically occurs up to around 3,000 feet altitude in areas which have an annual rainfall of at least 80 inches, fairly evenly distributed throughout the year. Climax evergreen forests have remained unchanged for thousands of years; their foliage typically forms three major layers--shrubs and young trees making up a relatively open layer near the ground, an almost continuous middle canopy of tree crowns at 50-75 feet above the forest floor and, finally, an upper canopy of relatively isolated trees rising to 150-180 feet. These forests represent the richest and

*This discussion is based largely on material drawn from Richards [23], Williams [30], Fisher [15], Canada Department of Mines [14] and Tung [16].

**Five hundred years after Angkor was abandoned, for example, the forests there are still distinguishable from neighboring primary forest, though they closely resemble them [15].

most intricate environments in the world; the diversity of their flora and fauna is unsurpassed. Unfortunately, areas of primary tropical rain forest are shrinking rapidly the world over due to human encroachment. Though some areas of primary forest still exist in Indochina, much of the evergreen rain forest is secondary growth resulting from succession on land once used for shifting cultivation. In secondary forest the foliage is generally lower and denser; it is not so clearly stratified and the diversity of species is lower.

2. *Montane Forest* is limited to misty higher slopes; such forest is much less extensive than that of the evergreen rain forests and little appears to be known of their exposure to herbicides.

3. *Coniferous Forests* are of limited extent and have apparently not been treated extensively with herbicides.

4. *Monsoon Forests*, also known as semi-deciduous, seasonal, or dipterocarp forests, receive between 50 and 80 inches of rain annually and have well-pronounced wet and dry seasons. They contain many deciduous tree species, which lose their leaves during the dry season. In comparison with the evergreen forests much more light reaches the forest floor and undergrowth is denser in consequence.

5. *Dry deciduous Forests* replace monsoon forests as annual rainfall drops below 50 inches and the dry season lengthens to six months. These are much more open forests, with more grasses and undergrowth. Though still widespread in Indochina, both monsoon and dry deciduous forests have been extensively cut or burned by traditional shifting agriculture. The dry season makes these forests particularly susceptible to burning. Together with the evergreen forests, the monsoon and dry deciduous forests account for most of South Vietnam's forested areas and they have borne the brunt of the herbicide operations, for example in the Iron Triangle near Saigon, in the A Shau Valley and along the Ho Chi Minh trail in southern Laos [2].

6. *Savannah*, dotted with scattered trees and shrubs, is extensive in certain areas, especially in some highland plateaus. These grasslands probably represent secondary growth following destruction of the original forests.

7. *Mangrove forests* are characteristic of many coastal regions and river estuaries, especially the Mekong Delta. Comprising several different species, mangrove forests colonize and stabilize the shore line, consolidating the soil, and, after some decades, building up a climax dry land forest association ('rear mangrove') dominated by the cajeput tree (*Melaleuca leucadendron)* and the nipa palm *(Nipa fruticans)*.

Behind the coastal mangroves may develop freshwater swamps. Succession of various aquatic plants in these swamps deposits organic matter and traps silt, carried in by river waters. Gradually a tall forest emerges as the climax vegetation behind the coastal mangroves, though the ground level remains at water level since silting has ceased. As well as forming and slowly extending the Mekong and other delta lands, much of which have been converted to rice-growing, mangrove forests provide timber, fuel and charcoal wood, and essential habitat for stages in the food chains supporting some commercially important fish and shellfish. Having formed and extended the coastline, mangrove forests also protect it from erosion by the sea. In a region subject to frequent typhoons this function can be crucial.

8. *Coastal Pine Forests* are relatively open forests occurring on poor seashore soils. They contain few species and cover relatively small areas.

9. *Bamboo Forests*, mostly in dense stands, occur in almost all parts of Indochina. Invasion by various species of bamboo is considered by many to be one of the greatest threats to forest regeneration, as discussed later.

The areas covered by forest in Indochina have been estimated as follows [31]:

	Total Forest (km^2)	Percent of total area
Cambodia	133,720	74
Laos	140,500	59
North Vietnam	79,000	50
South Vietnam	56,000-100,000*	33-60*

The areas occupied by the different formations have been estimated for South Vietnam as follows [1, 2, 16]:

	Area (km^2)
Evergreen and Montane Forests	40,000-50,000
Monsoon and Dry deciduous Forests	10,000-20,000
Coniferous Forest and Coastal Pine Forest	1,500-1,800
Mangrove Forest	2,800
Rear mangrove (*M. leucadendron*)	2,000
Savannah	1,300
Swamps and Marshes	8,500
Bamboo	1,000-8,000

Published estimates for bamboo differ widely. The remaining land area,

*The upper limit is quoted from Westing [25, 32]. Discrepancy with the FAO figures may reflect different interpretations of what should be considered as forest.

originally mostly forest, has largely been modified for human use, primarily for agriculture. The most recent available figures for arable and permanently cropped land are as follows [31]:

Cambodia	29,840 km^2
Laos	8,000 km^2
North Vietnam	20,180 km^2
South Vietnam	28,370 km^2

Extent of bombing and aerial spraying

In South Vietnam, a total of about 21,000 km^2 of forested land is estimated to have been sprayed one or more times with herbicides through 1970. This represents about 35% of the total forested land in the country [26, 32].* The sprayed area includes approximately 13,500 km^2 of fairly mature, merchantable hardwood forest (almost one quarter of South Vietnam's total), mainly evergreen rain forest, monsoon and dry deciduous forest. Also included is approximately 1,400 km^2 of coastal mangrove forest in the Mekong Delta region, representing about one half of this forest type [1]. About one third of the hardwood forest treated with herbicides was sprayed more than once. Much additional spraying along roads, near military installations and in forests has been carried out by helicopters or ground equipment, for which records have been less systematically kept. Herbicides have evidently also been sprayed in southern Laos (Ho Chi Minh trail system) and northeastern Cambodia (Sihanouk trail system), though figures for the sprayed acreages are unavailable [1, 9, 26]. About 700 km^2 have been sprayed in southeastern Cambodia (the Fishhook region) [9].

In addition to the cratering caused by 500 and 750 lb. bombs, discussed earlier, a mighty new 15,000 lb. bomb, the BLU-82/B "Daisy Cutter," has now become operational in Indochina. Probably about 150 of these weapons, used largely to clear jungle areas for helicopter landing zones, have been exploded so far, killing or injuring wildlife in an estimated area of 470 km^2 [32].

Ecological Damage to Vegetation

a. *Mangrove forests*

Mangroves are especially susceptible to herbicides, a single application almost completely destroying all vegetation [1, 4]. Moreover, areas sprayed as long ago as 1961 had shown little or no signs of regeneration eight years later [11]. Vast wastelands of dead trees are now all that remains of 50%

*Westing [25] gives lower figures. Before the war, more than 100,000 km^2 of South Vietnam were covered by forest. So far, the war has claimed at the very least 12,000 km^2 of the forest cover. Rather more than a third of this is due to herbicide spraying, somewhat less than a third to bulldozing, and the remainder to bombs and other munitions [25].

of South Vietnam's coastal mangroves. Regeneration of the mangrove forest may be very slow, except along river banks, because the seeds are dispersed by water at an early stage of primary succession. In many areas of mangrove forest the soil level has risen sufficiently to prevent flooding except by the highest tides. It is likely, however, that mangrove regeneration might occur more rapidly following extensive soil erosion which would lower the land to a level more suitable for colonization.

Such erosion may be already occurring, and dredging operations have had to be substantially increased in the Saigon River ship channel as a result of extensive mangrove defoliation in its vicinity [2]. Dead mangrove roots once decayed will no longer stabilize the soil and trap silt. The emerging land is once again at the mercy of floods and tides, and considerable shifting of river channels and mud flats, as well as loss of soil to the ocean can be expected in the future, especially if the region is struck by a major typhoon [1, 4, 10, 11, 23, 33].

b. *Hardwood Forests*

As mentioned earlier, most of the herbicide treatment has fallen on the evergreen rain forests and monsoon (seasonal) forests, though studies of effects of herbicide treatment have largely been restricted to the seasonal forest type [2]. A single application of agents Orange or White kills some of the top story trees of a tropical seasonal forest, though lower vegetation is largely protected by the upper canopy and, barring further treatment, such a forest can regenerate itself within several years [1, 2, 4, 11, 32]. However, a second spraying on a forest which has already been partially defoliated by the first treatment has a disastrous effect, killing almost all woody vegetation, including seedlings [1, 11, 24, 32]. Regeneration of such a forest will be exceedingly slow, for the following reasons:

(i) *Loss of nutrients*, discussed in the earlier section on soils, seems to be an inevitable consequence of severe forest defoliation. When the outflow of various nutrients (nitrate, potassium, calcium, etc.) was carefully monitored in stream water leaving a clear-cut forest in New Hampshire, it was found that loss of nutrients from the ecosystem increased dramatically a few months after defoliation. This rate of loss, many times higher than that in adjacent uncut forest watersheds, was maintained for several years following defoliation and, indeed, still continues [34]. Since so little is known about the structure and function of tropical forest ecosystems, it is unfortunately impossible at present to make accurate predictions about them on the basis of data from temperate forests such as the one in New Hampshire. We can guess, however, that nutrient loss following defoliation would be more severe in a tropical forest for the simple reason that almost all the organic matter is present in the vegetation itself rather than in the soil. In a temperate forest, by contrast, a very large proportion of the ecosystem's nutrients at any time are present in the soil, with a correspondingly lower percentage in the vegetation [19].* Organically-poor soils would be less able to 'trap' nutrients as they are released from plant decay and they are less able to withstand the physical impact of heavy rain, leading to a greater risk of erosion. Moreover the tropical soils would have far lower nutrient reserves available for regeneration than do their temperate counterparts.

Certain root-associated fungi called mycorrhizae, which are especially abundant in nutrient-poor tropical forest soils, may be responsible for the transfer of nutrients from decaying organic material to plant roots. They may, in effect, close the nutrient cycle and prevent minerals from being lost into the soil where the water could leach them away. Mycorrhizal fungi are destroyed by the cutting, burning and cropping of shifting cultivation, and this may contribute to the rapid deterioration of the soil under this agricultural system [35]. Thus the effect of herbicides on mycorrhizal fungi in Indochina, about which little is known, may be crucial to the ability of sprayed areas to be revegetated.

Loss of nutrients, of course, has a profound effect on the process of revegetation. Thousands of years may be required to rebuild the system to the extent that it could once again support, say, an evergreen rain forest.

(ii) *Invasion by grasses.* Tropical forests are amazingly diverse and finely structured systems. Ten acres of Amazon rain forest, for example, may contain almost 200 species of tree; more than 3,000 species of higher plant have been counted from only 3 square miles of Brazilian forest [36]. Each of these species is so narrowly adapted to a particular range of physical and biotic conditions within its habitat that it cannot survive even relatively minor disturbance. Following defoliation, the wider variations in temperature and humidity, the depletion of available nutrients and the disappearance of other interacting species all combine to bring about local extinction. Defoliated areas in Indochina are generally invaded by grasses (such as bamboo) and other hardy 'pioneer' species which are adapted to exploiting full sunlight and can thrive on depleted soils. Such invasion is a normal stage in the secondary succession of cut forests in Indochina but it apparently maintains itself almost indefinitely in severely cleared areas by inhibiting the growth of other plant species which would otherwise replace it [4, 11, 23].**

*Typical figures (kg/ha) for total mineral elements in plant biomass/total mineral elements contained in forest floor are 745/2,221 for subarctic taiga pine forest, 5,800/800 for temperate zone oak forest, and 11,081/178 for tropical rain forest [19].

**In fact all the extensive grasslands and savannahs in Southeast Asia may be the result of such invasion of destroyed forests [23].

(iii) *Low dispersal rates.* It is entirely possible that recolonization of extensive areas of defoliated forest may be prevented or greatly retarded simply because of the lack of nearby seed sources. This problem would be exaggerated further for the many plant species which rely on dispersal of their seeds by birds, mammals or insects which themselves have been depleted or eliminated as a consequence of widespread defoliation [23].

(iv) *Persistence of herbicides.* The continued presence in the soil of persistent herbicides (such as picloram from agent White) or their break-down products may prevent recolonization by some plant species. To what extent, however, we cannot judge in the absence of relevant information on the properties of these compounds under the conditions in Indochina [4, 10].

(v) *Extinction of species.* As a consequence of the high species diversity of tropical forests, any one species is normally rather uncommon [38]. Moreover, because of the narrow tolerances of tropical climax forest species to environmental variation, there may be only small geographical areas within the overall forest formation within which a particular species can survive. If such habitats happen to have been destroyed or badly disrupted, local extinction of such a species would be very probable. Several tree species in South Vietnam (not necessarily rain forest species) are already known to be in danger of extinction [39];* others may disappear before they are ever known to science.

C. *FAUNA*

The countries of Indochina contain an enormously rich and diversified fauna. The teeming life of the rainforests in particular, along with that of other fast-shrinking tropical rainforests around the world, represents one of the most striking products of biological evolution and should be regarded as one of the Earth's most treasured possessions. With the possible exception of the birds and mammals, many species are undoubtedly not yet known to science. In many areas of Indochina the human population has traditionally made use of the fauna in various ways, as a source of food and as pack animals. Particularly important are the marine and freshwater fisheries, since fish represent the second most important item of food to most inhabitants of Indochina. The fauna of Indochina has been affected by the air war in several ways which we will consider in turn.

Direct Effects of Habitat Destruction by Defoliants, Bombing and Fires

As might be expected, the most obvious direct effect of the air war on

*These include the endemic species of pine with flattened leaves, *Pinus krempfii*, as well as *Pinus dalatensis*, *Libocedrus macrolepis*, *Dacrydium pierrei*, *Podocarpus imbricatus* and *P. neriifolius* [39].

fauna is widespread local extinction resulting from habitat destruction. Any given species of animal is biologically adapted to exploit a more or less specific kind of habitat [22]; as is the case with plants, the range of tolerances for tropical species is believed to be much narrower than that for temperate zone species [40]. The flora and fauna of mangrove forests, for example, are totally different from those of rain forest which in turn are totally different from those of dry deciduous forest. Populations of animals in defoliated areas are thus faced with extinction since they cannot move into other kinds of habitat nor can they adapt to the drastic alterations in their original habitat. Although there is evidence that some larger animals (ungulates, monkeys, etc.) have migrated from damaged areas to other areas of suitable habitat, this only postpones their eventual demise. A given area of suitable habitat can only support a certain population of any one species at any one time. This level may fluctuate somewhat, depending on food supply and other factors which may regulate the population; it cannot, however, be permanently augmented by invasion of individuals from other populations since the resources of the habitat will not support these [41].

The fauna of the sprayed areas of coastal mangrove forest in South Vietnam has almost totally disappeared, with the exception of hordes of crabs and a few species of fish-eating birds which are not directly dependent on the mangrove ecosystem [11, 33]. The effects of destruction on the inland forests must have been equally catastrophic. In nearby Malaysia, the rain forest fauna has totally disappeared from areas where the forest has been destroyed, as one might expect [37].

Habitat destruction has a particularly disastrous effect on those species which already have small populations, or inhabit limited areas. Ten species of Indochinese mammals and birds, the best known components of the fauna, are listed by the International Union for the Conservation of Nature and Natural Resources as being rare and endangered [42], and at least six additional species are said by other authorities to be threatened with extinction [4, 43].* Some of these animals have such a limited range that their maintenance of a breeding population would be jeopardized by destruction of any significant area of their habitat. War-related hunting of some

*The kouprey (*Bos sauveli*), a large bovine, is in particular danger of extinction as a result of the war. Other endangered species in the region are: two species of gibbon (*Hylobates pileatus* and *H. concolor)* and another primate, the douc langur (*Pygathrix nemaeus);* the Sumatran rhinoceros *(Didermocerus sumatrendis);* the Thailand brow-antlered deer *(Cervus eldi siamensis);* the pig-deer *(Cervus porcinus*); the serow *(Capricornis sumatrensis)*; the Malay tapir *(Tapirus indicus*); the otter civet *(Cynogale bennetti)* and Owston's banded civet *(Chrotogale owstoni)*; the local species of bear *(ursus tibetanus*); the giant ibis (*Thaumatibus gigantea*); the black-necked crane *(Grus nigricollis*); Edward's pheasant *(Lophura edwardsi)* and the Imperial pheasant *(L. imperialis)*.

of the larger animals and birds is an added threat to many species. The full extent of the danger of species extinctions can only be determined by extensive field investigation [11, 24].

In areas which have been totally disrupted by herbicides, bombing, bulldozing, or fires, any toxic effects of herbicides themselves are of academic interest only; the fauna is doomed anyway by habitat destruction. However, in rivers and lakes (and possibly also the ocean) and in hardwood forests which have received only one spraying of herbicide and can thus regenerate themselves within a relatively short time period, such toxicity of herbicides provides an additional threat to the fauna. Different species of animals appear to have widely different susceptibilities to the herbicidal agents used and it is almost impossible to estimate the impact of these compounds in Indochina, especially since most of the research has used temperate rather than tropical species for toxicity determinations. The following examples give some indication of possible problems for animal species:* About 40% of a reindeer herd died and a further 15% aborted their young when they fed on coniferous vegetation treated 9-10 months earlier with a mixture of two parts, 2,4-D and one part 2,4,5-T at about 2.5 lbs./acre; the foliage, when eaten by the animals, contained 25 ppm of 2,4-D and 10 ppm of 2,4,5-T [44]. Spraying a field with 2,4-D at 3 lbs./acre resulted in the death of 22% of the honeybees working the field (possibly due to a toxic metabolite secreted by plants into the nectar) [45]. In many plants, treatment with 2,4-D may result in much higher levels of nitrates (which can be fatal to animals feeding on the plants) [7]. 2,4-D and 2,4,5-T have been found to be toxic, at widely ranging concentrations, to many species of fish and to invertebrates which serve as food for fish [7]. Dioxin, a contaminant of some commercial 2,4,5-T is stable, toxic to some animals and is concentrated up food chains. Fetus deformities in several species have resulted from various dosages of 2,4,5-T. Dioxin has caused special concern as a potential teratogen in man [1, 4, 10, 11, 24]. On the other hand, other experiments have indicated that herbicides have little or no effect on many animal species [7]. It is clear that no generalizations can be made and that the impact of these compounds on the fauna of Indochina can only be assessed after appropriate experiments on the component species of that fauna.

Indirect Effects on Ecological Balance and Stability

Because of the intricate interdependence of all the species which make up a functioning ecosystem, removal of any part of such a system inevitably

*The effects of pesticides, including the herbicides used in Indochina, on non-target organisms have been summarized recently by Pimentel [7].

affects many other parts, often causing imbalances which may set off a chain reaction. It has been demonstrated experimentally, for example, that the existence of many species in a food-web may be dependent upon the continued presence of a single overall predator species [46]. If the predator is removed, former prey species increase in numbers to the extent that they compete with each other for food or space. The less efficient species are then eliminated and the more efficient may reach outbreak levels, in turn depleting their food supply, and so on. The greater the number of species in an ecosystem, the more 'checks and balances' exist and the more stable the system is believed to be [22, 40]. The high species diversity of tropical ecosystems is believed to be due in part to the higher proportion of predators in the fauna [38, 40, 46]. Unfortunately, it is the predators which suffer most from small amounts of pesticides in the environment since many of these compounds tend to be concentrated from one step in the food chain to the next [22]. Although the forest areas which have received only one application of herbicide will probably recover fairly quickly (with the exception of mangroves), there is a continued danger to the predatory fauna of accumulation of herbicides or their metabolic products with consequent risk to the species diversity and stability of the forest ecosystem in general. Of concern, also, are the effects on forest regeneration of damage to the vital populations of insect, bird and mammal pollinators and to those species which act as dispersal agents for plant seeds and fruits.

Many of the relationships between organisms in natural communities are mediated by a complex array of naturally occurring chemical substances, the 'pheromones' and 'allelochemics' [47]. These compounds are usually unnoticed by man but are of vital importance to many species in reproduction, defense or food location and identification. Disruption of this complex chemical structure by even very small amounts of man-made chemicals could have profound effects at all levels in an ecosystem and yet almost no research has been conducted on this subject.

Effects on Economically Important Animal Species

Of prime importance to the population of Indochina are fish. Marine fisheries are of greatest importance in North and South Vietnam (85% of the total catch); freshwater fish are most important in Cambodia, where fishing is mainly carried out in the richly productive Great Lake [48].

It is impossible to decide whether or not the fisheries in Indochina have suffered any extensive damage as a result of the war. In fact, the total fish catch for South Vietnam has steadily risen between 1958 and 1969 [49, 50].*

*These figures probably merely reflect the increased mechanization of South Vietnam's fishing fleet over the past few years which would conceal any decline in fish production per unit area [32, 50].

Total Fish Catch (live weight) [49, 50]

1,000 metric tons

1958	1959	1960	1961	1962	1963	1964	1965	1966	1967	1968	1969
143.0	153.5	240.0	250.0	255.0	378.7	397.0	375.0	380.5	410.0	403.0	463.8

However, some of the herbicides used in Vietnam are known to be toxic to fish [7] and a time lag might be expected before any effects of these materials became apparent. Much would depend on whether or not these compounds have reached concentrations in the water at which they affect the commercially important species of fish. Also important will be the effects of herbicides or their breakdown products on the various species of plankton or bottom fauna which make up the main food resources for the fish populations. In general, it seems that the impact of the air war will have been less severe in aquatic ecosystems than on the terrestrial flora and fauna, though it is too soon to be sure.

IV. CONCLUSIONS

It is clear that the natural as well as the human environment of Indochina has suffered extensive and in some ways irreparable damage as a result of the air war. Coastal mangroves and inland hardwood forests, in particular, have been radically altered over enormous areas and in many of these they have been totally destroyed. Without more detailed information, however, we cannot ascertain or predict with any accuracy the full effects of the war on the flora, fauna, soils, water, agriculture and fisheries of the region. Basic scientific information about the structure and function of tropical ecosystems, including those in Indochina, is meagre; moreover, the Herbicide Assessment Commission team and other scientists who have visited the region recently have been hampered by continuing hostilities and by inability to obtain certain needed statistics from government sources.

We can only add our voice to those of others in advocating urgently that thorough long term investigations of the ecological effects of the war be initiated as soon as conditions permit. In our view, priority consideration in such research should be given to the following:

1. The toxicity, stability and persistence, environmental concentration, and chemical transformation of herbicidal chemicals in the soil, water, flora and fauna. Of special concern are the possible health hazards to man of some of these materials (especially dioxin), either from direct exposure or when ingested in food.

2. Detailed study of the consequences to the major vegetation types of defoliation, bombing, fires and bulldozing. Of special concern here are the extent and effects of nutrient loss from soils, of invasion by bamboo and other

grasses, of elimination of species (such as mycorrhizal fungi and plant pollinators) vital to forest regeneration, and of economic consequences of forest defoliation, soil erosion and possible laterization.

3. The ability of mangrove forests to be regenerated, either naturally or with human help, and the role of mangrove forests in the ecology and stability of coastal regions. The role of the aquatic flora and fauna of mangrove areas on commercial fish production needs special attention.

4. The nature and extent of the impact of the war on rare animals and plants which may be in danger of extinction. Means to preserve these species should be investigated.

REFERENCES

1. Meselson, M. S., A. H. Westing, J. D. Constable and R. E. Cook, 1970. *Preliminary Report,* Herbicide Assessment Commission of the American Association for the Advancement of Science. Mimeo. 8 pp. Also reprinted in *Refugee Hearings* (1971), Part I, pp. 113-115; Meselson, M. S., A. H. Westing, and J. D. Constable, 1971. *Background material relevant to presentations at the 1970 Annual Meeting of the AAAS,* Herbicide Assessment Commission of the American Academy for the Advancement of Science. Mimeo. 47 pp. Also reprinted in *Refugee Hearings* (1971), Part I, pp. 115-131.
2. Lewallen, J., 1971. *Ecology of Devastation: Indochina*. Penguin Books, Baltimore. 179 pp.
3. Department of the Army Training Circular TC 3-16, April 1969. *Employment of riot control agents, flame, smoke, antiplant agents, and personnel detectors in counter-guerrilla operations*. Reprinted in Whiteside, T., 1970. *Defoliation*, pp. 73-84.
4. Tschirley, F. H., 1969. "Defoliation in Vietnam." *Science 163:* 779-786.
5. Flamm, B. R., 1968. *A partial evaluation of herbicidal effects to natural forest stands principally in Tay Ninh Province*. U.S. Agency for International Development publication. Flamm, B. R. and J. H. Cravens, 1971. "Effects of war damage on the forest resources of South Vietnam." *Jour. Forestry 69:*784-789.
6. House, W. B., L. H. Goodson, H. M. Gadberry, and K. W. Dockter, 1967. "Assessment of ecological effects of extensive or repeated use of herbicides." *Final Report* AD 824, 314. Midwest Research Institute, Kansas City, Missouri. 369 pp. (Distributed by Clearing House for Federal Scientific and Technical Information, Washington, D.C.)
7. Pimental, D., 1971. *Ecological effects of Pesticides on Non-Target Species*. Publication of the Executive Office of the President, Government Printing Office, Washington, D.C., 220 pp.
8. Cook, R. E., W. Haseltine and A. W. Galston, 1970. "What have we done to Vietnam?" *The New Republic 162*(2):18-21. Also reprinted in Weisberg, B. (ed.), 1970. *Ecocide in Indochina*, pp. 89-94.
9. Whiteside, T., 1970. *Defoliation*. Ballantine Books, New York. 168 pp.
10. Stanford Biology Study Group, 1970. *The Destruction of Indochina*. Stanford. 9 pp. Also reprinted in *Bulletin of the Atomic Scientists 27*(5):36-40 (1971).
11. Orians, G. H. and E. W. Pfeiffer, 1970. "Ecological effects of the war in Vietnam." *Science 168:*544-554; Pfeiffer, E. W., 1971. "Land War: (I) Craters." *Environment 13*(9):3-8.
12. *San Francisco Chronicle,* July 4, 1968, p. 11.
13. Westing, A. H. and E. W. Pfeiffer, 1971. *Science 174:*547.

14. Department of Mines and Technical Surveys, Geographical Branch, 1953. *Indo-China: A Geographical Appreciation*. Ottawa, 88 pp.

15. Fisher, C. A., 1964. *South-East Asia*. Methuen & Co., London. 831 pp.; Spencer, J. E., 1966. *Shifting Cultivation in Southeastern Asia*. University of California Press, Berkeley. 247 pp.

16. Tung, T.-C., 1967. *Natural Environment and Land Use in South Viet-Nam*. Directorate of Agricultural Research, Ministry of Agriculture, Saigon. 156 pp.

17. Moormann, F. R., 1961. *The soils of the Republic of Viet-Nam*. Ministry of Agriculture, Saigon. 66 pp.

18. Dudal, R., and F. R. Moormann, 1964. "Major Soils of Southeast Asia." *Journal of Tropical Geography 18:*54-80.

19. Rodin, L. E., and N. I. Bazilevich, 1967. *Production and Mineral Cycling in Terrestrial Vegetation*. Oliver and Boyd, Edinburgh and London. 288 pp., p. 246. (Translated from Russian edition, 1965).

20. Bormann, F. H. and G. E. Likens, 1967. "Nutrient cycling." *Science 155:*424-429.

21. Whittaker, R. H., 1970. *Communities and Ecosystems*. MacMillan, New York. 158 pp.

22. Odum, E. P., 1971. *Fundamentals of Ecology*. 3rd edition. W. B. Saunders Co., Philadelphia. 574 pp.

23. Richards, P. W., 1952. *The Tropical Rain Forest*. Cambridge University Press, New York, 450 pp.

24. Westing, A. H. 1971. "Ecocide in Indochina." *Natural History 80*(3):56-61; Pfeiffer, E. W., 1969. "Ecological effects of the Vietnam war." *Science Journal 5*(2):33-38.

25. Haseltine, W. and A. H. Westing, 1971. "The Wasteland: Beating Plowshares into Swords." *The New Republic 165*(18):13-15. Westing, A. H., 1971. "Land War: (II) Levelling the jungle." *Environment 13*(9):8-12.

26. Weisberg, B. (ed.), 1970. *Ecocide in Indochina*. Canfield Press, San Francisco. 241 pp.

27. Development and Resources Corporation, 1967. *The Joint development planning effort in Vietnam*. An initial report by Development and Resources Corp. to U.S. Agency for International Development . New York, 79 pp. Mimeo.

28. Nuttonson, M. Y., 1963. *The Physical Environment and Agriculture of Vietnam, Laos, and Cambodia*. American Institute of Crop Ecology, Washington, D.C. (Silver Springs, Md.), 137 pp. plus Appendix.

29. Pendleton, R. L., 1941. "Laterite and its structural uses in Thailand and Cambodia." *The Geographical Review 31:*177-202.

30. Williams, L., 1965. *Vegetation of Southeast Asia: Studies of Forest Types, 1963-65*. Agricultural Research Service, U.S. Department of Agriculture, Publ. No. CR 49-65. Washington, D.C. 302 pp.; Williams, L., 1967. *Forests of Southeast Asia, Puerto Rico, and Texas*. Agricultural Research Service, U.S. Department of Agriculture, Publ. No. CR 12-67. Washington, D.C. 410 pp.

31. "Food and Agricultural Organization of the United Nations, 1971." *Production Yearbook, 1970*, Vol. 24. FAO, Rome. 822 pp.

32. Westing, A. H., 1971. "Ecological effects of military defoliation on the forests of South Vietnam." *BioScience 21:*893-898; Westing, A. H., 1971. "Land War: (II) The big bomb." *Environment 13*(9):13-15; Westing, A. H., 1971. "Forestry and the war in South Vietnam." *Journal of Forestry 69:*777-783.

33. Constable, J., and M. Meselson, 1971. "The ecological impact of large scale defoliation in Vietnam." *Sierra Club Bulletin 56*(4):4-9.

34. Bormann, F. H., G. E. Likens, D. W. Fisher, and R. S. Pierce, 1968. "Nutrient loss accelerated by clear-cutting of a forest ecosystem." *Science 159:*882-884; Likens, G. E., F. H. Bormann, N. M. Johnson, D. W. Fisher and R. S. Pierce, 1970. "Effects of forest cutting and herbicide treatment on nutrient budgets in the Hubbard Brook Watershed Ecosystem." *Ecological Monographs 40:*23-47; Bormann, F. H., and G. E. Likens, 1970.

"The nutrient cycles of an ecosystem." *Scientific American 223*(4):92-101.

35. Went, F. W., and N. Stark, 1968. "Mycorrhiza." *BioScience 18:*1035-1039.

36. Cain, S. A. and G. M. de Oliveira Castro, 1959. *Manual of vegetation analysis*. New York: Harper & Brothers. 325 + XVII pp.

37. Harrison, J. L., 1965. "The effects of forest clearance on small mammals." In L. M. Talbot and M. H. Talbot (eds.), 1965, *Conservation in Tropical South East Asia,* pp. 153-158. IUCN Publications New Series No. 10, International Union for Conservation of Nature and Natural Resources, Morges, Switzerland. 550 pp.

38. Janzen, D. H., 1970. "Herbivores and the number of tree species in tropical forests." *American Naturalist 104:*501-528.

39. Ngan, P. T., 1965. "The status of conservation in South Vietnam." In L. M. Talbot and M. H. Talbot (eds.), 1965. *Conservation in Tropical South East Asia,* pp. 519-522.

40. Brookhaven Symposium in Biology No. 22, 1969. *Diversity and stability in ecological systems*. Brookhaven National Laboratory, Upton, N.Y. 264 pp.

41. Lack, D., 1954. *The Natural Regulation of Animal Numbers*. Oxford University Press, New York; Lack, D., 1966. *Population Studies of Birds*. Clarendon Press, Oxford. 341 pp.

42. International Union for Conservation of Nature and Natural Resources, Survival Service Commission, 1966 and 1969. Red Data Book. Vol. 1, *Mammalia* (compiled by N. Simon, 1969) and Vol. 2, *Aves* (compiled by J. Vincent, 1966). Morges, Switzerland.

43. Harrisson, B., 1971. "Conservation of Nonhuman primates in 1970." *Primates in Medicine,* Vol. 5. S. Karger, Basel. 97 pp.; and Vollmar, F. (ed.), 1970. *World Wildlife Yearbook 1969*. World Wildlife Fund, Morges, Switzerland. 343 pp.

44. Lundholm, B., 1970. *Alvsbyn reindeer mortality*. Smithsonian Institution Center for Short-Lived Phenomena. Event 51-70.

45. Palmer-Jones, T., 1964. "Effect on honeybees of 2,4-D." *New Zealand Journal of Agricultural Research 7:* 339-349.

46. Paine, R. T., 1966. "Food web complexity and species diversity." *American Naturalist 100:*65-75.

47. Whittaker, R. H., and P. P. Feeny, 1971. "Allelochemics: Chemical interactions between species." *Science 171:*757-770; Sondheimer, E., and J. B. Simeone (eds.), 1970. *Chemical Ecology*. Academic Press, New York and London.

48. Mizuno, T., and S. Mori, 1970. "Preliminary hydrobiological survey of some Southeast Asia inland waters." In *Biological Journal of the Linnean Society 2*(2):77-117.

49. Economic Commission for Asia and the Far East, 1970. *Statistical Yearbook for Asia and the Far East, 1969*. United Nations, Bangkok. 381 pp.

50. Brouillard, K. D., 1970. *Fishery development survey: South Vietnam*. U.S. Agency for International Development, 41 pp.

STATISTICAL SUMMARY

The numerical information tabulated here has, for the most part, been presented in graphical form in the text. Source references are keyed to bracketed numerals and are listed in Section SS-11. [Int] signifies that the information was obtained from personal interviews.

CONTENTS

SS-1. DEFINITIONS

a. *Aircraft*. Attack aircraft are classified as fighter-bombers (or attack bombers), strategic bombers, fixed-wing gunships, and helicopters. [Cf. Appendix C-1.]

b. *Activity*. The basic unit of aircraft activity is the *sortie*, which corresponds to one aircraft taking off on one or more missions and landing again.* A *mission* consists of one or more aircraft on a given task; thus a B-52 mission typically involves from 3 to 30 sorties, and an armed-reconnaissance mission may require two sorties. *Strike* is a loose term often used interchangeably with mission.

Sorties are further divided into attack sorties and others, the latter including reconnaissance, FAC, electronic countermeasures, and logistic tasks. Just how many of the support aircraft accompanying a given attack mission are counted as making attack sorties is a flexible decision; there is therefore no detailed agreement in the numbers of attack sorties reported by various sources.**

c. *Munitions*. Air-drop munitions, strictly speaking, include only those delivered by free fall and thus exclude rockets, cannon shells, and bullets. However, there is a tendency to slur over this distinction and to count as aerial munitions all ordnance delivered by an aircraft.

---

*Helicopter sorties may be multiple-counted, however, if more than one mission is performed, even if no intermediate landings are made.

**In addition, confusion arises because of carelessness or deliberate obfuscation in official releases. For example, the MACV monthly summaries [2] listed fighter-bomber attack sorties in South Vietnam under the heading "tactical sorties" through May 1970, under "air missions" from June to September, and under "tactical air strikes" since October. Concurrently with the last change of heading, additional types of sortie such as FAC sorties were enumerated separately, and there was a simultaneous sharp decline in the number of attack sorties recorded. The MACV data cannot be brought into concordance with the figures released by the Comptroller's Office [1], but the latter also show a sharp decline in attack sorties in October 1970. To pursue this numerology into too much detail seems futile, but conversely not too much detailed significance should be attached to the actual numbers reported.

SS-2. UNCLASSIFIED STATISTICS ON SOUTHEAST ASIA

Published by the Comptroller,
Office of the Secretary of Defense
[1]

UNCLASSIFIED
Statistics on Southeast Asia

Table 6

	1966												
	Jan	Feb	Mar	Apr	May	Jun	Jul	Aug	Sep	Oct	Nov	Dec	Cum
Friendly Military Forces in South Viet-Nam (000) a/													
United States	196	208	231	245	255	268	277	297	313	342	356	385	
Third Nation b/	22	23	23	28	29	30	31	35	47	52	52	53	
Casualties													
United States													
Deaths from hostile action c/	282	435	507	316	464	507	435	396	419	340	475	432	5,008
Deaths from other causes	83	55	51	67	90	69	100	74	85	137	149	85	1,045
Wounded d/													
Hospital care required	721	1,444	1,626	1,320	1,589	1,527	1,291	1,370	1,473	1,206	1,639	1,320	16,526
Hospital care not required	597	1,180	1,334	1,150	1,293	1,252	1,036	1,100	1,179	983	1,359	1,104	13,567
SVN													
Deaths from hostile action	903	1,359	1,145	945	961	1,185	1,006	914	803	844	907	981	11,953
Wounded e/	1,557	2,095	1,961	1,522	1,454	1,800	1,639	1,491	1,554	2,118	1,933	1,851	20,975
Missing	450	477	466	121	196	183	242	209	185	216	200	338	3,283
Third Nation													
Deaths from hostile action	74	58	59	30	19	41	32	44	30	63	87	29	566
Wounded e/	238	138	165	100	68	67	60	138	106	214	201	96	1,591
Missing	9	2	0	0	0	0	0	0	0	0	4	0	15
Enemy													
Deaths from hostile action	2,648	4,727	5,685	2,818	4,239	4,815	5,297	5,860	4,459	5,665	5,447	3,864	55,524
SVN Civilian Casualties Resulting from VC Terrorism													
Assassinated	163	98	153	181	210	134	80	122	135	189	123	144	1,732
Abducted	249	519	422	180	187	334	42	303	219	489	503	363	3,810
Land Operations (Bn Size or Larger)													
South Vietnamese Forces	286	304	376	337	354	304	328	338	345	345	297	328	3,942
United States/Third Nation Forces	41	57	64	67	72	92	94	98	98	95	89	89	956
Combined Forces	21	3	11	19	17	27	20	18	23	32	20	33	244
U.S. Air Operations in SVN-Sorties	(Data shown below are monthly averages for CY 1966)												
Fixed Wing													
Attack						10,754							129,050
Other Combat						3,478							41,730
Total						14,232							170,780
Helicopters													
Attack						27,648							331,777
Combat Assault						56,051							672,610
Combat Cargo						24,125							289,500
Other						141,721							1,700,650
Total						249,545							2,994,537
U.S. Aircraft Losses in SEA													
Fixed Wing													
NVN						23							280
SVN						6							69
Subtotal						29							349
Other f/						24							285
Total						53							634
Helicopters													
NVN						-*							1
SVN						10							123
Subtotal						10							124
Other g/						16							197
Total						26							321
Enemy Weapons Captured													
Crew Served	25	82	104	22	35	344	159	125	120	172	141	79	1,408
Individual	954	1,137	1,503	807	1,052	3,417	1,455	1,217	1,310	1,805	1,282	1,259	17,198
Total	979	1,219	1,607	829	1,087	3,761	1,614	1,342	1,430	1,977	1,423	1,338	18,606
Enemy Defections (Hoi Chanh)													
Military	886	1,547	1,345	1,133	848	885	894	791	626	1,089	1,457	1,396	12,897
Political	350	573	588	403	412	420	337	300	293	659	1,117	851	6,303
Other	17	94	49	88	82	74	76	82	56	81	74	269	1,042
Total	1,253	2,214	1,982	1,624	1,342	1,379	1,307	1,173	975	1,829	2,648	2,516	20,242
Terrorist Incidents h/	2,490	1,829	2,332	2,283	2,552	2,382	118	59	137	141	135	127	14,585
VC Armed Attacks	70	69	52	77	53	68	91	64	86	121	86	101	938

* Less than 1 per month.
a/ Strength as of end of month.
b/ Includes forces of Australia, Korea, New Zealand, Philippines, Republic of China, Spain and Thailand.
c/ Includes those who died of wounds and died while missing or captured.
d/ Approximately 85 percent of U. S. military personnel wounded recover sufficiently for return to duty.
e/ Includes only those seriously wounded.
f/ Combat type aircraft lost to non-hostile action, support aircraft losses, and all other fixed wing losses in connection with the war.
g/ Helicopters lost to non-hostile action, and all other helicopter losses in connection with the war.
h/ Terrorism and Harassment incidents were reported as terrorism prior to July 1966.

Page 6 of 6 pages

March 25, 1971

UNCLASSIFIED
Statistics on Southeast Asia

Table 6

	1967												
	Jan	Feb	Mar	Apr	May	Jun	Jul	Aug	Sep	Oct	Nov	Dec	Cum
Friendly Military Forces in South Viet-Nam (000) a/													
United States	403	414	421	436	443	449	458	466	460	467	470	486	
Third Nation b/	53	55	54	54	54	54	56	57	59	59	59	59	
Casualties													
United States													
Deaths from hostile action c/	520	662	944	710	1,233	830	781	535	775	733	881	774	9,378
Deaths from other causes	112	88	142	116	147	99	249	122	119	168	137	181	1,680
Wounded d/	3,456	3,853	6,314	4,964	8,380	4,946	5,471	4,604	6,909	4,122	4,165	4,841	62,025
Hospital care required	1,822	2,021	3,312	2,602	4,352	2,591	2,834	2,397	3,085	2,277	2,450	2,628	32,371
Hospital care not required	1,634	1,832	3,002	2,362	4,028	2,355	2,637	2,207	3,824	1,845	1,715	2,213	29,654
SVN													
Deaths from hostile action	914	885	1,297	1,057	1,184	981	676	1,068	1,090	1,066	1,299	1,199	12,176
Wounded e/	2,035	1,125	2,786	2,490	2,830	2,118	1,935	2,281	2,416	2,355	2,982	3,095	29,448
Missing	167	154	468	134	148	139	123	131	103	136	281	356	2,340
Third Nation													
Deaths from hostile action	77	95	54	56	112	74	102	90	149	96	98	102	1,105
Wounded e/	149	209	192	188	201	163	179	171	329	191	177	169	2,318
Missing	-	-	-	-	-	-	1	-	1	-	-	1	3
Enemy													
Deaths from hostile action	6,064	7,341	9,351	6,227	9,808	7,354	7,923	5,810	6,354	6,272	7,662	7,938	88,104
SVN Civilian Casualties Resulting from VC Terrorism													
Assassinated	128	171	181	226	263	439	224	447	444	229	389	565	3,706
Abducted	326	334	210	218	344	429	232	467	967	250	587	1,005	5,369
Hospital Admissions Attributed to the War													
SVN Hospitals	4,154	3,920	4,468	3,386	3,811	3,238	2,900	3,696	4,252	3,569	4,603	4,476	46,473
U.S. Hospitals f/				131	93	136	158	258	263	315	281	314	1,949
Land Operations (Bn Size or Larger)													
South Vietnamese Forces	368	281	340	299	274	286	304	392	318	342	339	331	3,874
United States/Third Nation Forces	109	117	115	120	122	121	118	125	111	124	140	129	1,451
Combined Forces	17	18	9	11	12	8	14	8	10	10	11	5	133
U.S. Air Operations in SVN-Sorties													
Fixed Wing													
Attack	12,598	12,272	14,875	14,092	16,912	15,106	16,557	15,021	15,624	14,975	14,437	13,968	176,437
Other Combat	4,443	4,691	4,983	4,731	4,538	4,154	4,026	3,840	3,465	3,752	3,547	3,549	49,719
Total	17,041	16,963	19,858	18,823	21,450	19,260	20,583	18,861	19,089	18,727	17,984	17,517	226,156
Helicopters													
Attack	48,966	37,255	49,307	48,963	59,304	49,881	52,722	48,903	57,424	54,319	54,909	65,465	627,418
Combat Assault	68,185	59,350	68,796	75,565	93,188	80,428	102,590	116,903	117,446	118,496	118,474	131,989	1,151,420
Combat Cargo	34,443	30,091	39,250	29,255	44,918	33,168	43,206	46,483	63,537	59,067	56,373	66,320	546,111
Other	211,975	203,596	224,096	227,537	278,184	240,685	294,189	344,206	285,830	281,731	275,669	324,978	3,192,676
Total	363,569	330,292	381,449	381,330	475,594	404,162	492,707	556,495	524,237	513,613	505,425	588,752	5,517,625
U.S. Aircraft Losses in SEA													
Fixed Wing													
NVN	20	7	24	28	40	26	38	39	15	39	34	16	326
SVN	7	6	10	3	12	4	7	8	4	4	3	5	73
Subtotal	27	13	34	31	52	30	45	47	19	43	37	21	399
Other g/	24	27	26	19	17	18	54	32	24	38	25	25	329
Total	51	40	60	50	69	48	99	79	43	81	62	46	728
Helicopters													
NVN	-	1	-	-	1	-	1	-	-	1	-	-	4
SVN	12	14	23	16	31	23	15	24	19	8	30	45	260
Subtotal	12	15	23	16	32	23	16	24	19	9	30	45	264
Other h/	27	26	33	24	40	24	39	37	29	45	41	34	399
Total	39	41	56	40	72	47	55	61	48	54	71	79	663
Enemy Weapons Captured													
Crew Served	94	188	236	143	254	185	325	159	168	367	429	328	2,876
Individual	2,266	2,207	3,590	1,975	2,527	1,794	3,183	1,909	1,709	2,936	2,150	2,076	28,322
Total	2,360	2,395	3,826	2,118	2,781	1,979	3,508	2,068	1,877	3,303	2,579	2,404	31,198
Enemy Defections (Hoi Chanh)													
Military	1,497	2,105	3,155	1,873	1,466	1,412	1,536	1,269	1,076	1,069	660	554	17,672
Political	802	939	1,358	1,031	773	535	433	515	385	396	351	359	7,877
Other	222	125	400	114	111	158	75	141	82	104	59	38	1,629
Total	2,521	3,169	4,913	3,018	2,350	2,105	2,044	1,925	1,543	1,569	1,070	951	27,178
Terrorist Incidents	134	123	111	200	202	158	181	219	209	141	123	162	1,963
VC Armed Attacks	142	117	219	162	193	168	197	204	260	264	264	286	2,476
Refugees (000)													
Current Number of Refugees												793,944	
In camp												297,108	
Out camp												496,836	
Re-established Refugees With GVN Assistance - Since 1/1/67												136,621	
Refugees Returned to Own Village - Since 1/1/67												315,499	
Tax Collections (Billions VN Piasters)													
Customs Receipts													13.40
Domestic Tax Receipts													17.22

a/ Strength as of end of month.
b/ Includes forces of Australia, Korea, New Zealand, Philippines, Republic of China, Spain and Thailand.
c/ Includes those who died of wounds and died while missing or captured.
d/ Approximately 85 percent of U. S. military personnel wounded recover sufficiently for return to duty.
e/ Includes only those seriously wounded.
f/ No data available prior to April 1967 for U.S. Hospitals.
g/ Combat type aircraft lost to non-hostile action, support aircraft losses, and all other fixed wing losses.
h/ Helicopters lost to non-hostile action, and all other helicopter losses in connection with the war.

UNCLASSIFIED
Statistics on Southeast Asia

Table 6

	1968												
	Jan	Feb	Mar	Apr	May	Jun	Jul	Aug	Sep	Oct	Nov	Dec	Cum
Friendly Military Forces in South Viet-Nam (000) a/													
United States	498	506	515	520	536	536	537	537	538	534	538	537	
Third Nation b/	61	60	61	61	61	63	65	66	66	66	66	66	
Casualties													
United States													
Deaths from hostile action c/	1,202	2,124	1,543	1,410	2,169	1,146	813	1,080	1,053	600	703	749	14,592
Deaths from other causes	118	169	178	133	147	164	196	134	177	205	141	157	1,919
Wounded d/	7,483	9,464	11,614	9,409	11,947	9,943	6,107	6,079	6,802	4,391	5,157	4,424	92,820
Hospital care required	4,004	4,955	5,591	4,645	6,687	5,046	3,312	3,374	3,339	1,816	2,107	1,923	46,799
Hospital care not required	3,479	4,509	6,023	4,764	5,260	4,897	2,795	2,705	3,463	2,575	3,050	2,501	46,021
SVN													
Deaths from hostile action	2,905	5,025	2,570	1,922	3,467	1,974	1,409	2,393	2,164	1,169	1,408	1,509	27,915
Wounded e/	6,819	11,451	6,060	4,530	8,569	5,244	3,441	6,495	5,918	3,631	3.929	4,609	70,696
Missing	336	1,138	158	105	127	97	60	128	170	29	48	64	2,460
Third Nation													
Deaths from hostile action	111	147	88	85	85	92	65	73	58	70	38	67	979
Wounded e/	252	270	151	157	263	169	123	165	130	125	51	141	1,997
Missing	1	1	0	6	1	0	0	0	0	0	0	0	9
Enemy													
Deaths from hostile action	15,217	39,867	17,371	12,215	24,086	10,319	6,653	15,478	12,543	8,168	9,632	9,600	181,149
SVN Civilian Casualties Resulting from VC Terrorism													
Assassinated	618	N/A	543	287	479	568	363	376	917	443	440	355	5,389
Abducted	861	N/A	1,133	828	871	588	529	429	952	1,430	430	708	8,759
Hospital Admissions Attributed to the War													
SVN Hospitals	5,277	18,968	8,645	5,867	8,256	6,647	5,071	5,589	5,695	4,294	4,333	4,557	83,199
U. S. Hospitals	642	694	298	616	688	55[illegible]	559	-	640	1,517	-	679	6,886
Land Operations (Bn Size or Larger)													
South Vietnamese Forces	351	275	474	444	607	611	634	747	660	682	664	824	6,973
United States/Third Nation Forces	129	115	129	104	96	81	91	65	70	85	89	84	1,1[illegible]
Combined Forces	3	0	13	80	28	41	38	60	40	42	47	48	440
U. S. Air Operations in SVN-Sorties													
Fixed Wing													
Attack	15,883	18,132	19,305	18,447	21,920	21,486	19,002	20,912	18,463	15,471	15,815	16,919	221,755
Other Combat	3,815	4,055	5,171	4,511	5,142	5,083	5,016	5,485	5,378	5,253	5,156	5,866	59,931
Total	19,698	22,187	24,476	22,958	27,062	26,569	24,018	26,397	23,841	20,724	20,971	22,785	281,686
Helicopters													
Attack	64,501	64,227	73,651	72,306	79,929	76,320	64,953	78,897	74,164	66,308	71,105	76,371	862,732
Combat Assault	118,653	109,360	136,553	135,353	150,721	144,066	147,462	158,132	160,463	142,774	132,436	150,976	1,686,949
Combat Cargo	53,108	54,573	55,200	69,066	68,663	69,235	81,045	81,030	73,624	73,815	64,374	75,307	819,030
Other	294,729	273,924	314,034	316,730	360,380	357,110	364,258	360,314	350,474	339,017	344,564	374,904	4,050,438
Total	530,991	502,084	579,438	593,455	659,693	646,731	657,708	678,373	658,725	621,914	612,479	677,558	7,419,149
U. S. Aircraft Losses in SEA													
Fixed Wing													
NVN	23	11	8	10	18	11	16	14	15	10	4	1	141
SVN	8	7	9	8	16	7	16	8	10	6	7	5	107
Subtotal	31	18	17	18	34	18	32	22	25	16	11	6	248
Other f/	43	49	48	36	41	32	30	22	29	29	24	26	409
Total	74	67	65	54	75	50	62	44	54	45	35	32	657
Helicopters													
NVN	1	-	-	-	-	-	-	-	-	1	-	-	2
SVN	50	55	54	43	52	35	24	43	43	27	42	28	496
Subtotal	51	55	54	43	52	35	24	43	43	28	42	28	498
Other g/	43	54	56	43	44	44	45	33	30	45	33	41	511
Total	94	109	110	86	96	79	69	76	73	73	75	69	1,009
Enemy Weapons Captured													
Crew Served	740	1,609	926	1,057	1,433	851	411	883	735	475	428	487	10,075
Individual	3,447	7,068	3,708	4,294	7,242	4,408	2,319	4,904	3,908	3,444	3,478	3,629	52,064
Total	4,187	8,677	4,634	5,351	8,675	5,259	2,730	5,787	4,643	3,919	3,906	4,116	62,139
Enemy Defections (Hoi Chanh)													
Military	965	586	427	654	635	857	954	1,088	1,020	1,476	1,681	2,226	12,569
Political	316	117	69	188	194	227	244	357	351	455	573	734	3,825
Other	22	17	22	326	73	49	423	189	130	184	154	188	1,777
Total	1,303	720	518	1,168	902	1,133	1,621	1,634	1,501	2,115	2,408	3,148	18,171
Terrorist Incidents	139	68	134	75	113	61	60	59	99	75	73	91	1,047
VC Armed Attacks	409	570	558	391	588	288	137	242	215	145	184	194	3,921
Refugees (000)													
Current Number of Refugees												1,328,517	
In camp												735,014	
Out camp												503.503	
Re-established Refugees With GVN Assistance - Since 1/1/68												235,043	
Refugees Returned to Own Village - Since 1/1/68												90,729	
Land Redistributed (000 acres)	2.2	7.1	1.8	3.7	6.3	12.8	4.1	1.4	12.0	5.6	4.4	.2	61.6
Tax Collections (Billions VN Piasters)													
Customs Receipts	.59	.84	1.27	1.60	..98	1.29	1.59	1.37	1.33	2.00	2.12	2.20	17.30
Domestic Tax Receipts	1.42	.68	1.30	1.95	1.76	1.43	1.48	1.99	1.75	1.92	2.10	2.10	19.88
Saigon Retail Price Index h/	326	360	323	351	401	350	396	417	409	397	407	408	

a/ Strength as of end of month.
b/ Includes forces of Australia, Korea, New Zealand, Philippines, Republic of China, Spain and Thailand.
c/ Includes those who died of wounds and died while missing or captured.
d/ Approximately 85 percent of U. S. military personnel wounded recover sufficiently for return to duty.
e/ Includes only those seriously wounded.
f/ Combat type aircraft lost to non-hostile action, support aircraft losses, and all other fixed wing losses in connection with the war.
g/ Helicopters lost to non-hostile action, and all other helicopter losses in connection with the war.
h/ 1 January 1965 = 100.

UNCLASSIFIED
Statistics on Southeast Asia

Table 6

	1969												
	Jan	Feb	Mar	Apr	May	Jun	Jul	Aug	Sep	Oct	Nov	Dec	Cum
Friendly Military Forces in South Viet-Nam (000) a/													
United States	542	541	538	543	540	539	537	510	510	495	480	474	
Third Nation b/	68	72	72	72	72	72	70	70	70	70	70	69	
Casualties													
United States													
Deaths from hostile action c/	795	1,073	1,316	847	1,209	1,100	638	795	477	377	446	341	9,414
Deaths from other causes	160	190	177	174	202	154	159	172	180	212	175	158	2,113
Wounded d/													
Hospital care required	2,292	2,457	3,589	4,401	4,029	3,851	2,945	2,712	2,463	1,397	1,469	1,335	32,940
Hospital care not required	3,277	3,509	4,315	5,325	3,606	3,780	3,054	2,579	2,993	1,525	1,762	1,551	37,276
Currently missing													
Currently captured													
SVN													
Deaths from hostile action	1,664	2,072	2,186	1,710	2,251	1,867	1,455	1,625	1,543	1,597	2,105	1,758	21,833
Wounded e/	5,154	6,167	6,781	5,425	6,501	5,937	3,904	4,832	4,919	4,500	5,758	5,398	65,276
Missing	56	78	109	64	130	96	56	36	92	46	93	67	923
Third Nation													
Deaths from hostile action	76	85	90	52	92	75	64	74	60	80	62	56	866
Wounded e/	152	168	193	163	241	276	238	221	168	166	108	124	2,218
Missing	-	-	-	-	-	-	-	-	1	-	-	-	1
Enemy													
Deaths from hostile action	10,955	14,086	19,805	14,539	17,443	16,825	10,237	12,373	10,369	8,747	11,639	9,936	156,954
Prisoners of War currently held											31,495		
SVN Civilian Casualties Resulting from VC Terrorism													
Assassinated	389	659	884	598	539	675	410	541	435	284	428	360	6,202
Abducted	1,387	615	1,217	628	323	546	227	429	288	193	282	154	6,289
Hospital Admissions Attributed to the War													
SVN Hospitals	4,338	4,551	6,030	5,447	5,678	5,682	4,742	5,007	4,949	3,982	3,893	4,122	58,421
U. S. Hospitals	749	899	402	795	878	735	481	850	518	481	547	470	7,805
Land Operations (Bn Size or Larger)													
South Vietnamese Forces	919	812	950	880	947	926	1,070	1,032	1,027	987	905	948	11,403
United States/Third Nation Forces	84	99	96	101	112	111	111	112	103	94	88	90	1,201
Combined Forces	74	42	38	18	31	26	51	45	61	41	7	10	444
U.S. Air Operations in SVN-Sorties													
Fixed Wing													
Attack	15,503	14,448	17,034	16,370	17,360	17,186	15,413	15,768	11,632	9,554	9,638	9,116	169,022
Other Combat	6,233	6,413	7,142	7,877	8,753	8,101	7,725	8,362	7,917	6,674	6,655	6,335	88,187
Total	21,736	20,861	24,176	24,247	26,113	25,287	23,138	24,130	19,549	16,228	16,293	15,451	257,209
Helicopters													
Attack	73,824	68,011	85,992	74,673	83,660	81,421	70,853	78,596	70,525	72,874	74,178	80,734	915,341
Combat Assault	154,530	138,371	155,578	150,251	169,068	159,735	159,956	159,066	145,897	153,784	138,654	140,966	1,825,856
Combat Cargo	67,644	68,021	74,550	78,414	66,338	66,828	65,763	68,194	56,331	55,734	59,425	70,551	797,793
Other	381,590	358,733	416,797	411,917	443,003	427,086	413,809	424,301	403,216	407,497	402,860	411,710	4,902,519
Total	677,588	633,136	732,917	715,255	762,069	735,070	710,381	730,157	675,969	689,889	675,117	703,961	8,441,509
U.S. Aircraft Losses in SEA													
Fixed Wing													
NVN	-	-	-	-	-	1	-	1	-	-	-	-	2
SVN	13	2	11	6	5	4	6	10	4	2	2	3	68
Subtotal	13	2	11	6	5	5	6	11	4	2	2	3	70
Other f/	38	36	47	36	33	26	31	27	22	32	35	33	396
Total	51	38	58	42	38	31	37	38	26	34	37	36	466
Helicopters													
NVN	-	-	-	-	-	-	-	-	-	-	-	-	-
SVN	31	33	51	51	51	38	30	40	35	25	50	24	459
Subtotal	31	33	51	51	51	38	30	40	35	25	50	24	459
Other g/	54	43	50	50	63	47	45	48	50	47	46	46	589
Total	85	76	101	101	114	85	75	88	85	72	96	70	1,048
Enemy Weapons Captured													
Crew Served	667	904	954	925	995	943	534	543	428	436	501	438	8,206
Individual	4,937	5,164	6,794	6,365	6,059	5,206	4,059	3,815	3,275	3,619	3,334	3,894	56,521
Total	5,604	6,068	7,748	7,290	7,054	6,149	4,593	4,358	3,703	4,055	3,835	4,332	64,789
Enemy Defections (Hoi Chanh)													
Military	2,114	1,621	2,776	2,603	2,574	2,056	2,594	2,447	2,340	2,979	2,450	1,851	28,405
Political	828	627	1,093	1,026	993	764	1,070	1,130	1,158	1,327	1,437	1,195	12,648
Other	204	141	459	584	359	336	1,427	729	426	656	419	230	5,970
Total	3,146	2,389	4,328	4,213	3,926	3,156	5,091	4,306	3,924	4,962	4,306	3,276	47,023
Terrorist Incidents	91	102	122	138	136	111	76	112	123	122	122	120	1,375
VC Armed Attacks	215	309	461	316	459	454	205	245	309	192	339	317	3,812
Refugees (000)													
Current Number of Refugees												268.3	
In camp												216.6	
Out camp												51.7	
Re-established Refugees With GVN Assistance - Since 1/1/69												586.4	
During Month												126.9	
Refugees Returned to Own Village - Since 1/1/69												488.2	
During Month												18.9	
Land Redistributed Since 1/1/68 (000 acres)												224.6	
Tax Collections (Billions VN Piasters)													
Customs Receipts	2.50	2.32	3.18	2.80	2.90	2.70	2.90	2.53	2.20	2.08	2.30	3.04	31.45
Domestic Tax Receipts	2.40	1.90	2.00	2.50	2.30	2.10	2.46	2.16	2.08	2.42	1.98	3.02	27.32
Saigon Retail Price Index h/	393	403	401	411	435	440	448	491	463	541			

a/ Strength as of end of month.
b/ Includes forces of Australia, Korea, New Zealand, Philippines, Republic of China, Spain and Thailand.
c/ Includes those who died of wounds and died while missing or captured.
d/ Approximately 85 percent of U. S. military personnel wounded recover sufficiently for return to duty.
e/ Includes only those seriously wounded.
f/ Combat type aircraft lost to non-hostile action, support aircraft losses, and all other fixed wing losses in connection with the war.
g/ Helicopters lost to non-hostile action, and all other helicopter losses in connection with the war.
h/ 1 January 1965 = 100.

UNCLASSIFIED
Statistics on Southeast Asia

Table 6

	1970												
	Jan	Feb	Mar	Apr	May	Jun	Jul	Aug	Sep	Oct	Nov	Dec	Cum
Friendly Military Forces in South Viet-Nam (000) a/													
United States	473	467	442	428	428	415	404	400	390	374	355	335	
Third Nation b/	70	70	70	70	69	69	69	69	69	69	68	68	
Casualties													
United States													
Deaths from hostile action c/	343	386	449	526	754	418	332	319	219	170	167	138	4,221
Deaths from other causes	141	171	208	135	166	129	171	129	146	155	133	160	1,844
Wounded d/													
Hospital care required	1,552	1,210	1,581	1,967	2,100	1,489	1,196	1,226	886	900	522	582	15,511
Hospital care not required	1,597	1,138	1,731	1,865	2,191	1,483	1,489	1,279	736	1,040	424	459	15,432
Currently missing												969	
Currently captured												462	
SVN													
Deaths from hostile action	1,768	1,417	1,674	2,642	2,851	2,873	1,711	1,720	1,734	1,491	1,619	1,846	23,346
Wounded e/	5,599	4,423	5,495	7,866	8,080	10,020	4,766	5,321	5,252	5,090	4,480	5,190	71,582
Missing	42	40	61	105	160	149	93	76	73	38	47	66	950
Third Nation													
Deaths from hostile action	69	36	75	79	58	63	71	63	46	57	48	39	704
Wounded e/	126	180	229	179	234	139	159	158	165	105	92	64	1,830
Missing	-	2	-	-	-	-	-	1	-	3	4	2	12
Enemy													
Deaths from hostile action	9,187	8,828	10,335	13,063	17,256	7,861	7,183	6,446	6,138	5,549	5,607	6,185	103,638
Prisoners of War currently held												37,353	
SVN Civilian Casualties Resulting from VC Terrorism													
Assassinated	411	304	452	785	861	805	492	435	368	381	275	378	5,947
Abducted	294	693	800	1,131	1,069	740	534	384	337	322	330	297	6,931
Hospital Admissions Attributed to the War													
SVN Hospitals	3,923	3,631	4,132	5,312	5,094	4,545	3,768	3,652	3,676	2,974	2,511	3,029	46,247
U. S. Hospitals	487	482	431	423	552	459	279	371	483	289	211	168	4,635
Land Operations (Bn Size or Larger)													
South Vietnamese Forces	1,026	787	888	882	819	706	811	791	812	807	749	826	9,904
United States/Third Nation Forces	88	58	56	48	56	64	69	74	92	80	64	90	839
Combined Forces	14	14	11	4	3	7	5	4	5	5	2	4	78
U.S. Air Operations in SVN-Sorties													
Fixed Wing													
Attack	9,234	7,413	8,608	10,034	9,089	7,774	8,245	7,339	5,985	2,869	2,540	2,268	81,398
Other Combat	6,336	5,363	4,948	5,111	5,016	3,787	4,151	4,068	3,625	2,646	2,384	2,631	50,066
Total	15,570	12,776	13,556	15,145	14,105	11,561	12,396	11,407	9,610	5,515	4,924	4,899	131,464
Helicopters													
Attack	77,081	73,645	77,814	81,682	78,290	68,546	62,502	68,663	61,347	49,585	49,546	50,275	798,976
Combat Assault	154,552	133,812	146,237	140,419	136,328	114,188	118,576	114,845	117,369	106,672	92,981	91,428	1,467,407
Combat Cargo	63,147	61,471	61,143	64,102	72,572	65,673	62,037	58,040	55,906	43,914	40,967	40,875	689,847
Other	427,223	395,713	419,434	428,773	428,873	406,417	405,883	392,411	372,585	328,066	299,655	302,563	4,607,596
Total	722,003	664,641	704,628	714,976	716,063	654,824	648,998	633,959	607,207	528,237	483,149	485,141	7,563,826
U.S. Aircraft Losses in SEA													
Fixed Wing													
NVN	1	-	1	-	1	-	-	-	-	-	1	-	4
SVN	2	4	1	4	6	4	4	3	1	-	-	-	29
Subtotal	3	4	2	4	7	4	4	3	1	-	1	-	33
Other f/	24	17	28	42	28	25	10	7	10	11	11	15	228
Total	27	21	30	46	35	29	14	10	11	11	12	15	261
Helicopters													
NVN	-	-	-	-	-	-	-	-	-	-	-	-	-
SVN	35	28	47	64	47	36	37	27	42	14	19	21	417
Subtotal	35	28	47	64	47	36	37	27	42	14	19	21	417
Other g/	28	41	54	38	82	41	35	30	30	24	13	20	436
Total	63	69	101	102	129	77	72	57	72	38	32	41	853
Enemy Weapons Captured													
Crew Served	499	377	497	701	2,259	698	402	351	253	351	226	416	7,030
Individual	3,459	3,394	3,835	5,231	16,396	9,925	3,815	3,217	2,225	2,733	2,349	2,529	59,108
Total	3,958	3,771	4,332	5,932	18,655	10,623	4,217	3,568	2,478	3,084	2,575	2,945	66,138
Enemy Defections (Hoi Chanh)													
Military	1,363	1,372	1,809	1,325	2,102	1,344	1,531	1,689	1,351	1,104	1,077	1,025	17,092
Political	810	835	1,098	842	933	709	924	1,239	1,065	1,058	961	887	11,361
Other	174	184	332	206	621	356	389	402	385	374	290	399	4,112
Total	2,347	2,391	3,239	2,373	3,656	2,409	2,844	3,330	2,801	2,536	2,328	2,311	32,565P
Terrorist Incidents	121	120	207	224	192	185	166	121	132	144	120	172	1,904
VC Armed Attacks	329	216	232	472	496	340	256	318	296	215	147	222	3,539
Refugees h/													
Current Number of Refugees												428,449	
In camp												213,679	
Out camp												-	
In return-to-village process												214,770	
Tax Collections (Billions VN Piasters)													
Customs Receipts	4.6	4.7	5.8	6.6	5.7	3.3	3.4	3.7	3.6	3.3	3.7	3.9	52.3
Domestic Tax Receipts	2.7	1.6	2.8	4.4	3.0	3.0	3.7	3.3	3.2	3.6	2.9	3.2	37.4

a/ Strength as of end of month.
b/ Includes forces of Australia, Korea, New Zealand, Philippines, Republic of China, Spain and Thailand.
c/ Includes those who died of wounds and died while missing or captured.
d/ Approximately 85 percent of U. S. military personnel wounded recover sufficiently for return to duty.
e/ Includes only those seriously wounded.
f/ Combat type aircraft lost to non-hostile action, support aircraft losses, and all other fixed wing losses in connection with the war.
g/ Helicopters lost to non-hostile action, and all other helicopter losses in connection with the war.
h/ Refugee reporting was revised with the April 1970 report.

P - Preliminary

Statistics on Southeast Asia

Table 6

	1971												
	Jan	Feb	Mar	Apr	May	Jun	Jul	Aug	Sep	Oct	Nov	Dec	Cum
Friendly Military Forces in South Viet-Nam (000) a/													
United States	336	325	302	270	250	239	225	216	213	196	178P	157P	
Third Nation b/	68	67	67	67	67	66	64	61	60	59P	59P	54P	
Casualties													
United States													
Deaths from hostile action c/	140	221	272	226	138	108	65	67	78	29	19	17	1,380
Deaths from other causes	103	135	104	100	63	73	61	48	53	91	102	35	968
Wounded d/													
Hospital care required	572	644	843	922	464	425	262	198	186	154	60	87	4,817
Hospital care not required	400	448	760	766	476	453	235	182	153	184	60	63	4,180
Currently missing												1,013	
Currently captured												478	
SVN													
Deaths from hostile action	1,616	2,435	3,676	2,198	2,091	1,846	1,389	1,488	1,607	1,574	1,161	988	22,069
Wounded e/	4,792	7,170	9,882	6,345	5,467	4,863	3,400	3,565	3,999	4,418	2,602	3,320	59,823
Missing	63	294	948	318	198	106	58	72	81	83	32	53	2,306
Third Nation													
Deaths from hostile action	30	48	104	86	50	44	44	32	27	20	14	26	525
Wounded e/	118	156	214	130	123	91	102	56	73	22	26	37	1,148
Missing	1	1	-	-	-	-	-	-	-	-	-	-	2
Enemy													
Deaths from hostile action	6,155	11,704	19,858	10,457	9,094	7,648	6,247	6,165	6,300	5,744	4,283	4,439	98,094
Prisoners of War currently held												35,596	
SVN Civilian Casualties Resulting from VC Terrorism													
Assassinated	326	373	735	397	403	305	241	216	203	192	146		3,391
Abducted	454	318	930	683	874	356	338	344	206	285	218		4,788
Hospital Admissions Attributed to the War													
SVN Hospitals	2,777	3,029	3,824	3,969	4,060	3,515	2,513	3,440	3,279	2,711			33,117
U. S. Hospitals	162	190	187	185	83	56	48	27	25	79			1,042
Land Operations (Bn Size or Larger)													
South Vietnamese Forces	905	804	806	767	800	742	706	789	627	675	710	735	9,060
United States/Third Nation Forces	96	90	83	90	56	48	63	52	60	35	17	24	715
Combined Forces	4	4	5	7	7	5	4	4	5	4	4	5	58
U.S. Air Operations in SVN-Sorties													
Fixed Wing													
Attack	2,155	1,700	1,786	2,778	1,588	1,858	1,657	1,996	1,464	1,057	366	217	18,622
Other Combat	2,388	2,401	1,861	1,940	1,909	1,693	1,799	1,529	1,840	1,379	1,049	1,047	20,835
Total	4,543	4,101	3,647	4,718	3,497	3,551	3,456	3,525	3,304	2,436	1,415	1,264	39,457
Helicopters													
Attack	49,667	50,072	47,802	38,475	36,432	32,417	32,739	31,984	29,634	27,178	21,901	18,866	417,167
Combat Assault	85,901	80,952	74,509	75,184	68,471	63,242	61,034	60,413	57,482	42,836	38,060	35,985	744,069
Combat Cargo	44,773	46,945	45,901	38,639	36,167	35,051	32,563	35,238	35,653	24,634	15,706	14,921	406,191
Other	287,920	261,446	273,289	235,681	238,641	212,812	216,934	226,323	204,720	187,399	165,358	135,885	2,646,408
Total	468,261	439,415	441,501	387,979	379,711	343,522	343,270	353,958	327,489	282,047	241,025	205,657	4,213,835
U.S. Aircraft Losses in SEA													
Fixed Wing													
NVN	-	-	1	-	-	-	-	-	-	-	-	5	6
SVN	1	1	1	3	5	-	3	-	-	3	-	-	17
Subtotal	1	1	2	3	5	-	3	-	-	3	-	5	23
Other f/	12	21	15	11	3	9	8	8	10	7	6	10	120
Total	13	22	17	14	8	9	11	8	10	10	6	15	143
Helicopters													
NVN	-	-	-	-	-	-	-	-	-	-	-	-	-
SVN	21	19	31	33	23	11	22	15	22	14	14	5	230
Subtotal	21	19	31	33	23	11	22	15	22	14	14	5	230
Other g/	14	52	93	17	14	9	13	10	12	25	11	14	284
Total	35	71	124	50	37	20	35	25	34	39	25	19	514
Enemy Weapons Captured													
Crew Served	291	655	1,912	350	396	363	238	288	244	231	137	198	5,303
Individual	2,432	4,730	6,074	3,039	2,558	2,402	2,322	2,031	2,087	1,886	1,612	1,678	32,851
Total	2,723	5,385	7,986	3,389	2,954	2,765	2,560	2,319	2,331	2,117	1,749	1,876	38,154
Enemy Defections (Hoi Chanh)													
Military	845	1,532	1,111	560	585	556	805	531	352	1,175			8,052
Political	730	1,204	987	491	484	453	564	387	272	322			5,894
Other	290	311	242	200	181	249	259	209	130	426			2,497
Total	1,865	3,047	2,340	1,251	1,250	1,258	1,628	1,127	754	1,923			16,443
Terrorist Incidents	201	174	262	212	282	258	245	150	195	148	146	60	2,333
VC Armed Attacks	166	266	336	246	239	241	133	148	144	125	103	97	2,244
Refugees h/													
Current Number											471,171		
In camp											94,967		
In Resettlement Process											69,996		
In return-to-village process											306,208		
Land Redistributed Since 1/1/68 i/ (000 acres)										1,701			
Tax Collections (Billions VN Piasters)													
Customs Receipts	6.6	8.1	3.0	15.4	8.8	12.7	9.6	7.0	16.6	10.5			98.3
Domestic Tax Receipts	3.4	2.8	3.5	5.4	3.7	3.2	4.8	3.8	4.2	5.0			39.8

SS-3. U.S. AIRCRAFT DEPLOYMENT IN SOUTHEAST ASIA

[Figure 13-6]

Category	End of Calendar Year						Nov	Feb
	1965	1966	1967	1968	1969	1970	1971	1972
Attack* [Int]	817	1098	1056	1104	1016			
Attack** [28]			1000	1140	950	590	355	
Attack** [31]								675
Non-attack** [Int]	706	1094	1473	1542	1779			
Helicopter** [Int]	1483	2008	3041	3323	3636			
Total [Int]	3006	4200	5570	5969	6431			
B-52 [Int], [10, p. 184]				100+				
B-52 [31]							45	80+

*Includes U.S. Navy Carrier-Based and VNAF

**Does not include VNAF

Air Force Planes in South Vietnam and Thailand, by Type, January 1971 [Int]

200 F-4s; 80 F-100s; 30 A-37s; 15 F-105s; 30 A-1s; 30 AC-119s; 10 AC-130s; 9 B-57s; 45 B-52s; 40 RF-4s; 20 EB-66s.

Add: Carrier-based attack planes, about 120.

U.S. Planes in Southeast Asia, by Base, February 1972 [31]

Fighter-Bombers: Thailand 400
South Vietnam 50
Carriers 225

B-52s: Thailand 50+
Guam 30

SS-4. INVENTORY OF THE VIETNAMESE AIR FORCE

[Figure 13-7]

	1960	Jan'62	1962	June'64	1965	1968	1969	Jan'70	June'70	Jan'71	May'71	Projection 1974
Fixed-Wing Attack Aircraft				75 [8]		87 [8]			100 [Int]	200 [7]		
Helicopter										300 [7]		500-600 [Int,9]
Total	150 [7]	110 [8]	180 [7]	230 [8]	380 [7]	350 [9] 300 [28]	375 [28]	400 [Int, 7]	660 [28]	700 [7]	800-850 [Int,9] 950 [28]	1200-1300 [Int,8,9]

SS-5a. U.S. FIGHTER-BOMBER SORTIES*

(i) *South Vietnam* [Figure 4-1, top]

Year	Source				Classification	
	[Int]	[1]	[4]**	[3]	Immediates	Close Air Support
1965			76,000	(75,000)		
1966	114,000	129,050	131,000			
1967	188,000	176,437	177,000			
1968	218,000	221,755		230,000+	55,000	18,000+
1969	155,000	169,022		192,200+	31,000	9,000+
1970	76,000	81,398		74,931		
1971		18,622		(7,666#)	(2,791#)	(448#)

*Check well with totals given in [28]. **Book 7, Vol. IV, p. 22.

#Air Force only, first 6 months.

(ii) *North Vietnam* [Figure 3-1]

Year	Quarter	[4] [Bk. 7, Vol. IV, p. 21]		[Int]
1965	1	1,000)	25,000	
	2	5,000)		
	3	10,000)		
	4	9,000)		
1966	1	6,000)	79,000	89,000
	2	18,000)		
	3	32,000)		
	4	23,000)		
1967	1	20,000)	108,000	109,000
	2	32,000)		
	3	33,000)		
	4	23,000)		
1968				82,000

(iii) *Laos*

Year	[Int] Total [Figure 13-3]	Trail* [Figure 5-2]	Northern Laos#
1966	48,000	48,000	
1967	53,000	53,000	
1968	88,000	78,000	10,000
1969	152,000 [6]	77,000	75,000
1970	101,000	61,000	40,000
"1971"	89,000	71,000	18,000

*Figures obtained by subtracting sorties for Northern Laos from total.

#Estimated from Figure 6-1; see section (iv), below.

(iv) *Northern Laos* [Figure 6-1]

1964: 20/year; 1965: 12/day; 1966: 20/day [11]

1968: Sept., 32/day; Oct., 22/day; Nov., 43/day; Dec., 52/day [12]
(Air Force, Thai bases only)

1969: "Continued almost exactly as it was from Nov. 68 through Feb. and early March 1969." [13]

July, Aug., Sept., 200-300/day [14]-[20]

1970: Jan., "Monthly (USAF) sorties in Laos reached a high point." [21]

1971: 65-75/day [22], [30]

(v) *Cambodia*

Period	[Int]
1970	14,040
1971: Jan	1,650
Feb	1,800
Mar	1,750
Apr	1,800
May	1,500
Jun	1,900
Jul	1,100
Aug	850
Sep	900
Oct	1,000
Nov	1,250
(Dec	1,500)
Total, 1971	17,000

SS-5b. VNAF FIGHTER-BOMBER SORTIES

[Figure 13-8] [Int]

Period	South Vietnam	Period	South Vietnam	Laos	Cambodia
1968: Jan	2,400	1970: Jan	3,600		
Feb	2,700	Feb	3,300		
Mar	2,700	Mar	3,000		
Apr	2,100	Apr	3,600		
May	2,400	May	1,500		
Jun	2,100	Jun	1,800		
Jul	2,100	Jul	1,800		
Aug	2,100	Aug	1,500		
Sep	1,800	Sep	1,800		
Oct	2,400	Oct	)		
Nov	2,100	Nov	) 6,300		
Dec	2,100	Dec	)		
Total	27,000	Total	28,200		9,800
1969: Jan	2,700	1971: Jan	1,950		1,400
Feb	2,400	Feb	1,950	6	1,300
Mar	2,400	Mar	2,100	230	1,250
Apr	2,100	Apr	2,600	16	1,060
May	2,700	May	2,625		1,100
Jun	2,700	Jun	2,300		900
Jul	3,000	Jul	2,860		830
Aug	3,300	Aug	(2,700)		)
Sep	3,000	Sep	(2,700)		)
Oct	3,300	Oct	2,688		) (5,000)
Nov	3,300	Nov	2,745		)
Dec	3,300	Dec	(2,700)		)
Total	34,200	Total	29,900	252	12,840

SS-6. B-52 ACTIVITY

a. *B-52 Sorties for Southeast Asia* [Figure 13-4]

Year	Total *Sorties* [Int]
1965	1,500 [27]
1966	5,200
1967	9,700
1968	20,500) [also 10, p. 184]
1969	19,500)
1970	15,100
1971	12,500

b. *Distribution of B-52 Missions, South Vietnam* [Figure 4-1, bottom], *DMZ,* and *North Vietnam* [2], [26], [29]

	MISSIONS*							
	South Vietnam					DMZ		North
Period	MR I	MR II	MR III	MR IV	Total	N	S	Vietnam
1967: Jan	18	14	27	1	60	2	7	
Feb	23	30	30	1	84	1		
Mar	45	23	32		100			
Apr	55	13	22	2	92	2	4	
May	55	27	23	1	106	1	3	
Jun	45	28	25	1	99			
Jul	44	31	22	3	100		3	3
Aug	26	28	24		78		24	1
Sep	13	9	6		28		57	15
Oct	17	15	20		52		30	27
Nov	13	47	16	1	77		12	9
Dec	6	19	22		47		27	8
Total	360	284	269	10	923	6	167	63
1968: Jan	59	22	23		104		4	1
Feb	204	53	34		291			
Mar	222	58	27	4	311			
Apr	173	66	19	7	265		2	
May	71	123	27	10	231		13	1
Jun	24	87	171	11	293	4	6	
Jul	28	34	152	26	240	7		45
Aug	71	55	161	13	300	8	8	8
Sep	51	55	167	18	291	1	10	8
Oct	86	33	128	25	272	2	1	15
Nov	45	36	109	17	207			
Dec	53	22	125	17	217			
Total	1087	644	1143	148	3022	22	50	78
1969: Jan	27	30	71	25	153			
Feb	23	18	144	10	195			
Mar	16	35	208	15	274			
Apr	13	14	152	2	181			
May	28	67	170	7	272			
Jun	23	86	145	6	260			
Jul	(27)	(39)	(151)	(9)	226	NOT	REPORTED	
Aug	36	32	197	6	271			
Sep	35	23	149	5	215			
Oct	42	24	149	5	220			
Nov	17	61	105	4	187			
Dec	27	29	119	5	180			
Total	(314)	(458)	(1760)	(102)	(2634)			

Period	South Vietnam MR I	MR II	MR III	MR IV	Total	DMZ N	S
1970: Jan	37	25	84	24	170	NOT	REPORTED
Feb	20	61	34	12	127		
Mar	33	33	68	23	157		
Apr	23	64	93	25	205		
May	56	55	26	12	149		
Jun	123	12	3	19	157		
Jul	127	14	23	22	186		
Aug	112	0	15	7	134		
Sep	79	5	14	4	102		
Oct	(10)	(4)	(6)	(3)	(23)		
Nov	4	0	0	0	4		
Dec							
Total	(624)	(273)	(366)	(151)	(1414)		
1971: Jan	85%				17		
Feb					14		
Mar					8		
Apr					96		
May					69		
Jun					102		
Jul					103		
Aug					125		
Sep					114		
Oct					57		
Nov					46		
Dec					10		
Total					761		

*Reported totals occasionally do not agree with individual figures, so small adjustments have been made. Numbers in parentheses represent deduced values, not stated explicitly in the source material. Blanks are shown when it is not clear whether there were zero missions or whether the particular item was not reported.

c. *Average Ordnance Tonnage per B-52 Sortie*

1965	17 tons
1966	20
1967	24
1968	26
1969	27
1970	28
1971	28

These figures were estimated from a smoothed curve, based on reported modifications of the B-52s and their maximum load capacities, and fitted to scattered data detailing the average load tonnages actually realized in service.

SS-7. HELICOPTER ATTACK SORTIES

South Vietnam [Figure 4-1, center] See data given in SS-2 [1]

SS-8. TONNAGE OF AERIAL MUNITIONS

a. *Southeast Asia, U.S. + Allied Total* [Figure 13-1] [5]

Period		Tons	
1965		315,000	
1966		512,000	
1967:	Jan	63,039	
	Feb	68,142	
	Mar	77,384	
	Apr	77,393	
	May	80,587	
	Jun	78,042	
	Jul	80,035	
	Aug	79,535	
	Sep	78,885	
	Oct	83,497	
	Nov	83,088	
	Dec	83,136	total = 932,763
1968:	Jan	90,036	
	Feb	103,000	
	Mar	123,672	
	Apr	124,660	
	May	127,942	
	Jun	125,159	
	Jul	128,407	
	Aug	126,379	
	Sep	117,569	
	Oct	122,233	
	Nov	114,925	
	Dec	127,672	total = 1,431,654
1969:	Jan	129,684	
	Feb	115,759	
	Mar	130,141	
	Apr	125,080	
	May	128,300	
	Jun	121,775	
	Jul	122,793	
	Aug	111,047	
	Sep	102,084	
	Oct	99,907	
	Nov	100,509	
	Dec	100,158	total = 1,387,237
1970:	Jan	117,675	
	Feb	100,639	
	Mar	100,358	
	Apr	97,494	
	May	97,323	
	Jun	80,682	
	Jul	79,582	
	Aug	70,867	
	Sep	59,390	
	Oct	54,538	
	Nov	58,434	
	Dec	60,464	total = 977,446
1971:	Jan	71,792	
	Feb	66,500	
	Mar	92,191	
	Apr	85,000	
	May	76,463	
	Jun	60,803	
	Jul	49,196	
	Aug	51,171	
	Sep	51,177	
	Oct	47,315	
	Nov	50,649	
	Dec	61,838	total = 764,095

b. Computation of Tonnage per Sortie

Year	B-52 sorties (1)	Tons/ sortie (2)	B-52 tons (3)	Total U.S. tonnage (4)	F-B tonnage (5)	F-B sorties (6)	Tons/ F-B sortie (7)	VNAF F-B sorties (8)	VNAF tonnage (9)
1965	1.5k	17	26k	315k	289k	114k	2.53		
1966	5.2k	20	104k	512k	408k	266k	1.53		
1967	9.7k	24	233k	933k	700k	338k	2.07		
1968	20.5k	26	533k	1392k	859k	392k	2.19	27k	40k
1969	19.5k	27	526k	1336k	810k	321k	2.52	34k	51k
1970	15.1k	28	423k	920k	497k	196k	2.54	38k	57k
1971	12.6k	28	352k	701k	349k	125k	2.80	42k	63k

(1) From SS-6a.
(2) Average estimated from B-52 modification data, cf. SS-6c.
(3) Column 1 times column 2.
(4) DoD figures for total SEA allied tonnage, less VNAF contribution from column (9).
(5) Column 4 minus column 3.
(6) U.S. fighter-bomber sorties, SEA, from SS-5.
(7) Column 5 divided by column 6.
(8) VNAF fighter-bomber sorties, SEA, from SS-5.
(9) VNAF fighter-bomber tonnage, assuming 1.5 tons/sortie.

c. Distribution of bomb tonnage by theater

The steps by which this distribution was estimated are outlined below. Several errors and approximations are involved, which may compound in the course of the calculation. The results should be regarded as a rough approximation only.

1. Fighter-bomber tonnage: Apportion fighter-bomber tons (SS-8b, column 5) in proportion to the number of sorties flown into each theater (SS-5).

2. B-52 tonnage: Apportion B-52 tons (SS-8b, column 3) between the theaters, using the published B-52 missions in South Vietnam (SS-6b) as a guide to the number of sorties there. (7 sorties per mission up to 1969, decreasing somewhat in the last two years.) The remainder of the B-52 tonnage is divided between the theaters in a "plausible" manner, using Press reports as a guide.

3. VNAF tonnage (SS-8b, column 9) is divided between South Vietnam and Cambodia in proportion to the sorties in the two theaters.

BOMB TONNAGE BY THEATER
(thousands of tons)

	South Vietnam	North Vietnam	Northern Laos	Trail	Cambodia
1965 F-B	192	63	10	23	
B-52	26				
Total	218	63	10	23	
1966 F-B	198	136	11	63	
B-52	104				
Total	302	136	11	63	
1967 F-B	365	226	19	91	
B-52	233				
Total	598	226	19	91	
1968 F-B	486	180	22	171	
B-52	533				
VNAF	40				
Total	1059	180	22	171	
1969 F-B	426		189	194	
B-52	480			46	
VNAF	51				
Total	957		189	240	
1970 F-B	204	3	100	154	35
B-52	265		28	112	17
VNAF	42				15
Total	511	3	128	266	67
1971 F-B	52	6	74	170	47
B-52	143		41	126	42
VNAF	43				20
Total	238	6	115	296	109

[Figures 1-1 and 13-2]

SS-9. CASUALTIES

a. *U.S. Deaths from Aircraft Losses* [23]

		1961-1967	1968	1969	1970	Total
As a Result of Hostile Action	Fixed-wing	538	250	165	87	1040
	Helicopter	640	631	638	610	2519
	Total	1178	881	803	697	3559
From Operational Causes, Accidents	Fixed-wing	378	120	106	118	722
	Helicopter	632	360	461	426	1879
	Total	1010	480	567	544	2601
Hostile + Non-hostile	Total	2188	1361	1370	1241	6160
Hostile Air Deaths as % of Total due to Hostile Action		7.4%	6.0%	8.5%	16.5%	8.0%
Non-hostile Air deaths as % of Total Non-Hostile Deaths		31.7%	25.0%	26.8%	29.5%	28.7%
Total Air Deaths as % of Total Air + Ground Deaths		11.4%	8.2%	11.9%	20.5%	11.6%

b. *U.S. Air-Related Deaths Due to Hostile Action* [Int]
[Through early 1971]

Service	Army	Navy	USMC	USAF	Total
Fixed-wing	83	155	139	687	1064
Helicopter	2143	62	429	59	2693
All Aircraft	2226	217	568	746	3757

SS-10. AIRCRAFT LOSSES

[Int]		1961–1965	1966	1967	1968	1969	1970	1971 [2 mo]	Total
INDOCHINA (All Causes)	Fixed-wing	462	634	728	657	466	256	(45)	3248
	Helicopter	275	321	664	1008	1048	832	104	4252
	Total	737	955	1392	1665	1514	1088	149	7500 [cf.23]
NORTH VIETNAM (Hostile Action)	Fixed-Wing	175	280	326	141	2	4	0	928
	Helicopter	3	1	4	2	0	0	0	10
SOUTH VIETNAM (Hostile Action)	Fixed-Wing	81	69	73	107	68	29	2	429
	Helicopter	106	123	260	495	459	393	42	1878
OTHER*	Fixed-Wing	206	285	329	409	396	133	33	1791
	Helicopter	166	197	400	511	589	419	42	2324
LAOS*	Fixed-Wing						(70)	(10)	400 [24]
	Helicopter						(20)	(20)	
CAMBODIA	Fixed-Wing Helicopter						60 (from April 30, 1970 through Feb. 1971 [25])		

*"Other" includes losses to hostile fire in Laos through 1969.

SS-11. KEY TO SOURCE REFERENCES

[Int] Data obtained through personal interviews.

[1] Table 6, "Unclassified Statistics on Southeast Asia," Department of Defense, OASD (Comptroller), Directorate for Information Operations. This table is reproduced in SS-2.

[2] MACV Monthly Summaries, Office of Information, MACV, Saigon.

[3] MACV Annual Statistics.

[4] *United States-Vietnam Relations, 1945-1967* (USGPO, 1971).

[5] Figures supplied by the Department of Defense.

[6] "12,500 sorties/month, according to Pentagon statistics," quoted by Stanley Karnow, *Washington Post,* August 16, 1969.

[7] *Vietnam Feature Service,* TCB-089 (January 1971): "Vietnamization's Impact on the Air War."

[8] "How the South Vietnamese are Taking over their own Air War," Kenneth Sams, *Air Force,* April 1971.

[9] Craig Whitney, *New York Times*, May 20, 1971.
[10] Col. James A. Donovan, *Militarism, U.S.A.* (Scribner's, 1970).
[11] *Security Agreement Hearings* (1969), p. 712. These sortie rates are given as yearly figures [20, 4548, 7316, respectively] and cover both USAF and USN flights. They are stated as being "strikes," which we interpret to mean sorties, for consistency with the data which follow.
[12] *Ibid.*, p. 690. These rates are given as monthly figures [961, 687, 1304, 1622, respectively]. By implication they are for USAF sorties based in Thailand only; the USN was probably flying few sorties into northern Laos, its activity being concentrated on Trail interdiction.
[13] *Refugee Hearings* (1971). Ambassador Sullivan is quoted as saying, "the north Laos sortie level continued almost exactly as it was from Nov. 68 through Feb. and early March 1969. It was only in late March 1969 and subsequently . . . that there was an augmentation of air activity over northern Laos." [p. 49] This is clearly not a literally correct statement in view of the rise in sorties from Nov. to Dec. 1968; Sullivan is trying to indicate that the air escalation was a response to ground activity, rather than preceding it. The figures bear him out only partially; we assume the rates did not rise steeply at least for the early part of 1969.
[14] 200/day, *New York Times*, July 27, 1969.
[15] 200/day, T. D. Allman, *NYT*, 8/24/69.
[16] 200/day, *NYT*, 9/13/69.
[17] "As many as 500 total [into Laos], with over 300/day in the North," *NYT*, 9/23/69.
[18] 250/day, "with surprisingly good agreement between Communist and non-Communist sources," Murray Sayle, *London Times*, September 13, 1969.
[19] 200-300/day, R. Shaplen, "Our Involvement in Laos," *Foreign Affairs*, April 1970, p. 478.
[20] "More than 100/day," R. Paul, "Laos: Anatomy of an American Involvement," *Foreign Affairs*, April 1971, p. 533. In private communication, Mr. Paul indicated that this figure was arrived at by doubling the 52/day for Dec. 1969 (which he quoted), this being the best he could do in view of the classified nature of the data. He says his figure is a lower limit, not intended as denying a higher rate.
[21] "Laos: April 1971," Staff Report for the Subcommittee on U.S. Security Agreements and Commitments Abroad, Committee on Foreign Relations, U.S. Senate, 92nd Congress, 1st Session (USGPO, 1971). The overall sortie rate into Laos peaked in January 1970, but this almost certainly reflects heavy activity over the Trail. However, since about half the Laos sorties were previously over the North, it is unlikely that their rate could have declined sharply and still leave the total peaking so late. We take this to indicate a slow decline in the North Laos sortie rate after its peak in about Sept. 69.
[22] *Refugee Hearings* (1971), p. 43. Ambassador Sullivan: "About 80% of the air sorties flown by U.S. air power are concentrated [over the Ho Chi Minh Train area]." Since the present total sortie rate for Laos is about 340/day [cf. ref. [21], p. 7], this leads to an estimate of about 65/day over the North.
[23] *Armed Forces Journal*, January 18, 1971, pp. 28-29: "total losses = 7351 at end of 1970." As of March 16, 1971, the Department of Defense recorded 7602 total aircraft losses, of which 3284 were fixed-wing and 4318 were helicopter. [*Impact of the Vietnam War,* Report prepared by the Congressional Research Service for the Committee on Foreign Relations, U.S. Senate, 92nd Congress, 1st Session (USGPO, 1971), p. 7.]
[24] *New York Times*, December 14, 1970.
[25] *NYT*, 3/2/71.
[26] *Science*, Vol. 168, p. 553 (May 1, 1970).
[27] "Counterinsurgency from 30,000 Feet: The B-52 in Vietnam," *Air University Review*, XIX, No. 2 (January-February 1968).
[28] News Conference, Secretary of the Air Force Robert C. Seamans, Jr., December 16, 1971.
[29] MACV Data, private communication from OASD, Public Affairs.
[30] "Over two thirds" of the bombs dropped in Laos fall on the Trail. [Secretary Seamans, quoted in *Washington Post*, January 17, 1972.] If this is interpreted to mean about 70%, and the sortie rate over Laos in 1971 averages 250/day [Int], the sorties over Northern Laos are 75/day.
[31] Craig Whitney, *New York Times*, February 14, 1972.

INDEX